Philosophical Enactment and Bodily Cultivation in Early Daoism

Also Available from Bloomsbury

Buddhist and Christian Responses to the Kowtow Problem in China, Eric Reinders

Religion and Orientalism in Asian Studies, Kiri Paramore

Philosophical Enactment and Bodily Cultivation in Early Daoism

In the Matrix of the Daodejing

Thomas Michael

BLOOMSBURY ACADEMIC
LONDON • NEW YORK • OXFORD • NEW DELHI • SYDNEY

BLOOMSBURY ACADEMIC
Bloomsbury Publishing Plc
50 Bedford Square, London, WC1B 3DP, UK
1385 Broadway, New York, NY 10018, USA
29 Earlsfort Terrace, Dublin 2, Ireland

BLOOMSBURY, BLOOMSBURY ACADEMIC and the Diana logo are trademarks of
Bloomsbury Publishing Plc

First published in Great Britain 2022
This paperback edition published 2024

Copyright © Thomas Michael, 2022

Thomas Michael has asserted his right under the Copyright, Designs and Patents Act,
1988, to be identified as Author of this work.

For legal purposes the Acknowledgments on p. viii constitute an extension
of this copyright page.

Cover image © Devin Araujo/EyeEm/Getty Images

All rights reserved. No part of this publication may be reproduced or transmitted in any
form or by any means, electronic or mechanical, including photocopying, recording, or
any information storage or retrieval system, without prior permission in writing from the
publishers.

Bloomsbury Publishing Plc does not have any control over, or responsibility for, any third-
party websites referred to or in this book. All internet addresses given in this book were
correct at the time of going to press. The author and publisher regret any inconvenience
caused if addresses have changed or sites have ceased to exist, but can accept no
responsibility for any such changes.

A catalogue record for this book is available from the British Library.

Library of Congress Control Number: 2021938995

ISBN:	HB:	978-1-3502-3665-3
	PB:	978-1-3502-3669-1
	ePDF:	978-1-3502-3666-0
	eBook:	978-1-3502-3667-7

Typeset by Integra Software Solutions Pvt. Ltd.

To find out more about our authors and books visit www.bloomsbury.com
and sign up for our newsletters

For Serge and Tara

Although the text has five thousand words, there is a single thread. Although its profusion of ideas is vast and abundant, they are of the same kind. Comprehending and thereby sheltering its one word, then nothing hidden in it is not known, but if each theme is taken independently, their analysis breeds confusion.

文雖五千貫之者一義雖廣贍眾則同類解其一言而蔽之則無幽而不識每事各為意則雖辯而愈惑

Wang Bi, *Laozi weizhi lueli* 6:1

Contents

Acknowledgments	viii
Prologue Approaching the Matrix	1
1 Matrix Side A: Conventions of the Dao	3
2 Matrix Side B: Yangsheng, according to Ge Hong	13
Part One Yangsheng Daoism and the Matrix	21
3 Uncovering Yangsheng Daoism	23
4 The Measurability of *Chang*	65
5 The Temporality of *Heng*	87
Part Two Huang-Lao Daoism and the Matrix	117
6 Yan Zun and Heshang Gong	119
Part Three Ge Hong and the Matrix	155
7 Ge Hong and the Philosophy of the Pristine Dao	157
8 Ge Hong and Yangsheng Daoism	183
Epilogue Yangsheng Daoism and Comparative Philosophy	213
9 Heidegger and the Philosophy of the Dao	215
Notes	235
Works Cited	255
Index	270

Acknowledgments

The seed of this book is American, but the soil, water, and moonlight that brought it to life are Chinese. Taken in the widest sense of the term, philosophy is among the most fun things to do, on top of which this book has also been one of the greatest intellectual journeys that I have ever taken. Much like being a sage or a ruler, a chess player or a flower arranger, philosophy too has its own particular *dao*, its own particular methods and rhythms, and it too takes a lot of practice. The *dao* of philosophy is not infinite, but neither is it uniform; it is not performed in the public square, but neither is it performed in isolation: there are better and worse ways of doing it. Sometimes, depending on the day, good ways of doing philosophy can include seminars, workshops, and conferences. Other good ways of doing philosophy are gathering with fellow colleagues on the train from Beijing to the conference in Zibo, there to talk about the significance of why the received text of the *Daodejing* says that "the myriad beings are born form somethingness, and somethingness is born from nothingness," while the Guodian *Laozi* manuscript says that the "myriad beings are born from somethingness and from nothingness" (my thanks to Zheng Kai and Cao Feng, and the other usual suspects typically seen on the Daoist conference circuit). Another good way to do philosophy is by staying in the mountain retreat at the top of a peasant village but at the foot of the Great Wall with some of the best Chinese scholars of Daoism (my thanks to Chen Xia). It is also good to do philosophy on top of a Chinese mountain just climbed (which means no pitons required) (my thanks to Li Shaomeng). Another fine way to do philosophy is after a Peking University philosophy workshop, sharing one of those archetypal Chinese dinners on a table that spins because there are so many different and delicious foods on it, but the good philosophizing begins with the baijiu (my thanks to Wang Zhongjiang, Chen Guying, and their entourages that irresistibly enliven all discussions of Daoism). Another very good way to do philosophy is by gathering other Beijing ex-pats and Chinese colleagues to form a WeChat group called "Beijing Daoism" that invites distinguished Western scholars, passing through Beijing on their way to other gigs in China, to give us a lecture followed by a non-spinning table Chinese dinner, of course with the proverbial Qingdao (my thanks to all members past, present, and future of the "Beijing Daoism Group," and also to the many scholars who gave us their presentations, including Graham Parkes, Paul Unschuld, David Chai, and Livia Kohn). Then there is one of my own preferred methods of doing philosophy, namely, in a dark corner of a smoky bar with a bottle of bourbon (my thanks to Danny Dunn, Soul Shake, JayZ and the two Wills, together with the many other "external kings-inner sages" who have kept the rhythms of the Dao vitally circulating in Beijing that has provided me with constant strength and inspiration during the composition of this book). Finally, one of my newly discovered ways of doing philosophy is by spending hours upon hours in deep discussion with one of Beijing's hidden treasures (my deepest thanks to Liu Yue; may our discussions continue long into the future …). But philosophy also requires a lot of work, especially when so much of it is in Chinese! This has been a delicious agony that has kept my hands constantly full, but with Guo Dingwei as my metaphorically literal right hand and Cui Xiaojiao as my literally metaphorical left hand, things have turned out more than quite alright. Dingwei has translated much of my work into Chinese, and Xiaojiao has fixed virtually every other thing involved with that, and together they have made some of the ideas in this book available to a wider group of Chinese scholars with whom I could further discuss them. Without the assistance over these years of three of my unbelievably invaluable Teaching Assistants, this book would be far less: Mehdi Arronis, Chu Ke, and Wu Zusong; all of them bookworms of the highest caliber: may each of you make your own marks when the time comes, and I will be there to see it). But there is a different side to doing the work of Daoist philosophy in China that can only be managed by having the right understanding of mercury versus lead, which I got from two different groups. The first group are my eminent elders, and they are Roger Ames, James Wang Qingjie, Barbara Hendrischke, and (the person I would thank twice if I could) James Sellmann. The second group includes my battle-hardened cohorts as well as formidable juniors who have had several years head-start on me living in China, and without whom this book would also be far less: Georges Favraud at first, but then Gilbert Feng, Li Xi, Li Ming, Magda Filipcz, Eric Nelson, David Chai (again), Misha Tadd, Paul D'Ambrosio, Dennis Schilling, and Sharon Small and Tommy. This book also would not have been possible without Dean Jiang Yi and Wang Chengbing, who brought me to Beijing Normal University; Dean Wu Xiangdong, who kept me at Beijing Normal University; and Jiang Limei, who made me feel right at home (i.e., not an outsider) at Beijing Normal University but who also taught me how to thrive in several different capacities there as well. My remaining acknowledgments are directed to all those both in and outside of China who, over the course of the last five years, challenged me to think more clearly and more deeply the many issues raised in this book, include my teachers, my colleagues, my students, as well as other associates, most of all of whom are also counted as friends. Not last and definitely not least, by once again fulfilling her role as *deus ex machina* by dropping in at the very last moment as all proper *deus ex machina*s do, the one to whom the phrase "without whom this work would not have been possible" takes on its own metaphysical value and significance, Robin Wang.

On the American side, my thanks go to Serge and Sarah and Cassandara in the northeast, Michael and Eugenia in the southeast, and Eric and Janelle in the northwest, each of whom from time to time gave me refuge and respite from Beijing. My last acknowledgment goes to my mother, who always afforded me the freedom to be whoever I was without trying to mold me into something that I am not, and, at the literal end of the end, has let me stay in her small place as I finished this work, stranded by Covid-19 far from Beijing.

Prologue: Approaching the Matrix

1

Matrix Side A: Conventions of the Dao

Of all philosophical traditions living and dead, the Daoist philosophy that was born of the *Daodejing* is among the most misunderstood. One reason is because, while this Daoism is indeed a philosophy, it is also something else in addition, which philosophy fundamentally cannot or temperamentally will not grasp in thought or word. Philosophy is certainly sensitive to this something else, yet for lack of viable options it continues to package the *Daodejing* in its own, strictly philosophical terms instead of letting it show itself to us as what it is, namely, a philosophy plus something else.

The dissonance between these two aspects of the *Daodejing* is a continuing source of misunderstanding Daoism. This study seeks to allow the *Daodejing* to unconceal itself as much as possible, given the formidable separations of time, place, language, culture, as well as different understandings of the basic nature and fabric of reality itself that stand between us. This study represents an effort at cross-cultural history of religions and comparative philosophy between the West and China, and it intends to reduce, even if only a bit, the misunderstanding of the Daoism of the *Daodejing*.

Another reason for the misunderstanding of this Daoism concerns sinology, and it is that the *Daodejing* is a text without a definite origin. Its earliest recorded appearances show that it was somehow born already fully fledged, philosophically speaking, but it somehow also was already demonstrating distinct marks of having been altered both textually and ideologically. Even so, nobody at that time had good explanations for where it came from, who wrote it, or what it was even about. Today there still are not any good explanations for the *Daodejing*: we cannot examine its philosophical influences because its original presentation of the Dao as an ultimate source was unparalleled and without historical model, and we cannot classify it within any particular philosophical tradition because the text itself birthed its own tradition—Daoism.

These two obstacles have a boomerang effect on each other: philosophy cannot entirely contain the Daoism of the *Daodejing* because of that additional something else, thus stranding sinology, and sinology cannot explain the origins of the *Daodejing*, thus stranding philosophy. This is to say, sinology would specialize in issues concerning the form of the *Daodejing*, but the formlessness of the text in its early oral circulations renders conventional sinological tools of little help. Philosophy would specialize in issues concerning the content of the *Daodejing*, but the *Laozi* manuscripts say things that are wildly incompatible, philosophically speaking, with the received text of the *Daodejing*, and this renders conventional philosophical tools of little help.

In these ways unable to come to each other's assistance for approaching the *Daodejing*, philosophy and sinology have been kept distanced from each other. The current study seeks to bring them a little closer together, partly by exploring those manuscripts philosophically and partly by examining that philosophy sinologically. Still, the questions herein asked of the *Daodejing* are neither entirely philosophical nor entirely sinological, even as the responses that the *Daodejing* gives are both philosophical and sinological. While this study simultaneously depends on philosophy and sinology and hopes to be useful to both in turn, it nevertheless remains a project of cross-cultural history of religions and comparative philosophy.

To discuss the *Daodejing* more clearly in the context of what in Chinese is called "*Laozi* Studies" 老學, this study relies on a set of conventions differently tailored from other scholarly works, and their application throughout represents one effort to bring sinology and philosophy closer. The beneficial utility of this label, "*Laozi* Studies," is that it allows a panoramic perspective on the *Daodejing* that has ample space for both philosophy and sinology. It is a challenging label for Western scholars because it does not necessarily distinguish between the values of what philosophy and sinology separately contribute, and it approaches the *Daodejing* as a cultural phenomenon more than a historical artefact.

The *Daodejing*'s deepest impact throughout traditional China was always as a cultural phenomenon, and the same can now be said of its impact throughout many parts of the modern world. But the *Daodejing* had already become a cultural phenomenon soon after its historical appearance in the Warring States, and even then, what the text literally said word for word was of less importance than its unprecedented vision of the world as generated from and ordered by the Dao—and yet at the heart of this vision there remains the historical text called the *Daodejing*.

As with many other cultural phenomena, the *Daodejing* is textless. It is not what so many people effortlessly read or recite; it is not "the received text" or even modern scholarly reconstructions of a received text; it is not any of the excavated manuscripts or any other historical or contemporary editions of the text; it is not any translation of an earlier *Daodejing* into a modern language like Mandarin or Cantonese, nor is it any translation into a different language like English, even if these translations incorporate or merge or add or delete as much as they find necessary or helpful to make its original or authentic philosophy more clear from among all of the many different things the *Daodejing* has said from its earliest excavated manuscripts to its many different editions in the hands of many different editors and many different commentators as well as many different readers.

This is the *Daodejing* that is referred to herein as "the *Daodejing*." When this convention is used with a specific chapter number, that is, *Daodejing* Chapter 2, the reference assumes a conventionally agreed-upon understanding of that chapter's position between 1 and 81, where that chapter begins and ends, as well as that chapter's general content.

Another convention concerns the issue of version, for which this study recognizes two, both of which are also textless. One version is the Laozi *Daodejing* and, being textless, it is nowhere seen but is nevertheless fortuitously reflected in a wide variety of early Chinese writings. These begin with the excavated manuscripts, including the Guodian *Laozi* with its partial transcription of the *Daodejing* and the Mawangdui *Laozi* with its complete transcription. This Laozi *Daodejing* is differently reflected in other excavated manuscripts, including the *Taiyi Sheng Shui*, *Hengxian*, and *Fanwu Liuxing*, and it is also reflected in a number of passages in the *Zhuangzi* and in a smaller number of passages in the *Huainanzi*, where it lingers barely visible.

The other version is the Huang-Lao *Daodejing*. This version historically appears after the Laozi *Daodejing* and, after that one had first been altered and then forgotten by the tradition, the Huang-Lao *Daodejing* quickly became the stand-alone version beginning in the Han Dynasty, a preeminence that it continues to enjoy even now, even after the discoveries of the *Laozi* manuscripts at the end of the twentieth century. There was a third version that appeared in the Eastern Han here referred to as the Tianshi *Daodejing*, but its shelf life was short and due to political circumstances of the time did not survive much past the end of the Han.

The next convention concerns the issue of manuscripts and editions. The excavated *Laozi* manuscripts are just that, manuscripts, and this study primarily discusses two sets of them, those of the Guodian *Laozi* and those of the Mawangdui *Laozi*. I do not have a lot to say about two other excavated *Laozi* manuscripts, the Beida *Laozi*[1] and Guben *Laozi*, not only because their dates and provenance are not certain but also because they offer very little for this study. Another group of manuscripts discussed herein, including *Taiyi Sheng Shui*, *Hengxian*, and *Fanwu Liuxing*, are separately referred to as the Huang-Lao manuscripts.

The next convention concerns editions. All known editions of the *Daodejing*, most importantly those of Heshang Gong and Wang Bi, derive from the Huang-Lao version of the *Daodejing*. Many of the important differences between these and other editions concern textual lineages more than internal content, but altogether they make up what is collectively referred to herein as the received edition, or sometimes for clarity in specific instances as the Heshang Gong edition. While there is only a minimal difference between what is referred to as the *Daodejing* and what is referred to as the received edition or the Heshang Gong edition, the term "received text" remains useful for analyses of specific terms or passages when discussed in the context of comparison with, for example, the *Laozi* manuscripts.

Rudolf Wagner's explanation of his own conventions for discussing textual issues surrounding Wang Bi's commentary mirror my own. Although our language and references differ and, unlike him, I am not attempting to reconstruct any original text, his explanation clarifies and partially justifies my own conventions; he writes:

> all received versions of the Wang Bi *Laozi* [are] referred to herein as "Wang Bi *Laozi Receptus*" ... I should emphasize that in the following discussion and examples, the term "Wang Bi *Laozi Receptus*" refers specifically and exclusively to the received "Wang Bi version" of the text. This should be strictly differentiated from what I will try to reconstruct as the original text known to Wang Bi, which I will refer to as "Wang Bi *Laozi Urtext*."[2]

Next to the cultural phenomenon called the *Daodejing* in two versions (the Laozi and the Huang-Lao), with its two groups of excavated manuscripts (from Guodian and Mawangdui), the received text and its editions (especially that of Heshang Gong), there is the issue concerning commentary. All known commentaries to the *Daodejing* are commentaries to the Huang-Lao *Daodejing*, including Xunzi's, with the possible exception of the Xiang'er commentary to the short-lived Tianshi *Daodejing*. This study particularly discusses the first two commentaries to the *Daodejing* composed in the Han Dynasty, one by Yan Zun and the other by Heshang Gong. Since their commentaries come with the actual text of the *Daodejing* upon which they commented, there is no need to complicate that by talking about any editions in particular.

The first look at the *Daodejing* above affirmed in it the presence of a definite philosophy, but also something else in addition. Both of them emerge from the particular notion of the Dao espoused by the *Daodejing* and understanding the connections between them leads the way into engaging with the matrix of the *Daodejing* itself, the subject of this entire study. Before starting down that path, however, a few words about the conventions for referring to the Dao adopted in this study are in order.

When scholars of Daoism talk about the Dao in English, it is in one of three ways: as "the Dao" with a determinative and capitalization; as "Dao" without determinative but with capitalization that is sometimes italicized as "*Dao*"; and as "*dao*" without a determinative or capitalization and always italicized. Because there is a lot at stake with these different conventions of referring to the Dao, I want to be clear about my own. To that end, it is worth reflecting on the following body of ideas from three eminent thinkers of the *Daodejing*; while I do not agree with everything that each one says, I fully support their general perspectives, which are of immense assistance for framing the issue.

Although scholars have long been discussing different conventions for referring to the Dao, the work of Chad Hansen was instrumental in taking them to a new level of critical reflection; about *Daodejing* Chapter 1, for example, he writes:

> The standard translation of the first line is "The *Dao* that can be told is not the constant *Dao*." (Translators usually capitalize *dao*—as they would *God*.) Note first that nothing in the Chinese corresponds to the definite article *the*. Translators conform to their own community practice of always putting *the* before *dao*. We could, in principle, take as interpretive hypotheses that the subject was *a dao* or *any dao*, or simply *Daos*. The translating convention embodies an ancient interpretive hypothesis that all Daoists must worship a mystical godlike *dao*. Thus they presume in translation what they cannot find in the original: assertion of the existence of a single, ineffable *dao*.
>
> It all seems so innocent. How can such a little, *nothing* word matter so much? The answer has been familiar to students of philosophy since Bertrand Russell. The usual effect of a definite article in English is to make a general noun, in this case the term *dao*, into a logically singular noun-phrase: *the* + general noun-phrase = a phrase that entails the existence of a unique object answering the description. Capitalization, on analogy with God (as against gods), has the same implication. It makes a general term a proper noun.[3]

Building on Hansen's comments, Steven Burik adds a succinct and very much to the point discussion of the philosophical consequences stemming from different conventions for referring to the Dao:

> [T]he temptation is always there to absolutize in a logocentric manner the "ideas" and "concepts" of East Asian traditions (an example being The Dao in capital letters translated back toward the reifying and "noun-thinking" substance

ontology connected to Western standards), and this temptation is apparent both in Western and subsequent Asian readings and interpretations of the Daoist tradition ...[4]

For reasons that are becoming more and more obvious, I think that writing Dao with a capital letter perpetuates the idea of reading it solely as a noun denoting a substance or a something, and thereby facilitating the idea of seeing "it" as a transcendent or metaphysical entity beyond the "ten thousand things." ... Chad Hansen, for example, has argued extensively against imposing such Western background assumptions on classical Chinese language and thinking. In unison with recent post-modern scholarship on, and the consequently non-metaphysical reading of, the Daoist classics, I therefore propose to write the Romanization of *dao* in lower case letters, not capitalized, except when it is capitalized in quotations.[5]

Burik heavily relies on continental philosophy, including notably the work of Martin Heidegger, in his reading of the *Daodejing*. Heidegger himself is famous for his non-metaphysical philosophy, generally recognized as phenomenology, and his critique of the Western metaphysical tradition. He also discussed the Dao at some length, which he interpreted phenomenologically (non-metaphysically), thus at the very least drawing our attention to the conventions of referring to the Dao much like Hansen did, although their starting points were different. Burik weaves together the critiques of Heidegger and Hansen, both of which are directed at the Western tendency to reify and essentialize notions, in this case the Dao, and he chooses to refer to "it" as *dao* because only in this way does the notion referred to not turn into a "transcendent or metaphysical entity."

Heidegger, however, is the original source for the critique of these conventions of referring to the Dao with their essentializing consequences. This critique is strikingly similar to his critique of the Western metaphysical tradition, which he accuses of essentializing the phenomenological notion of "being" (or "beyng" or "*ereignis*," etc.) and changing it into the metaphysical notion of Being. It seems that this is basically the same process undergone by the phenomenological *dao* that became the metaphysical Dao essentialized by Western thought.

However, when Western thought essentializes the Dao to make it into a metaphysical entity, doesn't this mean that it in fact exists? Or does it mean that it does not finally exist? But my thinking, which holds that this essentialized Dao does in fact exist, leads me to ask, where does it exist? Hansen and Burik would respond that it exists only in the mind of the Western thinker as a mistake of understanding, being anyway the consequence of the Western essentializing habit. Both of them also assert that this metaphysical Dao is nowhere to be found in traditional interpretations of the *Daodejing*, nor is it to be found anywhere in the *Daodejing* itself.

I can agree part way with what Hansen and Burik say about "*dao*" and "the Dao": I agree that "*dao*" intends to refer to a phenomenological something-nothing, and that calling it "the Dao" effectively turns that phenomenological something-nothing into a metaphysical thing, an essentialized substance, a metaphysical mistake. And if asked which of the two, "*dao*" or "the Dao," is the Dao of the *Daodejing*, they will certainly say only "*dao*" and not "the Dao." But because I see both a phenomenological "*dao*" and a metaphysical "the Dao" in the writing, I disagree with the other half of what they say. To better explain this, it is worth turning to Heidegger's famous characterization of the Dao, because it provides an important indication about the conventions for referring to it. Note that he translates "*dao*/the Dao" as "way" (*weg*), and he writes:

> The word "way" is a primal word of language that speaks to the reflective mind of man. The guideword in Laozi's poetic thinking is Dao, which "properly speaking" refers to way. But because we are prone to think of "way" superficially, as a stretch connecting two places, our word "way" has all too rashly been considered unfit to name what Dao says. Dao is then translated as reason, spirit, raison, meaning, logos.
>
> Yet Dao could be the way that gives all ways, the very source of our power to think what reason, mind, meaning, logos properly say—properly, by their proper nature. Perhaps the mystery of mysteries of thoughtful Saying conceals itself in the word "way," Dao, if only we will let these names return to what they leave unspoken, if only we are capable of this, to allow them to do so. Perhaps the enigmatic power of today's reign of method also, and indeed preeminently, stems from the fact that the methods, notwithstanding their efficiency, are after all merely the runoff of a great hidden stream which moves all things along and makes way for everything. All is way.[6]

Heidegger here also points to two different Daos, one that is phenomenological, whose presence in the world is that of "a great hidden stream which moves all things along and makes way for everything," and another that is metaphysical, born from the Western essentializing habit that derivatively recognizes it as "reason, spirit, raison, meaning, logos," an entity pushed outside of the world and into the realm of eternity/permanence/constancy. Given the existence of this metaphysical Dao, Heidegger encourages us to return to that phenomenological Dao, "if only we will let these names return to what they leave unspoken, if we are capable of this, to allow them to do so."

This study is constructed on the recognition of two separate Daos in the *Daodejing*; more precisely, it recognizes a phenomenological *dao* in the Laozi *Daodejing*, and a metaphysical Dao in the Huang-Lao *Daodejing*. Sinologically, the two Daos are differentiated by nothing so simple than that the Laozi *Daodejing* calls it *heng dao* 恆道 and the Huang-Lao *Daodejing* calls it *chang dao* 常道. To differentiate them philosophically, in this study "the pristine Dao" refers to the phenomenological, this-worldly Dao of the Laozi *Daodejing*, and "the cosmic Dao" refers to the metaphysical, transcendent Dao of the Huang-Lao *Daodejing*.

This study uses the convention of referring to "it" as "the Dao" to maintain the symmetrical connection between the pristine Dao and the cosmic Dao, not as two sides of the same coin because they really share little in common, but rather the symmetrical connection between it and other or identity and mimesis.

Grappling with how best to talk about the Dao of the *Daodejing*, I have discussed the ideas of Hansen, Burik, and Heidegger concerning different conventions and their consequences for an important reason: wittingly or not, each of them recognize two separate Daos, one phenomenological and the other metaphysical, but each also go on to reject the latter as a metaphysical mistake standing as the primary source of misunderstanding the authentic philosophy of the *Daodejing*. But if we can entertain the possibility of two different Daos, one pristine and the other cosmic, then we are in a better position to differentiate each according to which of the two versions of the *Daodejing* either is in play, the Laozi *Daodejing* or the Huang-Lao *Daodejing*. This study also discusses different groups associated with each version, Yangsheng Daoists with the Laozi *Daodejing*, and Huang-Lao Daoists with the Huang-Lao *Daodejing*. These subjects are here only introduced, being the matters that are explored throughout the course of this study.

One important reason that the *Daodejing* is difficult to understand is that scholars, including myself, have not had the proper tools with which to differentiate these two versions. The situation has changed a lot now that these tools are readily available in the form of the excavated *Laozi* manuscripts and, to a lesser degree, the excavated Huang-Lao manuscripts; taken altogether, they paint a different picture of the *Daodejing* than what we are familiar with.

Next to the *Daodejing*'s philosophy of the Dao, this study is equally focused on that something else in addition, which turns out to be indeed difficult to talk about directly. This study chooses to approach it indirectly, through the route of *yangsheng* 養生. Introducing this concept is the matter of the following chapter.

The outline of this study is not complicated. Part 1 focuses on Yangsheng Daoism and the Laozi *Daodejing*, Part 2 focuses on Huang-Lao Daoism and the Huang-Lao *Daodejing*, and Part 3 focuses on Ge Hong's understanding of Yangsheng Daoism and the *Daodejing*. The Epilogue discusses Heidegger's legacy for Daoist studies and comparative philosophy.

The issue of source texts and textual references is somewhat more complicated. Because the *Laozi* manuscripts demonstrate a tremendous number of textual variants, archaic characters, loan characters, etc., etc., there really can be no single standard edition, especially since there are no premodern commentaries. However, in this new age of digital resources, a vast number of Chinese texts meeting the highest scholarly standards are readily available on sites such as The Chinese Text Project at ctext.org, and this study joins with a growing number of contemporary publications that rely on those digital editions for citation purposes as much as possible. An additional benefit to this practice is that it makes the quotations from the original sources much more readily accessible to those readers who know at least a little Chinese but who are not specialists in the esoteric mysteries of modern sinological citation practices.

Most importantly, the major original source texts examined in this study are all found on ctext.org, including what is considered the received edition of the *Daodejing* 道德經; the *Laozi* manuscripts including the Guodian *Laozi* 郭店老子 and the Mawangdui *Laozi* 馬王堆老子; Yan Zun's commentary 老子指歸, Heshang Gong's commentary 河上公老子章句, Wang Bi's commentary 道德真經注, *Liexian zhuan* 列仙傳, *Shenxian zhuan* 神仙傳, and *Baopuzi Neipian* 抱朴子內篇. However, the *Shenxian zhuan* is a very problematic text, and when I discuss it herein, I rely on the two versions that, in their differences, are as close to standard as it gets, the *Longwei mishu Shenxian zhuan* 龍威祕書神仙傳 and the *Siku quanshu Shenxian zhuan* 四庫全書神仙傳. For other specific instances, many involving the *Baopuzi Neipian*, I also rely on the standard edition as noted.

All uses of English spelling variants of Chinese characters in transcription found in quotations of other works, if not given in pinyin have been changed to their pinyin equivalents, except for names and titles that remain unchanged.

One contribution of this work is to *Laozi* Studies first of all, and it is carried out as a project in the history of religions. Unfortunately, the term "religion" used in this way is probably not familiar to most Western readers, and the term is even harder to defend in China. From the Chinese perspective, this work would be in the area of cross-cultural studies. This is particularly the case with the examination of the philosophy and practices of Yangsheng Daoism.

Another contribution of this work is to what a Western reader might more readily understand as cross-cultural studies, namely, the discussions herein of a large number of contemporary works done by distinguished Chinese scholars, for whom the separation between sinology and philosophy is less pronounced but still exists. They include more sinologically oriented work by scholars such as Wang Zhongjiang as well as more philosophically oriented works by scholars such as Chen Ligui. Because of this feature of the present study, there are long quotations from contemporary Chinese scholarly works, all of which have been translated by me.

Many Western specialists in the field will be familiar with these folks, and they might even expect that this book had better heavily cite them. Which is odd because lots of Western scholars know very well the work of lots of Chinese scholars and the Western studies sometimes do a good job of citing the Chinese studies, it's just that they rarely discuss it in any detail. This void is seen in so much Western scholarship, and since non-specialists will not know about this Chinese work in other ways, this book brings that Chinese scholarship into direct conversation with Western scholarship.

Having lived in Beijing for many years now, I have had many exciting conversations with Chinese scholars. In the context of my Western education, it is amazing to witness and have direct access to their work, so it is my very good fortune to be able to bring their scholarship into dialogue with Western scholarship. And because contemporary *Laozi* Studies have been supercharged by the discoveries of the *Laozi* manuscripts, there is a pressing need to bring all of this work into dialogue—because is this not where cross-cultural dialogue begins?

2

Matrix Side B: Yangsheng, according to Ge Hong

Because this study of the *Daodejing* gives a more or less equal focus to *yangsheng* and to the philosophy of the Dao, and because *yangsheng* is somewhat unfamiliar in the West, it is important to have an idea about it before engaging with the *Daodejing*. This chapter analyzes Ge Hong's sophisticated systematization of the complete program of *yangsheng* as well as one of his illustrative depictions of *yangsheng* in action (he and his writings are discussed more fully in Chapters 7 and 8).

To be clear, Ge Hong's understanding of *yangsheng* does not explain the *Daodejing*'s understanding of *yangsheng*, not to mention that the *Daodejing* reveals *yangsheng* in its earliest stages while Ge Hong systematized it some eight centuries later. What we can say is that Ge Hong believed that the *yangsheng* he systematized was the same *yangsheng* of the *Daodejing*. Later chapters will independently examine the *yangsheng* of the *Daodejing*, but this introduction of Ge Hong's *yangsheng* should give a general idea of what it involves.

Yangsheng[1] is founded on the set of techniques that center on *qi* 氣 circulation. In Ge Hong's Daoist understanding of the world, *qi* is both the basic component of what exists and the most powerful. While it is not incorrect to understand *qi* as air or breath, Ge Hong understands it as the substance-energy of the pristine Dao, the fecund stuff from which Heaven, Earth, and existing beings are born. In its *yang* mode, *qi* forms Heaven above as well as the human mind or spirit; in its *yin* mode, it forms Earth below as well as the human body; and in its mixed mode, it is the breath that converges spirit with body: with convergence the person is born, and with dispersal the person dies. As the techniques of *yangsheng* replenish and revitalize the body's rhythmic systems of circulation thereby to prolong this convergence, there is long-life.

Referring to a specific technique, *yangsheng* refers to *qi* circulation 氣行 or 行氣, *qi* cultivation 氣功, and "spitting out the old and taking in the new [*qi*]" 吐古納新. The *Shenxian zhuan*'s biography of Peng Zu gives a striking instance of this:

He would often shut off his *qi* and breathe internally. From sunrise to mid-day, he would sit straight and rub his eyes, knead and squeeze his body and limbs, lick his lips, swallow his saliva, and ingest *qi* several dozen times. Only then he would get up and move, speaking and smiling as before. If his body felt any illness, fatigue, or discomfort, he would practice guiding and pulling and shut off his *qi* to attack the trouble. He would fix his heart on his body: his face and head, nine orifices, five viscera, four limbs, even his hair, fixing his concentration in each location. He would feel his *qi* circulate throughout his body, starting at his nose and mouth and reaching down to the tips of his ten fingers.[2]

Used as a category marker, *yangsheng* indicates four separate practices: *qi* circulation 行氣; dietetics including "avoidance of grains" 辟谷 or "ingesting medicines" 服藥 or 服飯; sexual arts or "the arts of the bedroom" 房中之術; and calisthenics or "guiding and pulling" 導引. Ge Hong appears as the first to systematize these four practices, reflected in this passage from the *Neipian* that mentions only three of them:

Although "ingesting medicines" is the root of longevity, if a person at the same time also is able to circulate *qi*, then the beneficial results will be experienced even more rapidly. If a person is unable to obtain medicines but circulates *qi* thoroughly according to the principles, that person will obtain several hundred additional years; a person must, however, also know "the arts of the bedroom" for that to happen. If a person does not know the methods of *yin* and *yang* [e.g., "the arts of the bedroom"], but consistently labors at it and depletes oneself, then it will be extremely difficult to have the energy for *qi* circulation.[3]

In this next passage, Ge Hong sets forth the full complement of *yangsheng* practices:

For anybody who practices *yangsheng*, you must desire to have extensive knowledge of it and learn to embody the essentials, experience it deeply and be good at selecting. Being partial to the cultivation of only one aspect of it is insufficient and unreliable but being overly fond of only one aspect also poses a danger to those students who only depend on those aspects of it for which they have an aptitude. Those who know the methods of Xuan Nü and Su Nü[4] claim that only "the arts of the bedroom" can enable a person to go beyond the world. Those who only understand "the way of spitting out and taking in [*qi*]" claim that only *qi* circulation can enable a person to extend the years of their life. Those who know the rules of "guiding and pulling" claim that only healing exercises can enable a person to retard old age. Those who know medicinal recipes claim that only "the ingestion of medicines" can enable a person to be without exhaustion. If someone studies the Dao without success, it is entirely due to such partialities.[5]

Because *yangsheng* is not self-taught, Ge Hong insists that finding an authentic master is the first order of business; he writes, for example, that "the selection of the correct master is more important than the hard work" 夫務學不如擇師.⁶ This requirement informs one aspect of Ge Hong's conception of Yangsheng Daoism that pertains to the functional structures of master–disciple transmissions, and Ge Hong's *Neipian* and *Shenxian zhuan* provide ample indications for reconstructing some of them. Unlike Chan Buddhism's *Transmission of the Lamp* writings, Ge Hong does not present systematically unbroken lines of continuous master–disciple transmissions from Laozi, but indications in the *Neipian* reveal something of his own line: Ge Hong received his teachings from Zheng Yin, who received them from Ge Xuan (Ge Hong's paternal grand-uncle), who received them from Zuo Ci, who received them from Li Zhongfu, who received them from Wang Jun. It is unclear if Wang Jun is Wang Zhongdu, "said to be a Daoist who studied the Dao on Liang Mountain under Taibo Zhenren (the Perfected One of Venus),"⁷ or Wang Yuan, who served as an official until he "quit his offices and entered the mountains to cultivate the Dao," where he found his own master whom the text does not name.

The master–disciple transmission primarily consists of writings and their accompanying "secret oral teachings" 口訣 or 訣言), also sometimes referred to as "essentials" (要). These transmissions are the core element of the master–disciple relationship and, according to Zhu Yueli:

> Ge Hong recorded two "secret oral teachings" 口訣 concerning "returning essence to replenish the brain" 還精補腦. He said that he received them through oral transmission and that he did not make them up by himself. The reason that he mentioned them was to prove to people that their existence was reliable. Ge Hong said that there were thousands of such secret oral teachings, although he did not completely reveal them so others would not be able to learn their secret contents. Most of the oral teachings were presented in esoteric language, and Ge Hong certainly treated them with confidentiality, so although we can easily understand his accounts of "the arts of the bedroom," it is difficult to know the central points of its inner contents without being a disciple. It's like "hearing somebody on the stairs without seeing anybody coming down," like "seeing flowers in the fog," or like "watching a movie without the curtain pulled back," you cannot really get it. This is exactly the result that Ge Hong wants to achieve without imparting the secrets. We have to give up the extravagant hope of peeping into the secrets, and only make our own assessments about what kind of bedroom arts these actually are.⁸

About these secret oral teachings, Ge Hong writes:

> The secret teachings concerning the highest truths were often transmitted orally; at other times they were written on a piece of silk not longer than eight feet that was worn around the neck and the waist; but these secret teachings could not be obtained without undergoing a long probationary period under a master who tested one's diligence.[9]

In a few passages, Ge Hong reveals some elements of the oral teachings that he received from his master, Zheng Yin.[10] Such transmissions were highly ritualized and often required the smearing of blood from a sacrificed animal on the disciple's lips as a guarantee that s/he would not divulge the secret oral teachings. The *Neipian* describes a little bit of the blood ritual:

> There are strict requisites for receiving the secret oral teachings concerning Truth-Unity: the lips are smeared with the blood of a white victim; the secret teachings are received on a propitious day; white gauze and white silver are used for the contract, and a tally of gold is used to engrave and split it. If one recklessly expounds these secret oral teachings or presumptuously transmits them, their gods will not operate.[11]

Since the arts of the bedroom often involve two persons working together, the necessity for the secret oral teachings in this case ought to be more urgent, but Ge Hong explains that each component of *yangsheng* has an equal necessity:

> The world says that the goodness of a single word can be worth more than a thousand in gold ... but when a person is told the secret teachings of long-life or given a prescription for deathlessness, it is worth far more than those good words of an ordinary person ... A person need only acquire the essentials, which consists in treasuring sperm, circulating *qi*, taking one great medicine, and that is enough, there is no need to multiply things. As for these three pursuits: one must return over and over to the shallow and the profound; nothing is worth more than an enlightened master; diligent effort cannot be shunned; and the utmost knowledge of them cannot be attained quickly. Although we speak of *qi* circulation [in the singular], there are a multitude of methods. Although we speak of sexual arts, there are nearly one hundred separate techniques. Although we speak of ingesting medicine, there are roughly one thousand recipes. When teaching these things, one starts with the shallow, and if the will of the disciple does not slacken and s/he is steadfast and diligent and can be taught, then s/he can be told the essentials.[12]

Precisely because these *yangsheng* techniques are so complex and their proper transmission requires an intimate relationship between master and disciple, Ge Hong says, "Authentic Persons have ever only transmitted these methods orally, and from the beginning they were never committed to writing," and he follows this with a dire warning coupled with a personal note:

> Unless one receives the secret oral teachings about these techniques, not a single person in ten thousand who attempts to perform them will fail to kill himself. Xuan Nü, Su Nü, Zi Du, Rong Cheng Gong, and Peng Zu likely recorded some general pointers about them, but they did not write down on paper their most essential principles. However, those committed to seeking deathlessness will devote themselves to seeking them out. I myself received the teachings from my master Zheng Yin.[13]

Ge Hong gives the *Daodejing* a pivotal position in the context of Yangsheng Daoist transmissions of secret oral teachings. As the matrix, it gathers the motherlode sources of Yangsheng Daoist knowledge pertaining to both the philosophy of the pristine Dao and practice of *yangsheng*, but in fact it is the transmitted record of Laozi's secret oral teachings. Since the time that Laozi was actively transmitting these oral teachings to his disciples, the text itself has become eminently public. Even though the *Daodejing* is the most important compendium of "Laozi's secret oral teachings" 老子之訣言[14] concerning the profound secrets of *yangsheng*, it nevertheless requires a secondary set of secret oral teachings to explain them; Ge Hong writes:

> Although *The Document in Five Thousand Words* [*Daodejing*] comes from Laozi, it presents only non-specific doctrines and approximate summaries. Its contents absolutely do not allow for a complete enumeration of matters from beginning to end, so how could a person rely on it for their own practice? To ignorantly recite this scripture without understanding the essentials of its Dao is an exercise in futility.[15]

Ge Hong's conception of Yangsheng Daoism depends on continuous transmissions from masters to disciples who in turn become transmitting masters. This structural component of continuous transmission is particularly demonstrated in the *Shenxian zhuan*'s biography of Peng Zu, whose *yangsheng* mastery has extended his life to nearly 800 years. Because Peng Zu stands out among all Yangsheng Daoists for his mastery of "the arts of the bedroom," Zhu Yueli writes:

> During the Jin Dynasty, there were different branches of "the arts of the bedroom," and Ge Hong pointed out more than ten, including those of Xuan Nü, Su Nü, Zi Du, Rong Cheng, and Peng Zu. Among these branches, Ge Hong most esteemed Peng Zu's. In the "Weizhi" of the *Neipian*, he wrote, "The techniques of Peng Zu are the most essential. Others are troublesome and difficult to pursue,

and their benefits are not worth the paper they are written on. People who can perform them are extremely few." Also during the Jin Dynasty, there were many names for the different techniques of "the arts of the bedroom," and Ge Hong pointed out more than one hundred of them. Of these, Ge Hong most valued the methods of "returning essence to replenish the brain" [particularly identified with Peng Zu].[16]

Peng Zu's biography in the *Shenxian zhuan* states that when the king learned about his long life, he sent one of his harem women, Cainü 采女,[17] to receive his oral teachings so that she could transmit them to the king so that he could extend his own life. Cainü "had attained the Dao in her youth and knew methods for nurturing the body; she was 270 years old but looked fifteen or sixteen."[18] After welcoming her, Peng Zu gifted her nine *yangsheng* writings that he had received from his teacher(s), including *Releasing the Nodes* 節解, *Sheathing the Body* 韜形, and *Opening and Clarifying* 開明,[19] telling her that these scriptures are appropriate for beginners. However, much like the Mawangdui *Daoyin tu* 導引圖 that contains forty-four color illustrations of various *yangsheng* "guiding and pulling" postures, such writings often took the form of "charts" 圖, for which oral teachings would be a necessary prerequisite for their proper exercise. The biography then states that Cainü "received all their essentials and taught them to the king,"[20] but it gives no indication as to how much time (hours, weeks, months, or years) that Cainü had spent with Peng Zu receiving his teachings.

The biography depicts a double transmission of texts and their "essentials" 要 (referring to their oral teachings) from Peng Zu to Cainü, then from Cainü to the king. After achieving some success, the king "promulgated a decree throughout the land that whoever transmitted Peng Zu's Dao would be executed, and he also wanted to kill Peng Zu so as to cut off the transmission of his teaching,"[21] but Peng Zu escaped unharmed.

This episode highlights Ge Hong's emphasis on continuous lines of transmission from masters to disciples. And while we never learn who was Peng Zu's master(s), the biography records his saying to Cainü,

> At present on Mount Dawan lives Master Qingjing who is said to be a thousand years old. His complexion is like that of a youth, and he can walk over three hundred *li* in one day. He can go a whole year without eating, or he can eat nine times in a single day. He is truly one who may be questioned.[22]

No further information is provided about this thousand-year-old Master Qingjing 青精先生, yet he remains there on Mount Dawan 大宛山, willing to accept worthy disciples: "He is truly one who may be questioned." It is not unreasonable to think that a committed seeker could go Mount Dawan with the expectation of having the opportunity to learn Master Qingjing's *yangsheng* techniques transmitted by generations of his disciples, some of whom themselves became masters in the lineage identified with his name. Finally, the *Neipian* underscores the centrality of master–disciple transmissions by recognizing "seven or eight of Peng Zu's own students … who lived for several centuries and departed as *xian* during the Yin Dynasty."[23]

This presentation of *yangsheng* according to Ge Hong offers a first introduction to its general ideas and practices that have informed all corners of Daoism from at least the Han Dynasty. How close or far it is from the *yangsheng* of the Laozi *Daodejing* is hard to discern, but both are squarely centered on *qi* circulation and lead to a physical embodiment of the Dao. This is enough to know for approaching the matrix of the *Daodejing*.

Part One

Yangsheng Daoism and the Matrix

3

Uncovering Yangsheng Daoism

Two Aspects of the Matrix

The basic perspective of this study is rooted in the difference between two separate versions of an early Chinese *Daodejing*, the first called the Laozi *Daodejing* and the second the Huang-Lao *Daodejing*. There are multiple ways to conceive of this difference, but they are possible only if one accepts that there are these two separate versions to begin with. Establishing this is the objective of this study and not its starting point, which begins by letting the two versions announce themselves by way of their English translations of the first chapter of the *Daodejing*. In order to display more clearly their difference, I set them against each other line by line, with the Laozi *Daodejing* on the left column and the Huang-Lao *Daodejing* on the right:

Dao's can guide, but they are not the temporalizing Dao.	The Dao that can be spoken is not the constant Dao.
Names can name, but they are not the temporalizing Name.	The name that can be named is not the constant name.
Nothingness names the beginning of Heaven and Earth	The Nameless is the origin of Heaven and Earth
Being names the mother of the myriad beings.	The Named is the mother of the myriad things.
For this reason,	For this reason,
Hold to the standpoint of Nothingness with the intent to witness its wonders.	Constantly be without desire to see its wonders.
Hold to the standpoint of Being with the intent to witness its manifestations.	Constantly be with desire to see its manifestations.

These two arise from the same but with different names.	These two are the same but diverge in name as they issue forth
and both can be called Mystery.	and they are called the profound.
Mystery upon Mystery: the gateway of the many and the wonders.	More profound than the profound: the gateway of manifold wonders.

The difference between the two versions is that the Laozi *Daodejing* is grounded in a phenomenology while the Huang-Lao *Daodejing* is grounded in a metaphysics. However, I do not here analyze just what the various terms in each version refer to or how they refer; I do not describe the differences between "Being" and "Nothingness" next to "the Named" and "the Nameless"; I do not discuss "the standpoints" of Being and Nothingness or their possible connections to "being with or without desire"; and I do not consider the consequences of "arising from the same" versus "being the same" in origin. I also do not here explain my use of Being and Nothingness to translate *you* 有 and *wu* 無; I do not discuss what I mean by phenomenology and metaphysics; I explore neither the historical nor the philosophical priority of either version; finally, I do not engage with the difference between "temporalizing" *heng* and "constant" *chang*.

These issues are the matter of everything that follows in this book. Nonetheless, equipped with these parallel translations of *Daodejing* chapter 1 in two versions, the reader is better equipped to follow the course of this study with a clear picture of what the destination will look like. In sum, the difference between the Laozi *Daodejing* and the Huang-Lao *Daodejing* is encapsulated in the difference between "temporalizing" 恆 *heng* and the pristine Dao, and "constant" 常 *chang* and the cosmic Dao. The reader will not be entirely wrong to expect that the matrix of the *Daodejing* should arise from the Laozi *Daodejing* rather than the Huang-Lao *Daodejing*.

The image of a matrix is useful in exploring the early career and vicissitudes of the *Daodejing* as well as the life course of Yangsheng Daoism. As a substance, entity, or environment, a matrix is a wellspring or ground source with two aspects: gestating, it inwardly contains and nurtures, while birthing, it outwardly generates and produces. This study more specifically concentrates on the matrix of the *Daodejing* with respect to two aspects or refractive perspectives on it: the first is nameable and the other is unnameable.

The *Daodejing* can be compared to an analogue program consisting of hundreds of semi-autonomous units of thought pulsating through the continuously variable time-space field that is the amorphous text itself. *Daodejing* chapter 1 displays several of these units of thought as it explores rich and various ways of conceiving the Dao, for which logical or epistemological standpoints are inadequate.

As the *Daodejing* presents a sustained meditation on the Dao, its first chapter presents a refracted reflection on the text as a whole. Even if we want to provide a more historically precise translation of the chapter that turns out to be more philosophically accurate or more intellectually provocative than the standard translation that states, "The Dao that can be spoken is not the constant Dao," it still raises a host of intriguing questions. The understood claim of that standard reading is that we in fact speak about the Dao, but this speakable Dao, according to the strict terms of metaphysics, is not the real Dao because that lies beyond language. Therefore, it is fruitful to inquire into the relationship between the nameable Dao that we can talk about and the unnameable Dao that we cannot.

The first line of the chapter introduces the text as one that gathers into itself a profundity of words that are directed to something that cannot be put into words. Lines three and four initially introduce the two aspects of the matrix: "unnamed" 無名 and "named" 有名. In conjunction with line one, the text appears to identify (that aspect of) the Dao that "can be spoken" 可道 as "named," and (that aspect of) the Dao that cannot be put into language as "unnamed." Are these two separate Daos, or two conditions, modes, or aspects of the same Dao?

Immediately following this claim that implies that there are two aspects of the Dao, one of which is unnamed, the text proceeds to speak about the Dao at great length. Is this a contradiction or a paradox? Is the text's speaking about the Dao then an impossibility in some logical sense that it simply evades by way of sleight of hand? But it cannot be an impossibility, because this demonstration is right in front of us, we are holding it, reading it, possibly reciting it, and this "it" is itself the *Daodejing*. But we might rephrase the question and ask, Is the Dao about which the text speaks the nameable Dao or the unnameable Dao?

Line 6 tells us that these two aspects of this Dao "arise from the same but with different names" 同出而異名: the unnamed Dao "is the beginning of Heaven and Earth" 天地之始, while the named Dao is "the Mother of the myriad beings" 萬物之母. Line 8 further states that the "mystery upon mystery" 玄之又玄 lies precisely in the primordiality of the pristine Dao in both of its aspects.

Yoan Ariel and Gil Raz write that "the first chapter was consciously composed as an introduction to the *Daodejing*, and the author or redactor of the chapter in fact responded to the very questions concerning the possibility of discussing the Dao. This response is encoded in the first chapter."[1] Ariel and Raz discuss multiple instances throughout the *Daodejing* of these sorts of "encoded" double meanings, and they argue that they represent two different readings of the text. Accordingly, the exoteric reading sends a political message about ruling the country, and the esoteric is directed to the Dao. But this distinction is not so cut and dry, even and particularly with respect to *Daodejing* chapter 1 because, as they write,

> These two aspects are linked not as esoteric and exoteric aspects, but as parts of a single argument. The esoteric aspect, therefore, must lie elsewhere, and we suggest that the most fundamental implication of this interpretation is that the book itself is identical to the Dao, and that the language of the text needs to be read and understood as encoding deeper levels of meaning.[2]

The claim that the *Daodejing* is "identical" to the Dao deserves closer attention,[3] especially when considering which of its aspects (named or unnamed) is at issue. The text speaks of the Dao at great length, suggesting that this is the named Dao, yet at every point it also recognizes the inability of language to speak of it even as it continuously manifests through "encoded deeper levels of meaning," suggesting that this is the unnameable Dao. This recognition of two Daos or two components of a single Dao in the text's opening line serves as the starting point for an initial ingress into the organic and integral matrix of the *Daodejing* with its two aspects: unnameable, it is the source from which all existence springs; nameable, it manifests in and as the *Daodejing*. In other words, the unnameable Dao harbors and emits the nameable Dao as the *Daodejing*, and the nameable Dao harbors and reveals the unnameable Dao as the source of existence.

These two aspects of the matrix of the *Daodejing*, one outwardly burgeoning and the other inwardly gathered, have infused the tradition of Daoism as well as Chinese culture at large for thousands of years. Much like Einsteinian physics, we can perceive the matrix in terms of time or space, in terms of energy or substance, or in terms of light within darkness or darkness within light. Hence, my references to the matrix of the *Daodejing* intend to broadly designate unitary but enfolded phenomena that intertwine two refractive perspectives as a kind of rolling, roiling Möbius loop that propels itself outward while simultaneously gathering itself into its own non-externalized depths.

To be more precise with these two aspects, the unnameable Dao is that which refers to the plenitudinous font of existence that gives birth to and sustains life. The plenitude of life is enjoyed only as a being becomes and remains one with the Dao; the *Daodejing* understands this oneness as a bodily phenomenon, rather than mental or mystical. It is exclusively achieved by bodily cultivation, and thus it signifies the unnameable aspect of the matrix. On the other hand, the nameable Dao refers to that other aspect that can be talked about and that provides a reasonable understanding of existence. This understanding is intended to anchor the bodily cultivation that leads to oneness with the Dao. The *Daodejing* gives many words about this aspect of the matrix that, taken altogether, articulate its philosophy of the pristine Dao.

The unnameable Dao courses throughout all existence and stands as the foundational source and intended goal of *yangsheng* bodily cultivation. This cultivation becomes effective as it merges the body of the adept with the force, flows, rhythms, and movements of the Dao, endowing the body with long-life and lasting satisfaction; this is what *Daodejing* chapter 59 calls "the Dao of long-life and lasting vision" 長生久視之道. Described and demonstrated throughout, the text nowhere names this system of bodily cultivation, but the tradition quickly identified it as *yangsheng* 養生 (the nurture of life). It requires the practitioner to focus resolutely and unwaveringly on empowering the circulation of *qi* throughout all parts of the physical body. This *qi* has multiple referents: normal respiratory breath and even something like air more generally, but also, on a cosmic register, the breath of the Dao that can be conceived in terms of energy and/or matter that, concentrated, provides the substance for all things. If maintained in vitality life continues, but when depleted or dispersed then death. To infuse the body with this cosmic *qi* is to nurture and thereby extend one's life, thus *yangsheng*.

The nameable Dao that manifests in and as the *Daodejing* puts into words an authoritative and profoundly encompassing philosophy of the Dao that responds to fundamental questions of existence. To call on Western categories, the *Daodejing*'s philosophy of the Dao contains a cosmogony giving image to the formation of Heaven and Earth and the myriad beings; a cosmology answering to the contextualities and relationalities of the myriad beings existing in the world; an ontology uncovering the phenomenological workings of being and nothingness with respect to the myriad beings; and a soteriology offering scathing insights into how and why the world has gone wrong together with hopeful visions of a harmoniously functional world.

The nameable Dao of the *Daodejing*'s philosophy of the Dao was a radically novel notion in the philosophical thought of early China. Its most profound insight, that the Dao itself is that from which all life and existence is born, injected a transformational agent into the Chinese consciousness that provided the foundational blueprint for how people came to conceive the world in its cosmogonic origins as well as in its on-going condition of duration and change. It also informed the ways in which people thought about knowledge, language, and truth itself.

Some scholars have recognized the otherness of the philosophy of the *Daodejing*. Kristofer Schipper writes, "It is most likely that the tradition which produced, over a number of centuries, the aphorisms of the *Daodejing* was not that of 'philosophers' ... The background of the book of the Old Master [Laozi] is not with the schools of the young noblemen of feudal China, as other texts may be."[4] This otherness is recognizable even in the earliest excavated manuscripts of the work, and Barbara Hendrischke, in her study of the three Guodian *Laozi* manuscripts, writes of the "otherness" of its philosophy that she recognizes as peculiarly Daoist:

> The message of the three *Laozi* texts ... is in distinct contrast to that of the rest of the Guodian corpus. The *Laozi* texts do not differ in regard to the problems they raise and promise to solve. Their striking otherness lies in the approach to these problems. They start from different premises and use different methods of philosophical investigation, a difference that becomes easily manifest in their style of writing ... How the *Laozi* texts and their message relate to the bulk of the Guodian corpus ... enhances the impression of the otherness of Daoist thought.[5]

The otherness of this Daoist philosophy is the direct product of the otherness of its foundational concept, the Dao, in its two aspects.

Next to this nameable Dao, the *Daodejing* indirectly reveals, through its words and images, the unnameable Dao first of all by way of the non-mediated bodily experience of *qi*, the breath of this Dao, as it surrounds and pervades all living things at every moment in every place, and the worldly arena for this experience of the unnameable Dao is what *Daodejing* chapter 29 calls "a sacred vessel" 神器. The *qi* of this Dao suffuses the pores of the skin, hardens to form the sinews and bones, enters from the nose and the mouth and gathers in the lungs, from there circulating from the hairs of the head to the tips of the toes.

Although we name it with the word Dao, it is beyond designation and impossibly incapable of representation in language, thought, and art. The sages 聖人 constantly mentioned throughout the *Daodejing* are those who cultivate this Dao and nurture life.

The unnameable aspect of the matrix is that to which *yangsheng* cultivation is directed. In its differences from the nameable aspect, it has received less scholarly attention, particularly in the ways that the nameable Dao bonds to and anchors it, thereby providing to the practitioner a viable access into *yangsheng*.

The *Daodejing*'s philosophy of the Dao together with the *yangsheng* cultivation that it supports, when merged in philosophical enactment, represents the central core of Yangsheng Daoism. This designation differs from the more familiar "philosophical Daoism" 道家 and, although it seems to downplay its philosophical aspect by highlighting the cultivational, *yangsheng* cultivation is stranded without the philosophy of pristine Dao to anchor it. To recognize Yangsheng Daoism is also to distinguish it, not from the "religious Daoism" 道教 that originally formed in the Eastern Han, but from the Huang-Lao Daoism that formed at the end of the Warring States, long before the formation of "religious Daoism."

To recognize something called Yangsheng Daoism goes against the grain of much modern scholarship that restricts the *Daodejing*'s original environment to late-third-century BCE circles of philosophical debate. However, correctly assembled historical evidence, indirect though much of it is, strongly suggests that a group(s) of people enacted the *Daodejing*'s philosophy of the Dao by their practice of *yangsheng* cultivation long before the late third century BCE. An important impetus for reexamining the original environment of the *Daodejing* arises from the recent discoveries of the Guodian *Laozi*, unearthed from a tomb roughly dated to the fourth century BCE, and the Mawangdui *Laozi*, unearthed from a tomb dated to the second century BCE. Particularly the Guodian *Laozi* implies a much earlier original environment for Daoism that is probably best characterized in terms other than philosophical debate.

Daodejing Chapter 15: A Yangsheng Manifesto

The question of the *Daodejing*'s original environment requires a close reading of the text for signs of a target audience, but its ambiguous nature makes it difficult to clearly recognize. Much of this ambiguity derives from a common misreading of its major figures, the sages, who are often (mis-)identified as kings. This (mis-)identification is motivated by political interpretations of the text that readers have forced upon it since the rise of Huang-Lao thought. The resulting transformation of the Laozi *Daodejing* into the Huang-Lao *Daodejing* has made it difficult to see the former in social and historical context. That version characterizes the sages not as political rulers but as *yangsheng* masters, as demonstrated in the numerous depictions of their *yangsheng* mastery for which the text's philosophy of the Dao provides a powerful foundation. Perhaps its richest description of the sages' *yangsheng* is found in *Daodejing* chapter 15.

To demonstrate the *yangsheng* core of the Laozi *Daodejing* that was already fully manifest in the Guodian *Laozi*, this section examines and builds on the reading of *Daodejing* chapter 15 by the eminent Swiss sinologist, Jean François

Billeter. It should be noted that he focuses on the Mawangdui *Laozi* rather than the received edition, and his essay was published before the discovery of the Guodian *Laozi*. Billeter exhaustively examines chapter 15's many textual variations that I do not deal with in any detail, and Billeter too writes, "I forego giving a table of all the variants listed, all the proposed punctuations, all the attempted translations. The confusion would be too great, and the reader would not benefit."[6] But even accounting for all of these, a further reason for the textual complexity of *Daodejing* chapter 15 is that later readers consistently interpreted the chapter in strictly moral terms. However, once the identification of the sages as perfectly moral rulers is rejected, then the *yangsheng* thrust of the chapter is unmistakable.

> Formerly, those who excelled in the art of the Dao:
> Were subtle, mysterious, profound, and penetrating.
> So deep that they were unfathomable.
> Because they were unfathomable, I can only describe their manifest look.
> Hesitant, like one who crosses a frozen river in winter.
> Circumspect, like one who fears his neighbors.
> Reserved, like one who visits.

Daodejing chapter 15 opens with an explicit reference to the Dao as an art whose core practice consists of the techniques of bodily cultivation familiar as *yangsheng*, and the remainder of the chapter is devoted to describing the one who "excels" 善 at it.[7] The opening passage characterizes the adept as "unfathomable" 不可識, referring to the transformed inner dynamics of the adept's body brought about by the practice of *yangsheng* that are not directly demonstrable to an outside observer, so the text states that its description of the adept is limited to his/her outward appearance or "manifest look" 容.

The following section describes the adept through a series of similes. The first likens him/her to a person crossing a frozen river, "hesitant" 豫 in feeling the strength of the ice upon which one foot is placed in front of the other. Because one false move leads to disaster, the walker must perfectly focus the body and mind in order to maintain balance while completely refraining from unnecessary movements. The adept is "circumspect, like one who fears his neighbors" 猶乎其若畏四鄰, because s/he avoids external interference from other people and shuns social interaction and political activity. S/he is "reserved, like one who visits" 敢乎其若客 because, intent on the internal bodily changes and transformations taking shape, s/he does not actively initiate anything, but rather awaits their appearance while remaining ready to respond.

Billeter explains that this attitude to the body and the world is the result of "an inversion mechanism"[8] in which attention is turned from the world of external stimuli to the world of internal sensations. This inversion calls for all bodily faculties and energies to be inwardly mobilized, since this is where "this Dao" 此道, this art, is to be realized. Billeter writes: "In order to practice this art, a quiet place is needed, free from abrupt or noisy interference ... Respiratory techniques play an important role in this practice, but they are not described in our text or even mentioned. The text speaks only of the essential, that is to say, of the spirit in which the art is practiced."[9]

Billeter interprets these preliminary descriptions as indicative of a sequential progression through preparatory *yangsheng* exercises leading to a fully embodied cultivation that now begins to bear fruit, as described in the next series of descriptions.

> Dissolving, like melting ice.
> Elemental, like raw wood.
> Turbid, like cloudy water.
> Ample, like a valley.

This series of similes begins with the term *huan* 渙 that, written with the water radical, means "to disintegrate, dissolve, or disperse" as happens to ice when subjected to heat. As a moment or stage in this cultivation sequence that involves respiratory techniques intended to vitalize the flow of *qi* throughout the body, this "dissolving" describes what happens to the internal bodily blockages that heretofore posed obstacles to the free circulation of *qi*. Initially formed in the course of the socialization processes that begin at childhood when, for example, girls are taught to wear dresses and boys to wear pants, these internal blockages harden and metastasize, posing serious challenges to the body's optimal health. Under the heat of invigorated *qi* coursing through the adept's body, these blockages begin to dissolve and melt away. Billeter writes:

> There comes a moment when the circulation of the internal energies, blocked to one degree or another in every civilized adult, resumes. Breathing exercises a gentle action on the benumbed body, comparable to spring air. Under the effect of this action, the blocked energy is released gradually and begins to circulate. The sensation felt is that of a solid body that loosens and comes to life: the body proper decompartmentalizes, overcome by an intoxicating activity that it does not remember having known.[10]

The text then states that this decompartmentalizing body is revealed to be "elemental" 沌, referring to an experience of the body in its primordial wholeness before it has undergone the processes of socialization. This is an experience of the body in its original condition of fecund chaos in which nothing has been divided or separated, a condition that is further characterized as "thick" 樸, referring to the thickness of raw wood that has not yet been cut, carved, or worked over. It is an important term in the *Daodejing* that is used eight times in six chapters. With reference to the transforming body of the adept, "elemental" and "thick" describe the original condition of the body before it has undergone the processes of socialization, when it deeply absorbed the breath of the Dao, the *qi* that nourishes its life. Other sections of the *Daodejing* (chapters 10, 28, 55) liken this original condition of the body experienced by the *yangsheng* practitioner to the "elemental," "thick," and unsocialized body of the new-born baby.

The *yangsheng* cultivational method centers on the diffusive circulation of *qi* throughout the body. Although its circulation is fluid, it is not itself a fluid, even though it is often described with watery images. Thus, the next line describes the *qi* at this stage as "turbid" 混, another term with the water radical. "Turbid" normally describes water that is mucked with other matter, and here this condition is further specified by likening it to "cloudy water" 濁. The passage uses these watery images to represent primal *qi* that is mucky with substances best conceived as life nutrients that, in the initial formations of the world, infused the primordial wetness of elemental existence during the time of original chaos. The term "turbid" is often also coupled with the term "elemental" from the previous line to form the term *hundun* 混沌, which is a term rich in cosmogonic and mythological content referring to the primordial beginnings of life.[11] This passage describes a metabolic invigoration to the circulatory systems that follow as the result of the practice of *yangsheng* techniques.

The next line describes the transforming body as "ample" 曠, a term that has the meanings of "vast" and "empty." In the course of the *yangsheng* progressions, the body has become "ample" since its compartmentalizations have been dissolved, rendering it thick, turbid, and elementally whole. The body's "ampleness" is a function of its wholeness, and it is likened to a "valley" 谷, an empty space that gathers into itself. The body is here seen as a vast and empty valley that gathers primal *qi* into itself, infusing the body's ampleness.

> In this cloudy state, tranquility gradually clarified it.
> In this calmness was born a movement that gradually came to life.

These next lines continue the *yangsheng* sequence describing the transformation of the body's *qi* circulation from its "cloudy state" 濁 to one that has been "clarified" 清 because of the adept's "tranquility" 靜. This "tranquility" is capable of "clarifying" the body's cloudy state by what Billeter calls "un effet de decantation."[12] This "decantation" renders the *qi* transparent, bringing the adept close to the final stage of the art that is given in the next line: "In this calmness was born a movement that gradually came to life." Billeter's comments (slightly modified for clarity) to this line underscore the fundamental *yangsheng* tenor of *Daodejing* chapter 15 as a whole:

> This sentence, which repeats the previous one in terms of form, introduces something new from the point of view of meaning. The initial attitudes and experiences described were negative in character and recommended "hesitation," "circumspection," "reservation." The inner dispositions were next described with images of "melting ice," "raw wood," "cloudy water," and "valley," evoking the experiences of decompartmentalization, of the free circulation of energy, and of a generalized activity reduced to a perfect regime of economy. Together, these experiences form the steps of a single process of dissolution, and this phenomenon of dissolution is only the preparation of a positive phenomenon. When the preparatory stages have been traversed and the conditions are met, "a movement gradually comes to life." The undivided and perfectly calm energy field that has become the proper body engenders in its midst a nucleus of concentrated energy. This happens in the *dantian*, the "cinnabar field," a region located in the belly a little below the navel. From there, the new energy opens a passage downward, reaches the lower extremity of the body, ascends up the back following the spine, reaches the top of the head, and from there descends again along a central path to its point of departure. In general, this passage is made in stages, each step being felt both as a jolt and as a piercing energy. When circular communication is established, a new mechanism begins to operate: the energy begins to circulate in the loop thus created. As a result of this, as the consequence of training, a general synergy is established inside the body, which is animated from one end to the other and now knows a function superiorly integrated. In the loop, the energy flows in a variable rhythm that is coupled with that of the breath and that can therefore be adjusted at will. It is this event that is mentioned in this line, this circulation that, when the time comes, "gradually comes to life."[13]

The next two lines complete the chapter:

> Who preserves this art does not seek satiation.
> Not satiated, s/he is perpetually renewed.

These lines recognize the adept as one who "preserves this Dao" 保此道, referring to the *yangsheng* program of bodily cultivation. Even if the phrase "this Dao" was not already explicitly identifiable as *yangsheng* at the time of the text's earliest circulation, it soon would be; still, the content of chapter 15 leaves no doubt about its grounding in bodily cultivation. True to this *yangsheng* grounding, the final line directly points to its ultimate result: "renewal" 新成 of the body, which is the effect of the vitalized flow of clarified primal *qi*. This "renewal" has a regenerative effect on the body, and it evokes the Daoist ideal of an extended longevity, a key notion that marks an important goal of *yangsheng*.

More than any other part of the *Daodejing*, chapter 15 depicts in vivid detail the experiential basis of Yangsheng Daoism. Against many chapters of the *Daodejing* that are comprised of multiple transposable "units of thought," this chapter demonstrates an unusually extended, self-contained structure devoted to a detailed commentary of the experiential stages of *yangsheng* cultivation. In other words, chapter 15 represents the *Daodejing*'s primary *yangsheng* manifesto.

Many studies of the *Daodejing* often note the heavy emphasis on bodily cultivation only to dismiss it as incongruent with its philosophy. This is normally because scholars find it hard to reconcile this aspect of the text with the political message that many take as definitive of its teachings, a misreading that began in the Warring States. Because those non-early Daoist thinkers from early China likely had little experience with *yangsheng*, they interpreted chapter 15, and the entire *Daodejing* more generally, in terms more familiar to their own philosophical commitments revolving around political thought and morality in ways that continue to deeply influence modern interpretations of the text.[14]

Nevertheless, *yangsheng* cultivation supplies one of the two core components of the *Daodejing*, the other being, of course, its philosophy of the Dao. The *yangsheng* component is linked to the unnameable aspect of the matrix, whereas the philosophy of the pristine Dao component is linked to its nameable aspect. With the assistance of Billeter, I have spent a good amount of time establishing the *yangsheng* bona fides of chapter 15 in order to highlight the centrality of *yangsheng* for the text as a whole, while underscoring the fact that this is not a later addition to the text—it was there from the beginning.

Billeter's *yangsheng* reading of *Daodejing* chapter 15 is limited, and he did not attempt to integrate its teachings into a more global examination of an original environment for Yangsheng Daoism. Given the rigors, dangers, and complexities of *yangsheng* training, a serious disciple would have needed to study under a master to make progress in the art. If the normal model of *yangsheng* transmission is from master to disciple, then this provides a first indication for the attempt to reconstruct an original environment together with its attendant community for one possible social history of Yangsheng Daoism. It is to this attempt that the following section turns.

Three Staple Assumptions about the *Daodejing*

Ariel and Raz recognize two readings of the *Daodejing*, one exoteric and the other esoteric, and they suggest that these readings initially took shape in a knowledge community. They find some grounds for this in their translation from *Daodejing* chapter 65: "Of old those who excelled at practicing the Dao, did not use it to enlighten the people, but to hoodwink them," and they go on to write:

> Pertinent to our purpose is the claim that the overt teaching of the ancient sages, while claiming to elucidate, was actually meant to confound the people. That is, the words the sages used did not carry the real meaning of the teaching. The passage thus implies that there was an esoteric teaching that was kept secret from the masses, and that this teaching is in fact contained in the subsequent words in the passage. Claiming esoteric knowledge and ancient pedigree were characteristic of the culture of secrecy that was to imbue the political, intellectual, and technical traditions in the late Warring States and on into the imperial era.[15]

Although I hesitate to reduce readings of the *Daodejing* to exoteric and esoteric, these comments by Ariel and Raz open a way into exploring one possible social history of Yangsheng Daoism. Of particular interest is their associating a community, in this case a knowledge community, with an in-group reading of the text. Although they are not alone in this effort, in general the associating of a community of any kind with the earliest circulations of the *Daodejing* marks a notable difference of some current scholarship on Daoism in distinction to most twentieth-century scholarship. Still, the denial of any specific community implicated with the earliest circulations of the *Daodejing*, especially one committed to bodily practices, continues to enjoy a significant (but gradually eroding) consensus today. Chad Hansen, for example, also accepts the existence of what he calls a "text community" rather than a "knowledge community," and he writes:

> Current textual thinking tends toward the view that all classical Chinese texts were being continuously edited and maintained in textual communities over sometimes hundreds of years. This editing and emendation often reflected interaction with other text communities as they worked out alternative answers to shared questions. Clearly, such an accretion theory undermines the traditional goal of uncovering the 'original' in the sense of the earliest version of the text.[16]

Still, the position that denies an early community assumes the syncretic model, which holds that the earliest composed *Daodejing* was the product of a process of compilation. Although I reject it in favor of the synthetic model, which holds that the earliest composed text of the *Daodejing* was the product of a process of transcription, it is nevertheless important to examine its three staple assumptions.[17]

Its first staple assumption is that the *Daodejing* gradually took shape in a chronologically linear process whereby it accumulated from a proto-text such as the Guodian *Laozi* by the inclusion of new materials until it reached a stable stage of maturity as seen in the Mawangdui *Laozi*. This view sees no particular author but rather a congeries of various and anonymous "editors" who compiled disparate materials from diverse sources whose final product became the *Daodejing*.

Its second staple assumption is that the earliest circulations of the *Daodejing* occurred only after the closing of the Guodian tomb in the mid-fourth century BCE, but likely long after.[18]

Its third staple assumption is that there was no distinct social community active in the production of the *Daodejing*, which simply represented one more player among many others in the early Chinese forum of political debate. The syncretic model is thus compelled to see the *Daodejing* as an orphan philosophical tract that other early Chinese knowledge communities, for example, the Mohist, Confucian, and Legalist ones, were only vaguely aware of if at all until the end of the Warring States, when adherents of the newly formed Huang-Lao knowledge community adopted it as their own before catapulting it onto the center stage of philosophical and political attention in the early Han Dynasty.

The last staple assumption is already sufficient unto itself as adequate support for the syncretic view and, barring new archaeological finds that could change this picture, it stands or falls with the question of social community in distinction to knowledge community. The denial of any such social community surrounding the early *Daodejing* received powerful support in the late 1970s with Nathan Sivin's influential claim that " 'philosophical Daoism' has no sociological meaning … The philosophical Daoists were not a group, but a handful of authors scattered through history."[19] Under the strict terms of this view, the *Daodejing* cannot even be considered Daoist in the first place.

Although I am not aware of anyone who has pursued the further implications, this line of reasoning, by historical necessity according to its own terms, must then assert that the *Daodejing* only became "Daoist" in the last decades of the Han Dynasty, when Zhang Daoling, founder of the Celestial Master Daoist religion and thus founder of Daoism tout court, adopted it as their primary scriptural writing; as Michel Strickmann writes, "I am proposing to use the word Daoist only in referring to those who recognize the historical position of Zhang Daoling."[20]

As another benchmark that shows the contentiousness of the debates concerning a possible and general early Daoism that would include the two most "philosophical Daoists," namely, Laozi and Zhuangzi, Hansen provides a judgment diametrically opposed to Sivin's, and precisely on the philosophical grounds that Sivin rejects:

> The concept of "Daoism" as a theme or a group did not exist at the time of the Classical Daoists, but we have some reasons to suspect the communities focusing on the *Zhuangzi* and the *Daodejing* texts were in contact with each other … Their metaethics vaguely favored different first-order normative theories (anarchism, pluralism, laissez faire government). The meta-ethical focus and the related less demanding first order ethics mostly distinguishes "Daoists" from other thinkers of the period.[21]

Claims concerning a knowledge community involved with the early *Daodejing*, for example, those by Arial and Raz, assist in opening cracks in the syncretic view. Still, rejecting the syncretic model once and for all begins with a simple question. Given the long-range processes of change undergone by the *Daodejing* throughout its extended history, do its internal contents exhibit an organic coherency, or do they stand in conflict and contradiction? The response to this question will be manifestly conditioned by whether one holds to the syncretic view that sees multiple and disparate sources for the text that can only reveal internal contradictions, or whether one holds to the synthetic view that sees a particular wellspring, a pliable *fons et origo*, from which the *Daodejing*, and with it a very particular interpretative stance, sprung.

Both models have been complicated by the discovery of the Guodian *Laozi* despite the fact that it provides no immediately decisive verdict for either. Even its title, "Guodian *Laozi*," is a misnomer, since it consists of not one but three separate *Laozi* manuscripts, as plainly evidenced by their different writing styles. The syncretic model, whose important proponents include D. C. Lau,[22] Michae LaFargue,[23] and A. C. Graham,[24] takes the Guodian *Laozi* to represent the original kernels of a future text just beginning the process of gradually accumulating unrelated aphorisms and other sayings,[25] while the synthetic model takes each of its three separate manuscripts as deliberate selections from an already existing and more complete version of the *Daodejing* singled out for specific polemical purposes. Edward Shaughnessy succinctly states this position thus: "Taken in total, it seems to me that the Guodian manuscripts demonstrate that when they were copied the text of the *Daodejing* was circulating in the form of intact chapters."[26]

Reflective of the contentious state of affairs surrounding these two options, William Boltz comments: "The first of these (assumptions) is circular and therefore meaningless and the second cannot be demonstrated from any presently known evidence and is therefore entirely conjectural; to believe it is an act of faith."[27] Shaughnessy[28] shows that these debates surrounding the coming together of the *Daodejing* were already raging in the Chinese academy from the first decades of the twentieth century, long before both the Mawangdui and the Guodian excavations. Liang Qichao, Gu Jiegang, Qian Mu, and Feng Youlan took the side of the syncretic model, in which they claimed that the *Daodejing* did not exist before the very late period of the Warring States, while it was the iconoclast Hu Shi who stood mostly alone in championing the traditional view that supported the text's antiquity. Shaughnessy does not mention the role played by Chen Guying[29] in more recent times who virtually single-handedly turned the Chinese syncretic tide back in favor of the synthetic view that, among a great majority of contemporary Chinese scholars, tends to support both the historical existence of Laozi and his authorship of the *Daodejing*.

The syncretic model uses the date of the Guodian *Laozi* to mark the genesis of the *Daodejing*. It would take another hundred years or so until its ideas publicly appeared at the court of Lü Buwei 呂不韋, the infamous statesman who sponsored the production of the *Lüshi Chunqiu* 呂氏春秋, a compendious volume that attempted to organize all of the philosophical and political knowledge available at the time.[30] According to the syncretic model, among the many thinkers invited to the court were those who had knowledge of the body of ideas that would soon be formalized into the independent text called the *Daodejing*. The proceedings at Lü Buwei's court assisted in the processing of those ideas, as evidenced by their inclusion in the *Lüshi Chunqiu*, thus making them ready for textual formalization. Those invited thinkers who knew those ideas comprised their own knowledge community, called Huang-Lao; they were also the ones who initially compiled the Huang-Lao *Daodejing* and associated it with Laozi.

On the other side, the synthetic model also has three staple assumptions. First, it sees in the Laozi *Daodejing* a thoroughgoing cohesion and coherency among all its parts (with only a few noteworthy exceptions[31]) that is not dependent on single authorship. Second, it recognizes a more or less complete *Daodejing* in limited oral circulation already before the composition of the Guodian *Laozi*. Third, it locates that oral circulation within a specific community.[32] In short, the three staple assumptions of the synthetic model are coherency, oral antiquity, and community.

I retain the characterization of this Laozi *Daodejing* as "more or less complete" partially based on Shaughnessy's comments to the Guodian *Laozi*, namely, that "there is no reason to think that this is all of the *Daodejing* material that was available at the time. Of course, we cannot determine from the Guodian manuscripts how many other chapters of the received text were already in existence, but it seems safe to say that a large percentage of them certainly were."[33]

Dependent on these three staple assumptions, the synthetic model is nevertheless pliable. Its coherency is not dependent on single authorship; its oral antiquity requires the circulation of a more or less complete Laozi *Daodejing* any time before the closing of the Guodian tomb, but even as early as the Spring and Autumn period; and the original environment within which it orally circulated could be (and has been) characterized as a political community,[34] a textual community,[35] a knowledge community,[36] a hermit community,[37] or a practice community.[38] Still, each of these staple assumptions needs further specificity.

The assumption of coherency is anything but self-evident and requires, according to Alan Chan, "a particular interpretative context" that he explains: "As distinguished from a linear evolutionary [syncretic] model, what is suggested here is that there were different collections of sayings attributed to Laozi, overlapping to some extent but each with its own emphases and predilections, inhabiting a particular interpretative context" (2013). Jean François Billeter sees the coherency of the *Daodejing* in terms of its "philosophical unity" that he articulates in response to Jean Levi's comments about its "plurality of meanings":[39]

> If we take Jean Levi literally, then the very general character of Laozi's formulas would be sufficient to explain the plurality of levels of meaning. By their generality, their conciseness, their often enigmatic character, these formulas would have the power to elicit meanings situated on different planes: they would be forms almost meaningless, but which would have the property of stimulating the imagination, the wisdom, and the speculative vein of the best minds, and would be invested by them with various meanings, without any other connection between them than the forms which would have aroused them. But we can also think that if these formulas are capable of so many different interpretations, it is because they express data common to different domains of reality. In this hypothesis, the book would not be "multiple," as Jean Levi says, but one. It would set out principles that would be verifiable in different fields but would still be the same principles. The philosophical unity of the book would reveal a unity underlying the domains that we arbitrarily distinguish.[40]

Billeter's comments pinpoint the coherency at the heart of the *Daodejing*, which can only be perceived in its inter-weaving of multiple domains. Still, the two most immediate domains that typical readings of the *Daodejing* "arbitrarily distinguish" are theory/philosophy and practice/cultivation. The assumption of coherency has its source in the inseparability of theory/philosophy and practice/cultivation, and it intends to overcome the judgment of contradiction. Other domains, including the political, the psychological, and the social, are secondary off-shoots of that original inseparability.

The assumption of oral antiquity is not challenged by the mid-fourth-century BCE date of the Guodian *Laozi* since any earlier date can be taken as antique, even as far back as the Spring and Autumn period, according to the Chinese tradition. This assumption requires that the text circulated orally any time before the Guodian *Laozi*, thus making it available for transcription in the first place; this is despite the fact that it is virtually impossible to precise an origin date for originally oral texts, and the *Daodejing* is no exception. Given this unknowability, rejecting a late Spring and Autumn date range is no longer compulsory.

Victor Mair's (1990) study serves as a benchmark for serious considerations of an originally oral circulation of the *Daodejing* in Western studies, most of which focus on the text's syntax, particularly the rhymed and/or tetrasyllabic verse that are found throughout it.[41] Dirk Meyer provides a different but reasonable and well-informed explanation for the originally oral circulation of the *Daodejing* that he derives from his analysis of the Guodian texts taken altogether.

In keeping with the assumption of oral antiquity, Meyer does not posit any particular date for the earliest oral circulations of the *Daodejing* other than that they preceded the closing of the tomb. He takes the Guodian *Laozi* as a primary example of a "context-dependent text," a designation for texts that consist of discrete individual units of thought. In such texts, individual units do not combine in the erection of a systematic philosophy; rather, they "simply reflect a situational response to a given concern. The individual units remain ambiguous, sometimes even enigmatic."[42]

These units are gathered into what Meyer calls "modules," groupings that form the original structures for what would become recognizable to us as chapters of a written text. Thus, in part because of the "ambiguous" or "enigmatic" character of these units that make up modules, "the units of context-dependent texts (such as the Guodian *Laozi*) rely primarily on authority to advance their positions."[43] Meyer continues:

> This suggests that a—now lost—oral discourse underlying the process of meaning construction for the individual modules of context-dependent texts should be postulated. It connected the various modules to identified traditions and so contextualised them within a given intellectual horizon … The modules remain ambiguous on the literary level of the text, and so context-dependent

texts require both a predetermined acquaintance *with* and identification—and consent—*of* the cultural, that is, the group-based application of knowledge behind the stories and quotations referred to … This wider context of meaning construction was necessarily an oral one, and this is true even for those examples which at some point were copied on bamboo … In an environment where it is a largely oral—and group-based—exercise to give meaning to the modules of context-dependent texts, guidance becomes necessary … This guidance falls back on a mediator of meaning. The mediator of meaning could be envisioned as a master (or masters). Or it could be the preexisting cultural consent of defined groups, which, in turn, had to be established by some kind of masters.[44]

Meyer's final comments lead into the third assumption of the synthetic model, namely, that of a specific community within which the oral text originally circulated. Other than affirming that this original community comprised masters and disciples, Meyer does not attempt to characterize it in further detail, writing that "a *Gegentext*—the productive environment against which a given (context-dependent) text was produced—can hardly ever be reconstructed with certainty."[45] His resistance to characterizing this community is understandable since his focus is on the formal structures of the text's units of thought, and not on its internal contents, which for the *Daodejing* primarily include *yangsheng* cultivation and the philosophy of the pristine Dao.

Alan Chan goes slightly farther than Meyer in his characterization of the original community as the following that Laozi attracted and note his inclusion of the assumption of oral antiquity in his comments:

It seems reasonable to suppose that Laozi attracted a following and that some of his sayings entered the world of Chinese philosophical discourse during the fifth century BCE. A process of oral transmission may have preceded the appearance of these sayings in written form. As the archaeological evidence to be presented below will indicate, bodies of sayings attributed to Laozi were committed to writing probably from the second half of the fifth century BCE, resulting in different collections with overlapping contents. These collections grew, competed for attention, and gradually came to be consolidated during the fourth century BCE. By the middle of the third century BCE, the *Daodejing* probably reached a relatively stable form.[46]

Chan notes that early Chinese sources do not provide a title for the collection of "Laozi's sayings" until the middle of the third century BCE (the Guodian *Laozi* is also untitled), and neither do they provide solid evidence for any associated community. Nonetheless, since both original text and original community seamlessly flow into Daoist history and in fact instantiate it, then this is already sufficient reason not to concoct a different history for it. This same recognition leads Harold Roth, quoting Michael LaFargue,[47] to write,

> LaFargue asserts that those who created and transmitted the units of verse and later assembled them into a complete composition were probably members of a community, whom he prefers to identify simply as 'Laoists,' after the lead of A. C. Graham. There is no particular reason to doubt a theory as general as this, but with further research it may become possible to speak with more precision about this community, which, at the very least, amounts to one early Daoist lineage.[48]

It is exactly here, in the context of community, that Daoism finds its origins, but whether our conceptions of it can ever get beyond speculation is an entirely different question. My own efforts to "speak with more precision about this community" have led me to call it Yangsheng Daoism.

The Guodian *Laozi* does not directly speak to this Yangsheng Daoism, and the placement of its three manuscripts in the tomb also offers precious little information about its own proper community. Nonetheless, any exploration into a Yangsheng Daoist community is possible only by way of the Guodian *Laozi*, which by necessity will exert a guiding pull on the possible courses that that exploration can take. It will do so by delimiting the field of inquiry, whereby any descriptions of that possible community (other than those based entirely on speculation) will have to mesh with the relatively scant historical and textual data communicated by the Guodian *Laozi*.

The possible existence of a Yangsheng Daoist community is entirely dependent on the oral circulation of the more or less complete Laozi *Daodejing* from which the Guodian *Laozi* has taken selections. Next to the many claims recognized earlier in this chapter concerning this staple assumption, Barbara Hendrischke adds: "As a group, the three texts share terms and philosophical intention. They support each other. It has therefore been proposed that they are individual sections adapted from one larger identical bulk of materials."[49]

This picture presents a major challenge to the exploration of this possible community, regardless of how we might want to characterize it: to understand its connection to that orally circulating Laozi *Daodejing*. The remainder of this chapter attempts to make sense of what seem to be the echoes of a social history surrounding the Laozi *Daodejing* in the period of the Warring States and the Han Dynasty by examining its movement from a *yangsheng* environment to a therapeutic environment to a philosophical environment to a religious environment, each with their own community.

The first community called Yangsheng Daoism 养生道 inhabited a reclusive mountainous practice environment. According to traditional accounts, its earliest possible period of formation is the middle of the sixth century BCE.

Yangsheng Daoism comprised masters and disciples who integrated yangsheng bodily cultivation with a particular phenomenology of the pristine Dao. The Warring States *Zhuangzi* 莊子 provides tantalizing anecdotal evidence for Yangsheng Daoism, as does the Han Dynasty *Liexian zhuan* 列仙傳, as does the Jin Dynasty *Shenxian zhuan* 神仙傳. Yangsheng Daoism was centrally involved with the earliest oral circulations of the Laozi *Daodejing*.

The second community called Fangxian Daoism 方仙道 ("the Dao of Recipes and Longevity") inhabited a semi-public therapeutic environment. It formed as a practical offshoot of Yangsheng Daoism no earlier than the middle of the fifth century BCE, and the Han Dynasty *Shiji* 史記 provides the major historical data concerning it. Fangxian Daoism comprised *fangji* 方技, "masters of recipes and methods," ritual healers who applied *yangsheng* techniques to treat their clients. They were likely the first to have committed parts of the Laozi *Daodejing* to writing, for which the Guodian *Laozi* is representative, and they have bequeathed to us a breathtaking cache of their therapeutic writings, many of which were recovered from among the silk texts buried at Mawangdui.

The third community called Huang-Lao Daoism 黃老道 inhabited a public philosophical environment. It too formed as an offshoot of Yangsheng Daoism, but in the direction of thought rather than practice, in the middle of the third century BCE. Originally a Warring States philosophical lineage, Huang-Lao transformed into the ruling ideology of the first six decades of the Han Dynasty. Its members were responsible for the production of the Huang-Lao *Daodejing*, which, after the Laozi *Daodejing* completely vanished for two thousand years, became the standard version of the *Daodejing* familiar to us today.

The fourth community called Tianshi Daoism 天師道 (Celestial Master Daoism) inhabited a semi-reclusive religious environment. It formed in 142, when the Most High Lord Lao 太上老君 invested Zhang Daoling 張道陵 (34–156) with authority to establish the community in Sichuan. Its forced dispersal in 215 led to the disappearance of Tianshi Daoism's most important textual production, the *Xiang'er* 想尔 commentary, until it was discovered in the Dunhuang Caves in the early twentieth century. If not for its early disappearance, it might have come to rival the preeminent status of the Huang-Lao *Daodejing*.

Despite Strickmann's claim that has become near dogma in modern studies, namely that Daoism before the formation of Tianshi Daoism "has no sociological meaning," the last three of these communities are firmly established by the historical sources upon which such kinds of scholarly claims are usually made, but the first, Yangsheng Daoism, has never been recognized in this way before, and the fact that each of these communities carries the Dao label might lead us to think they are equally Daoist in a uniform way. Still, it is not important to force these seemingly incongruous squares into an essentialist circle and, one by one or altogether, each can be considered Daoist or non-Daoist entirely depending on how one chooses to essentialize the definition of *what Daoism is*. Looked at differently, it is also possible that the early Chinese use of the Dao label refers not to Daoism but to the *Daodejing*, in which case we should more precisely recognize them not as *Daoist* communities but as *Daodejing* communities, which seems to make eminently more sense. This becomes more reasonable in light of the name Huang-Lao, where the "Lao" refers to Laozi in his guise as the putative author of the *Daodejing*; in other words, Huang-Lao Daoism is already identified with the *Daodejing* with or without the Dao label supplement.

This study discusses the first three of these early Daoist communities but says little about the fourth. This is because, next to the fact that the *Xiang'er* commentary was quickly lost to history and therefore had little influence over later *Daodejing* commentary, it also came too late to exert any impact during the decisive periods of its textual formation, which is a primary concern of this study.

There is yet another strand of early Daoism regularly recognized herein that I call Zuowang Daoism, associated with Zhuangzi 莊子 and the collection of writings gathered under his name. Like Yangsheng Daoism but unlike Fangxian, Huang-Lao, and Tianshi Daoism, Zuowang Daoism is not explicitly recognized as a Daoist community in the historical sources. On one side, this strand of early Daoism is animated by the phenomenology of the Dao originally identifiable with Yangsheng Daoism rather than with the later metaphysics of the Dao identifiable with Huang-Lao Daoism. On the other side, although Zuowang Daoism's primary form of cultivation, called *zuowang* 坐忘 ("sit and forget") or sometimes *xinzhai* 心齋 ("fasting of the heart") significantly differs from *yangsheng* in being based on physical immobility (thus the term "sit and forget") rather than on physical movements, it was nevertheless the cultivation program adopted and absorbed by Huang-Lao Daoism, which largely ignored Laozi's *yangsheng*. And because Zuowang Daoism, much like Tianshi Daoism, had no impact on the *Daodejing*'s textual formation, I do not directly explore it on its own terms to any extent herein.

Yangsheng Daoism

The modern Chinese tradition differs from the Western tradition in its desire to maintain Laozi's status as the single, original, and historical author behind the

Daodejing; Liao Mingchun and Li Cheng provide a typical example of this where they write, "The author of the *Daodejing* could only have been the singular Laozi himself, and it could not possibly have been authored by scholars of different schools. Later editors of the *Daodejing* are one thing, but the original makeup of the *Daodejing* is another thing entirely."[50]

Still, the synthetic nature of the Laozi *Daodejing* does not require an individual author (or speaker, given its originally oral nature) named Laozi, "the Old One," and its genesis can be more reasonably attributed to a corporate group of mountainous *yangsheng* masters collectively called Laozi, "the Old Ones." Barbara Hendrischke writes, "The three texts [of the Guodian *Laozi*] are here tentatively read as deliberate selections from the same set of materials from which the received *Daodejing* originated. It is assumed that these materials convey ideas that were put forth by one author, or a group of anonymous authors."[51] Kristofer Schipper also discusses the original composition of the *Daodejing* by questioning its attribution:

> Why then is the book attributed to the Old Master? One should not see in this an attempt at falsification. It was very common, in classical China, for authors and editors to sign their works with the name of the founder of the school to which they belonged, rather than to use their own names ... Those who wrote the *Daodejing*—we do not know their names, but does that matter?—wanted to give a comprehensive summing up of the thought which tradition attributed to the Old Master, but in a version purified of mythical elements and detached from its historical context.[52]

These comments indicate that the oral genesis of the *Daodejing* need not be restricted to a single person or even necessarily to a single generation. They do, however, reinforce the suspicion that the text's original voices belonged to a specific community with shared philosophical commitments and shared cultivational practices. According to William Baxter, who recognizes a "tradition" rather than a "community," "A reasonable conjecture would be that the *Daodejing* and similar texts emerged from a distinctive tradition of philosophical verse with strong oral elements and little concept of individual authorship."[53]

Against the syncretic model that sees the original *Daodejing* as a text compiled from disparate sources, the synthetic model posits a single homogeneous source (the "Old Masters") inhabiting a *yangsheng* environment whose community members sought bodily well-being and longevity by harmonizing with the natural movements of the Dao, which they understood in terms of their philosophy of the Dao. Their philosophy conditioned their practice, and their practice honed their philosophy. As the original possessors of these teachings, they merged their philosophy and their practice in the Laozi *Daodejing*.

Modern Anglo-American scholarship downplays the centrality of bodily cultivation in the *Daodejing*, holding that the cultivational elements found in the text are secondary additions intended to bolster the status of the enlightened ruler. Modern French scholarship, on the other hand, more fully appreciates the organic position of *yangsheng* cultivation in early Daoism. Henri Maspero initiated this tradition in the first half of the twentieth century, and his second-generation student Kristofer Schipper advanced it in important ways. They had similar views about an early Daoist community that were arrived at from their understanding of the role of *yangsheng* cultivation. Schipper, for example, writes:

> The *Daodejing*, as a whole, was developed in a religious context … The whole philosophy of the book of the Old Master [Laozi]—and in this respect the work is entirely different from other classical philosophies—is borne out of the situation of the adept of the Mysteries, and of his search for Long Life … The chapters of the *Daodejing* refer to real body practices.[54]

Schipper associates "the Mysteries" or the "real body practices" with *qigong* 氣功, itself a modern alternative name for *yangsheng*, and he discusses several passages that refer to them, including one from *Daodejing* chapter 6: "The spirit of the valley never dies, it is called the Obscure female," and he concludes, "Only a few passages refer to the Mysteries … These passages are like signatures attesting to the original inspiration, the 'ancestor' of the book."[55] Schipper also notes that the commentarial tradition, particularly Heshang Gong's commentary, often strove to clarify this language: "The ancient commentaries speak about many body techniques, such as breathing exercises and sexual practices, in order to fill out the abstract thought of the *Daodejing* with concrete elements."[56]

Schipper consistently recognizes the original Laozi teachings as specifically oral, and he recommends interpreting them in their "religious context," by which he means a community setting populated by *yangsheng* "adepts" actively teaching their disciples. In this way, the original target audience for these teachings were not rulers (as maintained by the Huang-Lao *Daodejing*), but rather *yangsheng* masters and disciples. Among the few Anglo-American scholars to take early Daoist cultivation practices seriously, Harold Roth writes that texts like the *Daodejing* "represent the form that much of the early lore of inner cultivation took. This lore would have been transmitted by individual teachers to students, who would then have embellished it and adapted it on the basis of their own experience and circumstances … This lore of inner cultivation was most likely the basis of the early Daoist tradition."[57]

How one characterizes the *Daodejing*'s early community is largely dependent on how one determines priority of the political and the cultivational. Prioritizing the political (a hallmark of the Huang-Lao *Daodejing* that identifies its sages as rulers) is to characterize it as comprising politicians and philosophers who dabbled from time to time in cultivation, while prioritizing the cultivational is to characterize it as comprised of practitioners. Still, it can be difficult to determine the political and the cultivational. David Schaberg, who identifies its sages as rulers, writes,

> The connection [between the political and the cultivational] is so fundamental to the *Daodejing* itself that modern readers can sometimes entirely neglect the statecraft advice that is central to the text, regarding it as a metaphorical extension of directives on self-cultivation that are somehow more basic. In truth, however, the call for self-reform that is found in that text ... always makes the health of the ruler and of the collective (family, state, world) interdependent, and the cure for the latter proceeds from the cure from the former.[58]

Roth, who does not identify its sages as rulers, provides a different determination of the political and the cultivational:

> My hypothesis on the origins of Daoism is that it began as a lineage of masters and disciples that practiced and transmitted a unique form of guided breathing meditation involving this regular circulation of vital breath. Political and social concerns and naturalist techniques and philosophy represented later developments.[59]

Schipper, who also does not identify its sages as kings, provides an even more nuanced understanding of how the political and the cultivational are connected to each other:

> This physical dimension remains constantly of central significance, as it is from this very dimension—and this is confirmed time and again by the text itself—that the political begins. In other words: it is the way of perceiving the physical body that determines the vision of the social body. The autonomy of each individual ... is reflected in the unity of each village, a world closed in on itself but also a social unit, similar and equal to all other units. Together these ideal village communities are a vast network of alliances, of natural confederations, modeled on the great cosmic systems.[60]

The views of Roth and Schipper support characterizing that early community as comprising practitioners and, in a separate work, Roth states even more directly:

> The foundational texts of the Daoist tradition were produced within one or more closely related master-disciple lineages whose principal focus was on learning and practicing specific techniques ... The single most important technique was

of guiding and refining the flow of vital energy or vital breath (*qi*) within the human organism.⁶¹

I agree with the tenor of Roth's claim but not the details, including his preferred term, "lineages," that is meant to capture the essence of early Daoist social organization. The term implies an awareness of one's own master next to other masters with their own disciples in "lineages" that entails something more regimented than the more basic term, "community." I also disagree with Roth's use of the term "the Daoist tradition" because it cannot contain all the things that he attempts to force into it. The term "Yangsheng Daoism" is less ambitious and more precise, particularly since it emphasizes this community's intimate connection with the Laozi *Daodejing*.

As a community, Yangsheng Daoism is characterized as reclusive (or "hidden" 隱), in part since it celebrates *qi* in its most vital state, one that is normally encountered in a mountainous environment; this perhaps explains the absence of substantial historical records about it. Nevertheless, the *Zhuangzi* provides compelling anecdotal evidence of Yangsheng Daoism with its many colorful depictions of *yangsheng* masters, many of whom, including Gengsang Chu 庚桑楚, Guang Chengzi 廣成子, and even Laozi himself, are shown teaching disciples in a mountainous environment.⁶² The *Zhuangzi*, however, is representative of a different early Chinese strand of Daoism here called Zuowang Daoism (坐忘道), named after the specific style of spirit cultivation that Zhuangzi calls *zuowang* 坐忘 ("to sit and forget") that significantly differs from the bodily cultivation of *yangsheng* ("to nourish life"). The depictions in the *Zhuangzi* portray Yangsheng Daoists as living in mountain reclusion, but it depicts Zuowang Daoists as living in urban reclusion, as Wang Bo's⁶³ masterful study of *zuowang* reclusion demonstrates.

Still, the Laozi *Daodejing* as the original possession of Yangsheng Daoism remained hidden until it started to go beyond the original community and, according to the remarks of Alan Chan cited above, "entered the world of Chinese philosophical discourse during the fifth century BCE." This turn of events resulted in the Laozi *Daodejing* being embraced by a different community, Fangxian Daoism.

Although the reclusive nature of Yangsheng Daoism necessarily shrouds it from the historical gaze, it can be likened to the early Confucian community. The *Analects* depicts it as comprising not more than several dozen students; its teaching system was based on direct interactions between masters and disciples; Confucius was only one of several respected masters actively teaching there; students were, if not required, then at least expected to contribute to the economic well-being of the community; and their education consisted of physical performance and philosophy, and Robert Eno goes so far as to describe these early Confucians not as philosophers first of all but as "masters of the dance."⁶⁴

It should not be unreasonable to consider Yangsheng Daoism in similar ways. Certainly, we will likely never be in a position to answer too many questions about it: How large of a community did it comprise, less than a dozen or more than a hundred? Was it strictly limited to mountainous areas or was it also active in the arena of early marketplaces, even if only on the level of advertisement? Was there only one mountainous center where *yangsheng* masters congregated or did its reach go beyond? Did its practitioners participate in the community for a delimited period of time and return to society or did they remain as mountain hermits?

Fangxian Daoism

Yangsheng Daoists were committed to the mastery of *yangsheng* with the goal of becoming a sage. *Yangsheng*, then as now, was directed to the health and longevity of the individual, and its regimes demanded a rigor that could compare to that demanded by Confucius in his community; it was a full-time enterprise.

Although the *Daodejing* never displays *yangsheng* as a patient-directed therapy, at some point early on it became just that. The transfer of *yangsheng*'s subject from self to other coincides with the initial public appearances of the Laozi *Daodejing*. Who were those persons who had the position and authority to take the Laozi *Daodejing* together with its *yangsheng* teachings out of reclusive Yangsheng Daoism and introduce them to semi-public Fangxian Daoism?

According to Schaberg, the earliest transcriptions of the *Daodejing* were "efforts to represent speakable material accurately. But this is to beg a question: speakable by whom, then, and to whom, and in what settings?"[65] Although Schaberg implicitly distinguishes between those who had initial possession of the Laozi *Daodejing* and those who later transcribed parts of it, he does not consider if they were part of the same community or two different ones. I suggest that it is precisely here that the outlines of Fangxian Daoism come into focus.

Roth describes how a second Daoist community could have emerged from an original one, where "the lore of the Way" refers to early Daoist teachings generally: "This lore—both oral and written—was probably taught by a master to students and constituted a core of the teachings they carried with them when they finished their study and went elsewhere to teach on their own."[66] Roth pictures for this community a fair degree of traffic: freshmen arrive and seniors graduate. No matter that he identifies all early Daoist practice as mystical, which more closely approximates Zhuangzi's *zuowang* than Laozi's *yangsheng*, his hypothesis insightfully pinpoints a group of people trained both in Daoist practice and philosophy who would be equipped to develop *yangsheng* from a self-oriented bodily cultivation to an other-directed bodily therapy. These are the *fangji* 方技 of Fangxian Daoism.

Considering the early Confucian community where some members remained, others left to start their own, and others still went on to acquire positions in government, we can surmise that Yangsheng Daoism was not very different, where some graduated masters remained in the community and others departed to assume a semi-public role in society. Their motivations for departing probably included the relative ease of a daily life not dominated by the rigors of mountainous reclusion, the attraction of earning some degree of wealth, and the satisfaction of bringing health and comfort to their clients by applying their *yangsheng* skills in patient-directed therapy.

As a rule, historical records such as those in the *Shiji* have little to say about Yangsheng Daoism, but they provide several indications of Fangxian Daoism. Western studies rarely notice Fangxian Daoism and the *fangji*, and Chinese studies rarely discuss them in any detail. Sun Yiping provides an initial characterization where he mentions the complex term *xian* that here simply refers to the highest-level adept; he writes: "The highest objective of Fangxian Daoism is the pursuit of deathlessness and becoming a *xian*, and it is accompanied by worship and offerings to the spirits, circulating *qi* and performing *daoyin*, and undertaking the esoteric arts of alchemy and producing medicines."[67]

Fangxian Daoist *yangsheng* writings are being unearthed with some frequency and include those from Baoshan and Zhangjiashan,[68] but the motherlode collection was buried together with the Mawangdui *Laozi*.[69] They represent *yangsheng* as both a self-oriented bodily cultivation and an other-oriented therapy.

The term *fang* 方 ("recipes") in the phrase Fangxian Daoism normally refers to secret techniques committed to writing. This use of the term *fang* announces the proximity of this community to a different group called *fangshi* 方士 ("recipe masters"), whose founding is often attributed to Zou Yan 鄒衍 (305–240 BCE). The *fangshi* were eminently public, and their many extant biographies provide much historical detail including their names, their adventures, and where they were active. They were primarily occupied with "natural philosophy and the occult arts,"[70] and they prognosticated by relying on celestial and earthly phenomenon, theories of *yin* and *yang* and the five phases, and political geography. However, the *fangshi* had no substantial connection with Yangsheng Daoism or the *Daodejing*, partly because they are associated with the eastern seaboard while Yangsheng Daoists are associated the south, partly because they congregated in centers of power while Yangsheng Daoists were reclusive, but mostly because the methods and goals of each had little in common.

The term *xian* 仙 (or divine *xian* 神仙) originally referred to semi-divine beings before being adopted as the preferred term to designate masters of Yangsheng Daoism. The *Daodejing* did not use the term because it had not yet become associated with *yangsheng*; it uses the term "sage" 聖人, which itself was gradually becoming identified with enlightened rulers in non-Daoist Warring States writings and motivating Yangsheng Daoists to adopt the term *xian* instead.

Both *Shiji* 28 and *Hanshu* 25[71] state, "Song Wuji, Zhengbo Qiao, Chong Shang, and lastly Xianmen Gao, all of whom were from Yan, practiced Fangxian Daoism." Hu Fuchen's comments that refer to "the divine xian tradition," which is the same as Yangsheng Daoism, are highly instructive:

> Fangxian Daoism appropriated the theories of "long-life and lasting vision" [*Daodejing* chapter 59] from the divine *xian* tradition together with Zou Yan's *fangshi* theories. Its adherents spread and manufactured teachings about the divine *xian*, they studied all the divine *xian* methods and arts, and in the society of the time they formed their own professional group that relied on the divine *xian* and methods to earn their living.[72]

Much like Hu Fuchen, in a previous study[73] I erroneously followed the *Shiji* in considering Fangxian Daoism as a hybrid community cross-fertilized from Yangsheng Daoism and the *fangshi*, but it is more likely that it directly emerged from Yangsheng Daoism alone. Its members were well trained in *yangsheng* as well as in the philosophy of the Dao, but not so much in divination, which was a *fangshi* specialty. Hu's comments, however, show that Yangsheng Daoism had come to employ a *xian*-based terminology rather than a sage-based one, a move that may have been motivated with the formation of Fangxian Daoism. Seeing Fangxian Daoism as forming directly from Yangsheng Daoism is to see the *fangji* as originally the disciples of reclusive *yangsheng* masters, after which they became the primary agents responsible for developing an other-oriented *yangsheng* therapy out of self-oriented *yangsheng* bodily cultivation, which allowed them to forge their own social niche as ritual healers; as Hu writes, they formed a "professional group," namely the *fangji* community of Fangxian Daoism, in order "to earn their living" by administering *yangsheng* therapy to an elite clientele.

Hu provides a further introduction to Fangxian Daoism where he discusses the geographical spread of the *fangji* together with their regional masteries of *yangsheng* therapies:

> In the Warring States, the primary features of Fangxian Daoism in the states of Yan and Qi were the ingestion of *xian* herbs and the refinement of cinnabar and "the yellow and white" taught by Anqi Sheng and Xianmen Gao. Fangxian

Daoism in the areas of Qin and Jin offered the teachings of the arts of the bedroom and sexual intercourse. They believed that the mutual exchanges between a man and a woman could increase the body's *qi*, help to maintain a youthful appearance, and extend one's lifespan. They revered Peng Zu, Rong Chenggong, Xuan Nü, and Su Nü. In the regions of the southern states of Jing, Chu, Wu, Yue, Ba, and Shu, the [*fangji*] taught the arts of *qi* circulation, and [other *yangsheng* techniques called] *daoyin*, *tuna*, and *mingxiang*; they revered Wangzi Qiao and Chi Songzi.[74]

Fangxian Daoism and the *fangji* have been recognized in Western scholarship: Herlee Creel (1970) dubbed them "the *xian*-cult" and "the cult of immortality" and Robert van Gulik (2003) also had interesting things to say about them, but Donald Harper has made the greatest progress in uncovering their social position and activities in early Chinese society. Because I rely on and quote Harper's work over the following pages and since his heavy reliance on English analogues for original Chinese terms is a bit dissonant, I retain the original Chinese terminology that I have been using throughout this study. I retain the term *fangji* where Harper sometimes uses the phrase "*xian* cult" or, referring to them individually, "physicians"; I retain the name Fangxian Daoism where he uses the phrase "a medical tradition of macrobiotic hygiene"; and I retain the term *yangsheng* where he uses the phrase "macrobiotic hygiene." Since in fact I find these terms used in the received literature, I cannot easily accept his explanation for his word uses: "All of the material on macrobiotic hygiene belongs to a medical tradition of *yangsheng* 養生 (nurturing life), but neither this term nor several related terms in received literature occur in the manuscripts."[75]

This is not meant to take anything from the value of Harper's work, particularly regarding his translations of the Mawangdui *yangsheng* texts, because it has opened new inroads into relatively unknown sectors of early Chinese thought and practice. Still, he is more interested in uncovering actual *yangsheng* techniques while I am more interested in the significance of the *fangji's* introducing them as other-oriented therapies as well as their symbiotic connection to the Laozi *Daodejing*.

Different from Hu Fuchen's understanding of Fangxian Daoism as a hybrid of early Daoism and the *fangshi*, and different from my understanding of it directly forming from Yangsheng Daoism alone, Harper sees Fangxian Daoism as directly forming from the *fangshi* alone, and he associates it with natural philosophy, occult arts, and "fang-literature."[76] However, like Hu and myself, Harper equates the emergence of the *fangji* with the rise of a new professional class that he calls "the physicians" but that, following Schaberg, I call ritual healers.

Part of the reason for my and Harper's different understandings of the origins of Fangxian Daoism is that we also have different views on the origins of *yangsheng*. He sees it originating as one of the occult arts of the *fangshi* no earlier than the fourth century BCE, while I see it as originating with Yangsheng Daoism no later than the fifth century BCE. I think that the decisive factor is that *yangsheng* holds a central place in the Laozi *Daodejing*, but few *fangshi* writings deal with *yangsheng*, and anyway it was the *fangji* who developed *yangsheng* into an other-directed therapy and who also wrote about it.

Harper denies any connection between early Daoism and the origins of *yangsheng*, and he gives two reasons for this. First, holding to the syncretic model allows him to date the *Daodejing* to the third century BCE, which is about a century after the formation of Fangxian Daoism. Second, holding to the views of Sivin and Strickmann mentioned earlier that reject the historical presence of a Daoist community before the Eastern Han allows him to deny the existence of any early Daoism from which *yangsheng* could have originated.

Harper's views are largely based on his reading of the bellows analogy from *Daodejing* chapter 5 that he translates as "The space between heaven and earth is like the bellows bag and tube, is it not? When empty, not expended; when moved, emitting ever more." This passage correlates with one from the Mawangdui *Yinshu* that he translates as "When cultivating the body you want to seek conformity with heaven and earth. It is like the bellows bag and tube: when empty, not expended; when moved, emitting ever more."

Recognizing that there is a *yangsheng* component to the *Daodejing*, Harper writes, "A number of passages in the *Daodejing* were clearly written to present physical cultivation theory, and the early commentaries probably preserve an exegetical tradition that dates to the time of the book's original composition."[77] Nevertheless, he also writes that "the scholarly convention[78] is to treat the complex of ideas associated with [*yangsheng*] and the belief in *xian* as aspects of a belief system loosely called Daoism … efforts to understand the development of ideas concerning [*yangsheng*] and the *xian* cult are not well served by a too easy use of the label Daoism."[79] His reasoning follows:

> To be sure, the philosophy of the *Daodejing* itself embraces [*yangsheng*], and the presence of cultivation techniques in certain paragraphs is manifest. My point is that Warring States [*yangsheng*] did not originate from the *Daodejing*, and that the centrality of the *Daodejing* to Warring States [*yangsheng*] is arguable … In the past it might have been argued that the mystical vision of the *Daodejing* was adapted to [*yangsheng*] techniques, which gave the *Daodejing*'s figurative language concrete physiological application. Although the bellows analogy is firmly associated with the *Daodejing* in received literature, I suspect

just the opposite may have occurred; the analogy originated in literature like *Yinshu*, whence it found its way into the *Daodejing* text. I cannot definitively prove priority for the bellows analogy in medical literature of [*yangsheng*]; the *Daodejing* was already circulating in the third century BCE, and *Yinshu* is certainly a younger text.[80]

According to Harper, *yangsheng* content was included in the *Daodejing* as it was undergoing the compilation process in the mid- to late third century BCE, but this is beside the fact that the text is not about *yangsheng* but rulership.[81] My view is that the Laozi *Daodejing* and *yangsheng* were the original possessions of reclusive Yangsheng Daoism. At some point during the fourth century BCE, both were introduced into public society by the *fangji*, who were well versed in the philosophy of the Dao and well trained in *yangsheng* techniques that they developed into an other-oriented therapy and administered to clients, which resulted in a wider cultural awareness of *yangsheng* as well as of the Laozi *Daodejing*.

Next to the work of Harper, Schaberg's study of early Chinese tetrasyllables also opens new pathways into understanding Fangxian Daoism (he does not recognize the term). His study of early Chinese tetrasyllables isolates one type that he calls "*Laozi*-style tetrasyllables" to distinguish them as representative of an entire subgenre of prosimetric philosophical discourse. These *Laozi*-style tetrasyllables are judiciously found throughout the *Daodejing*, and *Daodejing* chapter 2 ("The difficult and the simple complete each other" 難易相成) provides one of the clearest uses of it.[82] According to Schaberg,[83] the tetrasyllabic form enjoyed a widespread presence in a range of early Chinese writings. It juxtaposes rhymed with unrhymed material, and it demonstrates an absence of narrative, a restricted vocabulary, and use of paradox.

Briefly noting an ancient style of rhymed tetrasyllables in the *Shijing*, Schaberg writes:

> By the late Spring and Autumn period, bell inscriptions were showing a coincidence of rhyming and tetrasyllabic tendencies in inscriptions that sought to capture and control the harmonious sociality of bell music. Meanwhile, sacrificial prayers, blessings, oaths and curses, wedding songs and marching songs, and many of the other occasional songs useful in the social interactions of the period were being sung in rhymed tetrasyllables. For the specialists and ordinary people who used these songs … the language of ritual authority was tetrasyllabic.[84]

Schaberg's comments have bearing on Fangxian Daoism. Although he emphasizes the ritual contexts of the tetrasyllabic form even as he highlights its close relation to orality, I understand the tetrasyllables in the Laozi *Daodejing* as the product of its original orality to the exclusion of other ritual contexts, since Yangsheng Daoism did not share the kind of ritual mentality exhibited by Confucius.

Different from Yangsheng Daoists, an important feature of the *fangji* was their professional specialization in ritual, as supported by Harper and Schaberg. It directed the ways in which they administered *yangsheng* therapies to their clientele in the highly ritualized world of early China, where ritual recitation, for example, of the *Shijing*, played an exceptionally pronounced role among the noblemen.[85] However, Schaberg writes that they normally looked upon rhyming as beneath them, whose ritualized provenance was more appropriately associated with "employed specialists, diviners and physicians in particular";[86] in other words, those who may have made the rhymed tetrasyllables of the *Daodejing* more culturally visible.

Harper's reconstruction of the social context of Fangxian Daoism is nicely placed next to Schaberg's reconstruction of its ritual context, who writes, "Assuming that there were indeed specialists in the oral delivery of *Laozi*-style tetrasyllables, (then) the broad diffusion of their form of verse in texts of the late first millennium BCE bespeaks the existence of a large group, even a class, of such practitioners."[87] These practitioners would be the *fangji* that Schaberg characterizes as ritual healers reciting verses from the *Daodejing* and that Harper characterizes as physicians administering *yangsheng* therapies. However, to recognize them as reciting the Laozi *Daodejing* simultaneously with administering *yangsheng* therapy is to recognize Fangxian Daoism's reconfiguration of the genetic relationship between the Laozi *Daodejing* and *yangsheng* that was first established by Yangsheng Daoism.

Since Harper denies the existence of early Daoism, it could have exerted no influence on Fangxian Daoism; on the other hand, Schaberg neither affirms nor denies the existence of early Daoism, and this leaves him without resources to account for the origins of Fangxian Daoism. According to him, the historical materials that might clarify the situation usually are couched in passages involving semi-legendary figures: "The richest source of anecdotes featuring performance of *Laozi*-style tetrasyllables is of course the *Zhuangzi*."[88] Moreover, he does not discuss connections between the Laozi *Daodejing* and the later *yangsheng* texts such as those from Mawangdui. It is not far off to say that Harper uncovers the *yangsheng* component of Fangxian Daoism but ignores the *Daodejing* component, while Schaberg uncovers the *Daodejing* component but ignores the *yangsheng* component.

Schaberg effectively distinguishes the performance of *Laozi*-style tetrasyllables in didactic scenes of teaching involving masters and disciples from curative scenes of healing involving ritual healers and clients. But it would be more precise to see an original association of these didactic scenes with Yangsheng Daoism. As for the curative scene, both Harper and Schaberg agree that the patient/client of Fangxian Daoism would likely have had an elite social status; Harper writes, "The Mawangdui and Zhangjiashan [*yangsheng*] texts provide a remarkably full record of a tradition of [*yangsheng*] which by all appearances was taught to the elite by physicians in the third and second centuries BCE,"[89] and Schaberg writes that these ritual healers "would perhaps have enjoyed a special access to the patron or ruler."[90]

It is possible to be more precise in understanding Fangxian Daoism, but the preceding exploration is sufficient to establish its rough outlines and to recognize the *fangji* as instrumental players in the Warring States history of the Laozi *Daodejing*, positioned as they were between Yangsheng Daoism and Huang-Lao Daoism.

Orality and the Laozi *Daodejing*

My approach to Yangsheng Daoism is largely structured on the distinction between the Laozi *Daodejing* and the Huang-Lao *Daodejing*. There are no purely textual editions of either, but the Guodian and Mawangdui *Laozi* manuscripts are more reflective of the former, and the Heshang Gong and Wang Bi editions are more reflective of the latter. I display this distinction by concentrating on a few key points of the excavated manuscripts that significantly differ from the received edition in the attempt to uncover a Yangsheng Daoist reading of the *Daodejing* that has been dormant for more than two thousand years. This should not be taken as an attempt to reconstruct an original *Daodejing*; others have already been doing that difficult work for several decades now.[91]

Ding Sixin asks the pertinent question about the possibility of an original text:

> Has an absolutely perfect "original version" of the *Daodejing* ever existed in history? ... In light of the unearthed manuscripts, the answer is undoubtedly no ... On the whole, we now ought to accomplish a big shift in ideas: turn from the reductionist search for the earliest originally intended text of the *Daodejing* to an affirmation of the historical evolution of this text, and see the particularity of the formation and finalization of the *Daodejing*.[92]

Much like Ding, I too am concerned with understanding the processes that led from the early *Daodejing* to its "finalization" or, as I put it, the processes that led from the Laozi *Daodejing* to the Huang-Lao *Daodejing*. Following the syncretic model, Western approaches to the *Daodejing* normally take it as a product of the late third century BCE that was compiled from disparate sources by various multiple editors. Important representatives of this approach include D. C. Lau, who famously wrote that "the *Daodejing* is an anthology in which are to be found passages representing the views of various schools,"[93] A. C. Graham,[94] William Boltz,[95] Michael LaFargue,[96] and more recently Hongkyung Kim.[97] This approach logically requires them to reject the possibility of the Laozi *Daodejing* and take the Huang-Lao *Daodejing* as the original version.

The ideas of Alan Chan and Jean François Billeter previously discussed provide initial support for the synthetic model, since each provides solid grounds for accepting an original interpretative context that I identify as Yangsheng Daoist that served as both a generative source for the inner content of the Laozi *Daodejing* and a filtering mechanism to prevent inclusion of disparate material not in keeping with its philosophy of the Dao or *yangsheng*. Other important representatives of this approach include Kristofer Schipper,[98] William Baxter,[99] and Rudolf Wagner.[100] Each of them sees in the *Daodejing* a fundamental coherency that is attributed to its pre-third-century BCE oral origins, so any exploration of the Laozi *Daodejing* will necessarily rely on their findings.

Wagner (1980, 2003) famously discovered the fluid coherency of a particular format that is functional throughout many parts of the *Daodejing* that he calls the "interlocking parallel style" (IPS) in which sections or chapters of the text are not meant to be read in a typical linear fashion. In the IPS style, for example, two consecutive sentences, A and B, are not read with A on top and B beneath; rather, A is to be read on a left-hand column and B on a right-hand column directly next to it; thus, A and B are parallel with each other. The main thematic content of A is typically contrastive, complementary, or connective with B, and thus the thematic content interlocks. In addition, there is often a middle column that progresses, contains, or links the A-B parallel. Wagner[101] 2003 and I[102] have separately published *Daodejing* translations that follow the IPS format.

Already present in the Guodian *Laozi*, the IPS format functions on a formal level of original orality that tightly organizes and uniformly designs the synthetic patterns that provide structure to separate blocks of text. Its employment throughout the *Daodejing* argues against the syncretic model that sees the text as compiled.

Baxter's findings are also based on close analysis of the *Daodejing*'s internal contents, and they too give strong support to the synthetic model. Wagner uncovered one central structuring characteristic of the text, but Baxter uncovered multiple others that are fundamentally changing the way scholars read it.[103]

Where Baxter conservatively dates the *Daodejing* to 400 BCE, Roth writes that "there is also some evidence that (the *Daodejing* is) based upon an even older oral tradition."[104] Because the *Daodejing* preserves certain rhetorical and phonological features of the ancient *Shijing* that had been lost in the *Chuci*, Baxter specifies its origins as standing somewhere between the *Shijing* (whose collected songs are dated from 1000 to 600 BCE) and the earliest poems of the *Chuci* (dated to the late fourth century BCE). He adds that "the *Daodejing* represents a specific genre,"[105] and this is the insight that led Schaberg to designate its specific genre as "didactic prosimetrum."[106]

Taking such these findings altogether reveals twelve privileged features of the original orality of the Laozi *Daodejing*. Without analyzing them in finer detail here, the first seven are general features of the text, while the final six are passage-specific, and instead of presenting textual examples, I simply provide chapter numbers for clear instances of them.

1. Interlocking Parallel Style
2. Rhymed passages integrated with unrhymed portions of text
3. Absence of narration in relation to persons, places, or times
4. Restricted vocabulary
5. Generalized present except for depictions of cosmogony
6. Introductions, transitions, or summaries that frame units of verse, often tetrasyllables
7. Literary gestures of questioning and exclamation and use of the first person
8. Rhythm of rhymed tetrasyllabic lines (9, 19, 30, 41)
9. Semantic parallelism and/or antithesis with corresponding words in adjacent lines (81)
10. Patterns of repetition of individual words or chains of words in consecutive lines (16, 59)
11. Foregrounding of dichotomies (2, 18, 38)
12. Paradox (22, 24, 36, 45)
13. Binomes that are mostly limited to descriptions of cosmic and natural phenomena (6, 14, 16, 20, 58)

Each of these characteristic features of the original orality of the Laozi *Daodejing* is already present in the Guodian *Laozi* and are not the result of a syncretic process of compilation; in addition, each feature also bolsters the staple assumptions of coherency, oral antiquity, and community. However, feature number 6 (introductions, transitions, or summaries that frame units of verse) is least pronounced in the Guodian *Laozi*, since it was largely the result of the later transcription processes, but it is more pronounced in the Mawangdui *Laozi*, and then even more pronounced in the received text. This accumulation does not demonstrate the validity of the syncretic model, since its primary purpose was to clarify and organize already existing content without adding new substance,[107] but it does provide a particular window into its early oral circulations. More specifically, it indicates that the Laozi *Daodejing* orally circulated as a structurally fluid text consisting of moveable parts without standard sequence.

Dirk Meyer focuses on precisely this element of the Guodian *Laozi*. He approaches it by first distinguishing two sorts of early Chinese texts, argument-based texts and authority-based texts, the latter of which he would later call context-dependent texts. Meyer recognizes the Guodian *Laozi* as a primary example of a context-dependent text.

According to Meyer,[108] authority-based texts construct their arguments on building blocks that contribute, step by step, to the construction of a larger whole, namely, the complete argument. Context-dependent texts, on the other hand, consist of what he calls "units of thought (that) put forward one isolated concern … Every new unit reflects a different concern and should thus be seen as a distinctive text in its own right."[109] These units present "a situational response to a certain concern,"[110] but "do not articulate any concern in writing beyond the level of the particular unit. The individual unit remains formally isolated and must be approached in its own right. No formal elements blend the different units into larger integrated wholes of … the text as a whole,"[111] and he concludes that "the units of thought thus become movable modules."[112] These movable modules, individually or in groups, served as the measure for what circulated.

Since these units of thought are generally unrelated to each other one to the next and do not construct a single argument or system as with argument-based texts, this might raise the specter of the syncretic compilation model except for the presence of the interpretative community standing behind the text that guarantees the synthetic assumption of coherency; Meyer writes that "despite their brief and at times even enigmatic nature, these rather simplistic statements [units of thought] were nonetheless considered important enough to make the effort of fixing them on bamboo."[113] So even if we call it "anthology," it still expresses a certain "macrocoherence" by which the text's "macrolevel consistency suggests that it is unlikely that this anthology is an accidental collection of otherwise-unrelated materials."[114]

Recognizing the Laozi *Daodejing* as context-dependent points to the local authority within the interpretative community of masters and disciples (which will change over time). This authority originates with the master(s) who initially articulated the separate units of thought, but then transfers to the units of thought themselves (bundled into modules), while the master(s) acquire a different authority based not on their articulations of additional units of thought but on their position as teachers and interpreters of those units of thought. Meyer writes:

> However, the fact that these units have already taken on the shape of authoritative ideas prevalent in some elite circles does not necessarily imply the inverse conclusion that the authoritative character of these statements results from the existence of a prevalent concept of one authoritative "Laozi" behind them. Without doubt, such a concept would connect these units of thought to one philosophically prevalent current, lending a group identity to those circles.[115]

Against Meyer, I find reason to keep ahold of "Laozi" as a collective place holder ("the Old Masters") rather than as the name of a particular person ("the Old Master"), where it simply refers to the source of the local authority from which these units of thought were initially produced. Because of this and much like Wagner and Baxter, Meyer rarely goes beyond the formal features of the text to engage its philosophy and practice content, making it difficult for him to characterize the community in any detail other than to call it "one philosophically prevalent current."

But this is Yangsheng Daoism, and once the gathered modules exceeded its community, they continued to be orally circulated in modules. Given their elite clientele, the *fangji* would not have recited the entire *Daodejing* in curative scenes but just sections appropriate for the situation, and while this kept the modules from acquiring a stable sequence, it also initiated the Chinese cultural familiarity with the text. This explains why modules that speak to the health of the person and the state were prominently included in the Guodian *Laozi*, so it is no surprise to find in it such a heavy *yangsheng* representation. Instead of a newly minted Fangxian Daoist reading of the Laozi *Daodejing*, the Guodian *Laozi* likely reflects not more than a Fangxian Daoist emphasis on *yangsheng* and statecraft. According to Wang Bo (2000) and Barbara Hendrischke (2019), Guodian *Laozi* manuscript A concentrates on cultivation and statecraft, manuscript B only on cultivation, and manuscript C only on statecraft.

In the absence of a standard sequence in curative or didactic scenes of recitation, there had to be at least a rudimentary organization of modules even if only by rhythm or in memory. Among differing views, Liao Mingchun and Li Cheng hold that the text circulated in two *pian* 篇 (parts or sections):

> We believe that the original makeup of the *Daodejing* is neither one *pian* or the other first. The *Daodejing* at its earliest was not an integrated monograph, not a work written at one time and place, but rather a collection of Laozi's writings. The two *pian*, "Way" [Dao] and "Virtue" [De], were originally two independent parts that Laozi wrote at different times, and that circulated separately. There initially was no fixed order between them—that is, there was no distinction between first and second or before and after. Later, when people merged the two into one book called the *Daodejing*, they did not particularly care about which should precede which, and different people had different compiling methods; both sequences existed.[116]

The Guodian *Laozi* gives no indication of separation into two *pian* and, whether the text circulated in multiple modules or in two *pian*, Liao's ideas are useful because they demonstrate that their unique content had already been linked by the interpretative community, making it extremely difficult to mix into the whole any non-Yangsheng Daoist units of thought. Liao also says that the normal manner in which texts circulated at least from the mid-fourth century BCE was in the form of *pian*; in the following quote, where he writes "compilation" I would write "transcription" without affecting his wider point: "In comparison with the works of the other pre-Qin masters such as the 71 *pian* of the *Mozi*, the 52 *pian* of the *Zhuangzi*, and the 55 *pian* of the *Han Feizi*, the *Daodejing* is much shorter with only two *pian* and 5,000 words. Thus, compiling it was the easiest and the time of compilation was the earliest."[117]

Knowing that the *Daodejing*, either from the beginning or at a later time, circulated in two *pian* still does not answer to how even that content was organized into two separate parts, much less chapter sequences. The *Daodejing*'s textual organization was not stabilized in terms of chapter divisions, chapter sequences, and the order of the two *pian* (i.e., the received version) until the Western Han Dynasty; Ding Sixing writes:

> In fact, from the Warring States period to the Western Han, the *Daodejing* text underwent continuous changes, and the editors of each version did not necessarily take the "original version" as the most necessary and most rational "final version." In addition, although the edition of more than 5,000 words had already taken shape in the mid and late Warring States period, it remains difficult

to know what the condition of the *Daodejing* text was at that time (including the word count, textual variants, parts and sections, their order, etc.).[118]

The "continuous changes" noted by Ding pertain to the text's formal organization and not its internal contents, which remained stable. Next to alternative characters and loans words, for example,[119] the received text, with only a few exceptions, precisely replicates the wording of the Mawangdui *Laozi*, which replicates that of the Guodian *Laozi*. Meyer also speaks to this continuity:

> The units of thought collected [in the Guodian *Laozi*] were handed down for generations. They all persisted in the later canonized compilation familiar to us as the *Daodejing*. Despite the fact that most of these units took on an appreciably different form (certain words may differ, the internal structure of these units is not the same, some units are significantly shorter than their transmitted counterpart, and so on), the thought and tone in most cases nevertheless remain largely unchanged in the received classic.[120]

The overall continuity of the *Daodejing* from early to late is also demonstrated by the continuity of its thematic content since none that is present in the Guodian *Laozi* was ever deleted in later editions. This also points to the difficulty of inserting new thematic content once the *fangji* began to introduce it into early Chinese society. Meyer writes:

> Because these units of thought were considered important enough to fix on bamboo and all units persist to the present day [in the received *Daodejing*], the units anthologized in [the Guodian *Laozi*] must have been commonly known and also highly respected, at least in some circles of intellectual activity in the Warring States period. That they were written down, anthologized, and, to some extent, remained unchanged [in the received *Daodejing*] casts light on the authoritative character of these statements.[121]

Manuscripts and editions postdating the Guodian *Laozi* continued to demonstrate leeway with chapter numbers, exactly where some chapters are divided or precisely how some chapters are combined, with the order of the *Daojing* and the *Dejing*, as well as with a small number of alternative characters and phrasings. The Mawangdui *Laozi* in 81 chapters and the Beida *Laozi* in 77 chapters place the *De* section first, as does Yan Zun's commentary, which is missing the *Dao* section. The *Xiang'er* commentary, which is without chapter divisions and only covers content from chapters 3 through 37, places the *Dao* section first. The commentaries by Heshang Gong and Wang Bi come with the standard division of 81 chapters, but some of their chapter divisions and sequences differ from the

Mawangdui *Laozi*, and they also place the *Dao* section first. Finally, of all known versions, only Heshang Gong's has chapter titles. Ding writes:

> The end of the Warring States period to the beginning of the early Han marks the second stage of development of the *Daodejing* text. This stage was the eve of canonization. In comparison with the [Guodian *Laozi*], the [Mawangdui] *Laozi* experienced much splitting, splicing, and displacement of sections, which includes such aspects as the composition of the [Dao and De] sections and the transformation of the sequence of these sections. And these active transformations laid the direct textual foundation for the emergence of the finalized versions of the *Daodejing* (for example, the edition that Emperor Jing canonized).[122]

One final difference between the excavated and transmitted editions of the *Daodejing* concerns the tabooing of characters in the name of an emperor when he assumes the throne. The first instance of this came with the enthronement of Liu Bang 劉邦 in 202 BCE. As a general noun, *bang* 邦 means "the state," and while Mawangdui *Laozi* manuscript A uses *bang* some twenty times, it has vanished in manuscript B, having substituted it with *guo* 國, which means "the country." This demonstrates that manuscript A was composed before 202 BCE and that manuscript B was composed after, but this hardly impacted the meaning of the text.

The second instance occurred with the enthronement of Liu Heng in 180 BCE, which rendered *heng* 恆, used more than fifty times in the two Mawangdui *Laozi* manuscripts, taboo. It was the preferred term for describing the Dao in the Guodian, Mawangdui, and Beida *Laozi* manuscripts before it was substituted with *chang* 常. Wang Qingjie notes that it was not just the *Daodejing* that fell victim to this:

> The substitution of the word of *chang* for *heng* in pre-Qin texts after Emperor Wen of the Han should be very common. For example, it happened in the *Analects*, e.g., 7:26, as Kong Yingda (孔穎達) mentioned in his commentary of the text. It also happened in the "Outer Chapters" of 莊子 (*Zhuangzi*). The other examples were the change of the name of Mountain *Heng* (恆山) to Mountain *Chang* (常山) and the change of the name of the legendary girl in moon from "*Heng'e*" (恆娥) to "*Chang'e*" (嫦娥), etc.[123]

This substitution had a dramatic impact on the meaning of the *Daodejing*. Understanding the positions and meanings of *chang* and *heng* in the excavated *Laozi* manuscripts is essential for distinguishing the Laozi *Daodejing* from the Huang-Lao *Daodejing*, and it is to the examination of these two terms that the next chapter turns.

4

The Measurability of *Chang*

The Eternal Dao Is Not Very Old

The eminent Chinese scholar Chen Guying, whose research on the *Daodejing* in the last decades of the twentieth century was instrumental in bringing Daoism onto the stage of internationally recognized world philosophy, unabashedly recognizes Laozi as "China's first philosopher."[1] If he is correct, then we might also recognize that the *Daodejing*'s opening line established the rich and decidedly non-Western tradition of Chinese philosophy: 道可道非常道.

This line offers two possible interpretations, two orientational attitudes, that apply to the text as a whole. The first is phenomenological, and it is particular to Yangsheng Daoism, while the second is metaphysical and is particular to Huang-Lao Daoism. This second interpretation effectively obliterated the first.

Both readings take the first and third *dao* as nominals, and the second as verbal. The phenomenological reading takes the first and the third *dao* as signifying "a way" of doing something in which there is no determinative "the" and the term *dao* is given in the lower case, where *dao* can also be understood as referring to a plurality of ways of doing something. Although Roger Ames and David Hall want to keep the verbal nature of the second *dao* as "to speak," they provide an important modern translation that embodies this phenomenological interpretation (but they would call it "process philosophy") of the nominal first and third *dao*: "Way-making that can be put into words is not really way-making."[2] However, taken verbally, the phenomenological reading takes the second *dao* not as "to speak," but rather as "to lead, to open up (a path or way of doing something)." A clear instance of this usage is from the Guodian *Ziyi* 緇衣,[3] which quotes Confucius to say: "The superior man leads people by his words and by his conduct" 君子道人以言而以行.

The phenomenological reading can translate the first line as "*daos* can lead, but these are not permanent *daos*."[4] It asserts that specific and pre-established ways of doing things, for example, "the kingly way" 王道 or "the way of tea" 茶道, can teach, lead, and guide people to perform those activities with efficiency and grace, but these ways of doing things are not permanently set and will change over time.

The metaphysical reading separates the realm of the "eternal Dao" 常道 (*chang* Dao) from the phenomenal world in which thought and language can only approximate but never directly apprehend or communicate the eternal Dao, and if this eternal Dao can be directly apprehended, it is only by way of a mysticism. Discussing the permanent Dao as ineffable is a staple feature of *Daodejing* scholarship; for example, Bo Mou writes: "The genuine *Dao*, as an ultimate concern, simply cannot be captured through language."[5] This metaphysical interpretation of the third *dao* as changeless starkly differs from the phenomenological that says that the *dao*s are subject to change. Chad Hansen, remarking on Max Kaltenmark's[6] early assertion concerning the Dao's ineffability, writes, "Strangely, practically everyone agrees with Kaltenmark's profile of the first line. They assume, with Kaltenmark, that it asserts the ineffability of the metaphysical, mystical object called *dao* ... That consensus is wrong."[7]

Although the phenomenological reading must contend with the term *chang* that affirms the Dao as changeless, changelessness itself goes against virtually everything else that the *Daodejing* has to say about the phenomenological relation between the Dao and the world. This compels the recognition that either the phenomenological reading is simply wrong and must be rejected, or the *Daodejing* is wrong and must be emended. Rather than stating this as an either/or decision, I suggest that this is an issue of sequence: first there was the phenomenological reading, and later there was the metaphysical reading.

Traditional Chinese readings long ago established the metaphysical Dao as one, eternal, and beyond representation, and English translations convey this by their use of a determinative and capitalization in "the Dao," where the addition of *chang* to modify "the Dao" as "eternal," "constant," or "permanent" it already superfluous. The metaphysical reading necessarily posits "the eternal Dao" as a thing, an entity, or an essence existing on a plane of existence that is ontologically different from that of the phenomenal world. Bo Mou provides one explanation of this:

> We first need to make clear what "*chang-Dao*" (the eternal *Dao*) means. In my view, what "*chang-Dao*" denotes is not something that is separate from the (genuine) *Dao* as a whole but one dimension or layer of the *Dao*: its eternal and infinite dimension that consists in the *Dao* going on forever and continuously transcending any finite manifestations of the *Dao* in "*wan-wu*" (ten thousand

particular, concrete, and individual things of the universe) in the course of its developing and changing process.[8]

According to Bo, there are several different but interrelated dimensions to the Dao, but the *chang*-dimension is the most metaphysically significant. Galia Patt-Shamir provides another illustrative example of this:

> The *Daodejing* suggests a twofold attitude toward *dao*. On the one hand *dao* is eternal, infinite, constant and indivisible and thus ineffable, while in some different sense there is a namable reality, which according to the common interpretation is inferior to *dao*, and yet it is called *dao* too; to be more precise it is the language of *dao* (*dao kedao*) as opposed to *dao* beyond language (*changdao*).[9]

These examples from a respected Chinese scholar and a respected Western scholar demonstrate representative interpretations of *chang dao* as the eternal entity beyond time and space that brings forth all existence. The Dao that is posited by the mind in language is either a weak reflection of "the Eternal Dao" or a different Dao altogether, depending if one believes that the Dao posited by the mind in language is weakly representative of "the eternal Dao" or not at all representative of it. Although such conceptions of "the eternal Dao" take it for granted that it is a metaphysical entity, they are incongruous with virtually everything else that the *Daodejing* says about *chang dao*.

In fact, *chang dao* is only a little more than two thousand years old. It was formally born on November 24, 180 BCE, the enthronement day of Emperor Wen, whose personal name was Liu Heng 劉恆. Up to that time, all previous editions of the *Daodejing* had used the term *heng* 恆 to modify *dao* in the opening line as well as throughout the text, but Liu's ascension immediately brought that to an end. In their search for an appropriate alternative, scholars and scribes resolved on the term *chang*.

In the course of the Han Dynasty, it became universally assumed that *chang dao* was the central feature of the original thought of the *Daodejing*, since no later scholars ever even off-handedly mentioned this substitution. The 1974 discovery of the Mawangdui *Laozi*, which had not yet substituted *chang* for *heng*, came as some surprise, and the usage was further verified with the 1993 discovery of the Guodian *Laozi*, which also did not have this substitution.

Few scholars have examined the significance of this and, already fifty years after the Mawangdui discovery, contemporary studies and translations of the *Daodejing* stubbornly maintain the phrase *chang dao* where the manuscript editions never once use it. Other scholars who recognize the substitution dismiss its significance by assuming that *heng dao* is synonymous with *chang dao*. Although after the fact, *heng* and *chang* were in fact made into synonyms, but their earlier meanings carried no metaphysical connotations and were anyway very far apart from each other.

This study explores the distinction between two orientational attitudes, phenomenological and metaphysical, standing behind interpretations of the *Daodejing* by exploring the significance of the substitution of *chang* for *heng*. Separately, the two terms serve as shorthand markers for the two components of the matrix of the Laozi *Daodejing*. The ancient meanings of *chang* pertain to the determinability of material extension, but the text deploys it for pointing to the unnameable Dao of *yangsheng* cultivation. The ancient meanings of *heng* pertain to the rhythms of temporal flux, but the text deploys it to discuss the nameable Dao of its philosophy of the pristine Dao.

Chen Ligui's comments offer initial direction for this study:

> As a source of Daoism, various philosophical concepts were derived from the *Daodejing*'s notion of the Dao and were widely disseminated until they came to thoroughly permeate every nook and cranny of Chinese philosophy. Among the several derivative concepts that later generations greatly elucidated and developed were the One, *chang*, and *heng* ... However, the concept of *chang*, according to the excavated texts of the *Daodejing*, originally had a specific philosophical meaning that was entirely distinct from *heng*. The versions transmitted in later generations had confused the meanings of the two and, because of this, the philosophical meaning of *chang* gradually became trivialized and neglected while *heng* acquired a signification that closely approximated that of the Dao.[10]

Although Chen does not go so far as to recognize that we are dealing with two entirely different versions of the *Daodejing*, she nicely pinpoints the core of the distinction between them. This has the potential to overturn many of our assumptions not only about traditional interpretations of the *Daodejing* but also about Yangsheng Daoism. None of this, however, can happen without first understanding the positions and meanings of *chang* and *heng* in the Laozi *Daodejing*, which is the matter of this and the next chapter.

Ancient and Early Uses of *Chang*

According to William Baxter, the *Daodejing* shows more influence from the ancient collection of songs gathered in the *Shijing* 詩經 than from any other Chinese writings. His insight serves as a cue for uncovering a Yangsheng Daoist reading of the Laozi *Daodejing*.

In the pre-philosophical songs of the *Shijing*, *chang* appears fourteen times, with typical meanings cohering around standard regularity or extended duration. "Juan A" 卷阿 presents well-wishing sentiments to the newly enthroned king: "May you fulfill your years/With genuine happiness your regular (*chang*) possession" 俾爾彌爾性/純嘏爾常矣.[11] "Bi Gong" 閟宮 offers words of encouragement to the young king, telling him that his ancestors will bless his rule and make it possible for him "To preserve this eastern region./ The state of Lu is determinably constant" 保彼東方/魯邦是常. "Wen Wang" 文王 declares: "the Mandate of Heaven is not determinably regular (*chang*)" 天命靡常.

Each of these three uses of *chang* denotes an extended duration in terms of determinable regularity or constancy: the regularity of an emotional condition in "Juan A," and the regularity of a political condition pertaining to the possession of a state in "Bi Gong" and the possession of the dynasty in "Wen Wang." Here, extended duration in terms of eternity is not the issue, but rather the determinable regularity of a positive condition that is not overcome by a negative condition. In other words, the first passage intends the determinable regularity of happiness not overcome by sadness, the second intends the determinable regularity of the possession of a state not overcome by invasion or insurrection, and the third intends the determinable regularity of Heaven not overcome by its bestowing its mandate on a different ruling lineage.

"Cai Wei" 采薇 notes the beauty of "the determinable regularity of flowers" 常之華, and "Chang Di" 常棣 more specifically notes the beauty of "the determinable regularity of the cherry flowers" 常棣之華. In these cases, *chang* expresses the determinable regularity of the condition of the flowers when they are in bloom—at those moments when they fulfill their fullness that is maintained for the short duration after they bloom but before they fade. Determinable regularity refers to a norm of fulfillment reached at a level of completeness that endures only so long as the fullness of that measure is maintained.

The condition of *chang* signals a norm of ontological plenitude that any other condition does not fulfill, and this is brought out in "Shi yue zhi jiao" 十月之交, which speaks of the natural regularity of lunar eclipses: "Lunar eclipses/Are only natural regularities" 彼月而食則維其常. However, *chang* also refers to a positive norm against which any condition that does not fulfill it is deemed deficient, as in "Bao yu" 鴇羽, which announces the complaints of the farmers who are not able to tend their fields because the king has requisitioned them for other purposes, likely a labor project: "When shall we return to our regular [responsibilities]?" 曷其有常.

Two further uses of *chang* develop the sense of the determinable regularity in relation to constant norms. In "Si wen" 思文, the norm refers to the agricultural methods incepted by Hou Ji, the legendary founder of the Xia Dynasty: "Without regard to territory or boundary/The regular norms [of agricultural methods] were diffused throughout the time of the Xia" 無此疆爾界陳常于時夏. "Yin wu" 殷武 describes the earlier tributes and acts of submission by the various tribal chiefs, referring to them as "the determinable norms [of political regularity] of the Shang Dynasty" 商是常.

Various commentaries of the *Yijing* 易經[12] also employ *chang* in the sense of a determinable constancy in relation to objects, events, or conditions. These employments are typical in the text and refer to a determinable course of behavior that remains within the bounds of what can be expected, calculated, and measured. The "Tuan Commentary" 象傳 to the Kun 坤 hexagram speaks of "acquiring the determinable course" 得常, the "Xiang Commentary" 象傳 to the Zhun 屯 hexagram speaks of "resuming the determinable course" 反常, and the "Xiang Commentary" 象傳 to the Xu 需 and the Shi 師 hexagrams speaks of "displacing the determinable course" 失常. Here as throughout these early Chinese writings, *chang* is used in senses that are not reducible to eternity/permanence/constancy.

Building on these meanings cohering around the notion of regular norms of determinable regularity, the *Shijing* uses *chang* to refer to objects, events, and conditions that can be expected, calculated, measured, or otherwise determined with precision with respect to extension, duration, occurrence, or appearance. "Liu yue" 六月 describes the preparations of the war carriages, and it points to "the determinably regular accoutrements hanging [on them]" 載是常服, while "Wen Wang" 文王 describes "the determinably regular robes and embroidered caps" 常服黼冔 worn at a ceremony. Both passages have the identical phrase, *chang fu* 常服, which is reflected in *Shuowen jiezi* 說文解字[13] 4845: "*chang* refers to the lower skirt" 常下帬也. To say that these accoutrements, robes, and caps are *chang* as determinably regular is to say that they follow a uniform measurement.

In his brief discussion of *chang*, Wang Qingjie writes, "The original meaning of *chang* as a unit of measurement or as a standard of things later attains its important philosophical significance."[14] Citing a work by Wu Chengluo entitled 中国度量衡史 (*A History of Measurement in China*) that provides information about *chang* as a precise measurement, he writes that "a *zhou chi* 周尺 is 19.01 cm. A *chang* 常 is two *xun* 尋 and one *xun* is eight *zhou chi*. For example, in the *Book of Rites* 禮記, we read, 'A short spear should be one *chang* and four *chi* while a long spear should be three *xun*.'"[15] Noting this precise measurement in relation to the *Shuowen*'s definition of *chang* as referring to a lower skirt, Wang writes, "The connection between these two meanings might be that *chang* was a standard measurement for a tailor to make a skirt and other clothes,"[16] where one *chang* is roughly equivalent to 76.64 centimeters or 31.35 inches. His intuition about the relation between *chang*, a tailor's measure, and clothing is supported by *Shuowen* 5398:

> One *chi* 尺 is ten *cun* 寸. The distance between the hand and its vessel is ten *fen* 分, which is called one *cun*. Ten *cun* makes one *chi*. A *chi* is that which is used to measure things precisely. The character consists of *shi* 尸 [as measurement] and *yi* 乙 [as a thing to be measured]. It is the thing that is to be known. According to the Zhou regulations, the measurements are *cun*, *chi*, *zhi* 咫, *xun*, *chang*, and *ren* 仞, all of which take the human body as the standard.

This passage concretely demonstrates one important meaning of *chang* as a precise measurement, while *Shuowen* 4845 gives another: "*Chang* is the lower skirt. Its root is cloth 巾 with *shang* 尚 as the phonetic" 常下帬也从巾尚聲. About the skirt 帬, *Shuowen* 4846 states, "It is the lower clothing. Its radical is cloth 巾 with *jun* 君 as the phonetic" 下裳也 从巾君聲. Finally, *Shuowen* 5228 states, "Clothing 衣 is what we depend on. Above it is called the upper garments 衣, below it is called the lower garments 裳. They cover both parts of a person. These terms for clothing all derive from the root *yi* 衣."

In general, these ancient uses of *chang* taken altogether show it as a precise measurement; the lower clothing that must be precisely measured by tailors; a precisely determinable course of action or behavior; and an object, event, or condition that is routinely expected, calculated, measured, or otherwise precisely determined with respect to extension, duration, occurrence, or appearance. It has no other philosophical content.

Because of this absence, Wang Qingjie argues that, where the term is found in the *Laozi* manuscripts, the reasons it was used instead of *heng* are trivial, and that "if we examine the three chapters where *chang* is used, we find that the use of *chang* is due to the rhyme scheme of the text."[17] He also writes: "As a philosophical concept, *chang* may appear for the first time in Mohism, one of the most important philosophical schools in Confucius' and Laozi's time."[18] He attributes this insight to Chad Hansen, who understands *dao* as a language-based "guiding discourse" that guides thought and behavior rather than as a metaphysical entity; Hansen writes:

> We have discussed the term *chang* in earlier chapters. There, too, it was as a linguistic pragmatic concept. Mozi was said to *chang* language that promotes

good behavior. Chinese philosophy had not made *chang* a metaphysical concept prior to this point. The standard interpretation needs to claim that it too now becomes a metaphysical concept. It appeals to the Greek and Indian metaphysical assumption that only the permanent is real to buttress their metaphysically monist interpretation that the *dao* is the only reality. Guided too quickly by the principle of charity, these interpreters grasp for the familiar before they explore the earlier, pragmatic, linguistic reading of the term.[19]

As a pragmatic discourse, a *dao* articulates a comprehensive set of norms pertaining to language, knowledge, and morality. Also, *dao*s are multiple, and different thinkers affirm different *dao*s. The Mohists applied a set of standards, primarily benefit and harm, to assess the rightness and wrongness or goodness and badness of a *dao*, but because standards are not constant, *dao*s also cannot be constant, thus there are multiple ones from which to choose. The standards themselves, however, should be made *chang*. Hansen shows the Mohist understanding of *chang* as both an adjective, "constant," and as a verb, "to make constant." A passage from *Mozi* 12, "Fuyi," repeated nearly verbatim in *Mozi* 11, "Gengzhu," illustrates his point: "Master Mozi said: If a teaching can modify conduct, then *chang* it; if it cannot modify conduct, then do not *chang* it. To *chang* (a teaching) that cannot modify conduct is only to agitate the mouth" 子墨子曰言足以遷行者常之不足以遷行者勿常不足以遷行而常之是蕩口也.[20]

When the standards for assessing *dao*s are made *chang*, then can the *dao*s themselves become *chang*; Hansen writes, "This explains Mozi's introducing the term *chang*[constant] into the debate. It gives his standard of *dao*s a point of contact with reality,"[21] and he goes on to discuss the measurability of *chang*:

> Mozi's position has an objectivist ring because he emphasizes external permanence as guiding our use of language. He advocates measurelike standards. Such standards are one component of a scientific perspective. Theories of measurement accompanied by operations that yield constant, reliable results for different evaluators are as crucial to science as is mathematics.[22]

Mozi "Canon 1" nicely illustrates the relation between *chang* and measurement: "Rotation: when the circumference has an acupoint, the shape is constant" 庫區穴若斯貌常. Because the circular shape develops an acupoint when in rotation, it therefore is *chang*, not in the sense of permanent, but in the sense of its measurability.

In the Laozi *Daodejing*, *chang* does not signify eternity/permanence/constancy; its range more points to norms of constant regularity that can be measured or otherwise determined. I disagree with the claims by Wang and Hansen that the *Mozi* turned *chang* into a philosophical term, because its uses there remain technical and concern how standards and *dao*s are to be made measurable.

A close approximation of the Laozi *Daodejing*'s pre-philosophical use of *chang* that is too easily interpreted philosophically can be found in the "Xiang Commentary" to the Guimei hexagram of the *Yijing* that states: "The gentleman makes constant his virtue and his conduct, and practices that which he has been taught" 君子以常德行習教事. This passage discusses the measurability of behavior, either good or bad or right or wrong, and not morality itself, such that an evil teaching or behavior can be made *chang* just as easily as a good teaching or behavior; *chang* as a term remains morally neutral. Interestingly, the *Analects* uses *chang* once to describe a person's regular teacher, whereas the *Xunzi* 荀子 has already fully moralized the term, which it uses sixty-eight times, referring to something like "constant morality." But even this usage is far removed from the Huang-Lao Daoist understanding of *chang* as eternal/permanent/constant.

In the Laozi *Daodejing*, the range of *chang* is severely circumscribed and only refers to the norms of constant regularity of the physical body. More precisely, *chang* signifies the changing measurability and determinateness of the condition of the physical body as it experiences the effects of *yangsheng* bodily cultivation. The text understands these changes as a "return" 复, since the body that has changed due the effects of *yangsheng* is not a categorically different body, but rather one that has returned to its natural condition, one that embodies the pristine Dao.

Uses of *Chang* in the Laozi *Daodejing*

Chen Ligui is counted at the top of the list of a small number of scholars to have engaged with a Yangsheng Daoist reading of the *Daodejing*, although she does not recognize the text in these terms and I do not fully endorse all of her interpretations. My main hesitation is with her tendency to spiritualize *yangsheng*, which is possibly explainable as a lingering habit of the metaphysical interpretation that she otherwise nearly conquers single-handedly. But because Western readers are not very familiar with her work, which is invaluable for this this study, I take the liberty of presenting several extended passages from it in this and the following part of this chapter. Pertinent to the immediate topic at hand, she writes:

Because all uses of *heng* were changed to *chang*, the special philosophical meanings of the original uses of *chang* in the *Daodejing* became obscured. Therefore, if we intend to examine its important meanings in the text, we must understand them based on the instances where they appear in three chapters of the Guodian *Laozi* and the Mawangdui *Laozi*.[23]

Following Chen, the analysis of *chang* in the *Daodejing* is limited to just three chapters; all other uses of *chang* in the received text were substitutions for *heng* and are here ignored. The Guodian *Laozi* employs *chang* only one time in a passage replicated in the Mawangdui *Laozi* corresponding to chapter 55 that itself has one additional use of the term. The Mawangdui *Laozi* uses it in two additional chapters, both of which have textual lacunae, that correspond to chapter 52 (where it is used one time) and chapter 16 (where it is used four times). Every use of the term in the *Laozi* manuscripts is retained in the received text, which has no additional uses of *chang* outside of its substitutions for *heng*. Thus, the following analysis is restricted to these three chapters.

None of these uses of *chang* express anything resembling eternity/permanence/constancy; rather, they share a uniform meaning within the field of *yangsheng* bodily cultivation that retains the ancient range of meanings cohering around standard regularities and extended durations that can be calculated, measured, and precisely determined in relation to objects, events, and conditions. The Laozi *Daodejing* systematically positions *chang* in reference to sequential stages of *yangsheng* cultivation that implicate two other central *yangsheng* terms, *he* 和 and *ming* 明.

This extended quotation from Chen Ligui offers a fitting starting point:

> What these three chapters (16, 52, and 55) repeatedly emphasize is the value of the notion of *chang* and "according with *chang*" 襲常 in the *Daodejing*. These several *chang*, which clearly have deep significance, are particular and deeply valued philosophical concepts in the *Daodejing*. They are related to two other concepts that are also highly valued in the *Daodejing*, *ming* 明 and *he* 和. "To know *he*" is called "*chang*," "to know *chang*" is called "*ming*," and to be able to "*ming*" is finally to be able to enter "the Dao" 入道. Bringing the meanings of the three chapters together, we see that these concepts are repeatedly emphasized. In other words, *he* and *chang* are both preliminary and necessary conditions for embodying the Dao 體道 and entering the Dao. But what is *he*? *Daodejing* chapter 42 states that in the Dao's processes of giving birth to the myriad beings, although they are "held up by *yin* and embrace *yang*" 負陰而抱陽, they still must have "blended *qi* as *he*" 沖氣以為和 before they are born, because without *he* they cannot be brought to life. *He* is a certain condition; it is the harmonious condition 和諧狀態 in which the processes of the Dao bring to birth the myriad

beings, and the two *qi* of *yin* and *yang* are balanced in equilibrium and stable. *Chang* too is a condition, but it is also a regulatory standard. It is a condition and a regulatory standard in which things return to the source in endless cycles of circulation without ceasing, called "returning to the root" 歸根 and "returning to the natural condition" 復命. In other words, *chang* is the operational condition 運作狀態 of the Dao, and it is also the regulatory standard of the operations of the myriad beings as well as the regulatory standard of their return to the source. Being able to clearly see and understand these conditions and regulatory standards is called *ming*. If one can be *ming*, then one can enter the Dao. Because of this, the *Daodejing* wants people to "use their light to return to their *ming*" 用其光復歸其明, and not become confused by "the side by side bursting forth" 旁作 and the "multitudinous arising" 芸芸 [chapter 16] of the myriad beings and the myriad manifestations of the phenomenal world. One must be able to clearly recognize the original source, return to the original source, and master the authentic truth before being able to enter the Dao. Because of this, *chang* refers to the operations of the regulatory standard of the Dao, and while *he*, *chang*, and *ming* only slightly differ in their references, they all mark preliminary conditions and necessary states for entering the Dao.[24]

Daodejing Chapter 55

In the Laozi *Daodejing*, *chang* primarily functions as a measure of knowability for the vitality of *de* 德, referring to the body's rhythmic systems of circulation. When the text mentions *de* in discussions of human virtue, it has its more familiar sense of "charismatic virtue," but it uses *de* in this technical *yangsheng* sense in discussions of the human body or the pristine Dao.[25]

Daodejing chapter 55 celebrates the physical vitality of *de* that it sees in the body of the infant. This body manifests physical perfection at one with the pristine Dao because it has not yet suffered the physically deleterious effects of socialization that wreak havoc on its natural conditions and that inevitably lead to its "early death" 早已, as the last line of the chapter states. The chapter opens with these lines:

> One who contains the fullness of *de* can be compared to an infant ...
> His bones are supple and his sinews are pliant yet his grasp is firm.
> Not yet knowing the union of male and female, his member is erect.
> This is the height of *jing*.
> He hollers all day and is not hoarse.
> This is the height of *he*.

This is a defining *yangsheng* passage that spotlights the sheer physicality of *de* devoid of moral connotation. It is recognized by the vitality of the infant's rhythmic systems of circulation, allowing it to experience the "the height of *jing*" 精之至也. In non-Daoist writings, *jing* 精 is often interpreted as a not-entirely corporeal "vitality" or "essence" of the body or the mind, but in the Laozi Daodejing it is fundamentally corporeal and refers to the body's hot internal fluids, primarily blood, and since the infant embodies "the height of *jing*," its member is constantly erect.

Among the infant body's systems of rhythmic circulation vitalized by *jing* is the respiratory system that, functioning in tandem with the lungs, is inexhaustible in the same way as "the space between Heaven and Earth" of *Daodejing* chapter 5 (the last chapter briefly discussed Harper's view on it), which goes on to state: "Is it not like a bellows bag and tube? Empty yet inexhaustible, when it is active, more always comes out."[26]

Because of the inexhaustibility of the infant's rhythmic systems of circulation, he can holler all day without depletion; this marks "the height of *he*" 和之至也 (*he zhi zhi ye*). In non-Daoist writings, *he* 和 is normally spiritualized as the "harmony" of the psyche or the spirit or as the ability to get along with others, but in the Laozi Daodejing its uses are fundamentally corporeal and signify the holistic integration of the body's various systems of circulation into a single body of circulation, as with the newborn body of the infant or the cultivated body of the sage.

More precisely, *he* is a condition of bodily ultimacy in which *qi* flows unimpeded throughout the integrated body. It designates a specific bodily condition in which *qi* circulation is proprioceptively determinable. Socialized bodies that remain uncultivated in *yangsheng* have a deficient flow of *qi* in which *he* is minimal and, thus, indeterminate.

The next two lines of the chapter further focus on the determinability of the corporeal condition of *he*. The Guodian and Mawangdui A manuscripts uniformly state:

He is *chang*.
To know *he* is *ming*.

The partially corrupted Mawangdui B manuscript likely is the same as the received text that adds *zhi* 知 (verbally as "to know" or nominally as "knowledge" or "the knowledge of") in the first line and substitutes *chang* for *he* in the second line:

To know *he* is *chang*.
To know *chang* is *ming*.

The passage emphasizes the particular relationship between *he* and *chang* (I turn to *ming* shortly) by stating that "*he* is *chang*" 和曰常 (where *yue* 曰 has the force of a copula as "X is Y" rather than as "X is called Y"). The condition of *he* is precisely determinable as *chang* insofar as its proprioceptive determinability does not waver or fluctuate. Awkwardly stated, *he* is determinable as *chang*, and what *chang* determines is *he*, and this seems to explain the addition of the second *zhi* in the received text, which is anyway either trivial or redundant since to "know" *he* (as bodily integration) is at the same time to "know" its *chang* (as determinability). But what about the other *zhi* (to know) in the second line?

More important than the relation between *he* and *chang* is the import of *zhi* in bringing the *he* "integrated" and *chang* "determinable" bodily condition to the level of *ming*. *Zhi* points to a specific kind of knowing that differs from rational intellection; it is a proprioceptive knowledge that is honed through one's cultivated awareness of internal bodily movements. This is the knowledge that Billeter recognized beneath the surface of *Daodejing* chapter 15 (discussed in the previous chapter) upon which the effectiveness of *yangsheng* depends; Billeter writes:

> To free ourselves from the influence (of our Western tradition) and to conceive of other ways of representing the human body to ourselves, let us oppose to the notion of the object-body that of the phenomenal body. The phenomenal body is a reality that we no longer grasp by sight, but much more immediately by proprioceptive sensitivity … the proprioceptive sense seems to us doomed to perceive the obscure, the indecisive, the subjective. It seems to us that the internal sensations, which cannot be represented or described in a precise way, cannot be used by the intellect because it cannot draw any knowledge from them. Especially since, unlike external objects, they are not manipulatable: we can neither preserve them, reproduce them, nor modify them at will, we believe, so that they escape our investigation … Thanks to their "energetic vision of the system," the Chinese have, on the contrary, disposed of a paradigm [*yangsheng*] perfectly adapted to the exploration of internal sensations since ancient times. This allowed them to explore this domain and develop a systematic knowledge of it. Where we have developed a knowledge of the body-object, they have mainly developed a knowledge of the phenomenal body.[27]

Especially cultivatable by *yangsheng* techniques, this proprioceptive bodily knowledge is capable of sensing and determining internal bodily conditions, "the obscure, the indecisive, the subjective" (*de l'obscur, de l'indécis, du subjectif*). It is capable of determining internal conditions of integration because they have now become, through the course of *yangsheng* cultivation, *chang*.

The final lines of the chapter:

> To add on to life is called inauspicious.
> If the heart controls *qi*, it is called aggression.
> When things attain their prime, then they age.
> This is called not-Dao.
> What is not-Dao dies early.[28]

If there was any suspicion that chapter 55's field of signification concerns anything other than the phenomenal body of *yangsheng* cultivation with emphasis on its unimpeded flow of *qi*, then these final lines leave no room for doubt. The first two lines raise the dangers of improper or misdirected *yangsheng* cultivation, calling it "inauspicious" 祥 and "aggression" 強 before bluntly asserting: "When things attain their prime, then they age. This is called not-Dao" 物壯則老是謂不道.

The improper or misdirected way of performing *yangsheng* is one that aspires to attain the "prime" 壯, an apex of attainment, but the efforts required to sustain it cause the body's *jing* to be overstretched and expended, leading to death. The passage is discouraging attainment of the state of "prime" because it goes against the grain of *yangsheng*, which teaches instead to conserve, retain, and continually revitalize inner *de*. Key technical terms that are found throughout the text that advocate such bodily conservation include "preserve the center" 守中 from *Daodejing* chapter 5, "preserve stillness" 守靜 from *Daodejing* chapter 16, and "manifest plainness and embrace simplicity" 見素抱樸 from *Daodejing* chapter 19. At the same time, the text also provides numerous negative depictions of those who have attained prime, including "One who is brave in being daring will be killed" 勇於敢則殺 from *Daodejing* chapter 73, and "One who stands high is not stable" 企者不立 from *Daodejing* chapter 24.

The *yangsheng* teachings of *Daodejing* chapter 55 discourage a person from attaining prime because to do so is to immediately begin to "age" 老, and this is "not-Dao" 不道. All editions except for the Guodian have the final line, "What is not-Dao dies prematurely" 不道早已, a final summary underscoring that the entire passage concerns the phenomenal body. Outside of war, execution, and other externally invasive death events, "premature death" 早已 is caused by the depletion of *jing* fueling the body's rhythmic systems of circulation.

The depleted condition that ensues from attaining prime begins the process of aging leading to death, and the text explicitly states not once but twice that this is "not-Dao." According to the logic of negation, if there is a condition of not-Dao, then there must also be the original condition that is negated in the first place, the condition of Dao, which also signifies the condition of being one with the pristine Dao characterized by not attaining prime, not growing old, and not dying prematurely: to be one with the pristine Dao is to enjoy longevity.

Longevity is not immortality,[29] but it still covers a vastly longer life duration (the Daoist tradition often mentions 800 years) compared to premature death. Even the Guodian *Laozi* recognizes this as a core *yangsheng* component in a passage from *Daodejing* chapter 44: "One can be long and lasting" 可以長久, where *chang* 長 and *jiu* 久 are, according to *Daodejing* chapter 59, abbreviations for long-life and lasting vision, the result of "the Dao of long-life and lasting vision" 長生久視之道, in other words the pristine Dao of *yangsheng*.

In *Daodejing* chapter 55, *chang* does not refer to a bodily condition but to the experiential determinateness and knowability of three higher bodily conditions: the height of *jing*, the height of *he*, and *ming*. This progressive order represents a *yangsheng* sequence that culminates in embodying the pristine Dao, and it is one of several sequences littered throughout the text normally presented in a sorites format.

This *yangsheng* sequence first recognizes "the height of *jing*," in which blood and other bodily fluids vitalize to expansively open their circulatory channels. It then recognizes "the height of *he*," in which unhindered *qi* pervades all parts of the body as a single circulatory system. It then recognizes *ming* 明 (to brighten or illuminate). In non-Daoist writings, *ming* is normally spiritualized as the "enlightenment" of the spirit, interpretable according to either traditional Western or Eastern notions of spirituality, but in the Laozi *Daodejing* its uses are fundamentally corporeal where it refers to a proprioceptive sensitivity, and the text reserves a particularly complex position for it.

Daodejing Chapter 16

Daodejing chapter 16 deploys *chang* within another *yangsheng* sequence. Chen Ligui and I both read it as a primary *yangsheng* chapter because of its emphasis on the connections between *chang* and *ming*, but she understands *ming* to concern a spiritual knowledge of the body of the Dao, and I understand it to concern a proprioceptive knowledge of the physical body. Chen writes:

> *Daodejing* chapter 16 teaches the way to penetrate the highest degree of emptiness and stillness to clear the mind and realize the operative conditions and regular norms of the natural Dao. Laozi recognizes that penetrating the clear mind, one can clearly see that the operative conditions and regular norms of the Dao are such as to ceaselessly return to the conditions and processes of

the original source, and that these conditions and processes are called "return." The conditions and processes of this return are a kind of absolute law, and the *Daodejing* calls it *chang*. To be able to comprehend the body of the Dao, the *chang* law of this return is called *ming*. To be able to see *ming* is to possess the wisdom of understanding that the body of the Dao has the principle of returning to the original source. The purpose of chapter 16 is to teach that possessing this wisdom of "knowing *chang*" and being able to be *ming*, one effectively manages every possible situation in the world and has success in everything.[30]

Although Chen takes *he*, *chang*, and *ming* as referring to the body of the Dao while I take them to refer to the physical body, her analysis nevertheless allows me to highlight the effective relationship between *chang* as the determining of the bodily condition of a unified system of rhythmic circulation designated as *he*, and *ming* as the ability to illuminate the ongoing changes in the bodily conditions. More precisely, *ming* signifies the functional activation of the proprioceptive sensitivity that recognizes incipient movements of the phenomenal body that lead either to benefit or to harm, or what Chen refers to as "success in everything."

In a previous study,[31] I examined *ming* as the type of "foreknowledge" 前識 mentioned in *Daodejing* chapter 38, "Foreknowledge is the flower of the Dao" 前識者道之華, that allows the sages as masters of *yangsheng* to restrain their urges to act directly on the world. There is a more important but very much related element to *ming*: as natural light is required to see the world, so *ming* as "brightness" is needed to see or, more precisely, proprioceptively sense the body's internal condition as it approaches ever so close to its union with the pristine Dao. *Daodejing* chapter 52 (discussed below) states: "To perceive the small is called brightness" 見小曰明.

Rather than internal illumination, Chen Ligui too understands *ming* as a foreknowledge that can be turned to achieving success: "one effectively manages every possible situation in the world and has success in everything." But these two interpretations of *ming* are not mutually exclusive and in fact complement each other as two sides of the same coin, with the caveat that *ming* as internal illumination is prior.

As with other uses of *chang* in the Laozi *Daodejing*, its meaning in chapter 16 is far removed from notions of eternity/permanence/constancy. In every case, *chang* holds a prominent position in *yangsheng* sequences, where its formal placements implicate it with the knowability and determinability of bodily conditions that are the result of *yangsheng* bodily cultivation. This *yangsheng* sequence most significantly differs from that of *Daodejing* chapter 55 in that it is situated in a natural world context that involves, as Chen notes, the cosmic processes of the generation and return of all things. Another significant difference between the two *yangsheng* sequences is that chapter 16 brings it to the ultimate conclusion: union of the adept with the pristine Dao. It begins:

> Take emptiness to the limit.
> Preserve stillness[32] in the overseer.[33]
> The myriad beings side by side burst forth.[34]
> By this, I see their return.
> Natural things multitudinously arise.[35]
> Each return to their root.

The chapter opens with two *yangsheng* dictums, "Take emptiness to the limit" 致虛極 and "Preserve stillness in the overseer" 守靜督. "Emptiness" 虛 has a somewhat complicated range of meanings in the *Daodejing*, but here it refers to the dissolution of physical blockages in the circulatory systems. Appearing in seven chapters, "stillness" 靜 is another highly complex term that does double duty in its application as both a key *yangsheng* term (as it does here) referring to the stillness of the rhythmic systems of the cultivated body, and as a key philosophical term referring to a central quality of the Dao's regulating the world,[36] as in chapter 45: "Tranquility and stillness are the regulators of the world 清靜為天下正.

Of further interest is the "overseer" 督. Robert Henricks briefly discusses previous scholarship that interprets it as "the central artery in the body for breath" or "the overseer channel," but he opts to maintain the received text's more philosophically mainstream interpretation of "sincere" 篤 taken to mean "center," a choice hard to understand. Still, the passage encourages the cultivation of the "stillness" of the breath in its circulatory passage through this "overseer," where it appears as a principle *yangsheng* teaching as displayed in the continuation.

> Returning to the root is called stillness.
> Stillness means to return to the natural condition.
> Returning to the natural condition is *chang*.
> To know *chang* is *ming*.

The passage establishes a context of phenomenal generation and return before setting forth the *yangsheng* sequence in three stages. The first stage is "the return to the root" 歸根 that is identified with the stillness of the *yangsheng* body. It is equivalent to "the height of *jing*" in which the body's hot fluids smoothly pulse at ease throughout.

The second stage is the "return" 復 to "the natural condition" 命 (*ming*). In early Chinese philosophical writings, the term *ming* often signifies "ordinance/mandate" and "destiny/fate" as decreed by Heaven as the moral authority of the world. Instead of moralizing the term in keeping with non-Daoist writings, the passage physicalizes it to refer to the body's "natural condition" in reference to its spontaneous rhythms and movements at play on a phenomenal, even biological level.

The "natural condition" is in fact the "fullness of *de*" manifesting in the spontaneously rhythmic systems of circulation of the sage's inexhaustible flow of *qi* as well as in the newborn that has not yet begun to suffer from the deleterious effects of socialization, without which it would naturally enjoy longevity. As the condition of inexhaustible *qi* flow, it is the same as the condition of *he* in which the body's several rhythmic systems of circulation function as an organic unity. As the stage of "stillness" equates to the "the height of *jing*," so too does "the return to the natural condition" equate to "the height of *he*."

This condition of *ming* is not yet ultimate, but just a "return" to the natural. The sequence invokes *chang* because the body's condition has only now become determinable as *he* (integrated), thereby allowing the proprioceptive sensitivity of *ming* to become effective. It is here that the *yangsheng* sequences of *Daodejing* chapters 16 and 55 arrive at the same point, but the sequence of chapter 16 will eventually go further.

> Not to know *chang* is to be presumptuous/reckless.
> To be presumptuous/reckless leads to misfortune.

These lines warn of the potential "misfortune" 凶 attendant upon the attainment of *ming* if one has the urge to apply it to the external world ("to have success in everything"). Mawangdui manuscript B identifies this urge as "recklessness" 芒, while manuscript A and the received text identify it as "presumption" 妄. However one reads it, the urge manifests in the form of bad knowledge[37] that tempts the sage to direct his/her *yangsheng* attainments to the political world with the intent to deliberately improve it, against which the text strongly cautions.

> To know *chang* is inclusiveness.
> Inclusiveness leads to impartiality.
> Impartiality leads to kingliness.
> Kingliness leads to heavenliness.
> Heavenliness leads to the Dao.
> The Dao leads to longevity and there is no decay to the end of life.

These lines display the final stages of the *yangsheng* sequence. Having already affirmed that "knowing *chang*" is *ming*, the text then applies *chang* to a higher level "inclusiveness" 容, referring to the physical inclusiveness of the *yangsheng* body with its unimpeded flow of *qi*; to apply *chang* to this "inclusive" body means that now it is open to a deeper, even more fundamental proprioceptive sensibility by which it is fully known and determinable. This then leads to "impartiality" 公 that has no further need to attend to any particular part of the *yangsheng* body such as the mind or any individual organ or system with determining the strength or weakness of its *de*.

This "impartial" *yangsheng* body has attained the optimum (different from the prime). These final lines gather from "kingliness" 王 to "heavenliness" 天, a progression that refers to neither a political nor a mystical ascension, but to a crowning or metaphorical enthronement. The *yangsheng* sequence culminates with the highest attainment, an embodied "union with the Dao" 乃道. This ultimate, embodied union endows the *yangsheng* body with "longevity" 久 qualitatively different from all other uncultivated bodies during which it experiences the radical physicality of "no decay to the end of life" 沒身不殆.

Daodejing chapter 52

Instead of its normal position within the *yangsheng* sequence, *chang* in *Daodejing* chapter 52 closes the chapter. Maintaining its close connection to *ming*, it refers to the determinably regular flow of *qi* in the *yangsheng* body that has its own measures, dimensions, functions, and natural conditions. It begins:

> The world had a beginning, which can be taken as the Mother of the world.
> The Mother can be attained by knowing her offspring.
> To know her offspring, return to preserve the Mother.
> Then throughout one's life there will be no danger.

Daodejing chapter 42 depicts the origin of the world from the Dao as a birthing process, and this final *yangsheng* sequence begins by reaffirming the Dao as "the Mother of the world" 天下母. It speaks of her "offspring" 子, but it is not obvious if it metaphorically refers to the myriad beings, as maintained by commentarial tradition, or a single child. However, given that the chapter's range of signification remains within the field of *yangsheng* sequences and not cosmological production, identifying "offspring" as the myriad beings is incongruous. The proper goal of *yangsheng* is not the knowledge or determination of external things in the world but the knowledge and determination of the own body and its natal connection with the pristine Dao as Mother. *Daodejing* chapter 28 describes the sage as one who has "returned to the state of an infant" 復歸於嬰兒.

The *yangsheng* sequence culminates with the embodied union with the pristine Dao, but this is described as not just a "return," but a return to the Mother. Returning to the Mother, the sage then "attains" 得 and "preserves" 守 her in his/her *yangsheng* body, an image that expresses the sage's embodied union with the Dao. These opening lines are a kind of *mise en abyme* that also foreshadow the ultimate *yangsheng* attainment.

> Block the holes and close the doors,
> Then to the end of one's life there is no exhaustion.
> Open the holes and add to one's projects,
> Then to the end of one's life one cannot be saved.

These lines maintain the focus on the physicality of the *yangsheng* sequence by attending to one specific technique of *qi* circulation, "blocking the holes" 塞其兌, including the ears, eyes, nostrils, mouth, and anus through which *qi* enters and leaves the body. This technique is reflected in the *Zhuangzi*'s story of the famous Hundun who had no bodily apertures, and when his guests carved them onto his body, he immediately expired. This *yangsheng* technique concerns imbibing and retaining vital and pristine *qi* (such as abundantly circulates in pristine mountain areas) in the yangsheng body where it internally circulates. This rejuvenates and revitalizes the body's rhythmic systems of circulation by increasing and empowering its *de*.

> To perceive the small is to be *ming*.
> To preserve pliancy is to be strong.
> Use the light to return to *ming*.
> Then the body will not be given over to disaster.
> This is to accord[38] with *chang*.

This final section returns to *ming* and begins by recognizing its proprioceptive effectiveness for "seeing the small" 見小 in the *yangsheng* body. It then underscores the physicality of the *yangsheng* body by recognizing one of its characteristic qualities, "pliancy" 柔, that expresses its nearness to the Dao.

The final reference to *ming* encourages continuous reliance on the "light" 光 of internal vision to sustain its proprioceptive sensitivity, ensuring that the *yangsheng* body "will not be given over to disaster" 無遺身殃. The sequence concludes with its single use of *chang*—"to accord with *chang*" 襲常—pointing to the determinable regularity of the corporeally manifested flow of *qi*.

The *Shijing* demonstrates that ancient significations of *chang* cohere around notions of determinability, but the Huang-Lao *Daodejing* uses it in the sense of eternity/permanence/constancy. In the Laozi *Daodejing*, the uses of *chang* are heavily weighted in the direction of the ancient range of meanings, but the text has modified it for application within the context of *yangsheng* bodily cultivation, where it is systematically positioned within specific *yangsheng* sequences to serve as a measure for the changes being undergone by the physical body.

The origin of the *Daodejing* is certainly an important topic in the history of Daoism, Chinese philosophy, and Chinese culture, but an equally important topic is the transformation of the text's philosophy from an original phenomenology to a later metaphysics. This transformation is demonstrated by way of its two important versions, the Laozi *Daodejing* and the Huang-Lao *Daodejing*. The most immediate difference between them is seen in the ways that each version uses *chang* and *heng*. To better understand the philosophy, as well as the cultivation practices, of the Laozi *Daodejing* and their differences from the Huang-Lao *Daodejing*, the current chapter has examined the significance of its uses of *chang*, and the next chapter examines the significance of *heng*.

5

The Temporality of *Heng*

Remembering *Heng*

This exploration of the early history of the *Daodejing* is anchored in the distinction between the Laozi version, visible through and behind the excavated *Laozi* manuscripts, and the Huang-Lao version that stabilized into the received text. This distinction is most visible in comparison between "the eternal Dao" 常道 and "the eternal Name" 常名 of the Huang-Lao *Daodejing* and "the temporalizing Dao" 恆道 and "the temporalizing name" 恆名 of the Laozi *Daodejing*. Wang Bo writes, "Laozi discussed the Dao and the Name, but it was not some general Dao and some general Name, it was the *heng* Dao and the *heng* Name. Given this, *heng* constitutes the core of Laozi's Dao."[1]

Wang Qingjie notes that "very few have paid attention to the philosophical importance of the re-discovery of the word *heng* in Laozi's philosophy … D. C. Lau might be the first one in the West who has discussed this change in the new introduction of his translation of the *Daodejing*. But his discussion focuses more on its philological aspect rather than philosophical meaning."[2]

The historical forgetting of *heng* is understandable, to a point, but already several decades after the 1973 Mawangdui and the 1993 Guodian excavations, there are no longer valid reasons to ignore the philosophical significance of that substitution, even if it threatens to overturn familiar readings of the *Daodejing*. Scholars who continue to read *heng* and *chang* as synonyms call on the support of *Shuowen* 8968, which succinctly states that "the meaning of *heng* is *chang*" 恆 常也. But the *Shuowen* was composed in the Eastern Han some three hundred years after the substitution, and their ancient meanings were not only not synonymous; they were also far from eternity/permanence/constancy. The process by which they became synonyms radically altered their ancient fields of signification, and the tabooing of *heng* in the Western Han brought that process to completion. Their ancient senses, the ones used by the Laozi *Daodejing*, had in the meantime been lost to memory, and no later writings ever mention or discuss this substitution. Imperial taboos are not without consequence.

The ancient meanings of *chang* are relatively straightforward and signify determinability of extension, whereas those for *heng* signify the rhythms of temporal flux. Inspired by the Laozi *Daodejing*, the excavated Huang-Lao manuscripts exploited a destined slippage between the two terms fated to become synonyms for eternity/permanence/constancy, even as ancient Chinese writings are without that notion. The Laozi *Daodejing* was the first Chinese text to discuss the very origins of the cosmos, and its cosmogony is a product of its philosophy of the pristine Dao which itself is centrally predicated on its understanding of *heng*. That cosmogony was a baseline upon which later Huang-Lao writings initially developed the notion of eternity.

Chen Ligui writes, "Originally, *heng* and *chang* were different: *chang* is a specific philosophical term, and *heng* just means frequently. But it gradually developed a meaning close to *chang* in terms of law, regularity, and order. After *heng* was changed to *chang* in the *Daodejing*, then *chang* in turn lost its specific philosophic meanings."[3] Wang Zhongjiang writes that a separate group of excavated Huang-Lao manuscripts, including the *Taiyi Sheng Shui* 太一生水, *Hengxian* 恆先, and *Fanwu Liuxing* 凡物流形, show that *heng* acquired an "independent meaning as a monosyllabic word expressing the origin and source of the cosmos and the myriad things."[4] Both agree that this change in the meaning of *heng* subsumed that of *chang*, substantially altering their ancient meanings to render them synonyms as eternity/permanence/constancy.

Chinese does not easily invent neologisms, and the normal practice for new words is simply to reinvest already existing characters with new meanings. Usually this does not impact the original meanings, but sometimes it happens that those new meanings are projected back into earlier meanings. When this happens, it can fundamentally alter a text's overall interpretation, as happened with the *Daodejing*.

Recent scholarship on the ancient meanings of *heng* focuses on the Huang-Lao manuscripts, particularity their cosmogonic descriptions and depictions. They shed much light on when and how the ancient meanings of *chang* and *heng* changed to become synonyms. Most of this scholarship is Chinese since they are best equipped to tackle ancient character etymology. Wang Qingjie cites the first important essay on *heng*, by Rao Zongyi (1993), but he does not then cite Chen Guying's equally important essay[5] that appeared next to Rao's in the same Guodian special issue of *Daojiao wenhua yanjiu*. Another work of particular importance is Wang Zhongjiang's 简帛文明与古代思想世界 *Civilization* of *Bamboo-Silk and the World of Ancient Thought*,⁶ a sprawling study of the Huang-Lao manuscripts. Its importance is underscored by the fact that many of its chapters were revised and published as independent articles in a variety of Chinese scholarly journals, and many have also been translated and published in two English language monographs.⁷

While this primarily sinological research has informed my own understanding of *heng*, its concentration on the Huang-Lao manuscripts is oddly not helpful for interpreting its uses in the Laozi *Daodejing*. Even the article by Wang Bo, entitled "恒先與老子" ("*Hengxian* and the *Laozi*"),⁸ hardly discusses the *Daodejing*. For this, the mostly philosophical research by Chen Ligui and Wang Qingjie is helpful, especially as it touches on issues of temporality; for example, Wang Qingjie writes:

> In the *Daodejing*, the word *heng* 恆, a key word in understanding Laozi's concept of temporality of *dao* 道, was missing during the past 2000 years. In most editions of the text, a synonym, *chang* 常, was substituted, which may refer to a totally different understanding of the temporality of *dao*. Second, based on an etymological study of the origins of the Chinese word *heng* and its philosophical use in the *Daodejing*, I shall claim that *heng* explores the temporality of Laozi's *dao* as *heng dao*. Unlike *chang*, which asks more for constant extension, and invariable and non-changeable movement, *heng* in Laozi's *heng dao* focuses more on "living longer" (長生) of the myriad creatures, and on the concept of "never dying" (不死) of *dao* as a natural way of giving birth.⁹

Although I do not entirely agree with the details of Wang's interpretation, I fully endorse his understanding of *heng* as temporality rather than as eternity as key for understanding the Laozi *Daodejing*.

Ancient and Early Uses of *Heng*

Because of its more complex set of significations, exploring the ancient uses of *heng* requires recourse to a wider variety of ancient writings than the previous exploration of *chang*. Since I am not deeply trained in sinological methods, I depend on the findings of those who are for direction and insight, and Wang Qingjie's comments are useful:

> The original meaning of "*heng*" may be traced back to two other ancient Chinese characters: *geng* 亙 and *gen* 亙. *Geng* means "to wax full" and "to navigate." In the oracle bone inscriptions, it is written as 𠄨 and 𠄭. The primordial image evoked by these variant characters may be that of the moving of the moon

across the sky, or the path of a boat on a river. *Gen* means to "flow through" and "to spread everywhere." Originally *gen* might be connected with another word *xuan* 𠬝. *Xuan* evoked an image of whirling water and was written in oracle bones as 𠬝 or 𠬛 ... Clearly, these two meanings of the ancient word *heng* are related, directly or indirectly, to movement on water, where a boat moves on an earthly river or the moon moves across the celestial "river." Thus understood, the original meaning of *heng* does not seem to have much to do with *chang*, if *chang* means "constancy" or "regularity." *Heng* as movement on water suggests a range of differentiated and even conflicting elements such as fast eddies and tranquil pools, shallow and deep water, movement forward and backward, up and down, slow and rapid, and so on. Given this original meaning of *heng* and the complicity of the world that the *Daodejing* seeks to characterize, it is not surprising that this text favors *heng* over *chang* in expressing *dao*.[10]

Wang raises several important points concerning *heng*'s ancient field of signification. First is "the primordial image" of the flowing of the moon across the nighttime sky (anciently reckoned as a celestial river) and the floating of a boat as the current takes it downriver. These images evoked by *heng* pertain not only to various flows of water, including those of eddies, pools, shallow waters, and deep waters, but also to the various rhythms taken by the different flows of waters.

The image of a boat being carried downstream by the changing currents of the river is taken from *Shuowen* 8698, whose first part, as noted above, defines *heng* as *chang*. The continuation states that the character *heng* has "the root of 'heart' and 'boat' between 'two' above and below: *heng* is a heart carried by a boat" 从心从舟在二之間上下心以舟施 恆也. This explanation breaks down the character into three parts. The first is on the left, "heart" 心, the second is the middle part on the right, "boat" 舟, and the third takes the two parts of the character "two" 二 and places the "boat" between them.

Wang Zhongjiang, who has extensively analyzed the etymology of *heng* from the perspective of the excavated Huang-Lao manuscripts, writes:

> The basic meaning of *heng* is *chang* and unchanging. At first it was often used for concrete things or people's behavior. When describing a specific property of a concrete thing or person, it means that this kind of thing or person in the passage of time maintains a fixed and unchanging nature: it is consistent and continuous. According to the *Shuowen*'s explanation, the original meaning of the character *heng* is *chang*, and it was written as 㪉 [heart and boat between two] ... [The *Shuowen*'s explanation] expresses that between the two riverbanks a boat comes and goes, yet the heart riding it is constantly stable. This kind of constancy is linked to people's mental psychology.[11]

Recognizing that the *Shuowen*'s moralization of *heng* is a late development, he continues:

> However, I am afraid that this is not the original character of *heng*, and it is also not its original meaning. Different from the structure of 恆 the *Shuowen* gives another ancient character for *heng* written as 死 with "moon" as root. It is related to the patterns of change of "the waxing of the moon" 月象之弦, and it is more likely to be the origin of the character *heng*. *Heng* in the oracle bones script is written as 𠄆, with the root of "two" and "moon," and its original meaning is "crescent moon" 月弦.[12]

Rao Zongyi's (1993) Chinese article first recognized the ancient association of *heng* with the crescent moon. Building on his findings, Wang Qingjie's (2000) article was the first Western study to analyze the Mawangdui *Laozi* through the ancient meanings of *heng* (he was not yet familiar with the Guodian *Laozi*) and their association with the moon in terms of its passage across the sky, overlooking the deeper point of association with moon's rhythmic cycles of waxing and waning. This is despite his recognition in a (2001) paper that understanding *heng* in the Laozi *Daodejing* calls for a radically different understanding of its "temporality of the Dao," a temporality that he saw reflected in the philosophy of Martin Heidegger.

The *Yijing*, a divinatory text structured by combinations of solid and broken lines in eight trigrams doubled to make sixty-four hexagrams, also reveals a complex connection between *heng* and the moon. Although different versions of the *Yijing*[13] and *Yijing* commentaries[14] present alternative sequences of the hexagrams, every known sequence systematically begins with the hexagram Qian that consists of six solid lines, but interestingly each one also systematically positions the Heng hexagram squarely in the middle, that is, the 32nd position.

The *Yijing* offers glimpses into the mythic consciousness of ancient China, and its association between *heng* and the moon reveals it. The *Gui cang* 歸藏,[15] excavated in 1993 from Wangjiatai and dated to the middle of the third century BCE, survives only in fragments. Structured by the sixty-four hexagrams, it provides no prognostications but largely consists of stories relating to them. It gives slightly different names for the some of the hexagrams, including for the Heng hexagram that it calls Heng E 恆我 [恆娥]. The fragments of its appended story oddly do not mention Heng E but rather Nü Wa, a mother goddess credited with creating humans. The story of Heng E is found under the Gui Mei 歸妹 hexagram, which states:

> [Hou] Yi requested the elixir of immortality from the Queen Mother of the West. Heng E stole it to flee to the moon. When she was about to go, she had

the stalks divined by milfoil by You Huang. You Huang prognosticated them and said: Auspicious. So soaring the returning maiden, alone about to travel westward. Meeting Heaven's dark void; do not tremble, do not fear. Afterwards there will be great prosperity. Heng E subsequently consigned her body to the moon, and this became the frog.[16]

This is the mythological Heng E, whose name was later changed to Chang E 嫦娥 after *heng* was tabooed; hers is the charter story for the Mid-Autumn Moon Festival. She was married to Hou Yi 后羿, the mythic archer famous for shooting down nine suns due to their combined great heat, leaving a manageable one. When the Queen Mother of the West rewarded him with the elixir of immortality, Heng E stole it. After having a divination performed, she ascended and became the frog in the moon; that is, she merged with the lunar essence, there to enjoy immortality.

The *Gui cang* suggests that the ancient meanings of *heng* developed in a mythic context centered on the Goddess of the Moon, a suspicion further supported by the term's ancient etymology involving the crescent moon, whose appearance late in the year marks the start of the Mid-Autumn Festival.

Looking forward, it is difficult to see how the term *heng*, with its deep associations with the cyclical waxing and waning of the moon, could come to be associated with notions of eternity/permanence/constancy of a person's moral structure, both of which factor into the *Shuowen*'s explanation. Edward Shaughnessy's comments are suggestive:

> Assuming that it is more likely for an abstract meaning to be derived from a particular concrete reference than the other way around, the Gui cang might have given the name—Heng E in reference to the mythological figure—to this hexagram, and Confucius, or someone else, to have derived from a part of the name a general notion of "constancy." Unfortunately, the manuscript text here is too fragmentary to allow for anything more than just a suggestion in this regard.[17]

Shaughnessy's suspicion about the moralization of *heng* helps to understand its uses in the Laozi *Daodejing*. It also goes some distance in explaining how the meanings of *heng* cohering around the rhythms of temporal flux became mixed with those of *chang* cohering around the constancies of material determination. Still, early Chinese writings use *heng* more frequently than *chang* and with a wider semantic range that also includes notions of temporal constancy, ordinariness, and moral constancy.

Texts such as the *Zuozhuan* 左傳[18] use *heng* in the sense of temporal constancy or "always." Xiang Gong Year 13 discusses the loss of a state due to moral decline and declares that such loss "must *heng*-ingly [always] derive from this" 恆必由之, and Xiang Gong Year 28 discusses the future demise of a certain ruler who is not fulfilling the obligations of a good father, and it states: "A man like this is *heng*-ingly [always] plagued by disasters instigated by his son" 如是者恆有子禍.

As "always," these uses of *heng* are typical for early Confucian writings, where its meaning is not constancy in the sense of a permanently enduring condition, but consistency in the sense of a situation whose effects can be expected from all similar situations. Although these uses have not yet acquired the meaning of eternity/permanence/constancy, they already diverge from the ancient meanings cohering around the rhythms of temporal flux.

In illustration of this, the Guodian *Lu Mu Gong Wen Zisi* 魯穆公問子思 states: "Those who *heng*-ingly point out to the ruler his own evils [can be called loyal ministers]" 亙(恆)稱其君之惡者. Wang Zhongjiang would translate *heng* in this phrase as "constantly," but this situation is very hard to imagine; rather, every time the ruler commits an evil act, the loyal minister will "consistently" point it out to him.

Another meaning of *heng* as "ordinary" or "common" is closer to consistency than constancy and depending on the context, the judgment of being "ordinary" can be good, bad, or neutral. In a neutral sense, *Mencius* 4A5[19] says that "the people have a common saying" 人有恆言. The "Qice" chapter of the *Zhanguoce* 戰國策[20] says that "Gan Mao is an extraordinary man, not an ordinary (*heng*) man" 甘茂賢人非恆士也. *Zhuangzi* 29,[21] "Dao zhi" (Robber Zhi), uses *heng* in a disparaging way where he says to Confucius: "Those who can be persuaded by considerations of gain and be swayed by reprimands are all ignorant, low, and ordinary (*heng*) people" 夫可規以利而可諫以言者皆愚陋恆民之謂耳.

These uses of *heng* have no particularly philosophical content, but an early instance is found in *Analects* 13.22,[22] in a passage that would become paradigmatic for Confucian moral philosophy. In it, Confucius says, "Not *heng*-ing [making constant] his virtue, someone will impute this to him as a disgrace" 不恆其德或承之羞. This phrase, "to *heng* one's virtue" 恆其德, is not unique to Confucius, in fact he is quoting a line from the Heng hexagram which is also found in the Heng E hexagram of the *Gui cang*. After Heng E stole the elixir of immortality, she had a divination and received an auspicious prognostication, so Confucius' follow up statement in *Analects* 13.22 makes more sense: "One does not just prognosticate and nothing else" 不占而已矣.

The "Xiang" 象 and the "Xici" 繫辭 Commentaries of the *Yijing*, both composed well after Confucius, support the meaning of *heng* in the quoted phrase as "to make constant," demonstrating how the later tradition understood it; the "Xiang" states: " 'Not *heng*-ing his virtue' means that he will nowhere be tolerated" 不恆其德无所容也, while the "Xici" states, "*Heng* refers to the stability of virtue" 恆德之固也. Still, it is not certain if Confucius was using *heng* as "to make constant," or even if this is its meaning in the Heng hexagram to begin with rather than "to make consistent (one's virtue)."

Wang Zhongjiang writes:

> Early Confucian texts expanded the meaning of *heng* by giving prominence to its understanding as permanence 常 and long-lastingness 久, and they also produced the idea of the constancy of material substance. The metaphysicalization of *heng* offered even more possibilities. The constancy 恆 of permanence 常 corresponds to notions of time. After the heart radical was added to *heng* 亙 [crescent moon] to become *heng* 恆, it referred to a person's willpower and behavior that was concentrated in terms of long-lastingness 久 and unchangeability. Therefore, the idea of "constant heart" 恆心 or of "having constancy" 有恆 was produced. For Confucius, a valued action was one that came from a person's "having constancy."[23]

The phrase "constant heart" to which Wang refers is first found in the *Mencius* and the phrase "possessing constancy" from the *Analects*. In stark contrast with "consistency," these two uses of *heng* have clearly acquired the sense of "moral constancy" as an unchanging state that does not come and go regardless of situational factors—it perdures through any and all circumstances. Confucius says in *Analects* 7:26:

> A perfectly good man I cannot hope to see; I would be satisfied only to see a man "possessing constancy" 有恆. Being without yet affecting to have, being empty yet affecting to be full, being reduced yet affecting to be at ease—it is difficult in such cases to maintain the possession of constancy 有恆.

Mencius 1A7 (repeated in *Mencius* 3A3) uses the term "constant heart" in the sense of moral constancy in one of the more popularly quoted passages from the text. Note that Mencius also uses *heng* in reference to the people's "constant means of livelihood" 恆產:

> Only a scholar is able to have a constant heart 恆心 despite being without a constant (*heng*) means of livelihood. Without a constant means of livelihood, the people will also be without a constant heart. If they are without a constant heart, then there will be no debauchery, depravity, deflection, or extravagance to which they will not succumb.

In true Daoist fashion, *Zhuangzi* 23 pushes back against the Confucian moralization of *heng* by using it to signify the constancy of one's bodily condition: "When a man has cultivated himself, he will thenceforth possess constancy 有恆. Possessing constancy, he gathers what is Human in himself while Heaven assists him."

These uses of *heng* diverge from the ancient range of meanings cohering around the crescent moon to move, ironically, in the opposite direction of unchanging permanence. They are without connection to notions of temporalization that characterize *heng* in the Laozi *Daodejing*.

Heng and Temporality

The ancient meanings of *heng* are not rooted in the crescent moon as such, but more particularly in the waxing and waning of the moon for which the crescent serves as synecdoche. This points to a lunar temporality with its temporal flux that moves back and forth between waxing and waning, swelling and dwindling, expanding and diminishing, accelerating and decelerating. Lunar temporality is difficult to *chang* in the sense of determine, unlike solar temporality, which is closer to the later sense of *chang* as eternity/permanence/constancy. That the Laozi *Daodejing* uses *heng* as the primary descriptor for the Dao does not first of all mean to identify it with the moon, but rather with the flux of temporality itself. This flux is not constant and not determinable, like the non-determinable movements of water in different moments such as "fast eddies and tranquil pools" as said by Wang Qingjie. This means to say that the movements of the Dao, its temporally fluxing flows, are indeterminable, and being indeterminable, they are *ziran* 自然, a term whose translations as "spontaneous" or "self-so" miss the deeper *ziran* quality of rhythmicality. This non-determinability further reveals the core of *heng*, as used in the Laozi *Daodejing*, as rhythmically fluxing temporality.

The *Shijing* uses *heng* to point to the rhythms of temporal flux, as seen in "Tian Bao" 天保 from the Lesser Odes, which presents wishes for the flourishing of the royal line; it says: "Like the *heng*-ing of the moon/Like the ascending of the sun" 如月之恆/如日之升. The line reveals the classic sense of *heng* denoting the lunar temporality of cyclical waxing and waning. This is very close to but not exactly identical with the primary uses of *heng* in the Laozi *Daodejing*, which do not signify temporality as such but rather the phenomena of temporalizing. This line uses *heng* verbally, where its direct association with the moon functions in complementarity, not with the sun as such but with the rising of the sun. It recognizes two separate temporalities or rhythms of temporal flux, one solar that concerns the sun's rise and the other lunar that concerns the moon's waxing and waning. Note that the following lines of "Tian Bao" refer to two further temporalities, that of mountains and that of the fir and cypress.

None of these temporalities are eternal or permanent; instead, they persist for varying durations, depending on the specific temporality (solar, lunar, geological, or biological). The flux of solar temporality is immediately available to the senses of sight and touch as the sun rises and sets, but the flux of lunar temporality is more subtly attenuated and concerns a different style of rhythm and repetition that incorporates the waxing and waning of the moon together with its full and black moons. Lunar temporality is richer, deeper, and darker than its solar counterpart and supplies the Laozi *Daodejing* with a powerful *heng* imagery for characterizing the pristine Dao.

Invested with notions of lunar temporality, the significatory field of *heng* as temporal flux sometimes allows the term to be translated as "lingering" or "abiding." To linger or abide is to temporarily remain in a place or a moment whose duration is enjoyed only for a time within a larger temporal movement of which it is a brief part during which one can contemplate, remember, rue, or enjoy. To linger also connotes a reluctance to quit those moments of lingering to resume work. To wrongly associate this with constancy, as in "to constantly linger," itself an oxymoron, is to displace this core sense of *heng*. To understand *heng* as a "constancy" connoting the enduringness of a place, or a time, or a situation is already to start from a prior metaphysical understanding of the term as eternity/permanence/constancy.

The sense of *heng* as "to linger" is brought out in "Xiao Ming" of *Shijing*; it states: "Ah, you gentlemen/Do not linger in your peaceful abode/But quietly carry out the duties of your office ... Do not linger in your peaceful repose/But quietly carry out the duties of your office" 嗟爾君子/無恆安處/靖共爾位 ... 無恆安息/靖共爾位.

These uses of *heng* are not hearkening to a permanent state of "abode" 處 or "repose" 息 as thought, for example, by James Legge,[24] but rather function to call the gentleman out of his reverie in which he lingeringly enjoys his position without conscientiously performing his duties. The security of his position of employment is not at issue, if *heng* were to be taken to mean constant, as if he could be fired; at issue is his leadership responsibility for the community.

The "Yueyu xia" of the *Guoyu*,[25] dated to the end of the fourth century BCE, is often noted for its Daoist tenor, and it uses *heng* in two instances. The first is found in the response of a minister, Fan Li 范蠡, to King of Zhao's question about how best to regulate affairs. After providing a run-down of necessary concerns to keep in mind, Fan Li says,

Because time has a way of returning and affairs have their intervals, there is a way to know the *heng*-ing system of Heaven and Earth; once known, then one can acquire the completed benefits of Heaven and Earth. When there are no intervals between affairs, and when time is not returning, then one must console the people and safeguard education in order to await them.

Here, Fan Li situates the existence of all things within a temporality that first emits then returns. He wants human affairs to be coordinated with that temporality by respecting the "intervals" 間 between, referring to the period after an affair (e.g., planting) has ended and before the next (e.g., harvesting) has begun. This coordinating depends on the ability to know the "*heng*-ing system of Heaven and Earth" 天地之恆制.

This "system" 制 is based on the phenomena of "temporalization" recognized as *heng*, or more precisely on the phenomena of "temporalizing" as *heng*-ing, which is to say that the cycles of time begin at one moment and end at another—time cannot in this sense be taken as constant or eternal, but rather as temporally rhythmic. Not being constant, this rhythm works on its own pace and, according to Fan Li, one must bide one's time to await the returning rhythm of time. This rhythm cannot be identified with Heaven and Earth since they only provide the spatial realm in which that rhythm is in play, and Fan Li provides no explanation about the actual source of this *heng*-ing. Given the opportunity, it would not surprise if he were to attribute it to the Dao.

Fan Li speaks of this worldly *heng*-ing in terms of a "system," but as such, what it is that this *heng*-ing *heng*s, what is it that temporality temporalizes? It is not Heaven and Earth, but rather time itself, which in ancient China was properly understood in terms of "seasons" 時. The *heng*-ing system is that which temporalizes time and makes possible the coordination of human affairs with temporalized time by way of its interstitial "intervals." This *heng*-ing is intimately related to the *heng*-ing of the Laozi *Daodejing*.

The second use of *heng* comes later in the same conversation between the king and Fan Li. After another run-down of necessary concerns for the king to keep in mind ("Don't disrupt the work of the people, don't go against the seasons of Heaven …"), Fan Li says: "Accord with the *heng*-ing of *yin* and *yang* and comply with the *chang* of Heaven and Earth; pliant but not bent, strong but not obstinate, virtuous and tyrannical behavior: accordingly use these as the measure" 因陰陽之恆，順天地之常，柔而不屈，強而不剛，德虐之行，因以為常.

Like the Laozi *Daodejing*, Fan Li's use of the terms *heng* and *chang* effortlessly evokes their ancient meanings. Fan Li advises "to accord with the *heng*-ing of *yin* and *yang*" 因陰陽之恆, where *yin* and *yang* serve as temporal markers by which the flux of temporal rhythms can be reckoned in terms of the seasons, and he recommends "to comply with the *chang* of Heaven and Earth" 順天地之常, where Heaven and Earth serve as spatial boundaries by which the constancies of material extension can be measured. More specifically, *heng* is identified with temporality and *chang* with spatiality, a fundamental distinction that is central to the Laozi *Daodejing*. That *chang* is a measure not only for material extension but also for events and conditions that can be expected, calculated, or otherwise determined explains why "pliant but not bent, strong but not obstinate, virtuous and tyrannical behavior" serve as solid measures for assessing proper kingship.

The *Jiapian* 甲篇, one of the excavated Chu silk manuscripts, decisively expresses this classic sense of *heng*: "Rain arrives and stops frequently, there is no determinable temporal rhythm" 時雨進退亡(無)又(有)尚(常)亙(恆).[26] Wang Zhongjiang's interpretation of the line is embedded in this comment: "This sentence means that the coming and stopping of the rain from time to time is not constant (not determinable),"[27] showing that he identifies *chang* with *heng* in this sentence, even as he qualifies *chang heng* as "not determinable" 不确定 in parentheses. However, here *heng* refers to the flux of temporal rhythms that themselves "do not have" 無有 *chang* in the sense of determinability.

This passage reveals Fan Li's distinctions between the temporality of *heng* and the determinability of *chang* by maintaining their ancient significations before each became synonymous with eternity/permanence/constancy. The frequent falling and stopping of rain is a clear example of a fluxing temporal rhythm that cannot be determined beforehand and it makes little sense to consider its falling and stopping in terms of constancy, at least from a phenomenal perspective.

This phenomenal perspective is opposed to a logical perspective that could make sense of the notion of the constancy of rainfall in a scientific meteorological model, but this is an untenable stretch. This underscores the sense of *chang* as the constancy of (predominantly material) extension that is measurable or determinable, and the sense of *heng* as the fluxing of temporal rhythms that are measurable and determinable only in a general way, for example, that each season roughly lasts for three months. Rainfall is even less amenable to accurate determinability, as the passage suggests. Whether it is a foggy mist or a thunderous downpour, the beginning and ending of rain is particularly difficult to determine, and quite often its beginning and ending *heng* in the sense of lingering or abiding. Thus, the rain abides in falling, but it lingers in coming to cessation. The temporal fluxing of falling rain is a near perfect analogue to *heng* in the Laozi *Daodejing*.

Turning once again to the *Yijing*, Wang Qingjie writes that "the centrality of the hexagram Heng in the *Yijing* system also suggests that *heng* is one of the most important concepts in the *Yijing*,"[28] and he continues:

> First, although the *Yijing* system as the system of changes can be organised in different ways, its process of changing and transformation is not totally "chaotic" or "disorderly". There must be some central axis around which the *Yijing* system moves like the eye of a hurricane in the natural world. Of course, such a pivot cannot be a fixed, absolute or unchanging point. Rather, it is only relatively unchanging, and it grounds all other things which are changing. Second, this observation may also encourage us to revise our understanding of the philosophical significance of *heng* as it appears in pre-Qin Chinese thought. For example, in reading the *Yijing* and the *Yizhuan* we generally assume that the hexagrams *qian* and *kun* are the two most important hexagrams in the *Yijing* system. But the central position of the hexagram *heng* in all four *Yijing* sequences discovered so far suggests that *heng* occupies, if not the most important, at least a very special place in the *Yijing*. That is to say, *heng* might well be 'the eye of the hurricane' in the *Yijing*'s conception of change.[29]

Wang's findings support the sense of *heng* as the flux of temporal rhythms, especially since the *Yijing* represents not only China's most sustained cultural project of reckoning the processes of change within the fluxes of time, but also its most sustained effort to *chang* (measure, determine) the *heng*-ing of time itself.

Another related concern of contemporary (mostly Chinese[30]) scholars of ancient texts is how to understand the connection between *heng* and *ji* 極, an issue that became a scholarly concern only with the excavation of the Mawangdui *Yijing* and its most important commentary, the "Xici." The commentary's seminal passage recognizes *heng* as Great Heng 大恆, the original and central source of all change. However, all later versions of the "Xici" replaced Great Heng with Supreme Ultimate 太極, where Ultimate 極 refers to the "ridgepole" that Wang Qingjie above referred to as "the eye of the hurricane," and on this point he also writes, "For almost two thousand years *taiji* 太極 [Great Ultimate] has been considered the most important philosophical concept in the Great Appendix ['Xici']."[31]

Among the recent studies on this substitution of *ji* for *heng*,[32] Wang Zhongjiang's is most insightful, and he writes:

> *Heng* originates from the notion of time while *ji* stems from the notion of space … From the perspective of the origins of the two terms *heng* and *ji*, the

original meaning of *heng* is the cyclicity of the changes in the shape of the moon, and the original meaning of *ji* is a pillar. In later developments, the former became a notion importantly related to time, and the latter became a notion importantly related to space. The extended meanings of *heng* are thus "long-lasting" 久 and "constancy" 常, while the extended meanings of *ji* are "peak," "extremity," and "boundary."³³

The complexities between *heng* and *ji* are also apparent in two chapters of the *Daodejing*. The Mawangdui and the received editions of chapter 16 open with the phrase: "To reach emptiness is the limit" 致虛極, whereas the Guodian *Laozi* has: "To reach emptiness is to be *heng*-ing" 致虛恆也. And although Mawangdui chapter 59 has been corrupted, the received edition states, "When there is nothing that cannot be overcome, nobody knows his limit. When nobody knows his limit, he can possess the state" 無不克則莫知其極莫知其極可以有國, whereas the Guodian *Laozi* has: "When there is nothing that cannot be overcome, nobody knows his *heng*-ing; when nobody knows his *heng*-ing, he can possess the state' [無]不克則莫知其亙莫知其亙可以有國."³⁴

This brief look at the relationship between *heng* and *ji* clarifies the importance of *heng* in the "Xici," where its ancient connection to the moon and the flux of temporal rhythms continues to echo. The *Yijing*'s most important discussion of *heng* is found in the "Tuan Commentary" to the Heng hexagram, but it already shows deep marks of *heng*'s gradual slippage towards eternity/permanence/constancy; it states:

> *Heng* means "long-lasting." The strong [trigram] is above, and the weak [trigram] is below: thunder and wind work together. Gentle yet moving, the solid and the broken [lines] all resonate with each other: this is *heng*. The Judgment states: "*Heng*: success. No trouble. Beneficial to determine." This indicates lasting long with the Dao. The Dao of Heaven and Earth is *heng*-ing and long-lasting and without cessation. The Judgment states: "Beneficial to have someplace to go." This indicates that completion is followed by beginning. The sun and the moon have Heaven and therefore are able to shine long-lastingly. The four seasons change and transform and therefore are able to complete long-lastingly. The Sage lasts long with the Dao and therefore the world transforms and completes. Observing this *heng*-ing, the nature of Heaven, Earth, and the myriad things can be seen.

The first part of this passage is explained by the two trigrams that make up the Heng hexagram: zhen 震 (thunder) above signifies powerful movement, and xun 巽 (wind) below signifies the reverberating wind that follows in its wake. Discussed in terms of "resonances" 應, the commentary depicts a plurality of phenomenal interactions between thunder and wind, the solid *yang* and broken *yin* lines of the two trigrams, Heaven and Earth, the sun and the moon, the four seasons, and the Sage and the world. Each of these resonances is the result of *heng*-ing. Without explicit attribute, the commentary is deeply influenced by the Laozi *Daodejing*'s understanding of the Dao that lingers/abides as the source for each of these phenomenal resonances. In its lingering/abiding, the Dao's particular activity is to allow each of these as well as infinite other resonances within the phenomenal world: this is its *heng*-ing.

The commentary defines this *heng*-ing (lingering/abiding) of the Dao in terms of "long-lasting" 久. However, the notion of long-lastingness is far removed from eternity/permanence/constancy in the same way that the Yangsheng Daoist ideal of long-life is different from the institutionalized Daoist ideal of eternal life. The commentary also articulates the essence of *heng*-ing: "Completion is followed by beginning" 終則有始也. The completions followed by beginnings are not themselves subject to the precise determinability of *chang* but instead to the *heng*-ing flux of temporal rhythms. Nothing could be further from eternity/permanence/constancy.

To be long-lasting is to be one with the Dao's lingering/abiding, a condition beyond the determinability of *chang*. While long-lasting is close in meaning to enduring, "to endure" implies a struggle against the passage of time, a connotation foreign to lingering/abiding. To say that the *heng*-ing of the Dao is long-lasting is to say that is primordial, the fluxing of the primordial rhythmicality of temporalization from within the womb of the phenomenal world. The Laozi *Daodejing*'s primordial phenomenology of the pristine *heng* Dao can be compared to the Huang-Lao *Daodejing*'s metaphysics of the eternal *chang* Dao that produces the world from outside of the world: these are two radically different ways of understanding the world and the human condition, and yet both have equal claims to the being called Daoism. How did that happen?

The Phenomenology of *Heng*

The Laozi *Daodejing* absorbed and philosophically developed the ancient fields of signification expressed by the two terms *chang* and *heng*. Each term separately points to one aspect of the matrix of the *Daodejing*: *chang* points to the unnamable Dao of *yangsheng* embodied by the sages, and *heng* points to the nameable Dao of the philosophy of the pristine Dao.

Precisely because it is nameable, the Laozi *Daodejing*'s philosophy of the Dao has much to say about the fundamental presencing, the modes of phenomenal expression, and the primordial generative movements of the pristine Dao. This is a philosophy saturated with *heng*, the source of the Dao's temporalizations that furnish the ground of the phenomenal world and the myriad beings.

Uses of *chang* and *heng* in the *Laozi* manuscripts announce their textual identity with Yangsheng Daoism, but the Huang-Lao thinkers were already far removed from its *yangsheng* context. Their metaphysical interpretation of the *Daodejing* became standardized for the tradition and rendered the Yangsheng Daoist phenomenological reading dormant until Ge Hong uncovered many of its important elements centuries later. Still, it was not until the recent discoveries of the *Laozi* manuscripts that contemporary readers have had the possibility to become aware of that Yangsheng Daoist reading that hinges on the proper understanding of *heng*. My own efforts to uncover that reading rely on the findings of scholars of the excavated Huang-Lao texts, like the *Fanwu Liuxing* and the *Hengxian*, who examine the Huang-Lao metaphysicalization of *heng*, even as few of those scholars have applied their findings to the Laozi *Daodejing*.

The *Hengxian* most clearly reveals the metaphysicalization of *heng* that was foundational for the formation of Huang-Lao Daoism. Wang Zhongjiang writes that "the image of *heng* in the *Hengxian* does not refer to experience of concrete objects but is an idea of the ultimate origin."[35]

The Laozi *Daodejing* grounds the experience of concrete things in primordial temporality, not in a metaphysics. With its source in the *heng*-ing of the pristine Dao, primordial time provides the basic ontological possibility for the temporal existence of the world and the myriad beings. According to this phenomenology of the pristine Dao, its *heng*-ing is simultaneous in time with the coming-into-being of the world and the myriad beings with nothing metaphysically prior. To identify the pristine Dao as primordial time is to recognize the *heng*-ing that temporalizes concrete things as well as the experience of them. The generatrix of temporality, the *heng*-ing Dao globally temporalizes: in birth, in movement, in enduring, in returning, in duration, in cessation, in concealment, in unconcealment; it temporalizes the past, the present, and the future.

About one ancient meaning of *heng* as "ordinariness," Wang Qingjie writes:

> Laozi's *dao* is *heng dao*. *Heng dao* should not be interpreted or translated as "invariable constancy" but rather as something always changing, growing and living. It is the differentiated appropriation of natural things in the world. By

"differentiated appropriation" I mean that *dao* manifests itself always in an interactive and transformative process in which the myriad beings find their consummation and express their particularity. *Heng dao* is not absolute and mystical "nothingness" either. *Heng dao* cannot be separated from ordinary things and ordinary life, as the original meaning of the word indicates. Without ordinariness there is no *dao* at all.[36]

While I generally agree with Wang's comments, *heng* in the Laozi *Daodejing* refers less often to the "ordinary" experience of concrete things than to the active conditions of beings being born into the temporalizations of the *heng*-ing Dao, if in fact this is a distinction with difference. Still, it is precisely this concrete experience of ordinariness that the Huang-Lao *Daodejing* conceals. *Daodejing* chapter 2 states:

Being and Nothingness are born from each other.
Difficult and easy are completed by each other.
Long and short are formed from each other.
High and low are filled out from each other.
Tone and voice are harmonized from each other.
Front and back are followed by each other.

No part of this passage posits a metaphysical ground of experience by which these distinctions can be known only subjectively as the product of the mind, as described by Ames and Hall: "Distinctions produce their opposites. For the Daoist, dividing up the world descriptively and prescriptively generates correlative categories that invariably entail themselves and their antinomies" (2003, 80). On the contrary, each line of this passage draws us more deeply into the ordinary phenomenal experience of concrete things temporalized by *heng*-ing. The Huang-Lao *Daodejing* has completely concealed this ordinariness by erasing the last line of the passage as found in the Laozi *Daodejing*, thereby severing its connection to the ordinariness of *heng*. One must look to the final line of the passage in the Mawangdui *Laozi*[37] to see that the arising of these phenomenal distinctions is inborn to the world, not the product of a correlative subjectivity; it states: "All of these (distinctions) are due to *heng*-ing" 恆也.[38]

These distinctions do not *heng* themselves, and since neither humans nor any other beings *heng*, and since the pristine Dao alone is described as *heng*-ing, then they can only arise as the concrete effects of the *heng*-ing Dao. Although Wang Qingjie[39] recognizes that "Confucius, for example, interprets *heng* as a virtue of the human being," this is not Daoism, and he goes on to explain: "Perhaps the philosophical meaning of *heng* gets its fullest expression and explanation in the

Daodejing. Here *heng* is interpreted not as a virtue of the human being, but as one of the most important 'virtues' of the Dao and of nature itself."[40]

Still, it is not entirely accurate to say *heng*-ing is an exclusive feature of the Dao since *Daodejing* chapter 28 discusses a "*heng*-ing *de*" 恆德 that the body acquires through *yangsheng* cultivation, a phrase that the Huang-Lao *Daodejing* has transformed into "permanent *de*" 常德 with all its metaphysical implications. In any case, human beings alone register these phenomenal distinctions of *Daodejing* chapter 2, which a metaphysical reading is compelled to recognize as "correlative categories" even as the phenomenological power of the final *heng ye* compels the recognition that in fact they are experienced first of all by the body in its basic motility.

Foundationally phenomenological, the Laozi *Daodejing*'s philosophy of the pristine Dao is directed to the world as the flourishing regionality of phenomenal temporalization inhabited by the myriad beings. Because they are temporalized by the spontaneous *heng*-ing exuded by the pristine Dao, the world and the myriad beings therefore exist.

The spontaneous *heng*-ing exuded by the Dao is a non-directed pan-horizontal diffusion through space with non-determinable starting and ending points. But the Dao exudes its *heng*-ing not through space but time; more precisely, the *heng*-ing exudations of the Dao are themselves the fluxing durationality of its rhythmic temporalizations. If these exudations were in fact spatial, they could be graspable by a metaphysics that would locate the Dao in a privileged transcendent position, but the pristine Dao is not locative or even an entity; *Daodejing* chapter 34 states that "the Dao is a drifting stream that can flow in any direction" 道渢呵其可左右也.[41]

Scholars have been especially intrigued by and attracted to *Daodejing* chapter 25 because of its residue articulations of many points of the Laozi *Daodejing*'s philosophy of the Dao. A close reading of the chapter demonstrates that its original Yangsheng Daoist phenomenology was transformed into a derived Huang-Lao Daoist metaphysics.

The chapter broadly consists of a terse cosmogony that seamlessly segues into a complex cosmology. It opens with a depiction of the cosmogonic movements of the Dao before the world came into existence:

There is a thing completed in chaos that was born before Heaven and Earth.
Empty and still, it stands on its own and does not change.
It moves in cycles and is never threatened.[42]
It can be taken as the Mother of Heaven and Earth.
Not knowing its name, I call it the Dao.

The Mawangdui and received editions already demonstrate their metaphysicalization by identifying the Dao as a substantive entity, a "thing" 物, requiring localizability in a privileged space from which it will go on to produce the world. The Guodian *Laozi* uses a starkly different term in recognizing the Dao as a "form" 狀[42] (or "condition") that conjures images of a non-substantial and non-localizable presencing or rhythm. In either case, it "formed in chaos before Heaven and Earth were born" 混成先天地生. Normally used to describe a state or a condition, the *Daodejing*'s use of "chaos"[44] 混 is rather more apt for describing the Dao's creative *heng*-ing, its temporalizing rhythm within the primordial time of origins, than for a substantive entity that produces the world as something outside of itself.

The Guodian passage continues:[45] "It stands on its own and does not *hai*" 獨立不亥. This use of *hai* is particularly vexing, and its primary meaning is as one of the twelve Terrestrial Branches. As Scott Cook notes,[46] the Mawangdui *Laozi* writes *hai* with the jade radical, the Beida *Laozi* writes it with the dog radical, Ding Yuanzhi interprets it with the earth radical in the sense of "limitless," Liu Xinfang interprets it with the speech radical in the sense of "dual," and Donald Harper interprets it with the sun radical in the sense of "unique." The meaning of *hai* here is anything but decided.

The Mawangdui and received editions have "It stands alone and does not change" 獨立不改, a reading permeated with the metaphysics that follows from identifying the Dao as an "unchanging" substantive entity 物. But it is difficult to imagine that *buhai* 不亥 means "not changing" 不改 (*bugai*), as explained by Ames and Hall: "While 'does not change' [*bugai*] might fall within the semantic tolerance of *gai* [改], this translation is hard to square generally and not insignificantly with everything else that is said about *dao* in the literature."[47] They consider two variants of *hai*, one with the jade radical meaning "without counterpart" and the other with the sun radical meaning "never complete," and write, "Or perhaps the text is making both of these points—*dao* has no counterpart and is never complete—at the same time." Either way, the traditional reading that "the Dao does not change" ought to be rejected once and for all.

The final lines once again identify the pristine Dao with the Mother and segue from cosmogonic depictions to the core of the *Daodejing*'s phenomenology of the Dao.

> Forcing a name on it, I call it "Great."
> "Great-ing," it is called "flowing forth."
> "Flowing forth," it is called "distancing."
> "Distancing," it is called "returning."

These lines are often interpreted as describing the processional movements and activities of the metaphysical Dao as departure—distance—return. Ellen Chen provides an illustrative example of this reading:

> "Great" is what has developed to the full. When a thing is full grown, the next stage is for it to recede or move away, i.e., to decline until it reaches the third stage "far away." While "great" depicts something in full bloom, "far away" is when a thing withdraws or ceases to exist. But Dao is the "far away" that "returns" (*fan*). *Fan* marks the return of Dao to the world. In this way, the cycle repeats itself. This is the reversive motion of the Dao. The name "Dao" thus describes this primal creativity as a movement in four stages.[48]

Wang Zhongjiang attributes this kind of reading to the mistaken view that this passage even demonstrates any movements of the Dao, which is itself a consequence of seeing the Dao as a substantial entity to begin with. He writes that the basic sense of "return" 反 in the *Daodejing* describes "a way of movement (or activation) that the Dao does to assist things and beings to return to themselves."[49] He continues:

> The character *fan* 反 in these citations are all used to imply "return" 返: indicating that when things or people depart from themselves they need to return to their own original authenticity or natural condition. Following this discussion, we notice that the sayings "distance means return" and "return is the movement of the Dao" in the *Daodejing* cannot simply refer to the Dao alone, but must be understood through the relationship between the Dao and the myriad things. Then again, we must also bear in mind that in the *Daodejing*, abnormalities and estrangements can occur only to the myriad things, not to the Dao. For if we maintain that the Dao can be abnormal or estranged then it loses its most fundamental meaning and function. So far, we can affirm that the three occurrences of the character *fan* 反 in the *Daodejing* mentioned herein do refer to the character *fan* 返, meaning "return"; furthermore, all three refer to the myriad things returning to their own authenticity and not to the return of the Dao.[50]

According to Wang, in the natural state of affairs no beings are "estranged" from the Dao, whose pervasive influence spontaneously maintains the natural balance. But human beings have become victims of the internal domination of knowledge and desire as well as more external forms of it such as tyranny, and this leads to "abnormality" and "estrangement." He continues: "To overcome various dominations or the centralization of power, the *Daodejing* proposed the fundamental idea of allowing things and people to self-transform through the non-coercive action of the Dao and the sages."[51]

Wang Zhongjiang reads *fan* not as a descriptive for the metaphysical processes of the Dao but as a possibility for the myriad beings to enhance their existence. There are alternative perspectives on *fan* that do not require the sort of salvation or redemption implied by Wang,[52] one of which centers on the view that the myriad beings including humans, as far as they exist in a natural state, have not yet achieved full authenticity and remain in need of something outside of themselves to achieve it.

The articulation of this perspective has an unavoidable Heideggerian flavor that Wang Qingjie, also a renowned Chinese translator of Heidegger's work, adopts in his reading of the *Daodejing*. His own understanding of *fan* is implicated with his understanding of *heng* as "the differentiated appropriation of natural things in the world. By 'differentiated appropriation' I mean that *dao* manifests itself always in an interactive and transformative process in which the myriad things find their consummation and express their particularity."[53] He isolates three key terms through which the *Daodejing* expresses this "differentiated appropriation," namely, *jiu* 久, *fan* 反, and *pu* 樸.

Noting that "*jiu* has often been understood and translated into English as 'invariable,' 'everlasting,' or 'unchangeable,'"[54] Wang relies on *Daodejing* chapter 16 for its definition as "to be free from danger throughout one's life" 沒身不殆, which also states that "to be one with the Dao is *jiu*" 道乃久. Wang's interpretation is, "*Jiu* in the *Daodejing* means becoming oneself and being underway in expression and consummation of one's natural being. In other words, *heng* as *jiu* is first of all 'self-soing' (*ziran*). It is the Daoist idea that if one expresses one's natural and authentic way of being, one not only survives, but flourishes."[55]

Turning to *fan*, Wang Qingjie writes that "the second connotation of *heng* as *fan* (reversion) provides insight into how to reach *heng* as *jiu* (and) refers to a way of repetition and renewing (or) 'tracing back' and 'starting again.'"[56] He recognizes two levels of meaning for *fan*, as the substantive interactions that concern the mutual formations of opposites (e.g., "long and short mutually form each other"), and as " 'the pre-substantive interaction' or the primordial 'gushing forth' [that] is the existential condition of both the existence of the opposite aspects and the 'substantive interaction' between them."[57]

Wang means that through the action of *fan*, the myriad beings revert to the non-substantive root of the Dao that *Daodejing* chapter 4 pictures as the first "ancestor" 宗 from which the myriad beings "gush forth" 沖 thereby to become differentiated by their own *ziran* 自然 or "self-soing." He writes in summary: "Thus understood, *heng dao* as *fan*, that is, as something both 'differentiated' and 'reversional' exposes the double-interactive nature of the myriad things in our world. *Heng dao* in the *Daodejing* is actually the '*heng*-ing' of the world. Because of or through this way of *heng*-ing, everything in the world is becoming itself, and keeps being itself."[58]

I have analyzed these (not necessarily exclusive) perspectives on *fan* by Wang Zhongjiang, who interprets it as a remedy for estrangement, and Wang Qingjie, who interprets it as a requirement for authenticity. While we three equally reject metaphysical readings of *Daodejing* chapter 25, my interpretation relies on a different Heideggerian notion, unconcealment (*aletheia*), to understand how the myriad beings are brought into the fullness of their being. My perspective is not entirely dissimilar from theirs since it too recognizes that the myriad beings require support in order to be brought into the fullness of their being—which I understand as unconcealment, not salvation or authenticity. I adopt this perspective for several reasons: it is grounded in an understanding of the pristine Dao's *heng*-ing; it recognizes that the myriad beings are in need of external assistance to achieve the fullness of their being; and it gives a prominent place to the notion of *da* 大 as more than adequate to bring beings into unconcealment.

The Four *Da* of *Daodejing* Chapter 25

Of all chapters of the *Daodejing*, chapter 25 provides the staunchest defense for the metaphysical reading, but it misinterprets the value of *da* 大. Continuing the analysis of chapter 25, the next lines of the Mawangdui and the received editions have:

> The Dao is great.
> Heaven is great.
> Earth is great.
> And the King too is great.
> Within the realm,[59] there are four greats,
> And the King occupies one place among them.

This ordering of "the four greats" 四大 immediately announces its metaphysical standpoint, in which the inherent greatness of each of the four greats shines forth; Heshang Gong explains:

> The greatness of the Dao is that it envelops Heaven and Earth and there is nothing that it does not enclose.

> The greatness of Heaven is that there is nothing that it does not cover.
> The greatness of Earth is that there is nothing that it does not uphold.
> The greatness of the King is that there is nothing that he does not control.

This passage depicts a descending hierarchical order of metaphysical greatness, with the Dao at the top, followed by Heaven and then Earth, and finally the King at the lowest position. The passage is rife with political implications; Daniel Fried writes that "the possibilities of political dissonance (if not dissidence) remain" because "in a feudal society, where ruling mandates are derived in principle from Heaven … there is nothing innately ethical in being forced to acknowledge the Other who must always-already have had an inviolable claim upon oneself … Only the nameless ultimate [the Dao] escapes this system," where even the king has "an inviolable claim upon himself" by Earth, then by Heaven, then by the Dao.[60] Chen Jing discusses the Daoist rationale behind this specific ordering of the four greats:

> Such statements place the Dao in the position of generating everything, which effectively expresses the chief aim of the *Daodejing* to place the Dao prior to the universe and all beings (and) it is also has deep internal consistency with the *Daodejing* text. It is beyond doubt that there are many sentences praising the Dao and positing the Dao as the foundation of all beings in the *Daodejing*.[61]

Next to this metaphysical order that presents the Dao as the substantive source that produces all things, there is an alternative order that places Heaven first, followed by Earth, then the Dao, then the King. This is found in the "Daoyuan" of the *Huainanzi* 淮南子, but scholarship has deemed it a copyist error and disregards it.

When the Guodian *Laozi* was discovered to have announced this order that begins with Heaven, it too was dismissed; the eminent scholar Liu Xiaogan writes that "the word order of the Guodian version is not right. Rendering it 'Heaven is great, Earth is great, the Dao is great, and the King is also great' is inconsistent with the received version and the Mawangdui versions, and moreover does not match the order of 'man–earth–heaven–*dao*' found in a following sentence. It is a copying error."[62]

When the Beida *Laozi* was also discovered to have this order, it was harder to maintain that it was the result of a copyist error. Tellingly, in their analyses of the philosophy of the Guodian *Laozi* that give particular attention to its differences with the received edition, both Franklin Perkins[63] and Barbara Hendrischke[64] translate and discuss this very passage without remarking on it. Ames and Hall, who said that their *Daodejing* translation features the Guodian *Laozi*, used the order that begins with the Dao. Each of these studies also continue to treat the Dao, as the first of the four greats, as the metaphysical entity par excellence. Chen Jing writes:

> If the [Guodian and Beida *Laozi*] had never been published, and we only had one citation from the *Huainanzi*, I am afraid that would still not be enough to awaken us to the fact that a version with "heaven is great" at the beginning had once existed. Unearthed manuscripts correct some of our fixed impressions of the *Daodejing* text, allowing us to see the complexity of the process of the *Daodejing* becoming a book: Even the simple ordering of the "four greats" involves a background with much complexity indeed.[65]

Chen's wider analysis of the complex background behind the two orders is an important contribution to uncovering the Laozi *Daodejing*'s philosophy of the Dao, and she writes that "there are two paths of reasoning … that respectively determine whether at the outset '*dao* is great' or 'heaven is great.'"[66] She attributes the separate reasonings to the differences between cosmogony ("the Dao gives birth to Heaven") and cosmology ("the Dao is under Heaven"):

> While the cosmogonic theory investigates how heaven and earth and all beings evolve out of a common source, the cosmologic theory forcefully describes the preestablished spatial structure of the cosmos and its internal order … If we link these two to the ordering of the four greats, the cosmogony matches the ordering of the four greats beginning with the Dao, while the cosmology matches the one beginning with heaven.[67]

Chen's intuition that leads her to uncover separate reasonings behind the two orders is generally correct, but her grasp of the philosophical stakes is limited and her historical explanation is a bit off. It attributes the alteration in the order to a vague notion of "Han Dynasty cosmology." Although the origins of this cosmology are traced back to the Warring States Huang-Lao manuscripts, she anyway writes that we must "wait until cosmology reaches maturity in the Han dynasty"[68] before we can appropriately understand why the order was altered; she writes:

> The divergence between Confucianism and Daoism in the Han dynasty was already marked clearly and the two schools were growing further apart in the direction of mutual rejection. So, when the Han dynasty commentators of the *Daodejing* were swayed by the spirit of the times to interpret such sections of the *Daodejing* through the lens of cosmos- related views … the arrangement of the four greats beginning with heaven, supported by the line of reasoning that "*dao* is under heaven,"

shattered in the eyes of the Han dynasty *Daodejing* commentators. Meanwhile, the line of reasoning that "*dao* begot heaven and earth" gained strength, and potentially pushed for the version beginning with "*dao* is great" to win out.[69]

Chen's historical explanation is based on the Beida *Laozi*, whose old order was changed due to Han Dynasty factors. But at its time of composition, the Beida *Laozi* was a relic: the Mawangdui *Laozi* already had the new order beginning with the Dao, despite the fact that the *Huainanzi* maintained the old order beginning with Heaven.

Chen attributes the new order to the Confucian conquest of Daoism in the Han Dynasty, but in fact it was the innovation of Warring States Huang-Lao thinkers who first transcribed the *Daodejing*. That the *Huainanzi* and the Beida *Laozi* still have the old order is a lingering residue of the Laozi *Daodejing* and not a copyist error.

Against the metaphysical Huang-Lao reading that interprets the greatness of the four greats as an inherent essence unique to each, the phenomenological Yangsheng reading understands their *da* ("greatness") differently. The first point to address is the status of *wang* 王 (King). Certainly due to political considerations, traditional commentaries usually identify *wang* with the ruler of the state, but some modern scholars take a more liberal view that identifies the term as a placeholder that represents and contains Humans or Humanity in general. Chen Guying provides persuasive historical support for this reading of *wang* as Humans in place of the singular King,[70] a reading also adopted by Wang Qingjie. I too read *wang* as referring to "Humans" since it more closely adheres with the Laozi *Daodejing*'s philosophy of the pristine Dao.

This reading rejects the interpretation of *da* as an enduring essence acquired by virtue of a thing's metaphysical position within separate realms of being to see it as a shared feature of what makes possible, not redemption or salvation, but the attainment of a being's fullness of being, its unconcealedness. Wang Qingjie identifies this fullness of being (that he calls authenticity) with *ziran* 自然, a term regularly translated as "spontaneity," "naturalness," or "self-soing." It often refers to a condition of one's being or to a quality of one's action or behavior.

When other scholars address this *da*, they usually understand it to refer to a quality that endows a thing with "greatness." Thus, the Dao is great because it envelops, Heaven because it covers, Earth because it upholds, and the King because he governs. But this is to understand *da* in terms of a metaphysics of presence, as a substantive quality that endows a thing with a particular and permanent essence. The phenomenological reading understands *da* rather as a kind of activity.

Da, however, is not easily characterized as an activity, because it is not performance-based with a start and an end and it is not the result of a conscious intentionality. Thus, *da* is not best interpreted as a substantive quality within a metaphysics of presence, but as a continuous style of *ziran*, a term that Wang Qingjie translates as a gerund; he writes:

> I do not follow the traditional understanding of and interpretation of the word *da* 大 (great) here as an adjective referring to a quality held by the very substance of Dao. I think that a more befitting interpretation of *da* should be found in understanding it as a verb (present participle), as a gerund, or more accurately as an "adjective" used as a "verb."[71]

In his published work, Wang has discussed elements of *Daodejing* chapter 25, but not the phenomenological order of the four *da*. Regardless, his work offers fruitful direction for this reading of the chapter, for which the next lines state:

> Heaven is *da*-ing.
> Earth is *da*-ing.
> The Dao is *da*-ing.
> And Humans too are *da*-ing.

This phenomenological order of the four *da* neatly sidesteps the metaphysics of presence informing the metaphysical order that positions the substantive Dao outside and beyond the world that it produces. This order situates the Dao within the world, in the space between Heaven and Earth. Heaven and Earth do not here stand as metaphysical boundaries, but rather signify the time-space presencing of the world that is announced in the phrase "Heaven is *da*-ing and Earth is *da*-ing" 天大地大. *Daodejing* chapter 7 states:

> Heaven is long and Earth is lasting.
> The reason why Heaven is long and Earth is lasting
> Is because they do not exist for themselves.

These lines present a pure expression of the *da*-ing of Heaven as being/doing "long" 長 and the *da*-ing of Earth as being/doing "lasting" 久. Their *da*-ing is not an intended activity with a start and finish performed for some desired outcome; rather, what they are (long and lasting) is explained as what they do (*da*-ing). The *da*-ings of Heaven and Earth are the same *da*-ings of the Dao and of Humans, and together they can be fruitfully interpreted in terms of the worlding of the world, a Heideggerian turn of phrase.

As an important aside, it is worth noting that while Heidegger of course was not as such a scholar of Daoism (see chapter 9), his thoughts about the worlding of the world open up a particularly incisive view of the four *da*'s of *Daodejing* 25. In his later writings, Heidegger discussed what he called the "fourfold" (*das Geviert*) that comprises the sky, the earth, gods, and mortals, and its deep resonance with the four *da*'s of the *Daodejing* has not gone unnoticed.[72] I mention this here because the language that I use to engage with Laozi's four *da*s, much like the language used by Wang Qingjie in his discussions, is directly inspired by Heidegger's notion of the fourfold, which was, to one degree or another, itself derived from and inspired by the four *da*. About heaven and earth, for example, Heidegger writes:

> Earth is the building bearer, nourishing with its fruits, tending water and rock, plant and animal … The sky is the sun's path, the course of the moon, the glitter of the stars, the year's seasons, the light and dusk of the day, the gloom and glow of night, the clemency and inclemency of the weather, the drifting clouds and blue depth of the ether.[73]

Informed by the potentially fruitful relationship between Heidegger's fourfold and Laozi's four *da*, the world painted by the Laozi *Daodejing* appears as something other than an extant objective presence or a substantive being. It is an emergent context as a generative doing ("worlding") within which the myriad beings appear, actualize, and flourish to realize the fullness of their being in unconcealment. The *da*-ing of the world signifies as a mobile temporalizing register for the rhythms and forms that underlie habitual temporalities and modes of being. This *da*-ing is not identical with *heng*-ing, although they are closely related. The *heng*-ing of the Dao exudes the fluxes of the rhythmic temporalizations by which the myriad beings come into existence, whereas its *da*-ing, understood in terms of "worlding," is what allows them to come into unconcealment.

In the Laozi *Daodejing*'s philosophy of the Dao, no being comes into unconcealment outside of the world's *da*-ing, and this is expressed by the force of the gerundive, where the worlding of the world only occurs through the *da*-ings of Heaven, Earth, the Dao, and Humans. According to Wang Qingjie, the four *da*-ings of the world are best understood as *ziran*, and he writes that "the ways of these great-ings [*da*-ings] are nothing but 'self-so-ing' (*ziran* 自然)."[74] To equate *da* with *ziran* is to recognize that the "greatness" at issue is not a quality possessed by Heaven or Earth or the Dao or Humans, but rather refers to their ability to allow the myriad things to achieve "greatness" understood as the fullness of being, as unconcealment.

By associating *da* with *ziran*, the phenomenological reading underscores that Heaven, Earth, the Dao, and Humans do not signify as substantive entities but as generative contexts by which the myriad beings come into unconcealment, in fundamental distinction from the metaphysical reading. Ames and Hall highlight this with their translation of "Dao" as a gerundive "way-making," and they write, "In early Chinese natural cosmology, there is no appeal to some substratum or independent metaphysical origin, no 'One' behind the many."[75]

Still, their reliance on the order beginning with the Dao cannot shake off the essentializing consequence of characterizing the Dao as an original metaphysical entity that produces a way that is subsequently followed by Heaven, then by Earth, and then by Humans. It is only the order beginning with Heaven that precludes the metaphysical trappings of positing a transcendental Dao as the "One behind the many," and it does this by enmeshing the *da*-ing of the Dao, together with the *da*-ing of Heaven, Earth, and Humans, squarely within the generative worlding of the world. More than this, since the pristine Dao is neither substantive nor an entity, it can have no spatial localization; *Daodejing* chapter 14, for example, depicts its non-localizable pervasiveness:

> Its top cannot be encompassed.
> Its bottom cannot be perceived.
> Boundless, boundless, it cannot be named …
> In front you will not see its head.
> In back you will not see behind it.

If the Dao were in fact a metaphysical entity, its "boundlessness" 繩 would point to its localization in an originally transcendent realm from which it produces the world, but the phenomenological reading denies such a realm outside of the world to begin with.

Not existing as substantive entities, the *da*-ings of Heaven, Earth, and the Dao are a function of their *ziran*, and therefore the myriad beings have the possibility to come into unconcealment and enjoy the fullness of their being.

Heidegger says that the worldling of the world is a gift to beings, and it conduces to unconcealment. To see the four *das* as gift in this way is to consider the myriad beings as not yet having come into their unconcealedness, and that they cannot do so without the *da*-ing of Heaven, Earth, and the Dao; thus Wang Zhongjiang introduces the salvation model and Wang Qingjie the authenticity model. But for the myriad beings to be brought into unconcealment and avoid oblivion, they require something in addition to the *da*-ing of Heaven, Earth, and the Dao: they need the *da*-ing of Humans.

The *da*-ing of Humans is not the *da*-ing of all humans generally, and like the *da*-ings of Heaven, Earth, and the Dao, it too is devoted to the work of allowing the myriad beings to come into unconcealment. At the same time, the *Daodejing* consistently exclaims on just the opposite condition, that humans themselves are the primary cause for the existential hardships experienced by the myriad beings, specifically in the form of war, tyranny, and injustice brought on by excessive knowledge and proliferating desires. The Humans of *Daodejing* chapter 25, however, refer to a particular group of humans whose *da*-ings are enmeshed with those of Heaven, Earth, and the Dao in the worlding of the world; these are the sages.

That the sages are agents of "salvation" 救 for the myriad beings is clearly stated in chapter 27: "For this reason the sages are constantly good at saving people and therefore none are rejected, and they are constantly goods at saving things and therefore none are rejected. This is called Actualized Brightness" 是以聖人常善救人故無棄人, 常善救物故無棄物, 是謂襲明. Is it possible to understand "brightness" 明 here in terms of the fullness of being in unconcealment?

The *Daodejing* gives a prominent position to the verb *sheng* 生 (to give birth, to be brought to birth), the pristine Dao's most vital activity; for example, *Daodejing* chapter 51 states, "The Dao *shengs* the myriad beings" 道生之. The phenomenological force of *sheng* is often lost in metaphysical readings that interpret the Dao as a substantive entity that *shengs*, typically understood in terms of producing, generating, or creating the myriad beings. Wang Qingjie proposes a phenomenological interpretation of the phrase, "through the Dao the myriad beings emerge," but I would rephrase it as "by means of the Dao the myriad beings are *sheng-ed*." Here, the "by means of" refers to the *heng*-ing of the Dao that allows beings to be brought into existence in conjunction with the *da*-ing of the Dao that allows beings to be brought into unconcealment. *Daodejing* chapter 2 clarifies the role of the sages who are one with the Dao and assist it in allowing beings to be brought into unconcealment; it says:

> For this reason, the sages carry out non-intentional service and spread wordless teachings.
> The myriad beings flourish therein and are never dismissed.
> By way of the sages they are *shenged* [brought to life] but are not possessed.
> They act for the myriad beings but do not make them dependent.
> They complete this merit but take no credit.
> It is only because they take no credit that (the myriad beings) are not displaced.

This passage depicts the *da*-ing of the sages in action. It consists of no action in particular and is identifiable with the *ziran* that informs the *da*-ings of Heaven,

Earth, and the Dao. Moreover, exactly like those other three *da*-ings, the *da*-ing of the sages also brings the gift of unconcealment and the enjoyment of the fullness of being "wherein the myriad beings flourish" 作焉, are "not dismissed" 不辭, and are "not displaced" 不去.

This *sheng* that refers to the coming into existence of the myriad beings and the *da*-ing that refers to their coming into "flourishing" unconcealment are activities that are shared not only by the Dao and the sages, but also by Heaven and Earth, as *Daodejing* chapter 7 demonstrates: "The reason why Heaven is able to be long and Earth is able to be lasting is because they do not *sheng* themselves, they are therefore able to lastingly *sheng*" 天地所以能長且久者以其不自生故能長生. The corollaries that connect the sages to this *da*-ing are from *Daodejing* chapter 63, "Sages never take themselves as *da*-ing" 聖人終不為大, and again from *Daodejing* chapter 7, "For this reason, the sages put their persons behind yet their persons are in front; they do not consider their persons but their persons are fine" 是以聖人後其身而身先外其身而身存.

In the current state of the field, the phenomenological reading of the Laozi *Daodejing* that relies on the excavated manuscripts remains in a state of infancy. My efforts to develop and bring precision to that reading are necessarily partial, and they center on forging an appropriate approach to two terms in particular, *chang* and *heng*, whose phenomenological force has been lost in the metaphysical readings of the Huang-Lao *Daodejing*, and this clear separation between *chang* and *heng* supplies a base standard with which to distinguish the phenomenological from the metaphysical reading. Informed by this distinction between the phenomenological Yangsheng Daoist reading of the Laozi *Daodejing* and the metaphysical Huang-Lao Daoist reading of the Huang-Lao *Daodejing*, the second part of this study turns to the Huang-Lao Daoist reading that, in the course of the Han Dynasty, became embedded in the tradition and continues to exert tremendous authority today.

Part Two

Huang-Lao Daoism and the Matrix

6

Yan Zun and Heshang Gong

Huang-Lao Daoism

The current chapter examines the effects of the Han Dynasty transformation of the Laozi *Daodejing* into the Huang-Lao *Daodejing*. It relies on two Han Dynasty commentaries, the first by the historical Yan Zun 嚴遵 (fl. 83 BCE–10 CE) and the second by the legendary Heshang Gong 河上公 (fl. first or second century CE).[1] The path of this transformation leads from the Laozi *Daodejing*, through to the forging of a novel Chinese metaphysics, finally to arrive at the Huang-Lao *Daodejing*, the text finalized by the librarian Liu Xiang 劉向 (77–6 BCE) that was canonized as a "classic" 經 during the reign of Emperor Jing (r. 157–141 BCE), the son of Emperor Wen (Liu Heng). This process is neatly summarized by Ding Sixin in the following:

> After Emperor Jing's canonization, the *Daodejing* text … was deeply impressed with the stamp of "canonization." What we call "canon" (*jing*) generally requires the possession of a high degree of indispensableness and authority in the formation of texts, teachings, cultural context, and official ideology. And canons themselves can only gain the necessary conditions of accomplishing their canonization when they possess a high degree of stability and self-identity. Concretely speaking, for the *Daodejing* to become a canon (a Classic), it needed to possess the following conditions: First, there needed to preexist a relatively stable version to serve as the textual precondition of its canonization, which at the time was found in the Silk Manuscript [Mawangdui] versions; second, there had to be a powerfully supportive trend of thought, at the time represented by the Huang- Lao trend; third, it had to come from the need and affirmation of constructing a state ideology, which may be observed in the act of Emperor Jing canonizing the Classic; fourth, on these three foundations, the *Daodejing* text itself had to attain a high degree of order, and it needed to harmonize with or manifest the philosophical ideas of the times … In the middle and late Western Han, the finalized versions of the *Daodejing* went through two formations, one

being the final canonized edition, which included the version canonized by Emperor Jing (and) the other was the final edition associated with the Masters, which included the Yan Zun and Liu Xiang editions. The latter was the direct source of the received edition (which split into the Heshang Gong and the Wang Bi versions).[2]

Ding astutely recognizes the four essential factors that led to the official canonization of the later *Daodejing*: its early transcriptions had worked to stabilize the originally oral teachings into a reliable text, an accomplishment attributable to late Warring States Huang-Lao thinkers; an authoritative tradition of thought, namely, Huang-Lao, had taken primary possession of the textual version; the teachings of the text had been made to conform to and support current state ideology, namely, Huang-Lao thought; and its thought was made to cohere with the philosophical trends of the times, namely, Huang-Lao metaphysics.

The origins of Huang-Lao were greatly clarified with the discovery of the recently excavated Huang-Lao manuscripts; they show that Huang-Lao emerged as a philosophical school from out of the thought of the Laozi *Daodejing*. The Huang-Lao community was primarily populated by philosophers and statesmen, and so its historical connection to Yangsheng Daoism was undoubtedly negligible. Scholars have long questioned the appropriateness of designating Huang-Lao as Daoist: does it represent early Daoism generally, is it one branch of Daoism, or is it entirely separate from Daoism? Arguments like those of Nathan Sivin and Michel Strickmann that deny the existence of anything that could be called Daoist before the formation of the organized Daoist religion in the Eastern Han short-circuit the issue and make no historical or philosophical sense. Other arguments for and against recognizing Huang-Lao as Daoist were not well informed until the discovery of the Huang-Lao manuscripts, and to date, given the recentness of their discovery, few scholars have as yet approached the issue from this direction. Is Huang-Lao Daoist?

Early Daoism comprises two main branches: (1) Yangsheng Daoism centered on the Laozi *Daodejing* identifiable by its *yangsheng* bodily cultivation based on physical movements that intend to fuse the body of the adept with the Dao; (2) Zuowang Daoism centered on the *Zhuangzi* identifiable by its *zuowang* spirit cultivation based on forms of sitting meditation that intend to release the spirit 神 of the adept into a condition of "free and easy wandering" 逍遙遊. Both largely share the same philosophy of the pristine Dao, but their philosophical styles differ as evidenced in the very different forms of the *Daodejing* and the *Zhuangzi*.

Huang-Lao was formed from major elements of both: from Yangsheng Daoism, it received the phenomenological *Daodejing* that it transformed into a metaphysics, and from Zuowang Daoism it absorbed *zuowang* cultivation that it used to replace *yangsheng* cultivation. The semi-dualistic *zuowang* cultivation that sought to release the spirit from the body was just more conducive to Huang-Lao metaphysics, at least as far as cultivation or practice had an important place in Huang-Lao thought at all.

The appeal of Zuowang Daoism to Huang-Lao thinkers is evident in the number of Huang-Lao writings collected in the *Zhuangzi*[3] by the "editors" gathered at the court of Huainan,[4] who themselves produced the most important collection of Huang-Lao writings called the *Huainanzi*.[5] Roth writes:

> The *Huainanzi* is a work of 21 essays on a wide variety of topics that was intended as a compendium of knowledge for the Daoist ruler. Completed in 139 B.C. by the retainers of Liu An, the second king of Huainan, it represents the final flowering of Huang-Lao thought before it was eclipsed by Confucianism under the Han Emperor Wu. It can be seen as a final attempt on the part of Liu An and his Huang-Lao philosophers to dissuade the emperor from his developing conviction that Confucian doctrines were best for ruling the unified empire.[6]

Other important Huang-Lao texts are the *Wenzi* 文子[7] and the *Heguanzi* 鶡冠子.[8] One feature that they all share is a concentrated engagement with the philosophy of the *Daodejing*, seen in its profuse quotations that they discuss, explore, pursue, and weave into metaphysical Huang-Lao thought. Each of them was composed in the span from the late Warring States to the middle of the Western Han, and they demonstrate the active Huang-Lao appropriation of the Laozi *Daodejing*, as do the later Han commentaries by Yan Zun and Heshang Gong that also systematically maintain its metaphysical reading.

It has never really been clear to what the term Huang-Lao refers. Anna Seidel was among the first Western scholars to discuss it, and she writes, "The Daoists, both the politically influential school tradition of the Yellow Thearch (Huangdi) and the adherents of Laozi, had by this time been joined in a single school, which was named the Huang-Lao school after its two patriarchs,"[9] and Roth notes that Huang-Lao "formed the first 'school' of Daoism."[10]

The habit of identifying Huang-Lao as Daoist has a long pedigree that stretches back to the *Shiji* 史記 and the *Hanshu* 漢書. In his famous "Treatise on the Essentials of the Six Schools" 論六家要旨 from the *Shiji*, Sima Tan, himself a Huang-Lao proponent, discussed "Daoism" 道德家 in terms that more appropriately characterize Huang-Lao, as recognized already long ago by Benjamin Schwartz (1985).[11]

To so easily identify Huang-Lao with Daoism is problematic. In connection to which part of Daoism is Huang-Lao to be identified: social community, philosophical school, or political faction? The complicating factor is that the only *Daodejing* with which we are today familiar is the Huang-Lao version, and since the *Daodejing* is normally recognized as Daoist, then Huang-Lao must also be Daoist. This picture assumes that there has ever only been this one version of the *Daodejing*, and also that there was ever only one kind of early Chinese Daoism.

But the excavated Laozi manuscripts and the excavated Huang-Lao manuscripts compel us to fundamentally revise this picture with the recognition of two versions of the *Daodejing*, namely, the earlier Laozi version and the later Huang-Lao version. Next to this is the recognition of multiple forms of early Chinese Daoism, including Yangsheng Daoism, Zuowang Daoism, Fangxian Daoism, Huang-Lao Daoism, and Tianshi Daoism. While the historical sources do not explicitly name one Daoism particular to Laozi and another particular to Zhuangzi, they do recognize, as shown in Chapter 3, the last three forms. Based simply on the addition of the term Dao to the titles Fangxian, Huang-Lao, and Tianshi, there is no question that they are forms of Daoism, but this then begs the question: what does the term Dao, as a designation of Daoism, intend to identify: a community, a school, or a faction?

Next to Seidel's pioneering work on Huang-Lao, other scholars have tried to see it through a group of early Chinse thinkers about whom little else is known except that many spent time at the Jixia Academy. Some of their ideas have been transmitted through fragments in the historical records, but they mostly do not reveal clear affiliation with other Warring States schools of thought.[12] Later generations of Huang-Lao thinkers are relatively easier to identify because they had prominent positions in early Han government administration, for which Huang-Lao thought served as the dominant political ideology, but they left behind few writings.

The discovery of the Mawangdui manuscripts greatly clarified Huang-Lao thought. Primary among them is the *Huangdi Sijing* 黃帝四經 (Four Classics of the Yellow Emperor[13]), which represent a sophisticated corpus of Huang-Lao writings. Randall Peerenboom interprets them as representing "foundational naturalism":

> Huang-Lao promotes a foundational naturalism: the way of humans (*ren dao* 人道) is predicated on and implicate in the normatively prior way of the natural order (*tian dao* 天道). Correlated to this foundational naturalism is the natural law theory of the [*Huangdi Sijing*]: the laws that govern society are constructed as objective laws of a predetermined natural order discoverable by humans.[14]

The *Huangdi Sijing* posits the cosmic Dao as the ultimate source that produces the *li* 理 ordering principles that regulate the world. That they are "discoverable by humans" means that it is only the enlightened ruler who discovers them because he has cultivated his mind to become tranquil and empty. Once discovered, the enlightened ruler implements them into the human world, and the empire is well governed. This foundational naturalism significantly differs from the Laozi *Daodejing*'s philosophy of the pristine Dao.[15] Rarely quoting the *Daodejing*, the *Huangdi Sijing* recognizes the Dao as the single source from which the world was produced, but its cosmic Dao has already become a substantive metaphysical entity, unlike the pristine Dao of Yangsheng Daoism. It also prioritizes many of the same principles of human action as the *Daodejing*, including *ziran*, *wuwei* 無為, and *jing* 靜 (tranquility), but achieving them is based on spirit cultivation, not bodily cultivation.

Recent additions to the growing collection of Huang-Lao texts include the excavated manuscripts *Taiyi Sheng Shui* from Guodian as well as *Hengxian* and the *Fanwu Liuxing* that were purchased by the Shanghai Museum in 1994 as part of a collection of bamboo strips looted from an unknown site but dated after the closing of the Guodian tomb.[16] Whereas the *Huangdi Sijing* situates its political thought within the metaphysics of a transcendent Dao, these manuscripts are predominantly cosmogonic in nature, and they shed much light on the processes whereby the phenomenological pristine Dao (*heng dao*) was transformed into the metaphysical cosmic Dao (*chang dao*).

Oddly, none of these manuscripts recognize the Dao as the ultimate source of cosmic generation: *Taiyi Sheng Shui* attributes it to Taiyi 太一 (Ultimate One), *Hengxian* to Heng 恆 (Constancy), and *Fanwu Liuxing* to Yi 一 (One).[17] Different from the pristine Dao, these ultimate sources are positioned beyond time and space. Despite this, each of them shows their deep influence by the original cosmogony of the Laozi *Daodejing* even as they attempt to distance themselves from it, a clear sign of the self-conscious emergence of Huang-Lao thought from the shadows of Yangsheng Daoism. Much like the *Huangdi Sijing*, these manuscripts also rely on many specific notions from the *Daodejing*, including *ziran*, *wuwei*, and *jing*, a practice continued in the *Huainanzi*, *Wenzi*, and *Heguanzi*.

Different from these manuscripts and demonstrating a heightened cultural status, the *Huangdi Sijing* is more sharply political; it pays less attention to the cosmogony to focus instead on methods of implementing the natural normative laws derived from the cosmic Dao into the political realm, and it relies on a set of privileged terms from the *Daodejing*, as explained by Ding Sixin:

Generally speaking, Huang-Lao political philosophy focuses on the effective rule of the monarch to the ministers and the monarch to the people, and it takes *wuwei* and *ziran* as its fundamental principles. Typically, Huang-Lao uses *wuwei* to regulate the monarch's rule or governance, and it uses *ziran* to stipulate his political effectiveness, which is commonly stated as "the ruler is *wuwei* and the people are *ziran*," or as Huang-Lao says, "the techniques of the ruler facing south."[18]

The "Jie Lao" 解老 and "Yu Lao" 喻老 chapters of the *Hanfeizi* 韓非子 reveal another step in the process of the metaphysicalization of the *Daodejing*. Although other chapters of the *Hanfeizi* quote it,[19] these two do not fit well with its overall Legalist thrust. Compared to the "Yu Lao," Sarah Queen shows that the "Jie Lao" is more consistent with the received text and argues that it was written after the "Yu Lao," although she dates both to the late Warring States. Likely postdating *Hengxian* and *Fanwu Liuxing* but predating the first complete transcriptions of the *Daodejing*, these two chapters demonstrate early Huang-Lao efforts to appropriate the *Daodejing*.

Early partial commentaries to the *Daodejing*, the "Yu Lao" is unusual in not attempting to explain the text's philosophical principles and it mostly consists of historical anecdotes intended to illuminate them, whereas the "Jie Lao" regularly focuses on explaining them. The "Yu Lao" is less of a commentary in the usual sense than an independent essay that judiciously quotes from the *Daodejing*. It has no overarching vision, and, while it mentions the king, it mostly provides general exhortations for ministers, as Queen also notes.

The "Jie Lao" is the first *Daodejing* commentary to interpret it as directed to the sage-king able to realize the *li* ordering principles of the natural world produced by the cosmic Dao, an ability acquired through inner cultivation. It is an important text that bridges the gap between the Laozi *Daodejing*'s philosophy of the pristine Dao and the Huang-Lao *Daodejing*'s philosophy of the cosmic Dao, a philosophy that became the backbone of the Huang-Lao foundational naturalism that would serve as the dominant political ideology of the early Han. Queen writes:

> [T]he "Dao" or "Way" in "Jie Lao" appears no less than 55 times (where) *dao* denotes, most importantly, the ineffable and meta-physical Way that is the source of all things in the world ... The Way, moreover, must be grasped through its "Ordering Principles" [*li*], a term that appears no less than 41 times ... Moreover, knowing and following the ordering principles of the Way is the key to success in cultivating a healthy state, a healthy body and well-being in general.[20]

This ability to know the *li* principles requires inner cultivation, loosely referring to *zuowang* by which the ruler empties the mind to grasp them; Queen writes:

> [W]e find a rich and varied vocabulary of inner cultivation in "Jie Lao" replete with glosses and definitions and chain syllogisms describing in great detail how the inner sacred landscape of the body may be disturbed and disoriented by the phenomenal world and what practices are most efficacious in staving off such undesired states. Thus the health and the longevity of the person/body complex forms a major theme of the commentary and this health and longevity is derived from inner cultivation practices.[21]

Turning to the title Huang-Lao, the "Lao" component derives from Laozi's authorship of the *Daodejing*, and the "Huang" component derives from the mythical Huangdi. Hardly mentioned in the familiar texts of early Chinese philosophy, his presence is otherwise pervasive in other early writings.

Huangdi's first textual appearances are dated to the mid-fourth century BCE, after which his figure rapidly assumed a privileged position as the supreme figure of early Chinese mythology. There are many sides to his character, but many scholars who discuss him limit it to his position as king, and Seidel (1992) primarily presents him as the Ruler personally advised by the Sage, but she also notes as the Sage, Laozi and Huangdi are never shown in company or conversation. Other important roles of Huangdi include Founding Ancestor of all the (Han) Chinese lineages,[22] First Emperor who established the throne in the center,[23] Master of War,[24] Master of Time and Space,[25] and Master of Yangsheng. Few studies focus on this last role, but it has an important place particularly in the Mawangdui *yangsheng* texts such as the *Shiwen* as well as other early Chinese medical texts such as the *Huangdi Neijing* 黃帝內經.[26] A closer examination of these writings is beyond the scope of this study, and here I only discuss some aspects of the regulating the body/state paradigm as it appears in the "Jingfa" of the *Huangdi Sijing*. The passage begins by referring to the (undefined) Five Regulators that likely refer to the powers of the five directions or the five phases; it states:

> Huangdi asked Yan Ran, "I wish to apply the Five Regulators; where do I stop and where do I begin?" He replied, "Begin with your body ... " Huangdi said, "I do not yet know my body; what should be done?" He replied, "If you, my lord, do not yet know your body, then hide yourself deep in a retreat in order to seek your inner form. When your inner form has been achieved, you, my lord ... will know your body completely." Huangdi said, "I wish to know my body completely. What should I do to achieve that?" He replied, "When the Dao of things is the same, their actions are the same. When the Dao of things is different, their actions are different. Now the world is fighting heavily, the time has come. Can you, my lord, be so cautious as not

to fight?" Huangdi said, "What should I do to fight?" He replied, "Anger is blood and *qi*. The outer fat of those who fight is greasy. If the anger does not issue forth, gradually it will form ulcerations. If you, my lord, are unable to purge yourself of these four, how will your dried-up bones be able to fight?" Huangdi thereupon yielded the throne to his nobles of the state, ascended Mount Bowang and calmly slept for three years to find himself. The battle was intense! Yan Ran then ascended and woke up Huangdi, saying, "It is permissible to take action. Now to fight is inauspicious, but not to fight will also not complete the task of bringing good order to the world. Anything is permissible." Huangdi … seized his weapons … and thereby captured (Chiyou).[27]

The phrases "regulate the body" and "regulate the state" are not found here, but this passage nonetheless establishes a direct connection between the body (of Huangdi) and the state (that he rules) that became a pillar of Huang-Lao Daoism, as seen particularly in the commentaries by Yan Zun and Heshang Gong. But although this development was well under way by the end of the Warring States, as shown by "Yu Lao" and "Jie Lao," it also far from completion. The difficulty in tracing it is the very small number of surviving writings that could further illuminate it. The most important of them are the commentaries by Yan Zun and Heshang Gong, but they come already after Huang-Lao Daoism had ceased to play a dominant role in state ideology. *Hanshu* 30 recognizes four additional *Daodejing* commentaries that were not transmitted; Alan Chan, who here mentions *Laoxue* (*Laozi* Studies) which is the common Chinese term for the study of the social, political, philosophical, and religious history of the *Daodejing*, writes that "the early history of *Laoxue* is difficult to reconstruct, for virtually all Han writings on the *Daodejing* have been lost."[28]

The *Huainanzi*, *Wenzi*, and *Heguanzi* judiciously quote from the *Daodejing*, but composing commentaries was not on their agenda. Other early Han writings more directly involved with court politics show influence from the *Daodejing*, notably the *Xinyu* 新语 by Lu Jia 陸賈 (200–169 BCE) and the *Xinshu* 新書 by Jia Yi 賈誼 (d. 170 BCE), but they are political court documents also not specifically focused on the *Daodejing*.[29] The official histories name around fifty politically important Huang-Lao proponents,[30] some of whom may have composed commentaries to, or other writings about, the *Daodejing* that were not transmitted; Xiong Tieji and Liu Lingzi write:

> In the early Han Dynasty, the ruling class advocated and applied the teachings of Laozi, and they stressed the advancement and elaboration of the political significance of the *Daodejing* … This period generally lasted from Han Emperor

Gaozu's founding of the dynasty [206 BCE] to the death of Empress Dou [135 BCE], and scholars use the phrase "Huang-Lao government" 黄老之治 to refer to this ... In the early Han, the rulers valued Laozi's techniques of *wuwei*, and those whom the histories clearly record as such include Emperors Hui, Wen, and Jing as well as Empress Dou.[31]

Xiong et al. provide a different perspective on Huang-Lao Daoism in the early Han:

In the early years of the Western Han Dynasty after the war, the rulers focused on the poverty of the people and the exhausted condition of the country, and in order to bring calmness and peace of mind to the people, they adjusted their ruling strategies. They introduced political theories based on Laozi's ideas of clarity, stillness, and *wuwei*, and by alleviating labor and reducing taxes, they created a more relaxed social environment. This resulted in a significant increase in national strength and laid an important foundation for the coming prosperity of the Western Han Dynasty. This is what history has called "the government of Huang Lao." Since that time, this kind of political ideology based on "tranquility" has become one of the well-known political models widely recognized among the people.[32]

Four people are particularly associated with early Han Huang-Lao thought: Empress Dou 竇皇后 (205–135 BCE), Liu An 劉安, the Prince of Huainan (179–122 BCE), Dong Zhongshu 董仲舒 (179–104 BCE), and Emperor Wu 漢武帝 (157–87 BCE). When Empress Dou, whose devotion to Huang-Lao Daoism is widely recognized, married Emperor Wen (Liu Heng), she brought him to admire and implement Huang-Lao policies. Also under her influence, her son who became Emperor Jing also became an avid proponent of Huang-Lao Daoism. Together, the reigns of Wen and Jing are collectively known as "the government of Wen and Jing" 文景之治, a catchphrase that refers to the golden age of Huang-Lao rule.

When Empress Dou's grandson, Emperor Wu, ascended the throne, he rejected Huang-Lao as a ruling ideology partly because he disliked the restrictions that it placed on his expansionist inclinations. In its stead, he adopted a more Confucian ideology. Emperor Wu's uncle, the Prince of Huainan, was an avid proponent of Huang-Lao with pretensions to the throne, and he created a Daoist academy responsible for the Huang-Lao collection, the *Huainanzi*. At that time, Emperor Wu elevated to a high position Dong Zhongshu, to whom is traditionally attributed authorship of the *Chunqiu Fanlu* 春秋繁露, a collection that served as the blueprint for the Confucian transformation of the early Chinese political landscape.[33] Confronted with the Huang-Lao thought of the

Huainanzi on one side and the Confucian thought of the *Chunqiu Fanlu* on the other, Emperor Wu had Liu An executed before clearing his own government of Huang-Lao proponents, replaced by officials educated in the thought of the *Chunqiu Fanlu* and the Confucian Classics.[34] Thus ended the political reign of Huang-Lao Daoism as the active political ideology the Han Dynasty.

Xiong et al. explain the consequences of these events:

> Beginning with Emperor Wu of the Western Han Dynasty, the "theological theory" 神学 of the "stimulus and response between Heaven and Human" integrated and brought to completion by Dong Zhongshu has always occupied the dominant position as the ruling thought that dominated the ideological field, supplying the people with common beliefs, values, ethics, and codes of conduct, and it kept the people's minds on a stable and orderly level.[35]

The Metaphysical Thought of Yan Zun

Emperor Wu's authoritarian reign, lasting fifty-four years, supported Confucian ideology based on Han cosmology. His armies ceaselessly clashed with "barbarian peoples" in his dedication to expanding the Han borders, squandering the wealth and vitality of the empire. His reign was followed by three shorter ones that barely managed the status quo. With the reign of Emperor Cheng (r. 33–7 BCE), change was ready; Alan Chan writes,

> When Confucianism triumphed over the other schools, the Huang-Lao tradition receded into the background. But during the reign of Emperor Cheng or slightly later, the time appeared ripe for a Huang-Lao revival … Yan Zun, too, was dissatisfied with the dominant [Confucian] view, and by the time of Emperor Cheng, it appears that the conditions were favorable to radical changes in the world of cosmological ideas and political practice.[36]

Yan Zun 嚴遵, living at the end of the Western Han,[37] made his living by divining in the Chengdu market and wrote extensively on the *Daodejing*, *Zhuangzi*, and *Yijing*. He resisted official position, and Alan Berkowitz writes that he "is commonly portrayed as a Daoist who exemplified Daoist reclusion; he was incorporated retroactively into the Daoist religion (where) he was said to have become an immortal."[38]

He wrote the earliest known commentary to the *Daodejing*, also called the *Laozi zhigui* 老子指歸 (Returning to the Meaning of the *Laozi*). Composed already after the *Daodejing*'s official recognition as the "Classic of the Dao and the De" 道德經, the text oddly has three uses of *heng* 恆, it places the *Dejing* before the *Daojing*, and it is given in 72 chapters.[39] Fan Bocheng writes, "The *Laozi zhigui* is Yan Zun's interpretation of the *Daodejing* from the late Western Han. As far as we can tell, the book is the first systematic interpretation of the *Daodejing*, and its importance is self-evident."[40] The original work comprised thirteen *juan* 卷 (books or scrolls), but the last seven that comprise the *Daojing* are missing, and only the *Dejing* portion in six *juan* exists. Still, this is enough to demonstrate its general outlines and main features; Chan writes, "Yan Zun's commentary ... is primarily concerned with a theory of Daoist government that promises to restore order and harmony to the empire. There is reason to believe that it represents the dominant interest of '*Laozi* learning' in early Han China."[41]

Yan Zun presents the first complete Huang-Lao Daoist commentary to the *Daodejing*. Different from the Yangsheng Daoist reading directed to sages-to-be, his is the first to interpret the text as systematically directed to the sage-king. One effect of this redirection was to clarify several ambiguous ideas such as from *Daodejing* chapter 38, "highest virtue" 上德. Where the "Jie Lao" took it to mean "a person of superior virtue" who is not necessarily a ruler, Yan Zun states: "The ruler of highest virtue: delicately wonderful his essence receives the Dao, profoundly subtle his nature gets the One. His essence and nature merge with *ziran*, and his emotions and thoughts unite with the numinous spirit. His actions cohere with the Ultimate harmony, and his decisions accord with Heaven's heart."[42]

Yan Zun's vision of ideal Huang-Lao Daoist government starkly contrasts with the Confucian correlative model represented in the *Chunqui fanlu* traditionally attributed to Dong Zhongshu.[43] Its thought is encapsulated by "the stimulus and response between Heaven and Human" 天人感應, a keyword for Han correlative cosmology that takes human actions, but primarily those of the king, as a stimulus to which Heaven responds—a positive action stimulates its positive reaction, and a negative action stimulates its negative reaction, such that if the king is derelict in his moral governance of the empire, then Heaven will send down an earthquake or a flood.

The cosmology of the *Chunqiu Fanlu* centers on the hierarchical system of *yin* and *yang*, where Heaven, the king, and the husband are *yang*, active, and dominant, and Earth, the minister, and the wife are *yin*, responsive, and yielding. But in fact, almost everything can be classified as either *yang* or *yin* depending on its position. So classified, things are established in continuous relations of "stimulus and response." This cosmology is complicated somewhat by the notion that *yin* and *yang* also manifest in "five phases" 五行 (water, wood, fire, earth, and metal) that are central to the functioning of systems of stimulus and response. According to Robin Wang, "The fact that tendencies and movements of things are located in complex systems of correlation suggests that things of the same kind can influence each other. This influence proceeds because there are mutual intrinsic links between things, since entities are mutually interconnected."44

For this correlative model, the sage-king is identified with heavenly *yang*, he actively initiates his policy, will, and decisions as a style of *youwei* 有為 (intentional action). The activeness of the sage-king is a foundation of the Confucian art of rulership that derives from an understanding of the Way of Heaven 天之道 whereby the sage-king, as "the Son of Heaven" 天子, infuses the realm with his personal virtue; Chan writes:

> Dong Zhongshu, for example, has come to the same conclusion: The Way of Heaven "employs virtue and not punishment." But the reason for this is because cosmologically heaven embodies the *yang* principle. Since the ruler represents the "Son of Heaven," he also embodies the *yang* principle and thus governs with virtue. Thus Dong Zhongshu writes, "The ruler represents *yang*, and the ministers represent *yin*" ... This contrasts sharply with the *Yan Zun* which comes to the opposite conclusion: "The ruler is *yin*, and the ministers are *yang*."45

The complete passage that Chan quotes from Shan jian pian 2 states: "In governing the world, the ruler is *yin* and the ministers are *yang*, the ruler is round and the ministers are square, the ruler responds and the ministers sing, the ruler is silent and the ministers speak" 治之于天下則主陰臣陽主靜臣動主圓臣方 主因臣唱 主默臣言. Chan continues, "In a Dao-centered world, the ruler embodies the *yin* principle and remains quiet, while the ministers assume the *yang* role and act for the ruler. Consequently, without active interference the ruler accomplishes all things."46 It is easy to see why the ambitious Emperor Wu would want to reject the Huang-Lao Daoist view that the ruler is passive *yin* and endorse the Han Confucian view that he is active *yang*. Still, Yan Zun and Dong Zhongshu equally ground their views on notions of the cosmic Dao, but any version of correlative cosmology, including Dong Zhongshu's, will significantly differ from the foundational naturalism promoted by Huang-Lao.

Confucian correlative cosmology views existence as nonfoundational and inherently dynamic. For it, the sources of change, mutation, and transformation are centered on the specific causes of any given stimulus, in which the agent of any stimulus is devoid of absolute identity but enjoys a developmental character (e.g., a younger brother is *yin* to his elder brother but *yang* to his sister).

Huang-Lao foundational naturalism, with its ordering principles that govern the world, views existence as constant and preconfigured. For it, the causes of change, mutation, and transformation are determined by invariant cosmic principles (e.g., in the transformation of a person's lifespan counted in decades to one counted in centuries), in which the essential natures of beings are predetermined and unchanging except when they undergo a fundamental transformation in conjunction with those cosmic principles.

That the nature of all things is predetermined is a staple feature of Yan Zun's thought and, unlike the Laozi *Daodejing* that twice uses *ming* 命 in the sense of "natural condition," Yan Zun systematically uses it in the sense of "destined lifespan," where it is often positioned next to "internal nature" 情. Separate beings are set apart from each other in terms of their defining qualities that are given with their nature and lifespan received at birth. Yan Zun uses the term "distinction" 分 to establish a being's internal nature in the context of the foundational nature of existence, and this too is a hallmark of Huang-Lao thought that distinguishes it from correlative cosmology. Ding Sixin writes, "Yan Zun gives great importance to the notion of 'distinctions,' and he provides a substantive meaning to the notion of 'distinctions in nature.'"[47] The full force of Yan Zun's use of "distinctions" is seen in the following passage from Ren zhi ji pian 2:

> In the Dao and De giving birth to people, there are distinctions. In Heaven and Earth's sufficiency for the people, there are distinctions. In the prince's and ruler's protecting the state, there are distinctions. In the salaries and positions of the ministers, there are distinctions. In the myriad beings protecting their bodies, there are distinctions ... If the distinctions of the Dao are lost, then nature cannot be so. If the distinctions of Heaven are lost, the families cannot be at peace. If the distinctions of the ruler are lost, the state cannot survive. If the distinctions of the ministers are lost, then lifespans cannot be complete. If the distinctions of the people are lost, then there cannot be birth.

In the correlative world, the internal nature that Dong Zhongshu discusses is constantly changing and must be strictly trained in youth to set on the proper path. For Yan Zun's foundational world, the nature acquired from birth cannot change except in those rare occasions when the Dao directly exerts its effects. This world is solidly structured by the *li* ordering principles that strictly govern it, and the main task of the sage-king is to grasp and then implement them in the human world. The world, however, is not limited by the ordering principles, and in fact there are changes and transformations occurring at every moment; it is just that all of these changes and transformations happen according to the *li* ordering principles determined by the Dao. Shan jian pian 2 states:

> The space between Heaven and Earth is vast and gigantic and has a very long history. There are diverse customs and different mores, and its kinds and categories are multitudinous. Change and transformation are inexhaustible, benefit and harm are uncanny and unpredictable. Therefore, if you try you cannot control it, if you act on it it cannot be acted on. I am the world, and the world is me.

Yan Zun's foundational world is rule-governed, but also infinite and beyond the control of any one person; strict compliance with its principles produces order, thus the sage-king is identified with *yin* responsiveness that does not initiate. The *Daodejing* associates *yin* responsiveness with *wuwei* 無為 (non-intentional activity) and contrasts it to *yang* initiative that is associated with *youwei* 有為 (intentional activity), but Yan Zun uses *wuwei* to mean "acting in accord with the *li* ordering principles of the Dao," with *youwei* as its opposite. This is not to say that *wuwei* is non-active; as performed by the sage-king, it is very active, and Yan Zun establishes it as the model behavior for the sage-king within the wider field of *ziran* 自然 (self-so-ness), where *wuwei* represents its concrete expression; Ding Sixin writes:

> Typically, Huang-Lao uses *wuwei* to regulate the ruler's governance, and it uses *ziran* to stipulate his political effectiveness … Yan Zun is no exception, and his political philosophy uses *wuwei* and *ziran* as core concepts (and) it uses "the theory of *yin-yang* and punishment-reward" and "the way of frugality" as its fundamental methods.[48]

Ding writes that Yan Zun's image of the Huang-Lao sage-king is constructed on the notions of *wuwei* and *ziran*, whose value in the commentary requires closer examination even before looking at the particular political methods that he endorses ("the theory of *yin-yang* and punishment-reward" 阴阳刑德理论 and "the way of frugality" 啬道). Where the *Daodejing* uses *wuwei* a total of five times, Yan Zun uses it ninety-one times, and where the *Daodejing* uses *ziran* eleven times, Yan Zun uses it ninety-six times—not counting their uses in the missing *Daojing* portion of the commentary.

Ding recognizes that Yan Zun uses *ziran* to describe both the fundamental regulating principle of the world and the inherent nature of all things; he writes, "*Wuwei* is the concept that is derived from *ziran*: *wuwei* belongs to *ziran* but *ziran* is higher than *wuwei*. This is a relationship of higher to lower … *Ziran* is the principle, and *wuwei* is the method" (2018, 58), where "method" is understood as the sage-king's *wuwei* method of regulating the empire. This gets close to the relationship of *ziran* as principle and *wuwei* as method.

Yan Zun recognizes *wuwei* as the fundamental characteristic of the cosmic Dao; Tianxia you shi pian 2 states: "*Wuwei* is the body of the Dao and the beginning of Heaven and Earth" 无为者道之身体而天地之始也. The Da cheng ruo pian 4 similarly states, "The Dao and the De perform *wuwei* and Heaven and Earth are produced" 道德无为而天地成. At the same time, *wuwei* is also the fundamental political activity of the sage-king, whom Yan Zun exhorts to perform *wuwei* because it is the essential principle for governing the world.

Even as it describes the life-giving, creative activity of the cosmic Dao, Yan Zun equally affirms the *wuwei* of the sage-king as the standard and norm for the *youwei* of the ministers, and this speaks to the proper place of *youwei* in the proper functioning of government. In contrast to the *wuwei* of the Laozi Daodejing's sages, Yan Zun holds that if *wuwei* is performed in isolation without the *youwei* of the ministers and the people, then it is a black hole. Although people typically want their ruler to be active in the performance of *youwei*, Yan Zun assigns that function to the ministers and people since *wuwei*, as the sole prerogative of the sage-king, serves as the central regulating mechanism for the performance of *youwei* by his ministers and people. Isabelle Robinet writes, "It must be noted here that for Yan Zun, it is the people who respond to [the *wuwei* of] the sage[-ruler] even though for earlier authors like Zhuangzi and Huainanzi as well as for later commentators, it is the sage[-ruler] who responds to the needs of the people."[49]

Chu sheng pian 4 illustrates the ideal sage-king's application of *wuwei* for regulating the body, and then the family, and then the state, and then the world before contrasting it with a less-than-ideal king's application of *youwei*; it states:

> His crown not seen, his cover without form, embracing emptiness and nothingness, treading on Highest Purity, holding the Dao and the De, floating with the numinous spirits, grasping Ultimate Harmony, galloping on Heaven and Earth, riding on *yin* and *yang*, dashing on the five phases, together with all things, crossing Profound Obscurity, roaming in uselessness, returning to the nameless: this is regulating the world by *wuwei*.

> Practicing filial piety and fraternity, honoring benevolence and righteousness, cultivating ritual and etiquette, teaching the people to know adornments, cultivating and regulating color and taste in order to set the hearts of the people, having the bells and drums and the *qin* and *se* performed in order to harmonize the people's will, the ruler speaks and the ministers listen, the ruler acts and the ministers follow, announcing merit and restricting behavior, enacting kindness and generosity, issuing orders and commands all by himself in a splendid voice,

causing the people to love and bow to him, all of the affairs well handled on his own, with all people from the four corners looking up and revering him: this is regulating the world by *youwei*.

For Yan Zun, the responsive *yin* nature of *wuwei* has an odd consequence that serves to initiate activity that he discusses in a secondary discourse of "effect" 驗; Herlee Creel[50] actually uncovered this initiating feature of *wuwei* that he called "purposive," but he wrongly ascribed it to the *Daodejing* itself. This too differs from Dong Zhongshu's correlative cosmology, where things affect each other in a miasma of horizontal interrelations. For Yan Zun, causes and effects are more vertical, even metaphysical, and work in a unidirectional manner. Da cheng ruo que pian 5 states, "The ruler of the world makes a sound, and the empire is the echo. The ruler of the world makes a form, and the beings and things are the reflection" 世主为声天下为响世主为形人物为影. Such statements are legion in Yan Zun's commentary, and they show that the *wuwei* of the ruler in fact initiates the causes that trigger effects. Zhi rou pian 4 states, "The Dao and the De perform *wuwei* and Heaven and Earth are produced, and Heaven and Earth do not speak but the four seasons proceed. In both cases this accords with the spirits and the people, and these are the effects of *ziran*" 道德无为而天地成，天地不言而四时行。凡此两者，神民之符，自然之验也.

About Yan Zun's understanding of the "effects of *ziran*" 自然之验, Ding writes:

> The effects of *ziran* that Yan Zun discusses have two levels of meaning. First, that "the effects of *ziran* are reflections 影 and echoes 响"[51] means that *ziran* has its "effects of *ziran*," which especially refer to the reflections of humans and the echoes of sound … "*Ziran*" and "the effects of *ziran*" are related to the movement from nothingness to somethingness, and from *wuwei* to *youwei*. "The common people say, we are all *ziran*"[52] is the effect of *ziran*, and "nothing not done"[53] is also the effect of *ziran*. Second, from the perspective of effects, "the effects of *ziran*" have a spiritual efficacy, and similar to the way that nothingness can produce somethingness, *wuwei* can produce Heaven and Earth, and Heaven and Earth make beings and things arise: all of these are the effects of *ziran*.[54]

Yan Zun's commentary has received scant scholarly attention, and the important studies by Robinet, Chan, and Ding hardly scratch the surface of its philosophical depth and beauty. I have had to pass over many of its primary ideas, including those concerning the relation between "regulating the body and regulating the state" that Heshang Gong will bring to full clarity. Nonetheless, Yan Zun's commentary remains a fascinating Han Dynasty text that further reveals the Huang-Lao appropriation of the Laozi *Daodejing*, and it leads the way to Heshang Gong's formidable commentary.

Heshang Gong's Reconfiguration of the Matrix

The abiding heart of Daoism resides in the matrix of the *Daodejing*, whose two aspects are immediately visible in the first line of Laozi *Daodejing* chapter 1: "The Dao that can be spoken is not the *heng* Dao." The first aspect is the nameable Dao upon which the text constructs its phenomenology of the *heng* Dao whose temporalizations allow beings to exist, and the second is the unnameable Dao with which the sages unite through *yangsheng* whose bodily experience cannot be articulated in language. However, these are not two separate Daos, since they are the same within the matrix: "These two are the same, but in their emerging they are called differently. Their sameness is called the Mystery."

Because eternity/permanence/constancy was not seen as a feature of the *heng* Dao, there was no particular political ideology that could be based on it.[55] But the Huang-Lao appropriation of the *Daodejing* transformed the pristine *heng* Dao into the cosmic *chang* Dao, thereby altering the structure and meaning of the matrix. It served to reconfigure the cosmos from one in which existence springs forth from the inside out into one in which existence descends from the outside in: the Dao produced Heaven and Earth, which produced the myriad beings. The functionality of this descending metaphysical order does not stop there, since it can be turned back on itself, opening the way to a different, political functionality: knowing the end-point of the processes of metaphysical production from its cosmic source with its *li* ordering principles in play throughout, humans (or at least the sage-king) can grasp those constant principles and implement them back into the socio-political order.

This Huang-Lao order is based on a normative foundationalism whose constant principles are realized by the enlightened sage-king who cultivates his sagely spirit to achieve tranquility and emptiness purified of worldly passions. A distinctive feature of Huang-Lao cultivation is the direct connection that it draws between "regulating the body" 治身 (*zhi shen*) and "regulating the state" 治国 (*zhi guo*). Actually, Huang-Lao Daoism pays much more attention to the spirit than the body, but there is a better theoretical symmetry between body and state than between spirit and state.

Huang-Lao cultivation intends the achievement of the tranquility and emptiness of spirit that the ruler uses to witness the cosmic Dao's natural *li* ordering principles. This cultivation differs from *yangsheng* bodily cultivation and is closely related to the apophatic meditation of the *Zhuangzi*'s *zuowang* that is also sometimes recognized as *xinzhai* 心斋 ("the fasting of the heart"). This spirit cultivation is clearly visible in Heshang Gong's commentary; noting that it "does not mention any form of physical exercise,"[56] Alan Chan writes, "The basic technique seems to involve deep and even breathing, concentrating on the succession of breaths, during which one visualizes the interior cosmos and listens to the movements of the [internal] spirits. This resembles what the *Zhuangzi* calls the fasting of the heart."[57]

Although both are focused on the circulation of *qi*, *yangsheng* intends physical longevity while *zuowang* (or *xinzhai*) intends spiritual emptiness. Without a metaphysical Dao, the highest attainment intended by Zhuangzi's *zuowang* was a non-centered liberation of the spirit called "free and easy wandering," but the cosmic Dao of Huang-Lao provided a specific target, namely, the substantial entity called the *chang* Dao that the "tranquil" 靜 *jing* spirit is able to grasp by way of its constant principles.

This notion of *jing* 靜 (clear, settled, calm, tranquil) is central to the *Daodejing*, and the possibilities of its significatory value, as seen, for example, in *Daodejing* chapter 15, were exploited in transforming the text's philosophy from a Yangsheng phenomenology to a Huang-Lao metaphysics, and it also demonstrates the substitution of *zuowang* for *yangsheng*. It states: "Who/what can be turbid and through *jing* become gradually pure?" 孰能濁以靜之徐清. In the phenomenological reading, the immediate referent of *jing* is to the process of beings in the world: it is the process of being/becoming "clear" for emerging beings, and it is the process of being/becoming "settled" for already emerged beings, but it also refers to the process of the *yangsheng* body being/ becoming "calm" with respect to its circulatory systems. Each of these processes is metaphorically congruent with muddy water becoming clear.

Huang-Lao's different interpretation of *jing* as a static condition of the enlightened spirit deeply informs Heshang Gong's conception of *zuowang* spirit cultivation. For him, *jing* in *Daodejing* chapter 15 refers to the spirit that has reduced the *zhuo* "turbidness" of its desires to attain the constant condition of *jing* "tranquility." It is only by the tranquility of his spirit that the sage-king witnesses the *li* ordering principles of the cosmic Dao that he will then implement in managing and governing the empire.

In comments to *Daodejing* chapter 1, Heshang Gong states, "'The Dao that can be spoken' is the Dao of the classics, the arts, and statecraft. That it is 'not the *chang* Dao' means that it is not the Dao of *ziran* and long-life." Xiong et al. write: "If we interpret 'the *chang* Dao' as the Dao of *ziran* and long-life, and the Dao of ruling the state as 'the Dao that can be spoken,' then in comparison the *chang* Dao is on a level many thousands of times higher."[58]

Zhang Zhenguo intuitively recognizes elements of the original phenomenology of the Laozi *Daodejing*, including that it does not posit transcendent principles by which to govern the state; he writes:

> Of course, those who study immortality do not necessarily have the talent to bring peace and stability to the country or managing the nation. Their value does not reside in their nobility. If the nation gets them, it won't experience much benefit, and if the nation rejects them, it won't experience much loss.[59]

The metaphysical philosophy of the Huang-Lao *Daodejing* in fact posits cosmic *li* ordering principles that can be implemented in statecraft even as it is devoted to cultivation of the spirit as the method for cognizing those ordering principles. This sophisticated coupling of a program of self-cultivation with enlightened political rulership is a characteristic feature of Huang-Lao thought, often discussed in terms of "regulating the body and regulating the state." This coupling also represents Heshang Gong's reconfiguration of the matrix of the *Daodejing*.

The Huang-Lao cosmology at the core of Heshang Gong's commentary starts from the multitudinous processes of change and transformation of beings in the world. Within the now-closed matrix structured by cosmic *li* ordering principles 理, natural law 法, *wuwei* 無為, and *ziran* 自然, the cosmos has become self-contained. Huang-Lao has made the process of world maintenance turn back into itself by grounding political activity in normative foundationalism. Even its understanding of self-cultivation has become closed by no longer being open to the infinite variety of existence: the *chang* Dao alone exists to be cognized by the spirit and implemented in policy.

Before Heshang Gong, Huang-Lao spirit cultivation was muted next to its political thought; Alan Chan writes, "Self-cultivation, for example, is hardly mentioned in the *Huangdi Sijing* (which) is generally more concerned with the art of rulership, especially with respect to the rule of law, the timeliness and fittingness of political action, and the correspondence between cosmic and human phenomena."[60] Still, the connection between regulating the body and regulating the state is already amply present there. Although Yan Zun began to emphasize cultivation by specifically coupling the regulating of the body with the regulating of the state, he encouraged a rudimentary self-cultivation based on lifestyle rather than on sophisticated techniques; Chan writes:

> The *Yan Zun* is concerned with the more concrete and practical issues of self-cultivation (*zhishen* 治身) and government. This does not mean that the *Yan Zun* seeks to promote any esoteric art of nourishing life [*yangsheng*]. On the contrary, like the *Zhuangzi*, it criticizes the kind of self-cultivation based on deliberate "effort" (*youwei* 有為), which includes breathing exercises, dietary practices, physical calisthenics modelled on animal movements and other techniques. This is contrasted with a higher form of self-cultivation that is modelled on the way of "non-action" (*wuwei* 無為).[61]

Ding Sixin provides a slightly different assessment based on a closer reading of the text. He argues that Yan Zun's self-cultivation, derived from lifestyle rather than particular techniques, has its basis in "frugality" 嗇, a term used nine times throughout the text; Fang er bu hai pian 5, for example, states: "Thus the Dao of governing the state and the root of nourishing the people takes frugality as the ancestor" 故治國之道生民之本嗇為祖宗. Ding writes,

> Frugality is a negative method and a method of protecting. The way of frugality appears in *Daodejing* chapter 59: "For regulating the people and serving Heaven, nothing is better than frugality." Yan Zun's notion of frugality has two meanings, the first is as a method for nourishing the breath or nourishing life, and the second is as a method for the ruler to govern the state, but of course there is a close connection between them.[62]

Heshang Gong for the first time reads into the *Daodejing* a sophisticated Huang-Lao cultivation showing muted signs of *yangsheng* techniques but that remains squarely in the field of *zuowang* spirit cultivation. His new emphasis on *zuowang* was instrumental in reconfiguring the matrix of the *Daodejing*, definitively severing any connection between Yangsheng Daoism and Huang-Lao Daoism. Based on some of these same considerations, Liu Gusheng claims that Heshang Gong was not a Daoist, but hedges on whether to call his commentary Daoist: "Although the author of the *Heshang Gong Commentary* is not necessarily a Daoist, the commentary is closely related to Daoism and has always been regarded as an important classic of Daoism."[63]

Liu Gusheng raises the specter of essentialized notions of *what Daoism is*, as if there is only one. Those who hold to such essentialized notions inevitably must decide if Heshang Gong or the *Daodejing* is Daoist. If the *Daodejing* is Daoist, then the Huang-Lao thinkers from the Warring States to the Han Dynasty who appropriated it were not, but if the Huang-Lao reading of the *Daodejing*, as evidenced by Yan Zun and Heshang Gong, is Daoist, then they were the ones who made it so. This also almost necessarily follows from the syncretic model of the origins of the *Daodejing* as a compiled text.

Relying on essentialized notions of *what is Daoism* to assess whether a person (like Heshang Gong) or a thing (like the *Daodejing*) is Daoist is to already displace most everything that Daoism is. To be disburdened of essentializing notions from the beginning is to see this variety of Daoism with what announces itself or is announced as Daoist, which turns out to be a plural phenomenon. Even the historical sources recognize this when they discuss Fangxian Daoism, Tianshi Daoism, and Huang-Lao Daoism, and this without even considering the validity of two further forms recognized in this study, Yangsheng Daoism and Zuowang Daoism. Of course these are all Daoist, including Heshang Gong and the *Daodejing*, and instead of denying them this recognition based on essentialized definitions of *what Daoism is*, it is better to understand why they are Daoist.

Certainly, the early Huang-Lao Daoists deliberately distanced themselves from the Yangsheng and Fangxian Daoists by identifying the ultimate source of the cosmos with entities other than the pristine Dao, including Taiyi, Heng, and Yi, before they collectively returned to the *Daodejing* to engage with its notion of the Dao, as evidenced in page after page of the *Huainanzi*. Their achievement was to have forged a different Dao that was no longer the pristine *heng* Dao of the Laozi *Daodejing* but the cosmic *chang* Dao of the Huang-Lao *Daodejing*. Next to this, Huang-Lao Daoism also replaced the *yangsheng* of Yangsheng Daoism with the *zuowang* of Zuowang Daoism. To say that Huang-Lao, or Heshang Gong, or the *Daodejing* is not Daoist is to shred the very fabric of Daoist history. The single-most outstanding contribution of Huang-Lao Daoism to this wider history of Daoism is its successful reconfiguration of matrix of the *Daodejing*.

The main content of the Warring States Huang-Lao manuscripts, including the *Taiyi Sheng Shui*, *Hengxian*, and *Fanwu Liuxing*, concerns cosmogony, and the Western Han Huang-Lao texts, including the *Huangdi Sijing*, *Huainanzi*, and *Wenzi* concern cosmology, particularly as it supports their political thought. During this time, when Huang-Lao thinkers began appropriating the *Daodejing*, they had naturally been drawn to its philosophy of the Dao but resisted the rigors of *yangsheng* bodily cultivation and replaced it with the less demanding *zuowang* spirit cultivation. This fit well with their cosmic Dao that could only be grasped by the spirit, not the body. Wang Bo writes:

> Purely from a textual perspective, Zhuangzi and Hanfeizi clearly represent two completely different directions of interpreting the *Daodejing* in the pre-Qin period. Zhuangzi transformed Laozi's transcendent attitude into the life of a hermit, who thinks about the world from the standpoint of life's foundation; Hanfeizi was bent of giving full play to the *Daodejing*'s political philosophy, and he brought it down into the real world ... The Han Dynasty's understandings and interpretations of the *Daodejing* generally fall under two different paradigms: one that focuses on political philosophy ... and another that focuses on the hermit and the concern for life.[64]

Taking Wang's reference to the *Zhuangzi* as synecdoche for early Daoism including Yangsheng and Zuowang Daoism, and his reference to the *Hanfeizi* (namely, the "Jie Lao" and "Yu Lao") as synecdoche for Huang-Lao Daoism, then this gives concrete form to the distinctions between them: Yangsheng Daoism is characterized by its phenomenology of the pristine Dao and its advocation of *yangsheng* bodily cultivation, and Huang-Lao Daoism by its metaphysics of the cosmic Dao and its advocation of *zuowang* spirit cultivation. First Yan Zun and then Heshang Gong, in their commentaries, recombined the new metaphysical philosophy of the *Daodejing* with the new *zuowang* cultivation of the *Daodejing*, impressive feats that generated a new configuration of the matrix of the *Daodejing*.

Huang-Lao's success in appropriating the *Daodejing* is due to this sophisticated reconfiguring of its matrix, even as it remains the historical product of its own Eastern Han era. Zheng Canshan writes:

> In the Han Dynasty, the notions of regulating the body (*zhi shen*) and regulating the state (*zhi guo*) that Huang-Lao advocated, at least from the perspective of the historical materials, basically derived from the importance that the Western Han Huang-Lao thinkers attached to regulating the state, while the Eastern Han gradually turned its attention to self-cultivation, the pursuit of long-life, and supplications and prayer.[65]

Zheng's comments illustrate that Heshang Gong closed the original matrix of the *Daodejing* not simply by merging cultivation and governance, but by simultaneously incorporating new religious practices and beliefs that would soon be firmly associated with Tianshi and later forms of institutionalized Daoism taking form at roughly the same time.[66]

Zheng indicates a different point of emphasis in Eastern Han Huang-Lao on a set of technical terms signifying techniques that, although dispersed in earlier writings, were brought together into a loose system of cultivation; these include *zhishen* 治身 (regulate the body), *xiushen* 修身 (self-cultivation), *yangxin* 養心

(nurture of the heart), and *yangxing* 養性 (nurture of the form). Each of these derives from *zuowang* meditative techniques, even though they are often miscategorized as *yangsheng*, as in the comments by Xiong Tieji and Liu Lingzi:

> After Emperor Wu, the *Daodejing* gradually withdrew from the political stage, and both the ruling classes as well as the general public started to study the *Daodejing* as an important part of self-cultivation 修身 and *yangxing* 養性. The *Daodejing*'s thought on *yangsheng* and *yangxing* was rapidly developed. In the time of the Eastern Han Dynasty, Huang-Lao thought was reduced to the study of pure *yangsheng*, and when people studied the writings of Huangdi and Laozi, their purpose was only directed to personal cultivation and *yangsheng*, and not to governing the state ... In addition, Heshang Gong's commentary, which can be said to represent one of the masterpieces of Daoist *yangsheng* theory, also focuses on the *Daodejing* from the perspective of *yangsheng*.[67]

Xiong and Liu's claim that "Huang-Lao was reduced to the study of pure *yangsheng*" is an overreaction to the fact that Huang-Lao, since the time of Emperor Wu, had minimal representation in actual state politics, and they too quickly discount the political component of Heshang Gong's commentary; still, their point that the tendencies of the Eastern Han were to decouple cultivation from governance remains eminently valid. Heshang Gong, however, serves as the exception to the rule, because he successfully recovered their intrinsic Huang-Lao connection and intertwined them in innovative ways. Ironically, this decoupling trend was beneficial for the development of self-cultivation practices and theories that allowed the Daoist tradition, and even the Chinese tradition as a whole, to recognize and accept Heshang Gong's commentary as orthodox Daoism.

One reason for the Chinese orthodoxy of Heshang Gong's commentary is precisely because of the manifest presence of the religious thought and practices, many of which involve figures known as *xian* 仙 (or divine *xian* 神仙). The history of the *xian* goes far back in Chinese antiquity and generally refers to semi-divine personages who enjoy longevity. Already in the Eastern Han, the term was used to replace the *Daodejing*'s preferred term for those who had become one with the Dao, namely, the sages 聖人, and *xian* became a staple feature of institutionalized Daoism. Liu Gusheng writes, "Eastern Han discussions of Huang-Lao give a high value to *yangsheng* and cultivating *xian*, and this differs from the Western Han Huang-Lao thought that gives a high value to statecraft. This was a new development whereby Huang-Lao thought 黃老學 gradually turned into Huang-Lao Daoism 黃老道" (2008, 56). Liu continues:

The *Heshang Gong Commentary* is the historical product of the gradual combination of divine *xian* theories and Huang-Lao political thought, and it marks an important transition from Daoist philosophy 道家 to Daoist religion 道教 … Because Heshang Gong's commentary gives high value to *yangsheng* and high value to the Dao of *ziran* and long-life, it was very much in line with the needs of the Daoist religion and, because of this, Daoists have always regarded it as a foundational classic of their religion.⁶⁸

The *Hanshu* records four lost commentaries to the *Daodejing*, and precisely how Heshang Gong's commentary fits into this wider line of Han Dynasty Huang-Lao commentaries remains unclear: is it a backward-looking political document desperately seeking to resurrect a dynasty on life-support, or is it a forward-looking scripture that portends the rise of an institutionalized Daoist religion? Or is it both at the same time? Isabelle Robinet writes:

> This "manual" directs behavior playing on two registers: "to regulate the self and to regulate the state" or, in other words: one does not govern the country without governing the self. Heshang Gong addresses his counsels equally to the person and the prince: philosophy and politics, the State, on one hand; morality and recipes of longevity on the other.⁶⁹

The Metaphysical Thought of Heshang Gong

The Heshang Gong Commentary to the Daodejing of Laozi 老子道德經河上公章句 is traditionally attributed to the reclusive hermit Heshang Gong 河上公 who is sometimes believed to have lived during the reign of Emperor Wen (r. 179–157 BCE). Most of what is known about him comes from the preface to the commentary written by Ge Xuan 葛玄 (164–244), the great-uncle of Ge Hong, which states that when the Emperor sought him out, Heshang Gong rose into the air to demonstrate his superior status before presenting him with the commentary. Discussing the commentary's Huang-Lao bona fides, Alan Chan writes, "The Huang-Lao tradition is also linked to a school headed by a legendary 'Daoist' figure known as Heshang Zhangren. Recluses, who might have tried to stay away from politics but were nevertheless much sought after by those in power, dominated the transmission of the school."⁷⁰ He is referring to *Shiji* 30, the "Biography of Yue Yi" 樂毅列傳, that mentions a certain Heshang Zhangren 河上丈人 from the late Warring States who is sometimes identified with Heshang Gong and who played an important role in the early formation of the Huang-Lao Daoism; it states:

Yue Chenggong studied the teachings of Huangdi and Laozi, and his important teacher was called Heshang Zhangren, but it is unknown from where he came. Heshang Zhangren was the teacher of An Qisheng, An Qisheng was the teacher of Maoxi Gong, Maoxi Gong was the teacher of Yuexia Gong, Yuexia Gong was the teacher of Yue Chengong, Yue Chengong was the teacher of Gao Gong. Gao Gong taught in the regions of Gaomi and Jiaoxi in the state of Qi, and he was the teacher of Cao of the state of Xiang.

Attributing the Eastern Han commentary to one of the Western Han founders of Huang-Lao Daoism was shrewd and serves to reinforce the text's Huang-Lao bona fides, and while there is some debate about the commentary's date of composition, I follow the views of Alan Chan[71] and Misha Tadd[72] that say it is an Eastern Han product of the first century.

Representing the dominant reading of the *Daodejing* throughout traditional China, modern scholars Western and Chinese have subordinated study of Heshang Gong's commentary to its less religious counterpart, Wang Bi's commentary. My necessarily partial examination of Heshang Gong's commentary explores the consequences of the Huang-Lao appropriation of the *Daodejing* that are seen in the commentary's focus on the cosmic Dao, the parallel structures of regulating the body and regulating the state, and the identification of the sage-king with *yin*.

Not only does Heshang Gong assume the cosmic Dao rather than the pristine Dao that had already been entirely forgotten as his commentary's fundamental starting point, he also holds that the cosmic Dao can be directly known. This is a spirit knowledge that wholly differs from the proprioceptive body knowledge of Yangsheng Daoism. This spirit knowledge of the cosmic Dao is the exclusive prerogative of the sage-king only because he has cultivated the tranquility of his desires and the emptiness of his spirit.

One stark difference between the Yangsheng and the Huang-Lao Daoist readings of the *Daodejing* is their different interpretations of the line from *Daodejing* chapter 1 that states *chang wu yu yi guan qi miao* 常無欲以觀其妙. The Yangsheng Daoist reading takes *chang* as a verb and *wu* as a noun: "Hold to the standpoint of nothingness in order to witness its subtleties." The Huang-Lao reading takes *chang* as an adverb and *wuyu* as a binomial: "Constantly be without desires in order to witness its subtleties."

The first interpretation directs perception to the phenomena of the world right at hand where the interaction of nothingness 無 and somethingness 有 plays itself out in the coming-into and going-out of existence of the myriad beings. It then interprets the next line in a complementary way: "Hold to the standpoint of somethingness in order to witness its manifestations" 常有欲以觀其徼, where the first line intends to witness the "subtleties" 妙 of the coming-into existence of beings and the second intends to witness their "manifestations" 徼 as they inhabit the world.

Heshang Gong's Huang-Lao reading takes the condition of being "constantly without desires" 常無欲 as the prerequisite for "witnessing its subtleties" 觀其徼 because they reveal the processes of the Dao on a transcendent realm outside of the everyday experience of things at hand, where the experience of phenomena is already the result of those transcendental subtleties. "To constantly have desires" 常有欲 means that one is locked into the realm of phenomena and is unable to go, or has not yet gone, beyond phenomena, and therefore the "subtleties" of the Dao cannot be witnessed, only its "manifestations." That Heshang Gong takes this metaphysics of presence as his starting point is amply illustrated in its comments to the passage:

> "Subtleties" are the essentials. If a person can be constantly without desires, then he can witness the essentials of the Dao. The essentials are called the One. The One manifests and announces the name of the Dao. It assists in ordering and illuminating what is true and what is false … [The One] eliminates emotions and dispels desires, and it protects Central Harmony. This is called knowing the gateway of the essentials of the Dao.

Two important points to note in this passage are that "to witness" is equivalent "to know," and that the One, defined as the "essentials" 要 of the Dao, is that by which the name of the Dao is "manifested and announced" 出布 but is not itself the Dao. The central claim here is that the cosmic Dao can be known through witnessing the essentials of the One by way of a spiritual emptiness devoid of emotions and desires. The "Central Harmony" 中和 refers to the "original qi" 元氣 that is the material expression of the One and that the commentary to *Daodejing* chapter 2 recognizes as the immediate source for the existence of the myriad things: "The original qi gives birth to the myriad beings" 元氣生萬物. Understanding the metaphysical structure of the cosmos assumed by Heshang Gong begins with understanding the One; Chan writes:

> Mediating between the formless Dao and the cosmos, (the One) forms the basis of Heshang Gong's entire intellectual enterprise. In itself, the Dao transcends the realm of human experience. Because of its "essence" and "virtue" [alternate names for the One] however, the creative and sustaining power of Dao is made manifest in the world. As the "breath" [qi] of the Dao, the "One" is at the same time materially conceived. It gives rise to "Heaven and Earth," which mark the boundaries of the physical universe … Together these form the basic elements of a cosmological vision, based ultimately on the idea of the "One."[73]

Heshang Gong assumes that the cosmic Dao exists on a transcendent realm outside of the phenomenal world, but it remains indirectly connected to the phenomenal world by way of the One that carries out its creative and ordering impulses. The commentary to *Daodejing* chapter 10 states, "The One is that which was born of the Dao's beginning and is the essential *qi* of Supreme Harmony," and the commentary to *Daodejing* chapter 52 states that the One is the first "offspring" or "son" 子 of the cosmic Dao, a line of thought that is more fully developed in the comments to the passage from *Daodejing* chapter 42 that states, "The Dao produces the One, the One produces the Two, the Two produces the Three, and the Three produces the myriad beings," to which Heshang Gong writes:

> What the Dao first produces is the One. The One produces *yin* and *yang*. *Yin* and *yang* produce the three kinds of *qi*—the harmonious, the clear, and the turbid—that separate to make the realms of Heaven, Earth, and Humanity. Together, the realms of Heaven Earth, and Humanity produce the myriad beings.

Heshang Gong depicts a strictly hierarchical cosmos that proceeds in descending stages from the cosmic Dao to the One that separates into *yin* and *yang*, which then further disperse before coagulating to form the realms of Heaven, Earth, and Humanity that lay the grounds for the existence of the myriad beings. This passage establishes the principal powers derived from the Dao that are active in the world, including the One first of all that Heshang Gong has already identified with original *qi*, but also *yin* and *yang* as two modes of it. The commentary to *Daodejing* chapter 42 goes on to state that all living beings acquire original *qi* at birth: "The myriad beings all possess original *qi* within" 萬物中皆有元氣.

The One bridges the metaphysical gap between the cosmic Dao and humanity but, in its life-giving presence within living beings, it is not normally knowable, even as it serves as the ordering principle for the world and all beings. For Heshang Gong's Huang-Lao Daoist political thought, it is precisely this One, and particularly in its service to the Dao as its "essential" ordering principle, that has taken the place of the foundational *li* ordering principles of earlier Huang-Lao thought that were to be realized by the sage-king. Heshang Gong's commentary to *Daodejing* chapter 14 states:

> The One is colorless and cannot be seen through the faculty of sight … The One is soundless and cannot be heard through the faculty of hearing … The One is formless and cannot be felt through the faculty of touch … Concerning [the One as] the colorless, the soundless, and the formless, the mouth cannot speak it and books cannot document it. It must be received through stillness and sought with the spirit. It cannot be obtained through inquiry or investigation.

The cosmic Dao produces the One, and from the One all things acquire existence. Heshang Gong has different names for it, including "original *qi*" and the "essentials," but most compelling is his identification of the One with the De 德 (often translated as "Virtue") that is also found in the title of the *Daodejing*, which could also be called *Classic of the Dao and the One*. Heshang Gong characterizes the activities of the Dao and the One in his commentary to *Daodejing* chapter 51 that states, "The Dao gives birth to them and the De nurtures them" 道生之德畜之; his commentary states:

> The Dao gives birth to the myriad beings. The De is the One. The One directs and dispenses *qi* to nurture and nourish their forms. The One establishes the forms and images of the myriad beings. The One made the conditions of winter and summer to complete them. There are none that are not impelled into activity by that which the Dao and the De enact. The Dao and the One do not give orders or decrees to the myriad things, but they constantly and spontaneously respond to them like shadows and echoes. The Dao does not only give birth to the myriad beings and that is all; it also grows and nourishes them, completes and matures them, fosters and nurses them, and makes integral their natures and lifespans. In regulating his state and regulating his body, the ruler should also be like this.

The first part of *Daodejing* chapter 51 depicts the activities of the Dao and the One (or the De) in the coming forth of beings into existence, and the important insight of Heshang Gong's commentary is that the Dao is relatively inactive in relation to the One that is supremely active. This recognition provides the first indication that Heshang Gong will identify the Dao with *yin* and the ruler, and the One with *yang* and the ministers. The second part of *Daodejing* chapter 51 singles out the activities of the Dao without mentioning the One, but the reason for this is clear: it is drawing a structural correlation between the Dao and the ruler where the ruler should "be like" 如是 the Dao and not like the One.

Because the commentary carves out a transcendent home for the Dao outside of the world and assigns active management of the world to the One, its identification of the ruler with the *yin* Dao instead of the *yang* One seems counterintuitive. But the values of Heshang Gong's Huang-Lao Daoism are different from those of Dong Zhongshu's Confucian correlativism that identify the ruler with Heaven and *yang*, and the ministers with Earth and *yin*. For Heshang Gong, the Dao as *yin* gives birth to the One as *yang*, thus elevating the value of *yin* over the value of *yang*, a hallmark of Daoist thought.

Misha Tadd convincingly uncovers the *yin* and *yang* mechanisms at play in the commentary that he treats in terms of mode and substance, and he underscores the ways in which the commentary employs *yin-yang* terminology in distinction from Dong Zhongshu's correlative cosmology. Heshang Gong's use of the *yin-yang* mechanisms that Tadd characterizes as mode and substance is a direct development of the cause and effect mechanisms that Yan Zun generally designated as "the effects of *ziran*." For that mechanism, *wuwei* does not signify an end in itself; rather, its performance is the cause for the *youwei* that is the effect in the way that a sound is the cause for the echo that is the effect. For Heshang Gong, as Tadd (2018, 12) explains, a *yang* mode such as life gives rise to a *yin* substance such as death, whereas a *yin* mode such as root gives rise to a *yang* substance such as branches.

Heshang Gong does not naively value *yin* over *yang*; he rather values *yin* mode over *yang* mode, but he also values *yang* substance over *yin* substance. *Yin* modes include *wuwei*, desirelessness, emptiness, and frugality, while *yang* modes include *youwei*, desirousness, fullness, and expenditure, such that *yin* is valued over *yang*. *Yin* substances include Earth, form, turbidity, and death, while *yang* substances include Heaven, spirit, clarity, and life, such that *yang* is valued over *yin*. Tadd writes:

> In summary, two inverted hierarchies of *yin* and *yang* coexist—*yin* mode over *yang* mode and *yang* substance over *yin* substance … In regard to cycles, this *yin-yang* cosmology distinctly involves the alternations of mode and substance. Most importantly, mode stands as the logically prior state, as the quality of behavior or existence that leads to a substantive result.[74]

Tadd points out that, for Heshang Gong, the Dao is the total *yin* mode with which the ruler is identified, and this shows once again the significant difference from Dong Zhongshu's political cosmology where Heaven is the total *yang* mode with which the ruler is identified, even though both views equally value *yang* substance over *yin* substance. The tension between them lies in how each understands the best way to bring about the flourishing of *yang* substance(s). Tadd writes:

> [Dong Zhongshu's] Confucian worldview arises from a fixed hierarchy in which all the *yang*, male, heavenly, virtuous, ritualized behaviors increase the *yang* in the world. Heshang Gong relies on the *Daodejing* tradition that prioritizes lowliness and emptiness, and valorizes these as paths to their opposites. From this practical and philosophical origin grows the split of substance and mode.[75]

The paradoxical nature of these mechanics of *yin* mode giving rise to *yang* substance is initially found in the *Daodejing* itself. Many of those passages concern *yangsheng* bodily cultivation, but Heshang Gong has stripped them of their physical applications to turn them into philosophical ideals. *Daodejing* chapter 24 describes the dangers of *yang* (as mode) increasing *yang* (as substance):

> One who stands high is not stable.
> One who strives does not go forward.
> One who displays himself is not bright.
> One who asserts himself is not prominent.
> One who brags does not achieve merit.
> One who praises himself does not live long.

This passage can be read in distinction to *Daodejing* chapter 22, which describes the benefits of *yin* (as mode) increasing *yang* (as substance), but note the final line's exhortation against using *yang* (mode) to increase *yin* (substance):

> Bending leads to intactness.
> Twisting leads to straightness.
> Emptying leads to fullness.
> Exhausting leads to renewal.
> Reducing leads to attaining.
> Excess leads to delusion.

The *yangsheng* ideals of the Laozi *Daodejing* devalue *yang* hardness that gives rise to *yin* softness as the strong army will be defeated, the strong tree will snap, the hard leather armor will split, and the hard teeth will break, insights that lead *Daodejing* chapter 76 to claim, "Hardness and rigidity occupy the inferior position, and pliancy and softness occupy the superior position" 強大處下柔弱處上. In the hands of Heshang Gong, these *yangsheng* ideals were transformed into metaphysical principles.

For Heshang Gong, death is the ultimate *yin* substance brought about by *yang* mode whose maximal expression is *youwei*, whereas long-life is the ultimate *yang* substance brought about by *yin* mode whose maximal expression is *wuwei*, which concretely manifests as either the long life of the individual body or the long life of the state. In order to acquire the One (or the De) as perfect *yang* substance, Heshang Gong exhorts the ruler to embody total *yin* mode by "being like" the Dao—empty, tranquil, still, desireless, and nameless. There is only one method to acquire the One, namely through "regulating" 治, but there are separate fields in which the method is applied, including the body 身 and the state 國. However, reducing Heshang Gong's metaphysical reading of the *Daodejing* to this two-part complementary structure does not yet get to the heart of the Huang-Lao cosmic Dao.

Two works by Lin Mingzhao (2014, 2015) are useful for understanding the position of the cosmic Dao in the commentary. She writes, "Judging from the various structures and mutual correspondences of the relationship between regulating the body and regulating the state in Heshang Gong's commentary, we can see that there are the following [three] significations" (2014, 135). Here is the first signification:

> From the perspective of structure, "regulating the body" refers to the ruler's regulating the domain of his personal spirit 精神 or soul, and from this producing the effect of prolonging his life; in other words, the intended effect of regulating the body is at the level of life. "Regulating the state" refers to the ruler's management or charge over the hearts of the ministers and the people and from this producing the political effect of long-term stability and enduring peace [of the state].[76]

The shared effect that follows from regulating the body and regulating the state is the prolongation of both. This parallel structure can be given as:

Ruler: Body->   regulate spirit->   long life of the body
Ruler: State ->   regulate ministers and people->   long life of the state

In this parallel structure, the "body" more properly signifies the spirit 神 than the integrated body of Yangsheng Daoism, while the "state" primarily signifies the hearts 心 of the ministers and the people. If the method of "regulating" is the same for both, then their sameness only refers to their structural positions that simultaneously bind the ruler to his spirit as well as his people, both occupying the same structural position, but it does not mean that these "regulatings" are the same in their methods of practice or implementation to the "body" and the "state." Thus, Lin's second signification:

> From the perspective of these parallel structures placed next to each other, when Heshang Gong brings together the relation between regulating the body and regulating the state, there is no assimilation of one to the other, but each rather retains its own independent character, and because of this they never form a single unified field. Based on a practical principle that they both share and because of the effects or objectives that each were intended to achieve, the methods of implementation and practice emphasized for each were different.[77]

Although its implementation is different in the two cases, "the practical principle that they both share" is the "regulating" that leads to the same intended effect, namely the long life of the body and the long life of the state. That they cannot be "assimilated" is because the methods at issue for regulating the body on one hand and for regulating the state on the other, despite sharing the same names, are not themselves the same in practice and implementation. The shared names of the methods are "loving" 爱 and "not harming" 不害, but for the case of regulating the body it refers to "loving" and "not harming" the spirit, and in the case of regulating the state it refers to "loving" and "not harming" the people. Lin explains this:

> In regulating the body, it is necessary to love and cherish the essential *qi* and not let it drain away, because one can then safeguard the effect for one's life. In regulating the state, it is necessary to love and protect the people, because then one can produce the effect of regulating the state and pacifying the people ... For regulating the state, it is important to not harm the people who enter it, because then one can have state security and long enduring peace ... For regulating the body, it is necessary not to harm the peace of the spirit, because then one can have bodily security with the effect of long-life.[78]

The basis for Heshang Gong's methods of "loving" and "not harming" is the *Daodejing* itself. The following sets forth the original lines from the *Daodejing* as read by Heshang Gong followed by his commentary to them.

Daodejing chapter 10:

In loving the people and regulating the state, can you do it without knowledge?

Heshang Gong:

One who regulates his body loves his *qi* and his body is intact.
One who regulates the state loves the people and the state is at peace.

Daodejing chapter 13:

To love one's body as the world.

Heshang Gong:

This means that only if the ruler can love his body without acting for himself can he hope to serve as the father and mother of the myriad people.

Daodejing chapter 35:

Hold to the Great Image, and the world will come to you. They will come and not be harmed because its security and peace are great.

Heshang Gong:

When the myriad people come and are not harmed, then the state and its families are secure and attain Supreme Peace. If you regulate the body without harming the spirit, then the body is secure and has long-life.

Lin's third signification concerns the cosmic Dao that Heshang Gong establishes as an absolute metaphysical foundation:

> From the perspective of structural correspondences, between the domains of regulating the body and regulating the state and in terms of their methods of implementation and effects, they each have their own separate characteristics and connections that, for example, contain identically specific meanings. And we can ask once again whether the correspondence between the structural fields of regulating the body and regulating the state, including the connection between their practical methods and their effects, have a metaphysical basis. In other words, why are there corresponding structures between the body and the state, and between regulating the body and regulating the state? Does Heshang Gong have a basic explanation for the structural characteristics and corresponding connections between the two fields?[79]

Lin asks the pertinent question about the metaphysical foundations of the regulating the state/regulating the body paradigm that other studies overlook or take for granted. Studies such as Tadd's focus on the complex relationship between the Dao and the One, while others such as Robinet's focus on the complex relationship between regulating the body and regulating the state. Lin, however, uncovers the genetic interrelations and mutual dependencies between the two foci that ultimately reveal Heshang Gong's commentary as a powerfully metaphysical Huang-Lao text. The parallel structures for regulating the body and regulating the state are functional, ideally or philosophically speaking, only because they directly emerge from the transcendent cosmic Dao that metaphysically anchors and effectuates them precisely in terms of their structural correspondence. Lin writes:

> Therefore, in terms of practical methods, Heshang Gong sometimes first establishes a common practical principle based on the foundational structure of the relationship between the Dao and the myriad beings. Then it takes that practical principle as the basis for the structural correspondence between the fields of regulating the body and regulating the state. Finally, it then juxtaposes the respective practical methods in those fields of regulating the body and regulating the state.[80]

Lin is spot-on in her recognition of the genetic interrelations and mutual dependencies between the cosmic Dao and the parallel structures of regulating the body and regulating the state, but she disregards the *yin-yang* mechanics that centrally inform them. Relying on Tadd's findings allows for a structural perspective that highlights the way that the *yin* mode and *yang* substance mechanism assist the cosmic Dao in regulating the world, where the dynamism of the world (understood in terms of cosmos, body, and state) is assumed as proceeding by the principles of *ziran*.[81]

Field= *ziran*	Yin=*wuwei*	Yang=*youwei*	Effect
Cosmos=	Dao->	the One->	Existence of the myriad things
Body=	Ruler->	the Spirit->	Long life of body
State=	Ruler->	the People->	Long life of state

The major effect of the Huang-Lao metaphysicalization of the Dao was to extract the pristine Dao from out of the phenomenal world to establish the cosmic Dao as a permanent and eternal entity existing on a transcendent realm outside of the world. This created a gulf between the phenomenal world and the transcendent realm that Heshang Gong bridged by way of the One (or the De or original *qi*). He grounded his cosmological model on the metaphysical sameness of three parallel and corresponding structures of the cosmos, the body, and the state that were inextricably bound together by their equal participation in the essential mechanism whereby a flourishing *yang* substance was bound to a creative *yin* mode.

Heshang Gong's commentary to the *Daodejing*, representing the Eastern Han culmination of Huang-Lao Daoism, dramatically reconfigured the Yangsheng Daoist matrix of the *Daodejing*. Situating its cosmic Dao in a transcendent realm outside of the world rendered it foreign to the flesh even as its *zuowang* spirit cultivation opened a new path of transcendental access to it. This *zuowang* spirit cultivation, based on meditative techniques leading to enlightened emptiness, allows the sage-king to sidestep the phenomenal world and directly apprehend the cosmic Dao that can then be directly implemented in the sage-king's regulating of his body and his regulating of the state.

Looking back over the course of the *Daodejing* from its original possession by a reclusive community of *yangsheng* masters and disciples to its near-total appropriation by empire building political ideologues, it is not unreasonable to affirm that there were in fact two different *Daodejing*s: a Laozi *Daodejing* grounded in the phenomenology of the pristine Dao and a Huang-Lao *Daodejing* grounded in the metaphysics of the cosmic Dao.[82] The Huang-Lao *Daodejing* became the orthodox version for the many later traditions of Daoism as well as the Chinese tradition more generally, while the Laozi *Daodejing* was relegated to oblivion, whose existence was unimaginable until the discoveries of the Guodian and Mawangdui *Laozi* manuscripts.

That the pristine Dao was rendered invisible with the enthronement of Liu Heng does not mean that Yangsheng Daoism simply evaporated. It continued as a rich, yet shadowy, tradition that surreptitiously wove its way through the Warring States and Han Dynasty, where it remains barely visible as good fiction embedded in a small number of writings like the *Zhuangzi*, *Huainanzi*, and *Shiji*.

Still, the most important records of Yangsheng Daoism were gathered together in a short text called the *Liexian zhuan* 列仙傳 that memorialized those *xian* who had successfully embodied the pristine Dao by *yangsheng* bodily cultivation. Systematically disregarded as fable, legend, and imaginative fiction by the majority of those who have read it, the text was taken very seriously by the one person who went on to reconstruct from it loose lineage-based traditions of Yangsheng Daoism; this was Ge Hong 葛洪 (283–343), who not only gave weight to this tradition by announcing his own membership in it but who also produced two further writings that displayed this tradition in even greater detail, namely the *Shenxian zhuan* 神仙傳 and the *Baopuzi* 抱朴子.

Following in the footsteps of Heshang Gong, Ge Hong in his turn attempted to re-establish the original Yangsheng Daoist matrix of the *Daodejing* by correctly calibrating its two aspects: a phenomenological reading of its philosophy of the nameable Dao and a *yangsheng* bodily cultivation that emerges from it by way of the unnameable Dao. The third part of this study is devoted in two chapters to Ge Hong's engagement with the matrix of the *Daodejing*: the first concerning the phenomenology of the nameable component of the pristine Dao, and the second concerning the *yangsheng* bodily cultivation of the unnameable component of the pristine Dao.

Part Three

Ge Hong and the Matrix

7

Ge Hong and the Philosophy of the Pristine Dao

Ge Hong and Xuanxue

The previous part of this study examined two Han period Huang-Lao commentaries to the *Daodejing*, by Yan Zun and Heshang Gong. Their Huang-Lao Daoist identity is announced in contradistinction to Yangsheng Daoism in three important ways: a rejection of the pristine Dao in favor of the cosmic Dao; a rejection of *yangsheng* bodily cultivation in favor of *zuowang* spirit self-cultivation; and a rejection of identifying the sage as sage in favor of identifying the sage as sage-king. In part due to the forgottenness of the Laozi *Daodejing*, and in part to the persuasiveness of the Huang-Lao *Daodejing*, this latter had already become the single version known to Yan Zun and Heshang Gong, which the present study now simply calls the *Daodejing* unless otherwise noted.

Standing between these two Han Dynasty Huang-Lao commentaries and the writings of Ge Hong is Wang Bi's 王弼 (226–49 CE) commentary to the *Daodejing*; he was a brilliant but ill-fated scholar who died of illness at the tender age of 23. His most important writings consist of three major commentaries, one to the *Analects*, one to the *Yijing*, and of course one to the *Daodejing*. The Chinese tradition long considered the *Yijing* commentary to be his master work until the Neo-Confucians elevated his *Daodejing* commentary to a position of Confucian orthodoxy, at least as far as they ever considered the *Daodejing* orthodox. The characteristic feature of Wang Bi's commentary is that it changed Huang-Lao metaphysics based on nothingness into Xuanxue meontology based on Non-being.

Wang Bi asserted that *wu* 無 as nameless Non-being is the ultimate source that produces *you* 有 as Being from which all beings exist. His major philosophical claims concern Non-being as eternal/permanent/constant, but where the *Daodejing* seems to consider *wu* as nothingness and *you* as somethingness as two original elements of the Dao, Wang Bi severs their connection and affirms *wu* as Non-being as the single fundamental root from which is produced *you* as Being. Since Non-being does not have a name, we just expediently call it the Dao. Oddly, this is a Daoism is without a Dao.

Wang Bi's meontological readings of both the *Daodejing* and the *Yijing* launched a new philosophical movement in the Wei-Jin period called Xuanxue 玄学 (Dark or Profound Learning), where the term *xuanxue* often just means "metaphysics." It is also sometimes called Neo-Daoism, which is something of a misnomer because the primary tendencies of many of its proponents, including Wang Bi, Guo Xiang 郭象, and Zhang Zhan 張湛, was to Confucianism, while others, including Ge Hong, Ji Kang 嵇康, and Ruan Ji 阮籍, was to Daoism.

Forming after the collapse of the Han Dynasty, the Xuanxue movement is often characterized by its search for an eternal source of existence in the face of life's unforeseeable vicissitudes, and Wang Bi helped to direct this project into the philosophical exploration of Non-being. Wang Bi's attention to the *Daodejing* also helped to partially exonerate it from its implications with the several Daoist millennial uprisings that fatally weakened the Han Dynasty. His meontological reading of the *Daodejing* would later be embraced in Chinese Buddhist circles before its adoption as the orthodox Confucian reading in imperial China that resulted in the demotion of Heshang Gong's Huang-Lao reading to a secondary position, and Wang Bi's Xuanxue reading continues to retain its status as the dominant reading in the academy today.

Still, there are no historical indications that Wang Bi's commentary, even after its Confucian ascendancy, had any impact on Daoist readings of the *Daodejing*. For the most part, Daoists continued to compose their own commentaries sometimes found scattered throughout the Daoist Canon, many of which incorporated teachings of internal alchemy 内丹 *neidan*, but none of them gained enough widespread traction to displace the tradition's adherence to Heshang Gong's commentary.[1] One fascinating counterexample to this is found in the writings of Ge Hong. Although he never composed an independent commentary to the *Daodejing* on par with Heshang Gong or Wang Bi, he nevertheless guaranteed the survival and continuing relevance of the Yangsheng Daoist reading that, we can only imagine due to its reclusive nature, helped to sustain the mountainous culture of Daoist hermits.

Ge Hong lived several generations after Wang Bi, and he considered himself an active member of the tradition of Yangsheng Daoism that he traced back to an ancient time predating even Laozi himself; because of this self-identification, I recognize Ge Hong as a latter-day member of Yangsheng Daoism, and I recognize his reading of the *Daodejing* also as such. Ge Hong's writings systematically give pride of place to the *Daodejing*, and whether he was familiar with Wang Bi's commentary (but he certainly was), he outright rejected metaphysical (and meontological) readings of it. Where Wang Bi grounded his reading on a single line from *Daodejing* chapter 40, "*you* is produced from *wu*" 有生於無, Ge Hong grounded his reading on a single line from *Daodejing* chapter 2, "*you* and *wu* are born together" 又無相生. Ge Hong affirmed the phenomenological co-primordiality of *you* and *wu* within the body of the Dao, and that it is from their interplay that all things come into existence. On the level of human existence, *you* manifests as the physical form and *wu* as spirit, and human existence continues so long as body and spirit are maintained together without separation.[2]

Ge Hong takes *yangsheng* as the core practice of the *Daodejing* that allows a person to maintain the continued co-presence of body and spirit, resulting in an individual longevity capable of spanning centuries. He termed practitioners who were content with this achievement "earthly *xian*" 地仙. But Ge Hong himself was not content with this kind of longevity, and he attempted to exceed even the limits of *yangsheng* longevity in his advocation of a more sublime achievement that was the result of a more profound practice, namely an alchemy that was capable of endowing immortality.[3] But the move from *yangsheng* to alchemy remained an individual choice for the practitioner who had already won longevity, and those who went on to achieve immortality were termed "heavenly *xian*" 天仙. Among many of Ge Hong's accomplishments, one that stands out is his formulation of a theoretical rationale for both longevity and immortality that was largely made possible by his Yangsheng reading of *Daodejing* chapter 2.

The legacy of Ge Hong's Yangsheng reading of the *Daodejing* is seen in the lasting impact it exerted on the Daoist quest for *yangsheng* longevity and alchemical immortality. It provided a powerful alibi for those who chose to take up mountainous reclusion in the hope of becoming an earthly *xian*, and it provided a blueprint for other institutionalized traditions of Daoism that would eventually make the move from external alchemy to internal alchemy, a core component in Daoist practice today. Unlike Heshang Gong's Huang-Lao and Wang Bi's Xuanxue readings, Ge Hong's Yangsheng reading of the *Daodejing* fully embraced the refusal to separate the *Daodejing*'s phenomenology of the Dao from its *yangsheng* bodily cultivation.

Ge Hong is a fascinating figure in the history of Chinese religion and philosophy, and one of the least studied by modern scholarship. His *Baopuzi Waipian* 抱朴子外篇 demonstrates his in-depth engagement with Confucianism, even though he self-identified as Daoist in the line of Yangsheng

Daoism that he traced all the way back to Laozi. He was devoted to alchemy and the pursuit of immortality, and although he had firsthand experience of the Tianshi Daoism sweeping China at the time (some of his family members had converted to it), he disparaged it. His great legacy to Chinese religious history is felt most powerfully by his uncovering of the two components of the Yangsheng Daoist matrix of the *Daodejing* comprising its philosophy of the Dao and its *yangsheng* bodily cultivation. This and the following chapter explore each component separately.

Ge Hong is counted among the ranks of Xuanxue scholars, and Teng Wei and Tang Juan introduce this facet of his career:

> During the Wei-Jin Dynasties, the scholar's awareness of individual life was awakened, but when they woke up, they found that they were in an era of brutal and precarious dark chaos. Experiencing the joy of life and self-existence, they also always had to confront the threat of death. As a result, some of these scholars were keen on religious fantasies and they sought to explore the spiritual destination of their spirits; some of them reveled in unleashing their bondage while others simply lived as recluses in the mountains and forests to enjoy a temporary physical and psychological liberation … Ge Hong manifested this life-consciousness of the Wei-Jin scholars both in theory and practice. He changed the illusion of immortality into an invisible reality that was within reach. His greatest achievements did not lie in his concrete methods for becoming an immortal, but in his providing a theoretical foundation for the state of immortality itself.[4]

Chinese scholars normally agree with this assessment of Ge Hong's important contribution articulated in his chef-d'oeuvre, the *Baopuzi Neipian* 抱朴子內篇. Zhang Zhenguo provides semi-mythic, semi-poetic context for this theoretical foundation:

> Turtles and cranes can have long-life, and people also can have long-life, and the myriad beings mutually transform. One day, people can undergo cultivation and become divine *xian*. But in the end, it is not the affair of a single day, and it is not easy to cultivate to become a divine *xian*. Ge Hong sought the grounds for these arguments in the ancient legends and used the legends as evidence to prove the correctness of his arguments. His intentions can be described as very painstaking.[5]

Still, hand in hand with the theoretical foundation for immortality went a set of practices involving *yangsheng* bodily techniques of *qi* 氣 circulation and methods of alchemy that he systematized in accordance with this theoretical foundation. He believed that would justify the pursuit of immortality, the successful achiever of which he called *xian* 仙.⁶ He constructed this foundation upon a specific discourse on *you* 有/*wu* 無.

The base meaning of *you* is "to have" and *wu* is "not to have." Despite A. C. Graham's hesitations,⁷ they are often translated as being and nothingness or non-being, which is for the most part warranted and non-problematic. Some philosophers continue to be struck by the resonance shared by these Chinese notions with Martin Heidegger's German notions of *sein* in their many variations (*dasein, mitdasein, nichtdasein*, etc.) and Jean-Paul Sartre's French notions, *être* and *néant*. Here, I leave *you* and *wu* in their transliterated form to highlight the continuity on this discourse from the *Daodejing* to Ge Hong (and Wang Bi).

Li Zongding writes: "Ge Hong employed *you/wu* for the production of an architectural structure for the metaphysics of cosmic generation, as well as for the methods of its application [for attaining immortality], and it became one of the most important elements of Wei-Jin Xuanxue."⁸ Li also recognizes that Ge Hong's discourse on *you/wu* is beholden to the *Daodejing*: "The terms *you* and *wu* began to be specialized philosophical terms from the time of Laozi."⁹ Thus, any exploration of Ge Hong's discourse on *you/wu* will need to examine its initial articulations in the *Daodejing*.

However, Ge Hong was not the only Wei-Jin thinker who saw himself as inheriting and developing the *Daodejing*'s discourse on *you/wu*; before him stood the towering figure of Wang Bi, who also established his Xuanxue reading of the *Daodejing* on that very foundation. Their developments and enrichments of that discourse, however, went in radically different directions: Wang Bi kept his strictly within the realm of a pure philosophy spiced with a dose of mysticism, while Ge Hong strove to maintain harmony between theory and practice. Thus, Ge Hong's discourse on *you/wu* can be clarified at times by comparison to Wang Bi's corresponding discourse as a counterpoint.

Throughout this chapter, I will continue to contrast Ge Hong's "religious" commitment to, or reading of, the *Daodejing* with Wang Bi's "philosophical" one. Hoping to curtail debate into the essential or defining differences between them, by "religious" I refer to the taking seriously of notions of long-life and immortality, and by "philosophical" I mean the refusal to entertain such notions. While this might come across as a refusal to engage, I appeal to the cultural history of Daoism, in which the possibility of immortality was not only taken seriously by practitioners, but also used as a badge of honor with the intent to differentiate themselves from the hegemony of dogmatic Confucian authoritarianism.

As important as this counterpoint is to approach the thought of Ge Hong, particularly given Wang Bi's dominance in *Daodejing* studies that hardly recognizes Ge Hong as having anything worthwhile to say about it, it is disappointing that he did not compose a complete commentary, unlike Wang Bi. Additionally, Western cultural resources for understanding Ge Hong, and Daoism more generally, are limited, and Wang Bi provides a relatively more familiar point *d'appui* for Western readers.

Ge Hong highly esteemed Laozi and Daoism, and Confucius and Confucianism followed second, but Wang Bi held the opposite assessment. This is not surprising, given that Ge Hong was a self-professed follower of Laozi, while Wang Bi famously revered Confucius as the greatest of sages. In other words, both considered Laozi to be Daoist, but Ge Hong read the *Daodejing* as a Daoist, and Wang Bi read it as a Confucian, and this matters for interpreting their writings: Wang Bi read the *Daodejing* as a philosophical treatise composed for the enlightened sage-king, but Ge Hong read it as a religious manual for the seeker of immortality.

Wang Bi was among the first major figures to engage the *Daodejing* after its incriminating associations with the popular rebellions at the end of the Han, and his meontological reading whitewashed many religious elements from the text. Ge Hong, on the other hand, not only rejected Wang Bi's meontology, but also the entire metaphysical edifice of Han period classical learning. Zhong Sheng and Luo Yi ask the question,

> Why does Ge Hong oppose Xuanxue [read: metaphysics]? In essence, Daoism and metaphysics not only do not conflict; they are inextricably linked. Moreover, as a master of Daoist theory, his thought incorporates many metaphysical components, and there are many academic studies on just this topic. So, we might ask, what factors contributed to his so strongly criticizing metaphysics?[10]

Their study goes on to explore many of the intellectual, sociological, and biographical factors behind Ge Hong's rejection of metaphysics,[11] but the core reason is that he was doing religion plain and simple, and his discourse on *you/wu* was put directly in service to that.[12] Sun Yiping writes:

> Religious faith as a type of genuine conviction represents a characteristically human value system and way of thinking, but if it only depends on the objects of worship as if they were vitally alive, as well as on certain social and psychological foundations, then it is insufficient; it also needs the support of theory and practice… After the philosophical arguments of Ge Hong's metaphysics, the divine *xian* 仙 transcended their non-logical and non-empirical features of myth and legend and became objects of religious belief and practice that were endowed with a rich philosophical content that was disseminated throughout Chinese society, and this objectively promoted the development of Daoist immortality.[13]

Wang Bi and Ge Hong on the *Daodejing*

The *Daodejing* established a discourse on *you/wu* that gathered and combined two separate domains: cosmogony and cosmology. The foundations of this discourse appeal to the condition and activities of the pristine Dao before the world had come to exist, and it conceives the Dao in terms of *you/wu*. Since *you/wu* exist prior to all things, they cannot be thought of as either energy or matter, fundamentally different from the somewhat parallel notions of *qi* and *yin-yang* generated by *you/wu* which are themselves identifiable as either energy or matter. *Daodejing* chapter 25 states:

> There was a thing completed in chaos that was born before Heaven and Earth.
> Empty and still, it stands on its own and does not change.
> It moves in cycles and is never threatened.
> It can be taken as the Mother of the world.
> I do not know its name; I call it the Dao.

This passage establishes the pristine Dao in the time before the primordial beginnings of the world, even before the initial stirrings of Heaven and Earth. The Dao "stands in its own" 獨立 and, entirely self-enclosed in its own (non-) presence, it churns through self-contained cycles 周行; without further activity or movement, it is recognized as "the Mother of the world" 天下母. *Daodejing* chapter 21 builds on this image:

> As a thing, the Dao is vague and diffuse.
> It is vague and diffuse, but inside there are images.
> It is diffuse and vague, but inside there are things.
> It is obscure and dark, but inside there are vitalities.

This passage provides additional perspective on what it is that churns through the cycles: "images" 象, "entities" 物, and "vitalities" 精, the cosmogonic components of the Dao in a state of turbid undifferentiation called "chaos" 混. They partake of being without being any specific or self-subsistent thing or entity, regardless that the *Daodejing* uses the abstract nouns to point to them; this is a function of the poetic nature of the *in illo tempore* language used to describe the genetic makeup of the Dao.

Referring to the life- and world-creating content on the verge of activating, these "images, things, and vitalities" are quasi-manifest reflections of the eternity of presence-suffused *you* within the infinity of the totality-field of *wu* that signifies the spatial non-presence into and out of which the *you*-presences churn. Another way of stating this is to say that *you* churns throughout *wu*, rendering what was a presence-laden *you*-space into an absence-laden *wu*-space, and rendering what was an absence-laden *wu*-space into a presence-laden *you*-space.

These passages envision the primordial origins of world. *Daodejing* chapter 42 depicts this with simultaneous vagueness and precision:

> The Dao gives birth to the One.
> The One gives birth to the Two.
> The Two gives birth to the Three.
> The Three gives birth to the myriad beings.

Ge Hong read the numbers (or states or stages as the case may be) from the cosmogonic sequence in terms of the Dao giving birth to *qi* as the One, *qi* giving birth to *yin-yang* as the Two, and *yin-yang* giving birth to the realms of Heaven, Earth, and Human as the Three. The *Daodejing*'s use of the term *sheng* 生, which is often translated into English as "to generate," also and more evocatively means "to give birth to," and this is how Ge Hong reads it, thereby maintaining the *Daodejing*'s consistent imagery of the Dao as the Mother. Wang Bi's commentary to *Daodejing* chapter 42 de-emphasizes this semi-religious image of the Dao as a Mother giving birth, and he reads *sheng* as "to generate":

> What the ten thousand forms of the ten thousand beings return to is the One. From what does the One come? From *wu*. From *wu* there is the One. Can the One then be called *wu*? As it is already called the One, how is it without a name? There is the word for it, and there is the One, so how could they not be the Two? There is the One and there is the Two, and the generation of the Three follows. The numbers arising from *wu* are exhausted at this point. Beyond this, there are no other things that belong to the class of the Dao.[14]

Wang Bi's comments make Ge Hong's reading of *sheng* as "to give birth to" more significant. When one thing generates another thing, the result is two separate things different in essence; when one thing gives birth to another thing, there are also two separate things but with a shared essence. In the cosmogonic sequence beginning from the Dao as the Mother and ending with the birth of the myriad beings, a shared essence is transmitted through the line. To call it *qi*, or *yin-yang*, or Heaven and Earth, is already too late and ignores the initial essence, which is itself eternally existing *you/wu*.

For Ge Hong's reading of *Daodejing* chapter 42, the separate operations of the birth of this very world and all things in it was initiated by the cosmogonic movements of *you/wu* from within the total field, or body, of the Dao, despite that it nowhere directly mentions *you/wu*. We must look to other passages from the *Daodejing* to understand how it applies the language of *you/wu* in relation to the very origins, and this begins with *Daodejing* chapter 1, which states:

> *Wu* names the beginning of Heaven and Earth.
> *You* names the Mother of the myriad beings.

These are controversial lines in *Daodejing* exegesis, and how one reads them says much about one's commitments, religious or philosophical, with respect to Daoism. Wang Bi demonstrates his philosophical commitment by reading the first two characters of each line as a compound noun, in which *wuming* 無名 refers to the "nameless" and *youming* 有名 to the "named." Doing so, he posits two ontologically separate levels of existence, the first characterized as "nameless" pointing to a transcendent (or logical) realm beyond time and space and beyond language and cognition, and a second characterized as "named" referring to the phenomenal realm in which language functions and knowledge can be secured. The first is metaphysically absolute, the second is contingent.

The alignment of Wang Bi's Xuanxue reading with the Confucian philosophical tradition followed by Western sinology's inheritance of that alignment persuades many modern readers that it represents the only valid reading. When Ge Hong's Yangsheng reading is recognized, it is usually rejected out of hand, and this itself is taken as sufficient reason to disassociate him from any relationship to a pure Daoism, for which the *Zhuangzi* is often held to represent the gold standard. Nonetheless, this is how Ge Hong reads the lines, and with purpose: to justify and stabilize his construction of a theoretical basis for the Daoist quest for longevity and immortality. But this requires a litmus; at a minimum, his reading of the *Daodejing* must be syntactically sound, especially if and where it diverges from Wang Bi's dominant reading. When Ge Hong is deliberately disassociated from Daoism, it is almost always on philosophical grounds, not syntactic ones.[15]

Ge Hong's reading of these lines takes *you* and *wu* as independent, stand-alone nouns and *ming* as a verb, thereby rendering *you/wu* amenable to language and cognition, and therefore the *Daodejing* is able to speak about both *you/wu* and the Dao. This helps to explain why Wang Bi's reading of the first line of *Daodejing* chapter 1 ("The Dao that can be spoken is not the eternal Dao") has been used as a bludgeon by the Confucian tradition as well as much of Western sinology to diminish, even ridicule, not only Ge Hong's "religious" (read: Yangsheng) reading of the *Daodejing* but also his career as a Daoist by celebrating the nonsensicality of spending five thousand words talking about something that cannot be talked about.

For Ge Hong, *Daodejing* chapter 1 demonstrates *wu* as the "beginning" 始 that situates temporality reckoned in terms of Heaven 天 and spatiality reckoned in terms of Earth 地, each together generating the worldly totality in which existence comes forth. *You* is the designation for the ultimate source of the plenitude of existence active within the spatiotemporal boundaries, and it is referred to as the Mother. By itself, however, *you*, as that which endows existence to every existent within the cosmos, is equated with no individually specific thing or being, in the same way that a mother can give birth to innumerable offspring without at the same time giving birth to herself. Significantly different from associations with a masculine-type god that creates *ex-nihilo*, *you* is a feminine generatrix.

Daodejing chapter 40 challenges Ge Hong's reading: "The myriad beings of the world are born from *you*, and *you* is born from *wu*." It appears to establish a logical sequence applicable to the coming-into-existence of living beings: *wu* gives birth to *you*, and *you* in turn gives birth to existents. Wang Bi asserts ontic and logical priority to *wu* over *you* on every level, and in fact reads these lines in precisely this way: "All of the myriad beings of the world take *you* for generation. That from which *you* begins takes *wu* as the root. In order to keep *you* complete, it must return back to *wu*" 天下之物皆以有為生有之所始以無為本將欲全有必反於無也. As Li Zongding explains, "Wang Bi separated *you* and *wu* into two levels, and put forth the propositions that '*wu* is the root' and '*you* is born from *wu*,' thereby transforming a developmental sequence of cosmology into a logical sequence of ontology."[16] But Ge Hong reads this cosmological sequence as giving only a limited logical priority to *wu* only in the cosmological field with respect to the coming-into-being of phenomenal existents; he affirms the equal priority of *you*/*wu* in every other way.

Wang Bi attaches more importance to the cosmological field of phenomenal existence than to the cosmogonic, and reads this cosmological sequence as providing precision to the lines from *Daodejing* chapter 1, but Ge Hong, who attaches more importance to the cosmogonic field in which *you*/*wu* remain in an eternal state of mutual interplay, minimizes *Daodejing* chapter 40 and takes the following line from *Daodejing* chapter 2 as providing precision to the lines from *Daodejing* chapter 1: "*Wu* and *you* mutually give birth to each other." Doing so, he thereby sidesteps the possible contradiction posed by *Daodejing* chapter 40 (but note that this line in turn poses a possible contradiction to Wang Bi's reading of *Daodejing* chapter 1).[17] This helps to explain the different directions taken by their separate discourses on *you*/*wu*.

Ge Hong nonetheless reads the *Daodejing*'s cosmological sequence as also prioritizing their mutual interplay within the spatiotemporal world of time and space. This reading too is often ignored or rejected by scholars who hold to Wang Bi's reading, which takes *wu* as the single, absolute, and transcendent foundation of *you*. For him, no matter if it is the cosmogonic or the cosmological level, there is only the logical sequence of *wu* generating *you*, and *you* generating things and beings. Ge Hong's reasons for seeing their equal priority even in the cosmological field are justified by two lines from *Daodejing* chapter 1 that demonstrate two distinct perspectives on existence that I call the *wu*-perspective and the *you*-perspective:

> Hold to the standpoint of *wu* with the intent to witness its subtleties.
> Hold to the standpoint of *you* with the intent to witness its manifestations.

Specialists of the *Daodejing* steeped in Wang Bi's reading will be struck by how differently Ge Hong interprets these lines; Wang Bi reads *chang* 常 as an adverb and *wuyu* 無欲 and *youyu* 有欲 as descriptive verbs: "When the myriad beings are constantly without desires, one can witness their subtleties; when they are constantly with desires, one can witness their manifestations." His point is that when things are without desires, they are in the state of beginning to come forth from *wu*, and when they are with desires, then they are already complete. In this way, Wang Bi again underscores his view of the strictly transcendental priority of *wu* over *you*.

Ge Hong takes *chang* verbally, and *wu* and *you* nominally. By "holding to the perspective of *you*" 常有, the typical mode of human perspective, one can "witness the manifestations" 觀其徼 of phenomenal existents as they ontically are; by "holding to the perspective of *wu*" 常無 one can "witness the subtleties" 觀其妙 of the interplay of *you/wu* in the ontic emergence and perdurance of things and beings, and this perspective is only possible because *you/wu* are never separated, even in the field of cosmology, despite the fact that it takes an altered perspective to "witness" this. I will return to the ways in which Ge Hong applies these two perspectives in his discourse on *you/wu* in the next section, but here it is sufficient to note how the *Daodejing* applies them by way of a set of vivid depictions of their mutual interplay, as in *Daodejing* chapter 11:

> Clay is kneaded to make a vessel, but the use of the vessel lies in the configuration of its *wu* and *you*.
> Doors and windows are cut out to make a room, but the use of the room lies in the configuration of its *wu* and *you*.
> For this reason, the service of a thing lies in its *you*, but its use lies in its *wu*.

These striking images depict the mutual interplay of *you/wu* in relation to all existing beings. A vessel exists and functions as a vessel only by virtue of its material clay, the existent stuff directly generated by *you*. It is strictly bounded by its material extensions, surrounded on all sides (top, bottom, inside, and outside) in its specific measures as an extended thing by that which it is not, its *wu*. Its inside possesses two aspects: the inner surface that can be felt, and the contained space that cannot. It is because of the interplay of these two aspects (*you/wu*) that the vessel can contain other matter (water or wine, or gold and dirt), and this provides for its service. In the same way, a room is built of walls, floor, and ceiling, the material stuff generated from *you*, but it is only a room because of the spaces cut into it in the form of a doorway and windows, without which the room would only be a cube: this is its *wu*.

Does the vessel strictly consist of only the extended material clay, or is the internally contained space also part of what it is? Does the room strictly consist of the extended material of walls, floor, and ceiling, or is the empty space of the door and windows also part of what it is? This entirely depends on the adopted perspective: either the *you*-perspective or the *wu*-perspective. The *you*-perspective reveals things in their condition of presence, by which they can be known physically (or chemically or atomically), but also, for example, politically, psychologically, and historically. The *wu*-perspective, on the other hand, reveals things with respect to their metaphysical absence(s), and this is the perspective by which to know the Dao. The *wu*-perspective can be extended to all existing things, from the *wu* of a clock face with the *you* of its hands, to the *you* of the fingers with the *wu* in-between: all things and beings, each entirely unique to themselves, everywhere and at all times express the constant interplay of *you/wu*.

The *Zhuangzi* does not challenge the *Daodejing*'s discourse of *you/wu*, but it did not rely on it for understanding the existence of things; for that, it developed a more materially based theory of *qi* involving *yin-yang*. It affirmed *qi*, not *you/wu*, as the primary stuff of the Dao, and attributed the differences between things to different *qi* concentrations: the *qi* of some things is predominantly clear and light (*yang*), while that of others is predominantly turbid and heavy (*yin*). This theory of *qi* had deep consequences for the *Zhuangzi*'s wider understanding of the transformation of things, which I will not go into here.

Ge Hong applied the *Zhuangzi*'s theory of *qi* as life for explaining death, but he harbored reservations about its value for explaining life, since it nullifies immortality as a viable existential possibility. Embracing the strict terms of this theory, the *Zhuangzi* only advocated for forgetting the body through *zuowang*, whose intended goals radically differed from the long-life of *yangsheng* or the immortality of alchemy. While this theory cohered nicely with Wang Bi's thought, it was anathema to Ge Hong's.

Herlee Creel[18] was among the first Western scholars who saw the "Daoist" thought of Ge Hong as contradictory to the "Daoist" thought of the *Zhuangzi*, while Chinese scholars explore their connections. Yuan Long, for example, writes:

> On one hand, Ge Hong fully advocated the *Zhuangzi*'s thought about "valuing life" concerning the survival of the body, but on the other hand he strongly rejected its theories about "the equalization of life and death," and he ultimately decided on the belief in the divine *xian* 仙 ... The *Zhuangzi* thought that, after the death of the person, there is no value in regretting the death of the fleshly body, because it is only one among the myriad beings, and the transformations of things can never cease ... Ge Hong attached great importance to the belief that the spirit depended on the existence of the body, and he believed that the continued existence of the flesh was extremely important for cultivating divine *xian*ship, so he adopted multiple methods to maintain the fleshly body.[19]

In the same vein, Li Songrong writes,

> *Daojia* ("Daoist philosophy") and *daojiao* ("Daoist religion") are both "Daoism," but the former is directed to the philosophical faction and the latter to the religious faction. Between *daojia* and *daojiao*, there are similarities and differences. *Daojia* pursues the realm of absolute happiness, *daojiao* pursues the results of immortality. One is directed to the conditions of life, the other is directed to the goals of religious practice. The *Zhuangzi* is a classic of Daoist doctrine, and its Dao encompasses the meanings of ontology. It takes the perspective of the Dao to observe death, and it solves the problem of the transcendence of death from the spiritual level. The *Baopuzi* is a classic of early *daojiao*, and although its Dao inherited the ontological characteristics of the *Zhuangzi*'s Dao, it connected the Dao to the divine *xian* of *daojiao*. Since becoming a *xian* became the mark of whether one has attained the Dao, how to become a *xian* comprises the core contents of the work.[20]

The relations between the thought of Ge Hong and the *Zhuangzi* are ripe for Western scholarly attention and this should prove beneficial for our understanding of Daoism, but the next section of this chapter turns to Ge Hong's own discourse on *you/wu*.

The Mystery

Ge Hong's discourse on *you/wu* emerges from the *Daodejing*'s discourse on *you/wu* and its corresponding conception of the pristine Dao. One aspect of its discourse was directed to the cosmogony pertaining to the origins of time, space, and cosmos, in which *you/wu* continuously "give birth to each other." Another aspect was directed to the cosmology pertaining to the continuous birth of all phenomenal existents, in which "the myriad beings are born from *you*, and *you* is born from *wu*." The *Daodejing*'s discourse on *you/wu* also recognized two independent modes of perception: a metaphysical *wu*-perspective and a physical *you*-perspective.

An additional feature of the *Daodejing*'s discourse on *you/wu* is its exploration of their functional interaction on an existential level, as represented by two different modes of behavior that it distinguishes in terms of "intentionality" 有為 and "non-intentionality" 無為, the latter exclusively pertaining to the behavior of the sage. This aspect of its discourse attends to other *wu*-type activities and behaviors, including "non-intentional desire" 無欲 and the carrying out of "non-intentional projects" 無事. All of this serves to underscore the fact that, for Ge Hong, the *Daodejing* never opposed *you/wu* but rather perceived them as equal partners in an eternally continuous state of mutual interplay, whereas Wang Bi consistently refers to *wu* as the self-subsistent root independently existing on its own with absolute priority over *you*.

Ge Hong's discourse on *you/wu* further developed the *Daodejing*'s by his injection of an innovative body of technical terminology. Much like the *Daodejing*, he conceives of the Dao in two ways: as the source from which all existents are born, and as the path leading to long-life and immortality consisting of the techniques of *yangsheng* and the methods of alchemy. Li Zongding writes:

> Although Ge Hong's theories were placed in the same relative position as Wang Bi's theories, his discussions of *you/wu* did not have the same ontological meaning of Wang Bi's *wu*, which gave *wu* a marked emphasis in the original production of the myriad beings, and this is evidenced in the methods that Ge Hong adopted in his theories about bodily cultivation.[21]

Ge Hong first applies this new terminology to the Dao in the cosmogonic *illud tempus*. As the continuous source from which all things and beings are born, he maintains that the body of the Dao consists only of *you/wu*, and this from eternity. From within this eternity (if indeed this wording has meaning), the origins of the cosmogony spontaneously set in motion, eventually generating temporality as Heaven and spatiality as Earth. Contained by *wu*, all that preceded the formation of Heaven and Earth was the primordial chaos of *you*, consisting of "images, entities, and vitalities." The *Daodejing* simply calls this primordial chaos *hun* 混, but Ge Hong calls it *hunmang* 渾茫. The *Daodejing* does not attach a name to these events, but Ge Hong calls it the "Great Beginning" 泰初.[22]

In the primordial *hunmang* of the body of the Dao, there was only *you/wu*. Relying on the cosmogonic sequence of *Daodejing* chapter 42, Ge Hong writes:

> When *hunmang* divided, the clear and the turbid were organized. Some of it ascended and became energized while some of it descended and became stabilized. Neither Heaven nor Earth knew how it was that they became thus. The myriad beings were touched by *qi*, and this too was so of itself.[23]

The cosmogonic "division" of *hunmang* does not refer to *you* and *wu*, because they never can be divided; instead, it refers to the division or distancing of the clearness of *you* from the turbidness of *you*, neither of which ceases to interact with and within *wu*. The rising clearness of *you* ascends to form Heaven and the falling turbidness of *you* descends to form Earth, but neither are things or beings as such: the "energized" 動 *you* of Heaven manifests as time, and the "stabilized" 靜 *you* of Earth manifests as space, thus providing the temporalized and spatialized dimensions of the world within which all existents come to birth. The passage continues:

> Every single thing and being together with Heaven and Earth constitute a single body.
> However, some were formed earlier and others later.
> The bodies of some are enormous while the bodies of others are miniscule.
> The immensity of Heaven and Earth is felt by the smallness of the myriad beings.
> The smallness of the myriad beings is felt by the immensity of Heaven and Earth.[24]

These lines establish the existence of phenomenally distinct realms, each emerging in a sequence of worldly unfolding. They include the antecedent realm of Heaven and Earth and the subsequent realm of existents, but these are in addition to the even prior realm of the eternity of *you/wu*, which never ceases to exist over and beyond time and space. Because the body of the Dao contains all this, and all that comes into existence is born from this body, receiving its essence as the offspring receives the essence of the mother, all realms "constitute a single body" 各為一物.

The realm of Heaven and Earth is phenomenally distinct and provides the time and space within which all existents come to be; Ge Hong underscores this with his use of the temporal markers "earlier and later" 先後 with reference to Heaven, and the spatial markers "enormous and miniscule" 巨細 with reference to Earth. Next to phenomenal distinctions between time and space and individual existents, there is no separation of *you/wu*, transcendent or otherwise (again in stark contrast to Wang Bi); *you/wu* continue to mutually interact, driving on the continuous coming forth of existents that are themselves constituted by *you/wu*. How can this be understood? Ge Hong writes:

> The Dao contains Heaven and encloses Earth, its root is without name.
> From the perspective of *wu*, then even shadows and echoes are replete with *you*.
> From the perspective of *you*, then even the myriad beings are replete with *wu*.[25]

This is an essential passage in Ge Hong's discourse on *you/wu*, and it demonstrates the *wu-* and *you*-perspectives first established in *Daodejing* chapter 1: "Hold to the standpoint of *wu* with the intent to witness its subtleties. Hold to the standpoint of *you* with the intent to witness its manifestations." Ge Hong alters the initial verbs of each line from *chang* 常, meaning "to frequent, to hold to" to *lun* 論, which has a complex set of meanings including verbally "to discuss" and nominally "view, theory, measure," but he uses the term prepositionally in another of its meanings as "by, in terms of."

Ge Hong is aligning without collapsing into each other the *Daodejing*'s *wu-* and *you*-perspectives. Doing so, he offers an organic view of existence by which the *wu*-perspective, in addition to the *Daodejing*'s "subtleties" 妙, also reveals *you*, even in the most translucent of existents including "shadows and echoes" 影響, and the *you*-perspective, in addition to the *Daodejing*'s "manifestations" 徼, also reveals *wu*, even in the most opaque of existents including "the myriad beings" 萬物.

With reference to *you/wu*, *Daodejing* chapter 1 continues: "These two emerge together," in apparent affirmation of the continuous co-presence of *you/wu* "emerging together" 同出. But from what do they emerge? The answer requires recourse to Ge Hong's understanding of the One 一.

Daodejing chapter 42 uses the One to designate the first offspring of the Dao, which then gave birth to the Two, where it serves as a kind of place-marker within the cosmogonic sequence. It is rhetorically different from other uses in the text where it refers to a specific thing or content in some way identified or associated with the Dao. The foundational discussion of the One is in *Daodejing* chapter 14, which *Daodejing* chapter 39 applies to the cosmology, while *Daodejing* chapters 10 and 22 remark on the sage's ability to hold onto it. *Daodejing* chapter 14 states:

> Looked at but not seen, it is called invisible.
> Listened for but not heard, it is called inaudible.
> Touched but not felt, it is called intangible.
> These three cannot be exhaustively analyzed.
> They merge together as the One.

Here are a set of qualities that lie beyond sensory perception and that are "merged together as the One" 混而為一 characterizing some specific unnamed thing or content. We might say that this is the Dao, but Ge Hong does not agree (nor does Wang Bi, whose commentary leaves these lines deliberately ambiguous). Whatever it is being referred to as the One, it is situated in the cosmogonic *illud tempus* depicted in *Daodejing* chapters 21 and 25. With attribution to Laozi, here referred to by his religious name Lord Lao 老君, Ge Hong writes:

> Lord Lao said: It is vague and diffuse, but inside there are images.
> It is diffuse and vague, but inside there are entities.
> This is called the One.[26]

Ge Hong even here does not specify a referent for the One, but it has two sets of content. The first set is worldly: that which is "invisible, intangible, and inaudible" within the realm of phenomenally existing things, and the second is cosmogonic: "images and entities" within the primordial *hunmang*. But he keeps his attention on the worldly content, because this is the same One involved with long-life and immortality.

The primordial body of the Dao, the Mother gestating *you/wu*, is not the One, but they share a particular relationship that Ge Hong clarifies: "The Dao springs from the One. Its value is without equal."[27] This seems counterintuitive, since the *Daodejing* seems to have described the Dao as that which pre-exists everything: is not the Dao the original existent from which all things are born? And yet Ge Hong unmistakably states that the Dao "springs" 起 from the One, thereby giving it cosmogonic priority. Ge Hong's phenomenological primacy of the One over the Dao could not be more contrastive with Heshang Gong's metaphysical primacy of the Dao over the One. A rich passage from *Daodejing* chapter 25 provides charter for Ge Hong's claim:

> Humans are modeled on Earth.
> Earth is modeled on Heaven.

Heaven is modeled on the Dao.
The Dao is modeled on *ziran*.

This reverse sequence leads from the world of phenomenal existence back to the Dao of the beginnings, but what is found at the very beginnings is not indeed the Dao, but *ziran* 自然 ("what is so of itself"). The key verb here is "to model" 法, which Wang Bi reads to refer to imitative behavior, where the ruler imitates one component of the activity of Earth, Earth does the same with respect to Heaven, and so on. Ge Hong reads "to model" in a much more active, even creative sense that verges on the meaning of "to give birth to" 生, such that what is modeled can be taken as a smaller-scale version of that which does the modeling. Thus, humans are smaller than and modeled on Earth; Earth is smaller than and modeled on Heaven; Heaven is smaller than and modeled on the Dao, as it is contained in the body of the Dao; and the Dao is smaller than and modeled on *ziran*, in an ultimate sense of infinity and eternity.

The Dao is not the ultimate source, because it is "modeled on," or follows from, *ziran*. But *ziran* is as much an activity as a state, while at the same time it is neither activity nor state. Yet even this is not what Ge Hong takes as the One; one must regress even further, before even *ziran* and Dao, to find what he calls Mystery 玄. This is Ge Hong's ultimate notion in his discourse on *you/wu*, so central to his project that it stands as the first word of the *Baopuzi Neipian*. The passage states:

> Mystery is the original ancestor of *ziran*, the ultimate progeniture of multitudinous diversity.
> Its minuteness and depth so profound, it can be called the subtle.
> Its capaciousness and distance so remote, it can be called the marvelous.[28]

This Mystery is the "original ancestor" 始祖 and the "ultimate progeniture" 大宗, marking the supreme source from which even *ziran* was produced, this same *ziran* upon which the Dao is modeled. Li Zongding writes:

> Ge Hong gives the Dao an extremely important position. The Dao, from which nothing does not come, is the original principle and the original standard that the myriad beings follow, and this is similar to Wang Bi's "There is no thing not based on it." However, Ge Hong understood Mystery as the original source and the ontological body from which the cosmos emerged. Wang Bi only described the character and function of the Dao by "mysterious," and he emphasized the deep meaning of "mysterious" to explain the Dao. Ge Hong elevated Mystery to the same level as the Dao, using different language for the same object. Like

this, Ge Hong's interpretation of Mystery has the same intention of religious Daoism, and the relationship between Mystery and Dao is that they produce change, and they are even combined in the phrase "Mystery-Dao" as the key to access immortality.[29]

Ge Hong's notion of "Mystery-Dao" will be introduced soon, but it is first necessary to understand how he resolves on Mystery as the supreme ultimate, and this leads back to *Daodejing* chapter 1:

> These two emerge together but have different names.
> Together they are called Mystery.
> The Mystery beyond mysteries, it is the gateway of the many and the subtle.

Ge Hong has already identified "these two" 此兩者 as *you/wu*, where the question concerning from what do *you/wu* emerge was left unanswered. This inquiry requires a brief examination of *tong* 同, which often means "the same" but is used here to mean "together," referring to the simultaneous "emergence" 出 of *you/wu*. For *tong* to mean "the same" would mean that *you/wu* share the same identify or essence, which would collapse *wu* and *you* into each other, which would, logically as well as by fiat, require that *wu* has ontological priority over *you*; but this is unacceptable to Ge Hong.

With this, Ge Hong reveals his identification of that to which the One refers: the eternal "togetherness" of *you/wu* that remains continuously functional on every level: the cosmogonic level in which *you/wu* mutually interact within the *hunmang* body of the Dao; the cosmological level in which *you/wu* mutually interact in the generation and perdurance of all existents; and also on the level of infinity and eternity in which *you/wu* mutually interact prior even to the first inceptions of the cosmogony (and, we can imagine, even after the cosmology will have come to a close). On each level, *you/wu* are co-primordial, co-existent, co-present, and coterminous, and it is precisely this eternal togetherness of *you/wu* that is designated by the One. Over and beyond the One, there is also Mystery, a designation that refers as the adjectival nominalization of the infinite and eternal togetherness of *you/wu*. This is far removed from Wang Bi's discourse on *you/wu*.

On this point, Li Zongding writes:

> Laozi used the phrase, "together they are called Mystery," to explain that *wu* and *you* together emerge from the Dao, although they have different names. Therefore, the Dao is able to give birth to *wu* and *you* simultaneously, and this is a subtle and deep theory. *Daodejing* chapter 21 depicts the Dao's pregnant condition, within it there are images and things, and this is the Mystery-Dao.[30]

The *Daodejing* conceives the togetherness of *you/wu* not from the perspective of eternity, but from the perspective of this very world, in terms of their interactions that brought about existence as we know it, expressed as emergence through a "gateway" 門 or "gateways," as the original Chinese does not distinguish the singular from the plural. Thus, *you/wu* emerge from a gateway, but it seems that there are two separate ones: from eternity to cosmogony, and another from cosmogony to cosmology.[31]

In sum, the One names the eternal togetherness of *you/wu*, and Mystery is the designation for their actively creative state of mutual interaction on every level. The Dao as the cosmic body entirely contains the interactive processes of transformation caused by *you/wu*, specifically in terms of the cosmogonic sequence of *Daodejing* chapter 42. Ge Hong starkly depicts Mystery's inception of the cosmogonic sequence:

> Mystery enwombed the Original One.
> It patterned and molded the Two Principles.
> It inspired the Great Beginning.
> It forged the multitudinous species.
> It initiated the cycle of the twenty-eight constellations.
> It fashioned primordial profusion.[32]

Next to *Daodejing* chapter 39's depictions of One in action, which show it establishing the world (Heaven, Earth, spirits, valleys, and the myriad beings) in terms of their "getting the One" 得一, Ge Hong provides other depictions of the One in action:

> The One is able to form *yin* and beget *yang*.
> It brings the cold and the heat.
> Spring gets the One and things sprout.
> Summer gets the One and things mature.
> Autumn gets the One and things are harvested.
> Winter gets the One and things are stored.[33]

Describing the continuous activities of the mutual interactions of *you/wu* within the phenomenal world, Ge Hong closes this passage by affirming that all this squarely remains within the specific parameters of his discourse of *you/wu*; he writes:

> Effecting the million kinds, it is *you*. Lodged in the obscure and silent, it is *wu*.[34]

Phenomenology of Form and Spirit

Ge Hong sees the interactions of *you/wu* in the makeup of all existents within the phenomenal world. Among them are included human beings, and with human beings there arises social existence, and social existence brings in its wake desire, greed, and selfishness. Falling victim to their individual desires by acting on their bias for themselves, humans assert their separate individuation apart from the One, inevitably leading them to value one side over the other: themselves over others, their bodies over their spirits, and their *you* over their *wu*, eventuating in their *wu* once and for all separating from their *you*, resulting in death. Ge Hong's understanding of the ways in which humans in social existence destroy their innate unity with the One derives from the *Daodejing*'s diagnosis of the sickness of human beings mired in social existence, once they have become separated from the Dao. While Ge Hong accepts the *Daodejing*'s diagnosis of this sickness, he analyzes it in slightly different terms.

For Ge Hong, as well as for Daoist discourse more generally, the Dao is the source of life, and either the process or the agent of change and transformation. *Daodejing* chapter 42 spoke of it in terms of the birth of the One to the Two to the Three to the ten thousand. But what form does transformation take in the existence of human beings? This exploration leads to one of the more stunning innovations in Ge Hong's phenomenology of form and spirit: in human beings, primordial *wu* transforms and manifests as spirit 神, and primordial *you* transforms and manifests as body or form 形.

These identifications reveal Ge Hong's discourse on *you/wu* and the theoretical foundation for immortality, and it is odd that they have received scant attention in Western scholarship. Li Zongding says that, while the "form-spirit" issue was long-standing in early Chinese philosophy, it was primarily Ge Hong who transformed it from a "dualism" 二元論 to a "monism" 一元論,[35] and this shows how some Chinese scholars, led by the eminent Hu Fuchen,[36] have closely attended to these identifications. For example, Zhu Zhanyan writes:

> Under the influence of Wei-Jin Xuanxue, Ge Hong used *you/wu* to explain the relationship between "form" and "spirit." What he called "form" referred to the human body-shape, and what he called "spirit" referred to spiritual awareness ... From a functional point of view, "shape" and "spirit" are the two sides of a single structure of existence, and both are indispensable. Between them, "shape" is the material carrier of human life, and "spirit" is the controlling master of human life. "Shape" and "spirit" are mutually independent and harmonious. They

manifest as actual living life, but when they become separated, it means that the original life ruptures and ceases to exist.³⁷

These scholars open paths into the Ge Hong's phenomenology of form and spirit, which can be said to start from his explanation of the birth of human beings: "Humans get the One and are born 人得一以生,"³⁸ where the One comprises *you/wu* in their transformed state of body and spirit. Reflecting the *Daodejing*'s statement that "The myriad beings are born from *you*, and *you* is born from *wu*," Ge Hong writes:

> *You* follows *wu* and is born.
> Form requires spirit and stands.
> *You* is the palace of *wu*.
> Form is the abode of spirit.³⁹

To exist as a human is to "get the One," signifying the togetherness of *you/wu* in their transformed state of body and spirit that relates human being to Mystery. Ge Hong characterizes the togetherness of body and spirit with the verb "to stand" 立 partly because it parallels *Daodejing* chapter 25: "There is a thing born in chaos before Heaven and Earth. Empty and still, it stands on its own." As the body of the Dao "stands" in the cosmogony, so do the bodies of human beings "stand" in the cosmology.

Human beings, born last in the cosmogonic sequence together with all other things and beings, manifest the purity of the eternal and primordial togetherness of *you/wu* in their natal reception of the One. However, they remain several steps removed from the Mystery; because of this, their individual manifestation of the togetherness of body-spirit is tenuous and liable to ruination. When that togetherness splits, it is due to the human bias of preferring either body over spirit or spirit over body. The former bias is an inevitable consequence of life in society, given the inherent pressures and seductions of pleasure, power, and profit, and Ge Hong expends much energy advocating for mountain reclusion. At the same time, he also recognizes the dangers of the latter bias, and he exhorts Daoists to commit to *yangsheng* bodily cultivation to preserve their body, a necessary requirement for long-life, but also alchemy for the highest-level disciples, a necessary requirement for immortality. For example, he writes:

> The Dao of humans is precisely to eat exquisite foods, to wear light and warm clothing, to indulge in sex, to enjoy high rank, to maintain keen hearing and

sharp sight, to keep the bones and physique strong and powerful, to have an attractive and pleasant complexion, [but] to abandon one's wife and children, to live alone in the mountains and marshes, to live detached and transgress human reason, like a clod having no other neighbors than trees and rocks, is also not to be encouraged.[40]

Ge Hong's discourse on *you/wu* now turns to death. He begins with Zhuangzi's theory of *qi* as life, which also holds that the body contains the spirit but that further holds that when the body exhausts due to the failings of *qi*, then the spirit simply disperses, leaving the body to decay; this does not affect the *qi*, which continues to exist in different forms. And although Ge Hong's "Daoist" thought is often seen as contradictory to the Zhuangzi's "Daoist" thought, his adoption of Zhuangzi's theory of *qi* as life to explain death is a counterargument against that view, as explained by Yuan Long:

> Zhuangzi thought that the life-vitality of all beings is attached to the body, and that the body depends on *qi* to be born, but *qi* is not an ultimate existent, it was produced "amidst the chaos" and was born from the Dao. Therefore, in Zhuangzi's philosophical thought, the Dao has ultimate reality, it indeed is ultimate reality, and *qi* has no meaning in terms of an ultimate body. Ge Hong inherited Zhuangzi's philosophical notion of the Dao as the one thing-in-itself of the entire cosmos, and he greatly enriched and developed the philosophical content of Zhuangzi's notion of *qi* in order to resolve the ways that Daoism engaged the core issues of life and death.[41]

Ge Hong's adoption of Zhuangzi's theory of *qi* does not mean that he resigns himself to the inevitably of death, only its inevitability for those humans unable to maintain the One. Death results from the exhaustion of *qi*, the consequence of the bias for the body over spirit or the spirit over body. Ge Hong says that the few and far between capable of maintaining the One, the unity of body/spirit, will achieve long-life and even immortality:

> Human beings live in the breast of *qi*, and *qi* is in the breast of humans. From Heaven and Earth to the myriad beings, there is nothing that does not depend on *qi* for life. Those who master the circulation of *qi* internally use it to nurture their bodies, and externally use it to banish evils. Common people, however, daily use their *qi* without understanding this.[42]

About the relation of Mystery to body-spirit, Ge Hong writes:

> When Mystery is present, joy is inexhaustible.
> When Mystery departs, the body decays and the spirit dies.[43]

He also writes:

> The Mystery-Dao is attained internally but lost externally.
> The spirit makes use of it, but the body forgets it.
> These are the essential precepts of the meditation of the Mystery-Dao.[44]

About Ge Hong's uses of the phrase "Mystery-Dao," Li Zongding says:

> The change from Mystery to Mystery-Dao marks an important transition from philosophy to religion, and Ge Hong often combines Mystery with other words, as for example in Mystery-Dao, Mystery-One, and other new words. On the one hand, he used the ethereal and profound meaning of Mystery to explain the wondrous Dao and the wondrous One; on the other hand, he also used Mystery-One to refer to the methods of cultivating immortality.[45]

Ge Hong next offers a series of images that illustrate the original unity and succeeding ruination of the togetherness of the body and spirit:

> To compare it to a dike: when the dike crumbles, the waters cannot be retained. To compare it to a candle: when the candle melts, the flame no longer exists. When the body is exhausted, the spirit disperses; when the *qi* is worn out, life ends. When the root is worn out yet the branches are abundant, the green leaves the tree. When *qi* is weary but desires are dominant, the pure soul departs from the body. For one who has passed, there is no time of return, and the decrepit is devoid of the principle of life. One who comprehends the Dao is deeply affected by this.[46]

Next to the *Daodejing*'s discussions of death as the exhaustion of the body, there are others that discuss long-life in terms of the preservation of the body, much like in Ge Hong's writings. However, when the *Daodejing* mentions the spirit, it is usually in a *yangsheng* context, as seen in *Daodejing* chapter 10, which mentions the "bright spirit" 營魄: "In keeping the bright spirit and embracing the One—can you do it without letting them leave?" and *Daodejing* chapter 22, which states: "The sage embraces the One and is the model for the world." Both passages show the *yangsheng* technique of "holding the One" 抱一 intended to maintain the togetherness of spirit and body resulting in long-life.

Ge Hong did not write in a vacuum, and there was a long history of philosophical debate concerning the relation between form and spirit beginning in the Warring States. Li Zongding (2012) shows that the early thinkers considered four basic positions: neither the body nor the spirit continues to exist after death; the spirit continues but the body perishes; the body continues but the spirit perishes; and the body and spirit exist together without death. Ge Hong maintained the fourth position for those capable of fusing spirit and body either for a period counted in centuries by way of *yangsheng* or for the immortality of alchemy. This refers, of course, to the *xian* 仙 who have locked the body into its eternal *you* source and the spirit into its eternal *wu* source. Li continues,

> Is that which is eternal without dying the form or the spirit, or the form permanently together with the spirit? Ge Hong's discussion of the relationship between form and spirit reflects the Daoist view of the divine *xian* at that time, and the discussion of the relationship between shape and spirit throughout the Six Dynasties was an important topic of debate. Ge Hong also used the metaphysical theories of *you/wu* and "branch and root," but his ideas were not identical with mainstream Xuanxue, because he brought forth the unique views of Daoist immortality theory … Ge Hong's discussions of the interdependence of form and spirit on the surface appears to give equal importance to both shape and spirit, but in actual practice he gave a special emphasis to bodily cultivation and the corresponding theories of alchemical elixirs, because they could change the physical properties of the body so that it would never die.[47]

These final passages bring Ge Hong's discourse on *you/wu* to conclusion:

> If they [body and spirit] are stored there is life, if not there is death.[48]

> Only the Mystery-Dao can confer permanence.[49]

> According to the *xian*-scriptures, those highest disciples who carry their bodies as they ascend into Heaven are called heavenly *xian*. Those middling disciples who roam in the famous mountains are called earthly *xian*.[50]

> The *xian* either ascend to Heaven or reside on Earth, but what is essential is that they have achieved long-life. As for where they go or stay, each chooses according to their own aspirations. … Those in the past who became *xian* would sometimes grow wings out of their bodies and, transforming, fly away. They had displaced the roots of what made them human and they acquired a new form, like the sparrow that transforms into a clam or the pheasant that transforms into an oyster.[51]

Planted at the historical crossroads between what has been called Daoist philosophy and Daoist religion, Ge Hong remains an enduring icon. His major contribution to Daoism as well as to Chinese culture more generally is largely due to his discourse on *you/wu* and its articulation of a systematic and theoretical foundation for long-life and immortality. That discourse together with the practices it seeks to justify reveals Ge Hong's Daoist sensibilities that inform his Yangsheng Daoist reading of the *Daodejing*.

Ge Hong's phenomenology of the pristine Dao represents his effort to strike out its Huang-Lao metaphysicalization into the cosmic Dao embraced by Yan Zun, Heshang Gong, and Wang Bi. Doing so allows him to undo the Huang-Lao reconfiguration of the matrix of the *Daodejing*. This chapter has examined his accomplishment with respect to the nameable component of the matrix, and the next chapter examines how he accomplished the same feat with respect to the unnameable component of the matrix.

8

Ge Hong and Yangsheng Daoism

Ge Hong and *Xian* Biography

In the "Bielu" 別錄 by Liu Xiang 劉襄 (77–6 BCE) that was enlarged and updated by his son Liu Xing who renamed it "Qilü" 七略 (Seven Summaries) before it was incorporated by Ban Gu into the "Yiwenzhi" in the *Hanshu*, Liu Xiang explained the origins of ten early Chinese philosophical schools. For the most part, his argument states that during the course of the early Zhou Dynasty education was the province of officials who ran the various government departments. When the Zhou lost its authority, these departments dispersed, and their former ministers began to teach and expand on the specialized content that once fell under their official purviews, thus resulting in the separate formations of ten schools of philosophers. Liu Xiang explained that in this way Daoism finds its origins with the official historians. Two thousand years later, Fung Yu-lan wrote that Liu Xiang was correct in his approach to the origins of these philosophical groups but mistaken in the details, and he then provides his own explanation for one of them: "Members of the Daoist school had their origin in the hermits."[1]

One must read further into Fung's work to understand his meaning, where his discussion of Daoism draws attention to Yang Zhu 杨朱 (440–360 BCE), a thinker famous for his idea that "if by pulling out a single hair from his own body he could have benefited the entire world, he would not have done it."[2] This leads Fung to claim that the Yangists (referring to Yang Zhu's school) were concerned above all with their own purity, and that "they were defeatists who thought that the world was so bad that nothing could be done for it."[3] Rejecting the world to live in seclusion, they "attempted to work out a system of thought that would give meaning to their action"[4] that Laozi and Zhuangzi would soon develop into Daoist philosophy.

Few thinkers, ancient or modern, have concurred with Fung's basic argument that Daoism originated with hermits, but Ge Hong is counted among them.

But he would say that Fung too was mistaken in the details, because Ge Hong identifies the origins of Daoism with Laozi and not Yang Zhu, and he associates it with a physical practice just as much as with a "system of thought."

For Ge Hong, a true Daoist is one who has achieved long-life by having mastered the *yangsheng* techniques transmitted from masters to disciples that go back to Laozi. He recognized many of these Daoists from their biographies in the *Liexian zhuan*, where they are indiscriminately mixed with other, not necessarily Daoist figures, all of whom are collectively called *xian* 仙. He furthermore gathered the biographies of many more in his *Shenxian zhuan*. I do not directly engage the formidable questions of date and authorship that surround the *Liexian zhuan* and the complexities of reconstructing the original collection of biographies in the *Shenxian zhuan*; for the present purposes it is enough to say that Ge Hong knew the *Liexian zhuan*, he compiled the *Shenxian zhuan*, and he composed the *Baopuzi Neipian* in which he provided a theoretical foundation for the attainments of the *xian*, as explored in the last chapter.[5]

This current chapter explores the continuity of Yangsheng Daoist biographies based on their textually demonstrable lines of *yangsheng* transmission that differentiate them from all other *xian* biographies recorded in these two works, in which the *xian* are used as representatives of reclusive Yangsheng Daoism. The *Liexian zhuan* is the single contemporary text that presents Han period biographies of Yangsheng Daoists, and the *Shenxian zhuan* provides Jin Dynasty support with its own. Each of these works clarifies the main features of Yangsheng Daoism to which Ge Hong self-identified.

The biographies of the *Liexian zhuan* and the *Shenxian zhuan* are not the creative works of an imaginative storyteller but rather are compilations of circulating stories about previously known figures. The standard version of the *Liexian zhuan* contains 70 biographies, the *Siku Quanshu* version of the *Shenxian zhuan* has 84, and the *Longwei Mishu* version has 92, each ordered in rough chronological sequence.

In the Chinese tradition, "biography" 傳 is a recognized literary genre for which those of the *Shiji* are taken as the model.[6] Writings sometimes called "reclusion biography" or "eremitic literature" 隱士傳 comprise a subgenre for which Huangfu Mi's *Gaoshi zhuan* 高士傳[7] is a model that typically encompasses figures, commonly represented as Confucian, Huang-Lao, or Xuanxue, who either held official position or were closely associated with officialdom before moving into reclusion. Finally, "*xian* biography" 仙傳 itself is also often considered as a subgenre that follows basic structures of the standard biography genre but with its own individual features.

Standard biographies target figures deemed more or less historical, but *xian* biographies have a wider range of potential subjects; Yao Shengliang writes,

> The biographies of the divine *xian* are different from the "authentic records" 实录 of the official histories [e.g. the *Shiji* biographies]. Many of their figures as well as their deeds are mostly from myths, fables, and fictions ... The *Liexian zhuan* and the *Shenxian zhuan* combined a historical style with the techniques of allegory and created the basic narrative mode of the early Daoist *xian* biographies.[8]

The typical structure of the *Shiji*'s model biographies is in three parts: origins of a famous person, his famous deeds, and his end,[9] and Zhang Yulian writes, "The *Liexian zhuan* is based on a chronological arrangement from the earliest to the latest biographies. The narrative structure of a specific biography is generally composed of three parts: the origins, deeds and final whereabouts of the *xian*."[10] Chen Hong echoes these ideas:

> Roughly speaking, for the purpose of promoting Daoism, the vast majority of the seventy stories of the *Liexian zhuan* have a deep narrative pattern that can be summarized in two major parts: someone becomes a *xian* by way of some method or technique, followed by the efficacious deeds of that *xian*. Corresponding to this pattern, we can see the surface stories of countless narratives.[11]

The discrepancy between Zhang's and Chen's comments concerns the final part of the *xian* biography structure. This is to be expected since it marks the major difference between the *Shiji*'s biography model and that of the *xian*, who are so designated because they are never shown to die. Yao Shengliang writes:

> The records of the *Shiji* pertain to real historical figures, and their end comes with their death; this so-called "not passing judgment until the coffin is closed" conclusion naturally marks the end of that figure's biography. The *Liexian zhuan* and the *Shenxian zhuan* were intended to imitate the style of the *Shiji*, and they also establish an ending for each biography, however, the *xian* are different from mortals and the end of their worldly experience is the beginning of their life in the realm of the *xian*. Because of this, unlike the biographies of the *Shiji*, the outcomes of the *Liexian zhuan* and the *Shenxian zhuan* demonstrate a uniquely open-ended continuation.[12]

In almost every case in the *Liexian zhuan* and *Shenxian zhuan*, the *xian* are either shown or are said to have disappeared into the mountains, where they lived for many additional centuries, or they ascend to a *xian* realm, a type of Daoist fairyland. The *xian* biographies primarily differ from standard biographies in that the *xian* have little attestation in the official histories, and they also do not die.

The original composition of the *Liexian zhuan* is covered in darkness and it is unlikely that its original date and author will be settled, even though the tradition credits Liu Xiang with its authorship. Chen Hong provides a useful introduction:

> People from traditional to modern times have disputed the authorship of the *Liexian zhuan* as well as when it actually became a book. Most modern Chinese studies of Daoist history either have accepted the hypothesis that Liu Xiang compiled it in the late Western Han Dynasty, or they have just avoided the issue. Therefore, discussions of the significance of the *Liexian zhuan* in the history of Daoism are often caught in a dilemma: if the work is a study guide to Daoist religion, then there is a contradiction between Liu Xiang's editing of the book and the period of the official formation of Daoist religion [in the second century AD]. If we say that the work is only a product of Fangxian Daoism and other influences since the Warring States and the Qin and Han dynasties, then this is to turn a blind eye to the vividly depicted methods and arts of the Daoist religion. Therefore, we have to say in general that the *Liexian zhuan* proclaims the idea that there are divine *xian* in every generation and in every place, that there are people everywhere who can become *xian*, and that there are many methods to becoming a *xian*. If not, then the records of the *Liexian zhuan* simply placed some Daoist ideas as well as some methods and arts, particularly those involving alchemy, that were only produced in the middle and late Eastern Han Dynasty into the Western Han Dynasty.[13]

On the other hand, the dates and authorship of the *Shenxian zhuan* and *Neipian* are not problematic; Keith Knapp writes,

> In 314, [Ge Hong] returned to his native place of Jurong ... It was during this long period of reclusion that he wrote his two-part magnum opus whose title bore his sobriquet: the *Inner Chapters of the Master Who Embraces Simplicity* [*Baopuzi Neipian*] and the *Outer Chapters of the Master Who Embraces Simplicity* ... Also at this time, illustrative of his aspirations, he compiled *Biographies of Divine Transcendents* [*Shenxian zhuan*].[14]

There is a close relationship between the *xian* biographies of the *Liexian zhuan* and the *Shenxian zhuan*. The former stands as the first Chinese collection of *xian* biographies, for which the latter can be taken as an updated and expanded sequel. Yao Shengliang writes, "Compared to the *Liexian zhuan*, the ways and methods of the *xian* contained in the *Shenxian zhuan* are more diversified, and the reason is because after the rise of the Daoist religion, the concept of *xian* experienced a renewed development."[15]

In putting together the *Shenxian zhuan*, Ge Hong avoided *xian* who had already received biographies in the *Liexian zhuan*, but figures like Laozi were too important to disregard. Chen Hong writes, "Although almost all the divine *xian* written about in the *Shenxian zhuan* do not appear in the *xian* biographies in the *Liexian zhuan*, it is indisputable that it was directly inspired by the style and intent of the *Liexian zhuan*."[16]

Scholars normally consider both works as literary fiction and not as historical records of Daoism. This reflects the traditional status of the *Daodejing* and the *Zhuangzi*, which were as often treated as literary fiction as works of philosophy. Exploring the *Zhuangzi*'s influence on *xian* biography, Yao Shengliang writes:

> Zhuangzi exerted his fanciful literary, imaginary, fictional, and exaggerated aesthetic qualities to an unimaginable height, and this had a profound effect on later generations of stories, especially on "the tales of the strange" 志怪小说. The *Liexian zhuan* and the *Shenxian zhuan* can also be counted among the earliest "tales of the strange," since they directly absorb and draw on the creative tactics of *Zhuangzi*'s fables.[17]

Chinese scholars are more and more looking into these two works as valid historical materials for the study of Daoism. This was also the manner in which Ge Hong approached *xian* biography, and I follow his lead in this. On this point, Chen Hong writes, "The *Liexian zhuan* was originally compiled to serve as a Daoist teaching manual. Therefore, it does not have the vivid and colorful imagery of ordinary folk tales,"[18] to which Yao Shengliang adds, "The *Liexian zhuan* and the *Shenxian zhuan* are Daoist *xian* biographies and they naturally serve a religious purpose: to promote the ideas of 'the true existence of the *xian*' (神仙实有) and 'the study of becoming a *xian*' (学以致仙)."[19]

Exploring the tradition of Yangsheng Daoism from Ge Hong's perspective means to prioritize the *Daodejing*, *Liexian zhuan*, *Shenxian zhuan*, and *Neipian* as foundational textual sources for it. Since the primary marks of the *xian* are that they have achieved long-life and are not seen to die, then this may or may not be sufficient reason for us to recognize them as Daoist, but it was sufficient for Ge Hong, who refers to "those who cultivate the Dao" 為道者 (*wei dao zhe*), a phrase used ten times in the *Neipian* to refer to persons we would normally call Daoists, as well as *daozhe* 道者, *daoshi* 道士, and *daojia* 道家, each of which is judiciously sprinkled throughout the *Shenxian zhuan* and the *Neipian* to refer to Daoists and Daoism.

Ge Hong used no other terms to name this tradition, but what he describes and portrays fits Yangsheng Daoism, even though only a small number of *xian* who receive biographies can be reckoned as such. Inclusion into the group requires demonstration of commitment to Ge Hong's nexus of Yangsheng Daoism, which consists of entrance into a network of master–disciple relations; deliberate practice of *yangsheng*; and mountain reclusion. Ge Hong's nexus of Yangsheng Daoism actually serves well as corresponding to the unnameable component of the matrix of the *Daodejing*.

Ge Hong's conception of Yangsheng Daoism stands in contrast to many modern conceptions of Daoism: Ge Hong's attribution of the *Daodejing* to Laozi contrasts with the view that Laozi had nothing to do with it; Ge Hong's assertion that *yangsheng* is the core of the *Daodejing* contrasts with the view that rulership is the core; and Ge Hong's affirmation of a Daoist tradition of mountainous reclusion contrasts with the view that Daoist mountain reclusion only began in the fifth century CE.[20] Since few scholars challenge these tenets, there has been little interest in Ge Hong's conception of Yangsheng Daoism and it is normally dismissed.

Scholars such as Robert Campany approach the *Shenxian zhuan* from Ge Hong's contemporary position in the Jin Dynasty, but this approach too easily sabotages the historical continuity of Daoist *yangsheng* transmission that anchors Ge Hong's conception of Yangsheng Daoism. Against this tendency, Zhang Yulian writes, "The origins of the *xian* in the *Liexian zhuan* are relatively complex, and they include mythological and legendary figures, historical figures, characters that may be actual but unexplored, and persons of unknown origin,"[21] and Chen Hong adds: "The *Liexian zhuan* consciously or unconsciously preserved and revealed the Daoism of the Eastern Han as well as the Fangxian Daoism and the Huang-Lao Daoism of the Warring States and Qin and Han Dynasties."[22]

Instead of analyzing the *xian* of the *Shenxian zhuan* as contemporary representations revealing Jin Dynasty sensibilities, it is more reasonable to see Ge Hong's own historical consciousness of the *xian* of the *Liexian zhuan* directing his choices of which other *xian* to include in his *Shenxian zhuan*. The *xian* of the *Liexian zhuan* taken altogether were representative of a wide range of Daoist notions and practices that long predated the Jin and provided Ge Hong much leeway to configure the *Shenxian zhuan* in demonstration of Yangsheng Daoism. Sun Yiping indicates as much: "Ge Hong's ideas about the study of *xian* were inherited from the traditions of Warring States Fangxian Daoism and the Han Dynasty *fangshi* study of *xian*."[23]

Campany in other ways recognizes the influence of the *Liexian zhuan* on *Shenxian zhuan* and writes that it loomed in Ge Hong's mind as the outstanding example of its genre to date; he mentions it repeatedly, refers to it in his preface in ways that match well with extant versions, and, at the end of his preface, seems to boast of having written a better hagiography. With rare and unavoidable exceptions, such as Laozi and Peng Zu, Ge Hong in [the *Shenxian zhuan*] does not cover the same figures as those included in [the *Liexian zhuan*] but instead covers ancient figures omitted from that work and more recent figures who were active since its time.[24]

In fact, Ge Hong's preface to the *Shenxian zhuan* more clearly specifies its relationship to the *Liexian zhuan* (even as it recognizes Liu Xiang's authorship of it):

> [Ge] Hong's [*Baopuzi*] *Neipian* discusses the affairs of the divine *xian* in 20 *juan*. The disciple Teng Sheng asked, "You, sir, have said that we can study how the divine *xian* achieved deathlessness. Who among the ancients are those who became *xian*?"
>
> Response: "In the past, the senior Qin official Ruan Cang recorded several hundred. Liu Xiang wrote about 71 of them. Of those *xian* who are hidden in the world, we learn about not more than one in a thousand. [There follows a very brief inventory of more than two dozen *xian*.] Now I too have transcribed and collected biographies about past *xian* that are found in the *xian* scriptures and esoteric recipes on dietetics, as well as in the documents of the hundred families; others that my former master recounted to me; and still others that are discussed by the learned scholars.[25] I have arranged them into ten *juan* to be passed down to scholars who recognize the true and discern the distant. Their disciples who are tied to the mundane, whose thinking cannot pass through the minute, are not capable of teaching them. Thus, knowing that what Liu Xiang wrote is exceedingly brief and simple and that he did not mention their marvelous deeds, these biographies are profound and marvelous, and they can never be exhausted. I should also say that this record of biographies contains on the whole even more than what Liu Xiang had.[26]

Still, neither Company nor Ge Hong's preface gets at the core difference between them: alchemical immortality is entirely absent from the *Liexian zhuan*, whose *xian* exclusively attain *yangsheng* long-life, but the *Shenxian zhuan* includes *xian* who have attained long-life and other *xian* who have attained immortality. The defining feature of any *xian* is that s/he has achieved a long life counted in centuries, and some of them will go on to acquire alchemical immortality as well. While there are many avenues to the attainment of long-life, *yangsheng* represents the most highly valued in Ge Hong's estimation. Immortality, on the other hand, is an achievement over and beyond long-life that can be secured only by exclusively alchemical means. This is to say that the *Liexian zhuan* biographies show at best a negligible awareness of alchemy, whereas alchemy appears as a sophisticated art in the *Shenxian zhuan*, about which Ge Hong in the *Neipian* had much to say.

Yangsheng has its roots in the hoary past of Chinese civilization, but alchemy historically appears only in the course of the Han Dynasty.[27] Ge Hong's writings bear witness that others before him had already coupled alchemy with *yangsheng*, but his groundbreaking innovation, arguably his most decisive and lasting contribution to the Chinese traditions of Daoism, was to provide this coupling with a theoretical foundation and a textual legitimacy that brought *yangsheng* masters and alchemical adepts together under a single blanket term: *xian*.

Bracketing the historical validity concerning Ge Hong's conception of Yangsheng Daoism while simultaneously assuming that he meant what he said allows for the pursuit of a heretofore neglected reading of the *Neipian* and the *Shenxian zhuan* that also accounts for their intimate relation to the *Daodejing* and the *Liexian zhuan*. Because this new reading treads on unexplored ground with few modern studies on which to rely, it is limited to what these works reveal about Yangsheng Daoism and Ge Hong's recovery of the matrix of the *Daodejing*. The following sections of this chapter explore, in this order, conceptions of Yangsheng Daoism in the *Neipian*, then in the *Liexian zhuan*, and then in the *Shenxian zhuan*.

Yangsheng Daoism and the *Neipian*

Since Ge Hong's conception of Yangsheng Daoism centers on the nexus of mountain reclusion, *yangsheng* and longevity, and master–disciple transmissions, we might be surprised that he does not identify Laozi as its founder. What we find at its beginnings are ancient, semi-mythic figures who have already discovered the core secrets of *yangsheng*: some pertaining to methods and techniques and others to the cosmogonic foundations upon which their effectiveness rests. Still, Laozi holds a preeminent position because of his "authorship" of the *Daodejing*, the decisive work that reveals *yangsheng*'s rootedness in the pristine Dao.

Ge Hong's great contribution to Daoism and Chinese culture is his formulation of a theoretical foundation for long-life. It heavily relies on the *Daodejing* in its claims to unlock the profound secrets of the Mystery 玄 from which emerged the Dao. In generating this Dao-centered world, the interplays of *you* 有 and *wu* 無 bring into being the world and all things in it, including the body and spirit of a human being. For Ge Hong, maintaining their vital and enduring union is the single requirement for long-life; this is the achievement of the *xian*, masters of the methods and techniques of *yangsheng*.

The *Daodejing* reveals the enigmatic anchoring of *yangsheng* to this Dao-centered world, providing an all-inclusive canvas of modal meaning oriented to longevity. Yangsheng Daoism positions *yangsheng* as its essential practice, whose techniques and effectiveness are woven into the fabric of existence. While neither is a practice manual, the *Daodejing* displays *yangsheng* without naming it as the *Neipian* revels in announcing it. A tradition without a founder, Yangsheng Daoism recognizes the *Daodejing* as its foundational text that discloses *yangsheng*'s rootedness in the world; still, the disciple stands in need of "Laozi's secret oral teachings,"[28] and although Yangsheng Daoism could have no original founder, it regards Laozi as its primary teacher; Ge Hong says:

> And so for all of the many hermits who honor the teachings of Laozi: externally they disdain glory and splendor and internally they "nourish life" (*yangsheng*), yet they experience no hardships in this dangerous world. The moisture of Laozi's vast spring that has long flowed forth is abundant, abundant, like this. How could he not have been established by Heaven and Earth as the teacher for ten thousand generations?[29]

This passage is key for understanding Ge Hong's views of Laozi, noting that "Laozi's enterprise was long-life and lasting vision."[30] In another passage from the *Neipian* that uses one of Laozi's alternative names, Ge Hong states: "Of all the eminent ones who got the Dao, no one surpasses Boyang."[31] The Yangsheng Daoist nexus of mountain reclusion, *yangsheng*, and the lines of ancient oral master–disciple transmissions of the *Daodejing* that binds together *yangsheng* adepts is firmly structured around Laozi, animating and giving the tradition concrete historical presence. The *Daodejing* recognizes these *yangsheng* adepts as sages 聖人, but the *Neipian* designates them as *xian* and characterizes them as "hermits" 隱士 *yinshi* or 幽隱 *youyin*.

Both *yinshi* and *youyin* include the character *yin* 隱, which verbally means "to hide" or adjectively means "hidden," but *yangsheng* hermits were not hiding from society, they rather were hidden within the mountains. In this sense, *yangsheng* hermits, those who are "hidden," live "hiddenly" 隱居, and in this they simulate the Dao, as *Daodejing* chapter 41 states: "The Dao is hidden and nameless" 道隱無名. This is reflected in *Neipian* 5:

> Those who achieve [longevity] are exceptionally rare and hidden, while those who do not succeed are extremely numerous and conspicuous. Worldly people cannot be aware of those who are hidden because they only see those who are

conspicuous, therefore they say that in the world there is indeed no such thing as the Dao of the *xian*.³²

Ge Hong's standard phrase to mark a person's becoming a *yangsheng* hermit is "to enter the mountains" 入山; the *Neipian* alone employs it more than 50 times and, together with the *Liexian zhuan* and the *Shenxian zhuan*, the reader comes to expect that for all of the *yangsheng* Daoists. This phrase is closely related to another frequently used one, "mountains and forests" 山林, which might sound odd to the Western ear because we do not usually think of hermits as living in forests, but Chinese mountains are not so dangerously high, and forests were typically understood as important components of mountain chains.

Neipian 8 gives several depictions of *yangsheng* hermits, including this:

> Why must a person completely abandon the affairs of the world to pursue cultivation in the mountains and forests in order to achieve success? There are [hermits] whose minds are calm in quietude and in silence, whose natures detest clamor and noise. Their pleasure comes from natural freedom, and they consider official appointments as nothing but grief. They wear strips of cloth with rope belts, they eat natural herbs, and they work the plough.³³

Neipian 15 gives a firsthand description of *yangsheng* mountain hermits practicing "avoidance of grains": "Several times I have seen people who had cut off eating grain for more than two or three years. Their bodies were slender, and their complexions were good. They could endure wind, cold, heat, and dampness, even though none of them were fat."³⁴ *Neipian* 10 provides a view from the other side of *yangsheng* mountain reclusion: "When Confucian scholars, looking through bamboo tubes and making assumptions like blind men, hear about those who live in the mountains and forests to pursue the patriarch Boyang's [Laozi's] course of study, they mock and vilify them, saying, 'This is all nonsense and they cannot be taken seriously.'"³⁵

When *Neipian* 17 states, "Many of those who cultivate the Dao live in mountains and forests,"³⁶ we might ask why such a dramatic move is necessary. Ge Hong's answer is based on a loose distinction he makes between ancient masters, who were so collected that they could master *yangsheng* even while holding office, and more recent ones. A student asked Ge Hong, "In antiquity, Chi Songzi, Wang Qiao, Jin Gao, Laozi, Peng Zu, Wu Cheng, and Yu Hua were all perfected yet held official positions with no urge to hide themselves far away. Beginning in the next age, however, Daoists made haste to disappear and live as hermits. Why?"³⁷

Ge Hong asks the same question slightly rephrased:

> In the past, Huangdi bore the burden of ruling the empire, but this did not prevent his ascension at Lake Ding. Peng Zu was a senior official for eight hundred years before going west to the desert [there follows eight more ancient *yangsheng* masters who did not enter the mountains]. Many of the ancients got the Dao but continued to hold public office; they cultivated it in the shadows of the court, because certainly they had an excess of energy. Why, then, must a person cultivate [the Dao] in the mountains and forests, and achieve it only after completely abandoning worldly affairs?[38]

Here is Ge Hong's reply:

> The Dao does not exist exclusively in mountains and forests, but those who cultivate the Dao must enter mountains and forests because they sincerely desire to distance themselves from the stench of society and go into places of purity and quietude ... It is best to live as a hermit and completely avoid the vermin of society. Do not those who go far away in solitude to pursue their aspiration in the caves of Mount Song have good reason for doing so?[39]

Ge Hong here mentions Mount Song 嵩岫, but that was only one of a long list of mountains that a *yangsheng* master could enter. *Neipian* 17 names the most important of them as Mount Taihua 太華 in the west, Mount Huo 霍山 in the south, Mount Heng 恆山 in the north, Mount Songgao 嵩高山 in the center, and Mount Tai 太山 in the east,[40] while *Neipian* 4 provides the names of twenty-eight further mountains, including Mount Luofu 羅浮, the mountain Ge Hong entered at the end of his public career.[41] However, entering these mountains is not to be taken lightly because of the extreme risks and dangers involved, and it warns that "Daoists must rely on their arts to protect themselves and the disciples who accompany them."[42] *Neipian* 17 offers a sobering catalogue of mountain dangers, including the kinds of noxious spirits[43] that inhabit them:

> All mountains, whether large or small, have many spirits and gods. The spirits of large mountains are very powerful, while the spirits of small mountains are less powerful. To enter the mountains without the proper arts will inevitably lead to disaster and injury. In some cases, people become seriously ill, injured in a fall, or immobilized with fear; in other cases, people see lights and shadows and hear strange sounds. At times great trees will be blown down when there is no wind, and at other times high rocks will come crashing down for no apparent reason, all of this causing horrible death or serious injury. Sometimes people get into a panic and madly run away, only to fall to their deaths in ravines; sometimes people are attacked by tigers, wolves, or poisonous insects. Mountains are not to be entered lightly.[44]

Neipian 17 is dominated with strategies for mountain survival. It discusses the proper times to enter a mountain, paying special attention to the numerous taboos surrounding all of them. It provides instructions for paying respects to the mountain spirits with the appropriate offerings, prayers, and propitiations. It offers strategies for dealing with snakes, poisonous insects and other harmful creatures, and toxic growths; for dealing with noxious spirits (many of which are the spirits of large trees and stones) and dangerous animals, many of whom take on human appearances; and for dealing with threatening weather conditions. The survival tools that he condones are medicines, pills, and potions; various kinds of visualizations and defensive projections of one's *qi* against noxious influences; magically empowered daggers; mirrors that show the true appearance of demonic spirits; various seals to use against, for example, tigers by stamping their tracks; and, most important of all, the numerous amulets and talismans that have protective and prophylactic functions. Neither the *Liexian zhuan* nor the *Shenxian zhuan* offer any such pragmatic and practical strategies, nor do they ever mention the risks and dangers of mountain living, but Ge Hong's description of mountain life presents itself as the true experience, including the risks and dangers, of the *xian* who flourished in them.

Likely because of the dangers of mountain life, many of Ge Hong's replies to the question of the necessity of entering the mountains are in the negative: to avoid the harangues of society. Although he does not dwell on them, there are many indications of the savory aspects of entering the mountains, but they are all trumped by the fact that mountains are the place to find a *yangsheng* master; his explanation for why Liu Xiang (the putative compiler of the *Liexian zhuan*) failed to become a *xian* is precisely this:

> There are certain matters that can only be transmitted orally and that must be received from a teacher. Also, one must go to a pure and clean spot deep in the mountains so that ordinary and unlearned people will not know about them. Liu Xiang, however, remained in the palace when he practiced them, and in letting the palace people attend to his wants, he necessarily could not maintain the required purity. Also, he was unable to cut off his involvement in human affairs with their comings and goings. Like this, how could he ever succeed?[45]

Ge Hong above admits to one of the savory aspects of entering the mountains: the "purity and cleanliness" 清潔 of the environment, referring first of all to the potent and invigorated mountain *qi* that provides the greatest *yangsheng* benefits. In the secular world, the practitioner constantly must deal with the grime of cities and villages, the pervasive depravity of moral corruption, and the constant vigilance of attending to one's duties and responsibilities. The world of mountains offers an entirely different environment. Instead of the goods sold at markets, there are deposits of minerals and ores, bushes with berries, and orchards with fruits. Instead of avenues leading to compounds, there are paths leading to lakes, copses, and groves. Instead of cliques, there are flocks, broods, herds, and swarms. Instead of lords and rulers, there are other kinds of spirits, forces, and energies, even and up to the Dao itself. As Livia Kohn writes,

> Mountains are sacred places that contain wondrous plants, animals, and beings who can help the practitioner's quest. They contain grottoes, caverns, caves, underground spaces, mountain hollows and inner corridors that all possess qualities manmade places do not have. They are archetypal chambers of reflection and the classical homes of immortals, where miraculous, inexplicable phenomena abound—such as lush growth despite droughts, or discovery of an ancient scroll within an uninhabited cave.[46]

Ge Hong himself entered the mountains twice, first in his early life when he worked on the *Shenxian zhuan* and *Neipian*, and then again toward the end of his life with his family and students; he writes:

> I have cut off all contact with my native village and relinquished the glories and splendors of the present world in my desire to go afar and ascend a famous mountain to finish my writings before preparing the divine medicine with a view to long- life … In the meantime, I write what is in my heart to inform those of the future who will value these same aspirations.[47]

Ge Hong's vision of Yangsheng Daoism centers on the nexus of reclusive mountain life, master–disciple relations, and *yangsheng*. The picture that he paints of the Yangsheng nexus that he believed came together many centuries before his time shows that it was still alive and flourishing in his own day. This provides the appropriate backdrop against which to read the *xian* biographies of the *Liexian zhuan* and *Shenxian zhuan* in exploration of the ways in which Ge Hong recovered the Yangsheng Daoist matrix of the *Daodejing*.

Yangsheng Daoism in the *Liexian zhuan*

Inclusion into Yangsheng Daoism requires that the practitioner deliberately commits to becoming a *xian*; that s/he participates in a network of master–disciple transmissions; and that s/he practices *yangsheng*. The *Liexian zhuan* provides biographies to seventy *xian*, but the majority are not Yangsheng Daoists since they demonstrate no deliberate commitment to becoming a *xian*, no participation in a master–disciple relationship, and no familiarity with *yangsheng*; they often become *xian* based on unwitting circumstances. Although they had different paths to getting long-life, they are still "Daoist" in the wider sense because of their attainment. Chen Hong writes,

> Of course, the seventy divine *xian* recorded in the *Liexian zhuan* not only have the flavor of Daoism, but they often present a diverse religious background that includes the Fangxian Daoism and the Huang-Lao Daoism of the Warring States and the Qin and Han dynasties. This is not only related to the organizational system of the deeds of the pre-Qin and Han Dynasty divine *xian* of the *Liexian zhuan*, but also to the original sources of the extremely heterogenous thoughts at play in the formation of early Daoism.[48]

Some become *xian* as a reward for a good deed, such as Ma Shihuang 馬師皇 who treated a dragon's tooth abscess after which the dragon carried him away as a *xian*. Others become *xian* by virtue of their idiosyncratic preference for a certain diet, for example, Wo Quan 偓佺 who ate pine needles or Gui Fu 桂父 who "often ingested cinnamon and sunflowers mixed with turtle brains,"[49] but they have no special reasons or recipes for this. Others still become *xian* for no apparent reason, like Ge You 葛由 who sculpted sheep out of wood that one day simply carried him away.

Several biographies identify their particular *xian* who live in mountain reclusion, or sometimes other mysterious figures who appear in them, as specifically Daoist 道士, as with Wang Ziqiao 王子喬, Jiqiu Jun 稷丘君, Zhu Zhu 主柱, Mao Nü 毛女, Zhu Huang 朱璜, and Nü Wan 女丸. But being specifically identified as Daoist while also living in mountain reclusion is still not sufficient for inclusion in the ranks of Yangsheng Daoists, since their biographies are conspicuously marked by the absence of *yangsheng* and their nonparticipation in networks of master–disciple transmissions.

Based on the *Liexian zhuan*'s demonstration of active involvement in the Yangsheng nexus of mountain reclusion, *yangsheng*, and master–disciple networks, only seven biographies are identifiable with Yangsheng Daoism. Each of them falls within the first 26 biographies of the work, thus speaking to the hoariness of their legends.

Rong Cheng Gong 容成公 has the earliest Yangsheng biography and the seventh overall. He was older even than Huangdi 黃帝, the mythological First Emperor of China (r. 2698–2598 BCE), since the biography states that he "named himself as Huangdi's master," but he was also "seen with King Mu of Zhou" (r. 956–918 BCE) more than 1500 years later.[50] Even if Rong Cheng Gong had a master (who anyway remains unnamed), and even if Rong Cheng Gong is older than Laozi, he still should only be considered a *yangsheng* pioneer rather than an original founder, since *yangsheng* can have no founder.

At the same time, Rong Cheng Gong (also known as Rong Cheng Shi 容成氏) has a wider coverage in other early Chinese writings. Both *Lüshi Chunqiu* 96 (容成造曆 *Rong Cheng zao li*) and *Huainanzi* 19 (容成作曆 *Rong Cheng zuo li*) recognize him as the inventor of the calendar.⁵¹ *Zhuangzi* 10 includes Rong Cheng as one among a larger group of sages who lived "in the age of perfect virtue," and *Zhuangzi* 25 quotes him as cryptically saying, "Take away the days and there will be no years; without the internals there are no externals."

"Yiwenzhi" of *Hanshu* 30.80b names two texts identified with Rong Cheng, the first called simply *Rong Cheng* 容成, and a second called *Rong Cheng's Yin Dao* 容成陰道, where *yin* refers to the sexual arts for which Rong Cheng was counted a master. This association is reinforced by the Mawangdui *Shiwen*, in which Rong Cheng, the *yangsheng* master, answers the questions of Huangdi, the *yangsheng* disciple, concerning sexual procreation, longevity, and the circulation of *qi*; Rong Cheng's answers demand a separate study, but Huangdi's questions give the flavor of the interview:

> When people first dispense the purity that flows into the form, what is obtained so that life occurs? When flowing into the form produces a body, what is lost so that death occurs? Among the people of the age, why are some foul while others are fair? Why do some die young while others are longevous? I wish to hear the reason why people's *qi* thrives or shrinks, why it slackens or expands.⁵²

The *Neipian* mentions Rong Cheng several times. *Neipian* 8 names him as one of five *yangsheng* masters who only wrote down some general points about the arts of the bedroom, and *Neipian* 19 may be referring to that where it lists a writing called *Cheng Rong Jing* 成容經. *Neipian* 20 tells the story of a certain Gu Qiang 古強 who "followed herbal recipes and practiced the methods of Rong Cheng and Su Nü."⁵³

Rong Cheng Gong's biography in the *Liexian zhuan* presents the most compelling instance of *yangsheng* practice in the entire collection. It states that he "excelled at supplementing and guiding" 善補導, referring to sexual techniques for retaining "essence" 精 (*jing* or sexual fluids, sperm) in the brain. In his commentary to the biography, Max Kaltenmark writes,

> This expression 補導 [supplementing and guiding] is often employed to designate Daoist sexual practices (房中之術 "bedroom arts"). It appears equivalent to the expression 還精補腦 "return the essence to repair the brain." The character 導 is one part of the expression 導引 that designates respiratory

gymnastics, the practices designated by the expression 補導 should equally include the respiratory movements; in effect, the circulation of the breath and the circulation of the sperm go together.[54]

The techniques of "supplementing and guiding" refer to general *yangsheng* practices, and Kaltenmark's comments demonstrate that they are fully consistent with Ge Hong's systematizing explanations examined in the Prologue. Rong Cheng's biography also states that he "drew essence from the Mysterious Female."[55] The name "Mysterious Female" 玄牝 occurs in *Daodejing* chapter 6, where it is identified with "the Valley Spirit (who) never dies." These passages situate Rong Cheng's *yangsheng* in connection with the cosmogonic passages of the *Daodejing*, again reinforcing the relationship between them.

Rong Cheng's *yangsheng* is not limited to the techniques of "guiding and pulling" and "the arts of the bedroom," but also include *qi* circulation. The biography states that his "essentials" 要 were that of "the Valley Spirit (who) never dies" and "guarding life and nourishing *qi*" 守生養氣, where "nourishing *qi*" is synonymous with, or one technique of, *qi* circulation and is focused on the physical body; thus, one immediate effect of Rong Cheng Gong's *yangsheng* was that his body rejuvenated and "his white hair turned black."[56] His biography ends with a claim that should not necessarily startle, namely that his "practices were the same as Laozi's," and this is explained by the fact that Rong Cheng Gong was "Laozi's teacher."[57] This marks the earliest recorded *yangsheng* transmission from master to disciple, thus fulfilling two of the three primary features of the Yangsheng nexus—but because Rong Cheng and Laozi were ancient *yangsheng* masters, they had no call to live in mountain reclusion.

The *Liexian zhuan*'s biography of Laozi is separated from Rong Cheng Gong's by one. Laozi himself is, arguably, the single-most mysterious Chinese figure in history: Was he the ritual master employed by the Zhou who was interviewed several times by Confucius, or was he a mountain hermit and *yangsheng* master? Did he compose or have any hand in the *Daodejing*, or did he in fact never exist and his eponym was conveniently created for its title?

These questions vex modern scholars as much as they have ancient scholars, both of whom have sought answers in the *Shiji*'s biography of him. It presents a loosely woven panoply of various legends steeped in conjecture and contradiction, but it has stamped Laozi since the time of its composition. There have been multitudes of Laozi biographies following the *Shiji*'s precisely because of the conjectures and contradictions in it that storytellers have exploited, and the *Liexian zhuan* is no exception.

The *Shiji* commands a certain gravitas, and the claims it makes about Laozi's life cannot be entirely ignored. The various ways that Daoist writings in particular managed the most important of them, namely that he was an employee of the Zhou Dynasty, offer a fascinating case for understanding Daoist thought and creativity. Partly this is because Laozi's mysterious name was appended to the *Daodejing*, itself a profoundly enigmatic text. Still, there is a difference between biographies associated with Huang-Lao, Xuanxue, and Confucianism that present Laozi as a wise philosopher, those associated with institutionalized Daoism that present him as a cosmic deity, and those associated with Yangsheng Daoism that present him as a *yangsheng* master who achieved long-life. It is this last sort of biography that is found in the *Liexian zhuan* as well as in the *Shenxian zhuan*.

The *Shiji*'s biography claimed that Laozi was at some point employed by the Zhou court, but in fact it also recognizes that Laozi was a *yangsheng* master where it states, "Laozi probably lived at least 160 years, and others say that he lived at least 200 hundred years, as a result of his cultivation of the Dao and his nurturing of longevity."[58] When the *Liexian zhuan* mentions his government employment, it states that he worked "for at least 80 years, but the *Shiji* says 'at least 200 years.'"[59] The *Liexian zhuan* cleverly misreads the *Shiji*'s claim that Laozi's age was 200 years to turn it into an employment period of 200 years, which allowed it to further extend Laozi's already long life.

The *Liexian zhuan* boldly declares that Laozi "was born in the time of the Yin Dynasty," thereby tacking on several additional centuries to his life. An added feature of this earlier than expected birth is that it more smoothly places him in company with Rong Cheng Gong, whom both Laozi and Huangdi served as disciples.

To be sure, the *Liexian zhuan* nowhere gives specific years for these figures whose dates are otherwise impossible to determine, but even so, it greatly expanded Laozi's life, thereby accomplishing three things. First, it endows a more awesome aura to Laozi. Second, it minimizes his status as "author" of the *Daodejing* because he received important teachings, including those concerning the Mysterious Female and the Valley Spirit, from his master, Rong Cheng Gong. Third, it provides a deeper cosmic pedigree to *yangsheng*, because Laozi did not discover it but learned it from Rong Cheng Gong, who also did not discover it. This reinforces the point that *yangsheng* is not the discovery of any one person but is rather woven into the very fabric of the Dao's reality.

In the end, the most important part of the lives of Rong Cheng Gong and Laozi is not that they mastered *yangsheng* to achieve long-life, but that they transmitted its teachings to posterity, thereby paving the way for later people to receive, master, and in turn transmit it to their own disciples. In the view of the *Liexian zhuan*, neither Rong Cheng Gong nor Laozi discovered *yangsheng*, but together they established something quite different: Yangsheng Daoism, cohering around the nexus of mountain reclusion, master–disciple transmissions, and *yangsheng* and longevity.

Juanzi's 涓子 *Liexian zhuan* biography is separated from Laozi's by one. It states that he "lived as a hermit on Dang Mountain" where he practiced a form of dietetics by eating atractylis, but was later seen in the state of Qi when he was more than three hundred years old.[60] It also situates him in a line of master–disciple transmission by stating that he "received the methods of the Nine *Xian* from Boyang," and it further states that these methods were transmitted through him all the way down to Liu An, the Prince of Huainan, who was unable to understand them, presumably because he never entered the mountains to find a *yangsheng* master from whom to receive their accompanying oral teachings. In this way, the *Liexian zhuan* inserts the *yangsheng* mountain hermit Juanzi squarely within the nexus of *yangsheng* Daoism. Additionally, his biography states that he composed the *Scripture of Heaven and Humans* 天人經, which *Neipian* 19 appears to recognize as *Juanzi's Scripture of Heaven, Earth, and Humans* 涓子天地人經. *Neipian* 13 also states that Huangdi once "entered Gold Valley to consult Juanzi."[61]

Peng Zu's is the next Yangsheng biography. It states that he lived in a "*xian* chamber" 仙室 (a mountain cave) and, when he reached eight hundred years, he "ascended as a *xian* and departed."[62] As for his *yangsheng*, he "often ate cassia and agaric (and) excelled at 'guiding and pulling' and circulating *qi*."[63] Oddly, the *Liexian zhuan* makes no mention of his mastery of the sexual arts, a feature emphasized in his *Shenxian zhuan* biography (discussed in the Prologue).

The next Yangsheng biography belongs to Qiong Shu 邛疎, and it states that he lived as mountain hermit on Mount Taishi where "his bed and pillow were made of stone."[64] I count him as a Yangsheng Daoist because of his methods: he "was able to circulate *qi* and refine his form," and he also "cooked stones and ate their marrow" by relying on a *fuyao* recipe for "concentrated stone milk."[65]

Lu Tong's 陸通 Yangsheng biography identifies him with "the Madman of Chu, Jie Yu" 楚狂接輿,[66] the famous hermit recorded in *Analects* 18.5. When passing by Confucius, he sang about the end of virtuous government and the futility of seeking office, a story that *Zhuangzi* 4 embellished. In *Zhuangzi* 7, a certain Jian Wu approaches Jie Yu who is once again talking about the end of virtuous government and the futility of trying to order the world, and in a famous passage from *Zhuangzi* 1, Jian Wu retells to a certain Lian Shu that he did not understand what Jie Yu said to him about the "spirit-person" 神人; Jie Yu's words to Jian Wu were:

> Far away on Gushe Mountain there lives a spirit-person whose flesh and skin are like ice and snow, and whose manner is gentle as a young virgin. He does not eat the five grains but breathes in the wind and drinks the dew. Riding on the *qi* of the clouds and driving flying dragons, he roams beyond the four seas. By concentrating his spirit, he can protect creatures from disease and pestilence and provide for an abundant harvest every year.

This spirit-person is strikingly similar to a *yangsheng* master, living in mountain reclusion and avoids grains. Probably because the *Zhuangzi* had already designated him as a spirit-person and not as a *xian*, he was disqualified from having a *xian* biography in the *Liexian zhuan*, which nevertheless finds a way to include him by a deft act of appropriation. It looks to Jie Yu, the "Madman of Chu" previously identified as neither a spirit-person nor a *xian*, and the *Liexian zhuan* binds him to an altogether different person about whom virtually nothing is known, Lu Tong, and it goes on to designate him as a *xian*. Doing so allows the spirit-person of Gushe Mountain to be indirectly included into the ranks of Yangsheng Daoists, but this requires that the *Liexian zhuan* provide *yangsheng* bona fides for Lu Tong himself, which it accomplishes in a heavy-handed way: his biography identifies him as a mountain hermit on the remote Emei Mountain in Shu far to west; it states that he practiced the avoidance of grains, eating only turnips and the fruits of the *tuolu* tree; and it most importantly states that he "excelled at *yangsheng*,"[67] marking the *Liexian zhuan*'s single use of the term. Doubling as Lu Tong, Jie Yu is smoothly (or not) brought to fit into the Yangsheng nexus, where Jian Wu and Lian Shu (about whom little else is said) stand in a kind of disciple relationship to him.

The last Yangsheng biography belongs to Qin Gao 琴高. It states that he taught techniques to an unspecified number of disciples, which it indirectly identifies as *yangsheng* by virtue of the fact that he "practiced the techniques of Juanzi and Peng Zu," both of whom were already recognized as *yangsheng* masters.[68] We see that already by the time of Qin Gao, *yangsheng* masters such as him have disciples so numerous that they are not individually named, and their *yangsheng* transmissions have taken on such definition that they can now be identified with specific lineages of the likes of Juanzi and Peng Zu. Such developed lines of master–disciple transmissions in the *Liexian zhuan* could only serve to fortify

Ge Hong's conception of Yangsheng Daoism in the *Shenxian zhuan*, as explored in the next section.

As a kind of afterword to the *Liexian zhuan*'s influence on Ge Hong's conception of Yangsheng Daoism, it is interesting to note that Qin Gao's biography states that, after announcing his final departure, he temporarily submerged himself in the Tang River to reappear riding a huge red carp after which he took his seat in a sanctuary where he stayed for more than a month, during which time ten thousand people came to see him. Recognizing that the biography is far from representing Qin Gao as a mountain hermit, Ge Hong in the *Neipian* uses this to his advantage by writing: "One who gets the Dao can raise his body into the skies above or submerge himself in rivers and seas below … The evidence for this is Qin Gao, who rode a red carp in the depths of the river."[69]

Yangsheng Daoism in the *Shenxian zhuan*

Ge Hong maintains a distinction between two kinds of *xian*: long-life *dixian* 地仙 (earth *xian*) and immortal *tianxian* 天仙 (heaven *xian*). *Dixian* exclusively master *yangsheng*; their diets and medicines consist of non-compounded products from the natural world; and they reside in mountain reclusion. *Tianxian* first master *yangsheng* before graduating to alchemy; their elixirs and drugs depend on compounded products and talismans; and they ascend to the heavens. Although Ge Hong held *tianxian* in higher esteem, he also recognized that *dixian* prefer to remain in the mountains to avoid the duties incumbent on *tianxian* who receive official appointments in the celestial bureaucracy.[70] In *Neipian* 3, he states, "I heard my late teacher say that some *xian* ascend to heaven and others remain on earth. What matters is that they all have achieved long-life; where they go to live depends on their personal preferences."[71]

Next to the theoretical foundation for long-life that represents Ge Hong's major contribution to Daoism and Chinese culture, another of his major contributions is the distinction he drew between *xian* who have achieved long-life and *xian* who have achieved immortality. By itself, the Chinese term *xian* does not make this distinction, but to call long-life *xian* who reside in mountain seclusion as *dixian* and immortality *xian* who ascend into the heavens as *tianxian*, while not exactly the same as the difference between long-life and immortality, does the job quite effectively. Robert Campany broke some ground in this by challenging the long-standing blanket understanding of the term *xian* as "immortal," but his solution was to call all *xian*, including *dixian* and *tianxian*, by a different Western term, "transcendents."[72] This does nothing to support Ge Hong's important distinction between *xian* with long-life and *xian* with immortality. My previous work[73] has examined this in more detail, and Zhang Ji also has this to say on the issue:

> There is a distinction in Ge Hong's writings between immortality and longevity. The former is unlimited existence, whereas the latter is a natural process. Long-lived people can still die, just as a long-lived turtle or a thousand-year-old pine tree can still perish. Even though longevity could turn into immortality, it is a lower form of existence. Longevity can be managed by cultivating natural life (*yangsheng*), whereas immortality can only be attained through alchemy. But longevity is a necessary step toward immortality that no one can bypass.[74]

In addition to this major distinction between long-life *dixian* and immortal *tianxian*, Ge Hong adds others whose importance is more or less, including a subcategory of *dixian* who depart from the strict terms of the Yangsheng nexus primarily because they divide their time between mountain reclusion and life in the world; I call them householder *xian*. Peng Zu is the primary example, and in his *Shenxian zhuan* biography he says this:

> The Dao of humans should allow them to eat sweet and delicious food, wear soft and beautiful clothes, have sex, and hold official position. With their ears and eyes acute and discerning, their bones and sinews firm and strong, their complexions smooth and moist, they grow old but do not age. Extending their years with lasting vision, they long remain in the world.[75]

Ge Hong takes advantage of Peng Zu's householder status to use him as a mouthpiece for articulating the ethos of all *dixian* generally. Because *dixian* living in mountain reclusion are notoriously silent and rarely seen, they lack voice and representation; householder *xian* like Peng Zu, with one foot in the mountains and the other in the social world, serve precisely to give voice and representation to *dixian*. Harper's comments on Peng Zu's dialogues in the Mawangdui *Shiwen* are appropriate also for Peng Zu's *Shenxian zhuan* biography, where he writes that these teachings are "directed to an elite, male audience; and it encompasses various activities that promote a healthy, enjoyable, and long life."[76]

Reclusive *dixian* appear in the *Shenxian zhuan* only when they descend from the mountains, typically to treat the sick, before quickly returning. This contrasts with the *tianxian*, who lead eminently public lives before entering the mountains and, after returning to the social world, strive to stay in the public spotlight. A driving factor was their need to secure wealthy sponsors to bankroll their expensive alchemical projects. But they too must enter the mountains to start their careers as a Daoist, because they too require the long life promised by *yangsheng* in order to have the extended years necessary to complete their elixirs of immortality. The *tianxian* are never shown in their laboratories, but once they have achieved their goal, their biographies are quickly dominated by their antics, adventures, and exorcisms in the public world.

The *dixian* master and remain with *yangsheng* throughout their lives, while the *tianxian* master just enough *yangsheng* to extend their years before graduating to alchemy. Ge Hong makes these distinctions explicit throughout the *Neipian*, and whatever the actual reality was, they provided him with an overarching directing structure through which he bound into his encompassing conception of Yangsheng Daoism alchemical adepts of immortality together with *yangsheng* masters of long-life.

Many of the *tianxian* biographies include detailed discussions of *yangsheng*, but only rarely does a *dixian* biography even mention alchemy. This present exploration thus restricts its attention to some of the important *xian* biographies in the *Shenxian zhuan*, regardless if they belong to *dixian* or *tianxian*, that focus on *yangsheng*, but it generally leaves aside the not entirely related issue of alchemy and immortality.

Much like the *Liexian zhuan*, the *Shenxian zhuan* dedicates biographies to a rich panoply of different kinds of *xian*, only some of whom are considered Yangsheng Daoists. But the *Shenxian zhuan* incorporates a higher ratio of them, partly because Ge Hong has expanded the parameters of who can count as a Yangsheng Daoist by including adepts of alchemy, who anyway began their careers by mastering *yangsheng*. In any case, the criteria for inclusion in Yangsheng Daoism, whether *dixian* or *tianxian*, remains active participation in the Yangsheng nexus of mountain reclusion, *yangsheng* and long-life, and master–disciple transmissions. Another way to put this is that all *dixian* and all *tianxian* are already Yangsheng Daoist without prejudice.

Several of the *dixian* biographies are remarkably sparse and specify not much more than their *yangsheng* practices and their medical treatments for the sick. The biography of Gan Shi 甘始 is typical:

> Gan Shi was a native of Taiyuan. He excelled at circulating *qi*. He did not eat a normal diet but only ingested asparagus root. He practiced the sexual arts, relying on the methods of Rong Cheng, Xuan Nü, and Su Nü; he [recorded] his extensions and supplements into a single *juan*, and they proved to be of immediate benefit. In curing the sick, he made no use of needles or moxa. He remained in the human realm for more than three hundred years, then entered Mount Wangshi and departed as a *xian*.[77]

Gan Shi is primarily defined by his *yangsheng* methods, noteworthy of which is his mastery of the sexual arts, and although we learn nothing of his master, we can be certain that he had one, as Ge Hong has made discipleship under a master a prerequisite for *yangsheng*. The same can be said of several of the other *dixian* biographies, including those of Shen Jian 沈建 who "practiced the arts of 'guiding and pulling' and dietetics, and also methods for extending one's years and reversing aging";⁷⁸ Dong Zhongjun 董仲君 who "ingested *qi* and refined his body; when he was more than two hundred years old he had not aged";⁷⁹ and Tianmenzi 天門子 who "was particularly enlightened about the essentials of supplementing and nourishing … at the age of one hundred eighty, he had the complexion of a child."⁸⁰

The *tianxian* sequence from *yangsheng* to alchemy is de rigueur for these *xian*, and their progress through *yangsheng* mastery is virtually indistinguishable from the *dixian*. This sequence is explicitly represented in several biographies, including that of Bo He 帛和. His *yangsheng* career was initiated when he entered Mount Difei and there served as Dong Feng's 董奉 disciple, himself a *yangsheng* master with his own *Shenxian zhuan* biography. In it, an official who had seen Dong Feng fifty years earlier noted that he had not aged and asked, "Is it that you possess the Dao?" to which Dong Feng replied, "It was only by accident."⁸¹ Bo He's biography states that Dong Feng "transmitted to him the methods of circulating *qi*, ingesting atractylis, and avoiding grains,"⁸² all standard hallmarks of *yangsheng*. Dong Feng then confesses to Bo He that his teachings are now exhausted and recommends him to find a *tianxian* to learn alchemy. Bo He then goes to Mount Xicheng and becomes disciple to Wang Jun 王君, who instructs him on how to acquire the *Central Scripture of Grand Purity* 太清中經.⁸³

I surmise that this Wang Jun is likely Wang Zhongdu 王仲都, whose biography states that he was ordered by Emperor Wen of the Han (r. 180–157) to gallop with a team of four horses around the imperial hunting grounds on a freezing night, wearing only a single garment. His driver, fully covered in fox furs, almost froze to death, but "Wang's body and breath were steaming as if he was cooking."⁸⁴ It is worth recalling that this Wang Jun, if he is in fact Wang Zhongdu, was the disciple of the deity Taibo Zhenren 太白真人 (Perfected One of Venus)⁸⁵ and then subsequently became the master of Li Zhongfu, who then himself transmitted the teachings to Zuo Ci, who transmitted them to Ge Xuan, who transmitted them to Zheng Yin, who transmitted them to Ge Hong. For his part, Bo He, who also received Wang Jun's teachings, is positioned in a separate line of transmission that goes from him to Sun Zhen 孫真. In brief, this set of intertwined biographies unambiguously demonstrates Ge Hong's conception of the Yangsheng Daoist nexus.

The biographies of Jie Xiang 介象 and Liu Gen 劉根 provide other notable portrayals of the *tianxian* sequence from *yangsheng* to alchemy. Unknowingly attempting to bypass *yangsheng* in order to immediately concern himself with the elixir, Jie Xiang entered the mountains in search of an alchemical adept. Instead, he encountered a Jade Maiden 玉女 (a lower-level female divine *xian*), who explained to him why he was incapable of ingesting the elixir: "Your blood-consuming *qi* is not yet exhausted. Abstain from grains for three years and then come back."[86] Jie Xiang did as directed, and after getting his body into good *yangsheng* shape, his quest for immortality was successful.

The biography of Liu Gen also shows him entering the mountains in search of an alchemical adept where he encountered a spirit-person named Han Zhong 韓眾, who explained the importance of *yangsheng* to him:

> You have the bones of a transcendent, and therefore you are able to see me. But at present your marrow is not full, your blood is not warm, your *qi* is slight, your brain is diminished, your muscles are nettled, and your flesh is damp. Therefore, when you ingest medicines and circulate *qi*, you are getting no benefit. If you wish to achieve long-life, you must first cure your illnesses; after twelve years you will be able to ingest the superior *xian* drugs.[87]

Liu Gen's biography provides a clear rationale for the necessity of undergoing the sequence from *yangsheng* to alchemy: as long as the body is not strong, revitalized, and healthy, it lacks the capacity to successfully absorb the drugs of immortality. His biography ends with a further nod to *yangsheng* techniques: after he has become a *tianxian*, Liu Gen had a disciple named Wang Zhen 王珍 to whom he transmitted *yangsheng* techniques, including *qi* circulation as well as another technique whose name is directly taken from *Daodejing* chapter 10: "guarding the one" 守一.[88]

Wang Zhongdu, Jie Xiang, and Liu Gen might at first glance appear disqualified from inclusion in Yangsheng Daoism because they did not receive teachings from a human *yangsheng* master, thereby defying the master–disciple transmission component of the Yangsheng nexus. However, the divine figures from whom they did receive their *yangsheng* instruction certainly themselves qualify as *yangsheng* masters despite their status as divine figures (respectively the deity Taibo Zhenren, a Jade maiden, or the spirit-person Han Zhong). The fact that Ge Hong attributes to them the quality of divinity 神 is likely another literary or structural ploy applied in the absence of clear knowledge as to precisely who their human teachers were. Of more importance is the recognition that the seekers received their *yangsheng* transmissions only after having entered the mountains as a prerequisite for their more advanced projects of immortality, thus bringing them squarely back into direct participation with the Yangsheng nexus.

The same is true of the biography of Lü Gong 呂恭, which states that after entering the mountains to collect medicinal herbs, he encountered three divinities. Recognizing his excellent character, they immediately accepted him as a student, and they "told Lü Gong the techniques of non-dying."[89] Lü Gong spent two days in the mountains receiving their instructions, but when he returned home, two hundred years had elapsed. His family long dispersed, Lü Gong tracked down Lü Xi 呂習, a descendent of his several generations removed who himself was a "practitioner of the Dao."[90] Lü Gong transmitted to him the *yangsheng* instructions as well as his *xian* recipes before reentering the mountains, where he lived several hundred more years, and Lü Xi's "sons and grandsons over many generations ingested the medicine without growing old or dying, and each of them became *xian*."[91] This last detail is interesting because it was not uncommon for masters to transmit to their own worthy off-spring and progeny.

The biography of the householder *dixian* Kong Anguo 孔安國 is likely a later addition to the *Shenxian zhuan*,[92] and its representation of Yangsheng Daoism, particularly in terms of the three-part nexus, is more highly developed and structured in terms of an actual public tradition than any of the other *xian* biographies. As such, Kong Anguo shares his time between the mountains and society. When living in reclusion on Mount Qian, he would "often circulate *qi* and ingest lead and cinnabar" staying for "a year and a half and return looking younger," after which he would "eat and drink normally in no way different from ordinary people."[93] Chen Bo 陳伯 was counted among "the hundreds of disciples who followed him," and to him Kong Anguo confessed that he had never encountered a master from whom he received instructions concerning the divine elixir, but "only received *dixian* methods appropriate for being able to not die."[94] He went on to tell Chen Bo that in fact he had once encountered a master named Fan Li 范蠡 who "transmitted to me secret methods for ingesting medicines with which to transcend the world,"[95] and he has now enjoyed more than three hundred years of age. He then directed Chen Bo to go and serve as Fan Li's disciple and, doing so, Chen Bo too "received his methods, transcended the world, and did not grow old."[96]

When residing in mountain reclusion, the householder *dixian* Kong Anguo performs "the secret methods" that he received from Fan Li, but when in public he teaches basic *yangsheng* methods to his many students. Throughout, he refrains from transmitting to any of them the secret methods, including even the best of his students like Chen Bo, most likely because his householder status does not qualify him to do so. If so, then his public face as a well-known (but not quite full-fledged?) *yangsheng* master attracts hundreds of students that he is able to assess; recognizing only those who are deeply committed to and capable of the rigorous *yangsheng* program, he recommends them to true mountain *yangsheng* masters such as Fan Li. In this we can clearly perceive the outlines of a network of *yangsheng* masters, some serving as public teachers and others as mountain masters. These public teachers introduce interested novices to the now-not-particularly-secret *yangsheng* teachings, performing a kind of public service advertising that allowed the tradition of Yangsheng Daoism to continue and thrive with new blood.

Coda: A Brief History of Yangsheng

I have refrained from discussing *yangsheng* as an independent subject of inquiry in this chapter because I have not wanted to divert focus away from its position and value in the *Daodejing*. Only now, at the close of this study, may a few ideas about it be ventured.[97]

In terms of theory and practice, the distinguishing feature of *yangsheng* bodily cultivation is its coupling of *qi* circulation with *daoyin* calisthenics. This immediately distinguishes it from other forms of cultivation and meditation like Hindu yoga (which concentrates on *asanas* or bodily positions), Buddhist meditation (which concentrates on bodily postures), or Christian prayer (another form of motionless cultivation). Daoist *yangsheng* is based on breath and movement, a feature that got the attention of the author of *Zhuangzi* chapter 15, who writes:

> To breathe out and breathe in, to inhale slowly and exhale slowly, to spit out the old and take in the new, and to practice bear-hangings and bird-stretchings with the intent to achieve longevity—such are the practices of *daoyin* adepts, those people who nourish their bodies and hope to live as long as Peng Zu.

This is already a developed understanding of *yangsheng*, but it does not appear in the literature as a fully systematized regime until Ge Hong's writings. The origin of *yangsheng*, however, is a different story and, buried in the hoary past of deep antiquity, lies outside the grasp of the modern gaze. Still, there are various views about it, and I am partial to Zhang Rongming's, even though he refers to *yangsheng* in the following passage as *qigong*, because it highlights the centrality of *qi* circulation merged with the *daoyin* modeled on animal movements highlighted in the *Zhuangzi* passage just quoted; Zhang writes:

> In the long period when humans survived by hunting, the ancient ancestors were naturally able to feel that abdominal breathing could quickly compensate for their depleted energy and effectively allow them to recover from their fatigues. In this way, they consciously repeated their abdominal breathing, thereby strengthening it. Over the course of time, abdominal breathing became established through a kind of popular usage that allowed it to gain a fixed regularity of practice. Because of this, modern *qigong* theorists recognize that this kind of abdominal breathing most likely marks the sprouting of Chinese *qigong*.… We obviously cannot make any quick judgments about whether or not the original *qigong* was started by the abdominal breathing produced by the stop and go of physical hunting and bodily breathing, but there is one thing that is evident and beyond doubt, which is that the origins of ancient Chinese *qigong* have a deep connection with the birds and animals that were the targets of hunting … "Bear-hangings and bird-stretchings" are phrases that express the *Zhuangzi*'s lively and vivid descriptions of the adepts of *yangsheng* who cultivated ancient *qigong*. This reveals that the beginnings of original *qigong* are connected to the different and unusual deportments of people who imitated the movements and postures of the animals of the natural world … In sum, the imitative movements of original *qigong* are for the most part patterned on the nearly infinite variety of animals from the natural world in all of their rich variety.[98]

Another interesting piece in the history of *yangsheng* comes with the excavated duodecagonal "Inscription on *Qi* Circulation," an excavated jade tablet dated to around 500 BCE, about the same time of the earliest circulations of the *Daodejing*, and it was likely connected to an early Yangsheng Daoist community. Its merging of *qi* circulation and *daoyin* in physical body movements is classic *yangsheng* practice; it reads:

> To circulate *qi*:
> Swallow it so that it will accumulate.
> As it accumulates, it will expand.
> As it expands, it will descend.
> As it descends, it will stabilize.
> As it stabilizes, it will consolidate.
> As it consolidates, it will sprout.

> As it sprouts, it will grow.
> As it grows, it will return.
> As it returns, it will merge with heaven.
> The heavenly impulses are revealed in the rising of *qi*;
> The earthly impulses are revealed in the descending of *qi*.
> Go along with this and you will live.
> Go against this and you will die.⁹⁹

By far the best representations of early Chinese *yangsheng* are found in two different sources. The first is the *Yinshu* manuscript excavated from the Zhangjiashan site dated to approximately 186 BCE that describes about one hundred different *daoyin* movements mostly modeled on animals.¹⁰⁰ The second is the *Daoyin tu* excavated from Mawangdui, which is actually a chart consisting of forty-four colored illustrations of human figures performing *daoyin* movements, most of which, again, are modeled on animal movements.

The next solid body of *yangsheng* writings are those of Ge Hong, through which he systematized an entire regime of *yangsheng* bodily cultivation. In this arena we once again find his powerful influence over institutionalized Daoism, particularly beginning with Shangqing Daoism 上清. Isabelle Robinet has written extensively on this tradition of Daoism and the ways in which it absorbed *yangsheng*,¹⁰¹ but exploring this too exceeds the scope of this study; it is sufficient to quote Robinet's general appraisal of *yangsheng* as practiced and absorbed by this and later traditions of Daoism:

> *Yangsheng* ... consists of adopting a way of life ruled by physico-mental hygienic principles. This is not specifically a Daoist art and derives from ancient Chinese practices; Daoists adopted, developed, and modified them by introducing the idea of the "primordial breath" (*yuanqi*), by associating them with the Daoist authorities and gods, as well as with certain more specifically religious practices, by giving them a cosmic dimension, and by adding the idea of purification and sublimation. Even when they seem to be eclipsed by new tendencies, the rules of this art remain a foundation of all Daoist practices in all areas—exorcism, therapy, liturgy, "interior alchemy"—and have never ceased to be the subject of many treatises during all epochs.¹⁰²

This note closes the study of the matrix of the *Daodejing*. It is not unfitting to close it with the unnameable component of the matrix, since so much has already been said about the *Daodejing*'s philosophy of the Dao. Fortified with a trove of recently excavated manuscripts that are trying hard to show us what they know about early Chinese Yangsheng Daoism, about Fangxian Daoism and about Huang-Lao Daoism, the field of *Laozi* Studies offers a breathtaking vista of future study that can prove more sensitive than what was previously possible to issues of philosophical enactment and bodily cultivation in the many historical traditions of Daoism as well as those that continue to this day.

Epilogue: Yangsheng Daoism and Comparative Philosophy

9

Heidegger and the Philosophy of the Dao

From the Pre-Socratics to the *Daodejing*

The Laozi *Daodejing*'s phenomenology of the pristine Dao lay dormant for more than two thousand years until the excavations of the *Laozi* manuscripts. Before their discoveries, there had been no textual basis upon which to even imagine that such a Daoist phenomenology was in fact possible in the face of the metaphysics of the Huang-Lao *Daodejing*, which established a cosmic Dao in its very opening line whose eternity/permanence/constancy is so transcendentally different from, prior to, and outside of the cosmos it produced that we cannot conceive of a proper name with which to talk about it. Metaphysics indeed.

Particularly since coming into possession of these manuscripts, a handful of contemporary scholars, several discussed herein, have attempted to discern, if not a phenomenology, then at least a philosophy of a distinctively non-metaphysical sort in the *Daodejing*. These scholars, much like Martin Heidegger, were troubled by the fact the metaphysics of the cosmic Dao were somewhat at odds with most everything else that the *Daodejing* had to say about the Dao.

Still, a prerequisite for uncovering the Laozi *Daodejing*'s phenomenology is an appropriate approach to and recognition of the pristine Dao, or what the *Laozi* manuscripts call *heng dao* 恆道, that sharply distinguishes it from the cosmic Dao, or what the received text calls *chang dao* 常道. Despite the fact that the recently excavated *Laozi* manuscripts have now in fact provided the textual basis for making such a distinction, so far not many scholars have explored this issue but doing so has been this study's main project. The very idea of a distinction between the pristine Dao of the Laozi *Daodejing* and the cosmic Dao of the Huang-Lao *Daodejing* is in itself compelling to contemplate and could even transform Daoist studies as well as comparative philosophy in interesting ways.

The modern foundations for uncovering the phenomenology of the Laozi *Daodejing* were laid by Martin Heidegger. He too was troubled by the dissonance between the cosmic Dao of the *Daodejing* (which always already announces the metaphysical bias that has exerted a dominant influence on interpretations of the text since the Han Dynasty), and everything else of philosophical interest, which is quite a lot, that the *Daodejing* has to say, most all of which is not difficult to recognize as non-metaphysical, if not outright phenomenological. In contrast to the many excellent studies that document the influence of Daoist philosophy on Heidegger's thought, this final chapter of the present study of the matrix of the *Daodejing* intends to shed light on Heidegger's decisive legacy for the modern enterprise of comparative philosophy as well as the contemporary engagement with the phenomenology of the *Daodejing*.

Throughout his long and storied career, Heidegger famously asked the following: "What is the meaning of the question of being?" which is the philosophically primordial question that follows from a previous first question, "Why is there something rather than nothing?" According to Heidegger, the question of the meaning of Being was originally raised by the pre-Socratic philosophers but was soon forgotten by the metaphysical tradition of Western philosophy. The question of the meaning of Being has been forgotten because Western philosophy has led itself into conceiving Being as itself an entity of absolute being that gives "being" to all beings. The consequences of this forgetting of Being is that it has ushered human civilization into a world of technological instrumentality in which existing beings are understood as resources.

Heidegger's thought from early on was decisively influenced by his focus on recovering the meaning of the question of Being, and it directed him back to the pre-Socratics, particularly Parmenides and Heraclitus.[1] His intent was to open the way for the inception of a new beginning for the questioning of Being by retrieving their ancient Greek ability to ask the same, but this time it is for the purpose of coming to terms with modern technology. His pursuit of the questioning of Being led him to the ancient Chinese philosophy of Daoism and the *Daodejing*.

Heidegger found in this short text a philosophy that was in many ways akin to that of the pre-Socratics in that both were, according to his understanding of each, radically non-metaphysical in contrast to the tradition of Western metaphysics that studies Being in terms of first principles existing outside and beyond the phenomenal world. In his engagements with the thought of the *Daodejing*, Heidegger sometimes expressed highly reticent and ambiguous remarks concerning a possible East–West dialogue. He was not entirely clear, in his writings and interviews, if he believed that the thought of the *Daodejing* could, like the thought of the pre-Socratics, open the way to raising again the question of the meaning of Being.

One instance among many is seen in his *der Speigel* interview, during the course of which he said, "And who of us would be in a position to decide whether or not one day in Russia or China very old traditions of 'thought' may awaken that will help make possible for man a free relationship to the technical world?"[2] But he then followed this by saying, "My conviction is that only in the same place where the modern technical world took its origin can we also prepare a conversion (*Umkehr*) of it. In other words, this cannot happen by taking over Zen Buddhism or other Eastern experiences of the world."[3] Still, his remarks on the issue have provided much fuel for debates that have been ongoing now for several decades concerning the possibility for such dialogue, and there remains to this day much controversy as to his final stance. It is within this general philosophical context that Heidegger approached the *Daodejing*.

The *Daodejing* was composed around 500 BCE, dates comparable to those of the pre-Socratics. It was the first Chinese text to introduce the notion of the Dao as the primordial source of existence. Although the *Daodejing* has been transmitted in different editions, this study has suggested that there were two master versions: the Laozi *Daodejing* and the Huang-Lao *Daodejing*.

Oddly, the Laozi *Daodejing* is both the most ancient version and the most recent. Originally circulating as an oral text, its earliest transcriptions date to the end of the third century BCE. The excavated *Laozi* manuscripts, from Guodian and Mawangdui, are the nearest that we will likely get that version. Its core notion is *heng dao* 恆道, where *heng* signifies the Dao's temporalizing nature. This "temporalizing" or pristine Dao exists between the space of Heaven and Earth, where beings come into existence by way of its interplay of *wu* 無 (absence) and *you* 有 (presence) within the world, and its philosophy is phenomenological.

The Huang-Lao *Daodejing* is the familiar version that has been transmitted to us today, best recognized by its two most important commentaries, one by Heshang Gong that identifies the Dao with Nothingness, and the other by Wang Bi that identifies the Dao with Non-being. The core notion of the Huang-Lao *Daodejing* is *chang dao* 常道, where *chang* signifies the Dao's eternity/permanence/constancy. This "cosmic Dao" exists transcendentally from where it produces Heaven and Earth and the myriad things also through the interplay of *wu* and *you*, but here understood by Heshang Gong as Nothingness and Somethingness and by Wang Bi as Non-being and Being, and its philosophy is metaphysical.

From Metaphysics to Phenomenology

Heidegger's overriding interest in the *Daodejing* stemmed from his inquiry into whether its thought spoke directly to the meaning of the question of Being. He believed that the world was threatened by the planetary Ge-stell of modern technology where beings are taken as standing reserve: "As the essence of technology, Ge-stell would be absolute. It would reduce man and beings to a sort of 'standing reserve' or stockpile in service to, and on call for, technological purposes."[4] Heidegger understood the Ge-stell of modern technology as the destined completion of metaphysics in a world that has entirely forgotten the question of the meaning of Being; as he remarks, "Not only have the gods and the god fled, but the divine radiance has become extinguished in the world's history."[5] As the destiny of metaphysics, Heidegger asserted that the movement from the origins of metaphysics to its completion in the Ge-stell was a function of the forgetfulness of Being where existence is shorn of meaning and plenitude.[6]

It is in this context that Heidegger raises the possibility of the second beginning that begins by returning to the ancient Greeks in order to reawaken the question of the meaning of Being. Only by doing so will beings once again be allowed to come into the plenitude of their unconcealment by which they shed their status as standing reserve. Thus, Heidegger encouraged the pursuit of this thinking that could uncover a more appropriate way for humans to exist fruitfully and flourishingly in accommodation with the Ge-stell, and this had to begin with once again raising the question of the meaning of Being. Could the *Daodejing* assist in raising the question and thereby play an important role in "the second beginning" and the overcoming of metaphysics? As Ma Lin and Jaap van Brakel note, "Despite Heidegger's general claim that the allegedly inevitable event of East-West dialogue can only be anticipated before the Western philosophical tradition gains maturity through its own self-transformation, East Asian sources have undeniably played a role in (Heidegger's) search for ways out of the Ge-stell."[7]

Heidegger's suspicion of the *Daodejing* led him to uncover a radically non-metaphysical interpretation of it that resonated with pre-Socratic thought, particularly in its attention to the phenomenological interplay of Being and Nothingness. This is in contrast to the metaphysics that was laid over the text with the appearance of the Huang-Lao *Daodejing*, where the metaphysical Dao was understood as an entity identified with *wu* as either Nothingness or as Non-being, which produces phenomenal *you* as Somethingness or Being. For the phenomenology of the Laozi *Daodejing*, the Dao cannot be identified with *wu* because they are not the same, where *wu* (as Nothingness considered in terms of absence) can only be conceived in its interplay with *you* (as Being considered in terms of presence). Whether Heidegger explicitly recognized the metaphysics of the standard Chinese interpretations of the *Daodejing* only to reject it or whether he remained unaware of it, it played no role in his reading of the text. He simply saw in the *Daodejing* a thought that was comparable to the pre-Socratics in that it was pre-metaphysical.

Western metaphysics separates Being as a first principle from the beings that it produces, but Chinese metaphysics (which developed directly from the *Daodejing*) separates Nothingness or Non-being as a first principle from the beings that it produces. On the other hand, phenomenology, whether of the sort articulated by the Laozi *Daodejing* or the pre-Socratics, integrates Being and Nothingness within the phenomenal world from where "poetic thinking" explores their interplay. For Heidegger, this involves the active involvement of humans able to allow things to be held forth in their unconcealment, often taking the form of art and poetry, for example, in the verses of the *Daodejing*, because of their ability to preserve the disclosures of being in aesthetic forms, linguistic, material, or otherwise. But the world has not yet overcome this destining of metaphysics, which alone will be the result of a return to the originary and primordial thinking that alone questions Being.

The line separating the Laozi *Daodejing* with its pristine Dao from the Huang-Lao *Daodejing* with its the cosmic Dao was established in 180 BCE, although the processes of metaphysicalization that led to the transformation from the former to the latter were already underway in the third century BCE. By a matter of coincidence, the name of the emperor who was enthroned in 180 BCE was Liu Heng 劉恆. Because the beliefs of the time mandated that upon enthronement the name of the emperor was tabooed, editors of the *Daodejing* had to find a different word to substitute for the tabooed *heng*, and they opted for *chang*.

There is a complex ancient history to both these terms, neither of which originally signified eternity/permanence/constancy. The Laozi *Daodejing* used *heng* to refer to the temporalizing and pristine nature of the Dao, whereas it used *chang* to refer to measurable extension. Largely due to the historical factors surrounding the substitution of *chang* for *heng* as well as to the philosophical factors involving the Huang-Lao philosophers who transformed the pristine Dao into the cosmic Dao by the beginning of the third century BCE, the terms had become synonyms meaning eternity/permanence/constancy.

Where *heng* in the Laozi *Daodejing* connotes notions of a watery presencing or a misty lingering, *chang* in the Huang-Lao *Daodejing* connotes a very different condition of eternity/permanency/constancy. The substitution of *chang* for *heng* used to identify the central feature of the Dao wrenched it out of the phenomenal world of the interplay of *wu* and *you* and re-situated it on a transcendent realm where *wu* was separated from *you* and given priority over it, standing as the original Nothingness outside of time and space that produces Being, that in turn produces the myriad things.

The metaphysicalization of the Dao of the *Daodejing*, itself deeply implicated with the origins of Chinese metaphysics, achieved completion with this term substitution, rendering to oblivion its phenomenology. Even the possibility of this phenomenology remained virtually inconceivable to readers both Chinese and Western of the *Daodejing* not yet equipped with the *Laozi* manuscripts to serve as roadmap back to the pristine Dao of the Laozi *Daodejing*, which should and likely will compel an interrogation of the traditional status of the cosmic Dao of the Huang-Lao *Daodejing*.

Either strangely or not so strangely, Heidegger had already uncovered the core feature of the phenomenology of the Laozi *Daodejing* long before the discovery of the *Laozi* manuscripts. Actually, he uncovered the two basic features of this phenomenology without which the metaphysics of the cosmic Dao could never be put into question. These are the pristine Dao that signifies a phenomenal, not a cosmic, source of existence, and the non-separation of *you* and *wu* in the phenomenal world. This is somewhat strange, given that Heidegger had negligible training in Chinese language, literature, history and, most importantly, negligible training in Chinese philosophy. But it is also not so strange, given that a non-cosmic, worldly source of existence as well as the co-primordiality, co-existence, and co-presence of *you* and *wu* (or presence and absence, or being and nothingness) are themselves the two basic features of phenomenology that Heidegger had already uncovered in the Pre-Socratics.

From his first encounters with the *Daodejing*, Heidegger deliberately approached it with an agenda: to assess if it posed the same primordial question of the meaning of Being that was posed by the pre-Socratics. While it is interesting to contemplate these possibilities, it is somehow of less importance at this point than the realization that it was precisely this question that gave Heidegger the possibility to bypass the traditional readings of the *Daodejing*, grounded as they almost entirely are in the metaphysics of the cosmic Dao, to confront the text directly. Ironically, this is something that scholars of the *Daodejing* including me have been unable to do because of our training from early on to learn the interpretative tradition rather than interrogate it.

There are three ways to look at Heidegger's uncovering of the phenomenology of the *Daodejing*. First, he was simply wrong and there is no phenomenology underlying the inescapable metaphysics of the text (which may or may not support other arguments that he seriously misread the Pre-Socratics). Second, he was right about this early Daoist phenomenology based on sheer coincidence, and the phenomenology of the *Daodejing* and the phenomenology of the pre-Socratics just happens to coincide in certain non-metaphysical ways. Or third, he was correct about the phenomenology of both the *Daodejing* and the pre-Socratics based on what he calls "the first beginning" in the face of the rapidly coordinating "destiny" of metaphysics. One consequence of this might be a possible realization that metaphysics, whether Western, Chinese, or any other sort, derive from a more primordial phenomenology. This is a question for comparative philosophy first of all, with all sorts of other implications (political in the widest sense of the term) to follow. From this perspective, Heidegger's uncovering of early Daoist phenomenology is not so strange, since his lifelong, overriding philosophical goal was to overturn metaphysics and with it the Gestell.

Throughout the course of the twentieth century, Heidegger's thoughts on Daoism were hardly entertained by sinologists, much as Western philosophy hardly entertained Chinese philosophy. For many years after the discovery of the pristine Dao in the *Laozi* manuscripts, sinologists still hardly interrogated the primacy of the metaphysical cosmic Dao, but the (English language) work of Wang Qingjie and the (Chinese language) work of Chen Ligui are two outstanding exceptions, from which much of the present work has taken direction. At present, a small cadre of scholars are beginning to rethink and cautiously distance themselves from the entire enterprise of interpreting the *Daodejing* according to the metaphysical dictates of the cosmic Dao, and in so doing, most all of them turn to Heidegger at one point or another.

Heidegger's legacy in opening the way to overcoming the metaphysical interpretation of the *Daodejing* should not be underestimated, nor should the differences in the total meaning of the text when interpreted metaphysically in conjunction with the cosmic Dao versus when interpreted phenomenologically in conjunction with the pristine Dao. Heidegger's phenomenological interpretation not only gives direction to contemporary phenomenological interpretations of the *Daodejing*, but it also continues to be intimately intertwined with them.

Heidegger and Comparative Philosophy

The philosophy of the Laozi *Daodejing* is not usually characterized as metaphysical, at least not explicitly. Interestingly, Ma and van Brakel come close to making this claim in their brief discussion of "Wang Bi's philosophical Daoism that advocates the centrality of the Nothing (無 *wu*) on the basis of the saying in chapter 40 of the [*Daodejing*] that what exists (有 *you*) comes from nothing," and they argue that "this approach [to the issue of emptiness in China] has the potential of being developed into an Asian version of metaphysics."[8]

Still, one cannot make a metaphysics out of something not-yet metaphysics without transforming its core meanings, but Wang Bi's metaphysical interpretation of the *Daodejing* was not "potential"; it was already actual. His metaphysical interpretation (together with Heshang Gong's earlier metaphysical interpretation) in fact had lost complete sight of the pristine Dao of the Laozi *Daodejing*, which long before had already been exchanged for the cosmic Dao of the Huang-Lao *Daodejing*.

As the ideas and methodologies of comparative philosophy continue to be developed, often through the auspices of "East–West Dialogue," it is a heavy order for scholars of Daoism, whether Chinese or Western, also to manage Heidegger as it is for Western philosophers also to handle the *Daodejing*. One major reason is that the tradition of Western metaphysics is not well equipped to manage the Chinese metaphysics of Nothingness, as Chinese metaphysics is not well equipped to manage the Western metaphysics of Being. Sinologists, usually without advanced training in philosophy, do not normally characterize the philosophy of the *Daodejing* as specifically metaphysical; for many of them, it is just Daoist philosophy.

Much like the pre-metaphysical philosophy of the pre-Socratics from which emerged Western metaphysics, the Laozi *Daodejing* is pre-metaphysical and from it emerged Chinese metaphysics. As Heidegger worked to uncover the pre-metaphysical thought of the pre-Socratics before the inception of Western metaphysics, so did he also see through the metaphysical veneer of traditional readings of the *Daodejing* to uncover its pre-metaphysical thought. In many ways, the question of the closeness between Daoist philosophy and Heideggerian philosophy is much less interesting than the question of the closeness between Daoist pre-metaphysical philosophy and Greek pre-metaphysical philosophy. But this is phenomenology, and there might be some value in distinguishing the pre-Socratic philosophy of ancient Greece and the Daoist philosophy of ancient China as ancient phenomenology or primordial phenomenology, in distinction to, say, the post-metaphysical philosophy of Heidegger.

The legacy of Heidegger's phenomenological reading of the *Daodejing* has two decisive aspects. The first, with respect to *Laozi* studies, was his success in entirely sidestepping the Chinese metaphysics of Nothingness (with Heshang Gong) and Non-being (with Wang Bi) brought to bear on readings of the text both traditional and modern to directly recognize the radically non-metaphysical core of its phenomenology. The second is that he established the *Daodejing* as canonical for the modern enterprise of comparative philosophy.

Ronnie Littlejohn characterizes comparative philosophy as "a subfield of philosophy in which philosophers work on problems by intentionally setting into dialogue various sources from across cultural, linguistic, and philosophical streams."[9] Still at a relatively undeveloped stage, comparative philosophy normally refers to encounters between Western and Eastern philosophy, but primarily Confucianism, Daoism, or Buddhism, where the comparative philosopher normally brings his/her training in Western philosophy to bear on Eastern philosophy, or vice versa. Littlejohn points out that the earliest works of comparative philosophy came from the Indian philosophers Sri Aurobindo (1872–1950) and Sarvepalli Radhakrishnan (1888–1975), and also the Japanese philosopher Nishida Kitarō (1870–1945), whose introduction of the Buddhist notion of Nothingness to Western philosophers was absorbed by Heidegger through several of Nishida's students who studied under him.[10]

Many others before Heidegger discussed Eastern philosophy, including the *Daodejing*, but they typically did so to introduce and explain it to the West or to remark on its deficiencies in contrast to Western philosophy; this is not comparative philosophy.[11] The collective enterprise of comparative philosophy itself as practiced today with respect to its parameters, methods, and objectives was largely formed and defined by Heidegger's understandings of and reflections on intercultural engagements and philosophical conversation between East and West. His most important articulations of them are dispersed among his later writings, but his 1959 essay, "A Dialogue on Language between a Japanese and an Inquirer,"[12] stands out among them.

This is to say that Heidegger is quite likely the founding figure of the modern enterprise of comparative philosophy. Although few have explicitly stated this in such straightforward ways, Ma and van Brakel come close; they write:

> The theme of "intercultural philosophical dialogue" has not received much focused attention ... Everyday examples of intercultural philosophical dialogue include: discussion between Heidegger and the Japanese Buddhist philosopher Hisamatsu Hōseke Shinichi; cooperation between the Chinese scholar Li Zhizao and the Jesuit Francisco Furtado in the seventeenth century; or the contemporary discussion between the American philosopher Rorty

and the Indian philosopher Balslev ... In German-language publications from the 1990's, a group of scholars ascribed to Heidegger's thinking a unique significance for the foundation, initiation, and orientation of cultural philosophy. According to them, Heidegger is the only great philosopher from the European traditions who took seriously the issue of East-West dialogue and hence something called intercultural philosophy. For example, Wolz-Gottwald argues that Heidegger has presented the "beginning of a 'creative' intercultural philosophy as a third way."[13]

Heidegger's legacy for comparative philosophy is matched by his legacy for *Laozi* studies. His familiarity with Daoist philosophy was, at least at first, channeled through a series of discussions throughout the 1920s and 1930s with several eminent Japanese philosophers studying in Germany. Although they were for the most part associated with the Kyoto School with its heavy influence from Buddhist thought, all of them were also familiar with the *Daodejing* as a classic of the Far Eastern philosophical and cultural tradition, but the *Daodejing* did not capture Heidegger's philosophical attention until after the Second World War.[14]

When the *Daodejing* did so, Heidegger read it without spending a lot of time with its European interpretations other than to reject their tendency to identify Laozi as a metaphysician; commenting on the unthoughtful discussions concerning philosophy among Europeans and "contemporary Indians, Chinese and Japanese," he writes that "everything is stirred up in a gigantic mishmash wherein it is no longer discernible whether or not the ancient Indians were English empiricists and Laozi a Kantian." [15]

Heidegger relied on several German translations of the *Daodejing* that were on hand. While some of them were more "philosophical" than others,[16] he approached the text directly in his own understanding and, although he had no training in Chinese, he went so far as to "translate" (the term is used with caution) at least eight of its chapters.[17] His colleague in this who assisted him to uncover the meanings of the *Daodejing* was the Taiwanese Paul Hsiao Shih-yi, a Roman Catholic studying theology in Italy who had dabbled with his own translation of the *Daodejing* into Italian. Given the state of *Laozi* studies at the time, it was probably more propitious that Heidegger studied with a non-specialist in *Laozi* studies who likely found it less disagreeable when Heidegger decisively broke with standard metaphysical interpretations of the text to think it phenomenologically on his own.

Next to Heidegger's widespread reception in the circles of Japanese philosophy, his thoughts on East–West dialogue have until recently been largely passed over by Western Heideggerian scholars who strictly attend to his position in and impact on Western philosophy. However, a watershed moment arrived in 1969 when Chang Chung-yuan, among the earliest of Chinese scholars to have attended to Heidegger's thought, organized an inaugural international conference on comparative philosophy at the University of Hawaii that was devoted to Heidegger's ideas about East–West dialogue.[18] To date, the work by the Chinese scholar Ma Lin has most successfully uncovered Heidegger's ideas about East–West dialogue, in part because of her advanced training in Chinese philosophy as well as in Heideggerian thought. Current trends of scholarship on East–West dialogue attend much more closely to Heidegger's ideas on the topic, with a great deal of success.

This study does not aim to further examine Heidegger's legacy for the modern enterprise of comparative philosophy to any extent, nor to rethink the influence of Asian thought including the *Daodejing* on his philosophy. Rather, it turns its focus to Heidegger's legacy that laid the foundations for contemporary interpretations of the *Daodejing* that strive to be cognizant of the dangers of subjecting it to traditional metaphysical interpretations, showing that Heidegger's engagement with the *Daodejing*'s pre-metaphysical phenomenology is bearing fruit.

Poetic Thinking and the *Daodejing*

Heidegger's interest in Asian philosophy stemmed from his conviction that the pre-Socratics were the first to think the question of the meaning of Being. By this, he meant that they contemplated the ontological difference between Being and beings, where the interplay of Being intertwined with Nothingness stands as the primordial ground from which all beings are brought forth as who or what they are; Heidegger writes, "Bringing-forth brings out of concealment into unconcealment."[19] Heidegger turns to the Greek term *aletheia* ("truth as disclosure") to refer to the phenomenal truth of this unconcealment.

The question of the meaning of Being thought by the pre-Socratics was, according to Heidegger, forgotten with the rise of Western philosophy beginning with Plato and Aristotle, a tradition that he consistently characterized as metaphysical. It conceives Being as a substantial entity, as with the eidos of Plato, the unmoved mover of Aristotle, or the God of Western monotheism. Heidegger recognized a distinct destiny for metaphysics that has already reached its completion in the planetary Ge-stell ("enframing"), a term Heidegger uses "as the name for the essence of modern technology."[20]

In the Ge-stell, beings are taken out of their lifeworld and fashioned into standing reserve for scientific manipulation. It signifies a condition in which the possibility for beings to be brought into their own unconcealedness is systematically strangled by "calculation, speed, and the claim of the massive."[21] The consequences of this are dire and threaten the well-being and survival of the planet as civilization turns to nihilism; Heidegger writes, "As soon as what is unconcealed no longer concerns man even as object, but exclusively as standing-reserve, and man in the midst of objectlessness is nothing but the orderer of the standing-reserve, then he comes to the very brink of a precipitous fall; that is, he comes to the point where he himself will have to be taken as standing-reserve."[22]

When Heidegger often speaks of the overcoming of metaphysics, he refers to a way of thinking that does not wrench beings out of their lived experience "in order to make them objects of investigation and to determine their grounds,"[23] but rather allows beings to be brought into their unconcealment. He intends that this way of thinking will offer new paths forward by which humans can find more appropriate relationships to the Ge-stell of modern technology, thereby to save the world. Heidegger writes that "only the greatest occurrence, the most intimate event, can still save us from lostness in the bustle of mere incidents and machinations. What must eventuate is what opens being to us and places us back into being and in that way brings us to ourselves and face to face with work and sacrifice."[24]

Heidegger conceives this "greatest occurrence" in various ways, but it primarily refers to an "inceptive thinking" that significantly differs from the scientific attitude. This inceptive thinking has its direct roots in the pre-Socratics who originally asked the meaning of the question of Being, an occurrence that Heidegger calls "the first beginning." For its part, the tradition of Western metaphysics was forged from out of the first beginning of the pre-Socratics and took shape as Being became an objectified essence or entity in the hands of the first metaphysicians.

Heidegger regularly encouraged a return to the pre-metaphysical thought of the pre-Socratics because doing so can initially direct the endeavor to develop our own ability to raise again the question of the meaning of Being within the Ge-stell of modern technology. The dawning of this inceptive thinking that will overcome metaphysics is what Heidegger calls "the second beginning" or "the other beginning"; he writes, "In this decisiveness [of renunciation as the highest form of possession], the open realm of the transition is sustained and grounded; this open realm is the abyssal in-between [where metaphysics reigns] amid the 'no longer' of the first beginning as well as of its history and the 'not yet' of the fulfillment of the other beginning."[25]

This is, in broad strokes, the context within which Heidegger approached Asian philosophy, to inquire if it too had ever raised the question of the meaning of Being. In line with this, Heidegger often discussed what it means to think the Same: is the question of the meaning of Being that he asks the same as the question of the meaning of Being that the pre-Socratics asked? His encounter with the *Daodejing* was directed by the inquiry into whether it too asked the same question of the meaning of Being, and if so, whether it too could be brought on board for the task of overcoming metaphysics; he asked, "whether in the end – which would also be the beginning – a nature of language can reach the thinking experience, a nature which would offer the assurance that European-Western saying and East Asian saying will enter into dialogue such that in it there sings something that wells up from a single source."[26]

That the *Daodejing* at present has a nearly canonical status in comparative philosophy is in large measure due to the prominence that Heidegger gave to it. He carved out a place for it in his own philosophy, and since there are not many other twentieth-century philosophies able to challenge its dominant standing in contemporary philosophy, the attention that Western philosophers give to Heidegger is also therefore attention that they give to the *Daodejing*. The irony in this is that Heidegger refused to recognize the thought of the *Daodejing* (but also of Asian philosophy more generally) as philosophy in the first place; for Heidegger, philosophy in the strict sense is exclusively and appropriately identifiable with metaphysics, and this of a definite Western sort: "The style of all Western-European philosophy – and there is no other, neither a Chinese nor an Indian philosophy—is determined by this duality 'beings – in being.'"[27]

In contrast to philosophy strictly understood as metaphysics, Heidegger found in the *Daodejing* what he called "thinking," "poetic thinking," or even "dwelling poetically."[28] Structurally, this thinking holds the same value in pre-Socratic thought as representing a pre-metaphysical philosophy, but given Heidegger's definition of philosophy, it is more appropriate to call that thinking pre-philosophical and non-metaphysical while remaining aware of the subtle difference between them.

Heidegger's resistance or refusal to identify the thought of the *Daodejing* as "philosophy" *sensu stricto* might appear to reflect the bias of Western philosophers that leads many of them to dismiss the *Daodejing* as non-philosophical and unworthy of their attention.[29] Ma Lin writes, "Although Heidegger was not the first to claim that ancient Greece is the sole and authentic birthplace of philosophy, his work has played the most crucial role in promoting the popularity this idea has come to enjoy."[30]

Heidegger's recognition of pre-Socratic thought as pre-metaphysical only makes sense with the subsequent formation of the tradition of Western philosophy itself understood as metaphysics. Since Heidegger did not recognize the tradition of Chinese metaphysics that was born from the thought of the *Daodejing* as the cosmic Dao was gradually being substituted for the pristine Dao, it could not be considered pre-philosophical, only non-metaphysical. But he indirectly established the structural relation between pre-Socratic thought and the thought of the *Daodejing* as "poetic thinking" in the deepest sense as the thinking of the question of the meaning of Being, and he goes on to recognize the *Daodejing* as the product of "Laozi's poetic thinking."[31]

Poetic thinking is non-metaphysical and, as demonstrated by the pre-Socratics if not also by the *Daodejing*, it is capable of thinking being, it is capable of assisting beings in being brought into unconcealment, and it is also capable of preserving them in their unconcealment. In this sense, poetic thinking differs from metaphysics in that it does not objectify beings but rather allows them to come into their unconcealment. The bringing-forth undertaken by thinking is, according to Heidegger, active and productive as a form of poiesis: "Not only handicraft manufacture, not only artistic and poetical bringing into appearance and concrete imagery, is a bringing-forth, poiesis."[32] He also states, "By no means, however, may the event [of the appropriation of Being] be represented as an 'incident' or a 'novelty.' Its truth, i.e., the truth itself, essentially occurs only if sheltered in art, thinking, poetry, deed. It therefore requires the steadfastness of the Da-sein [human being] that repudiates all the semblant immediacy of mere representation."[33]

Poetic thinking is inceptive because it gives rise to philosophy in the first beginning, but it is also a future activity that incepts the second beginning, which is capable of effectuating the release of beings (*gelassenheit*) from their subjection to the Ge-stell of modern planetary technology. Poetic thinking is inceptive because it opens the way to the second beginning that marks the overcoming of metaphysics; as Heidegger writes, "The thinking that is to come is no longer philosophy because it thinks more originally than metaphysics – a name identical to philosophy."[34]

Heidegger's resistance to recognizing the *Daodejing* as philosophy is the result of his identifying its thought as non-metaphysical. Although one need not agree with Heidegger's definition of philosophy as metaphysics that excludes the *Daodejing*, it is important to understand his intent and meaning in making that claim.

(Non-)Metaphysics and the *Daodejing*

The main reason that the *Daodejing* is foundational for Daoism as well as Chinese philosophy as a whole is because of its original introduction of a gathering of profound ideas about the Dao. The *Daodejing* conceives the Dao as the fundamental source for the existence of all things, as seen in *Daodejing* chapter 25: The Dao "was born before Heaven and Earth," and in *Daodejing* chapter 51: "The Dao gives birth to the myriad things."

Daodejing interpretation generally takes two forms: metaphysical and non-metaphysical or what can properly be called phenomenological. The differences between them is encapsulated by the following comments by Bo Mou, representative of the metaphysical interpretation, and by Roger Ames and David Hall, representative of the phenomenological (or, as they call it, process philosophy). Bo Mou writes:

> We first need to make clear what "*chang*-Dao" [the cosmic Dao] means. In my view, what "*chang*-Dao" denotes is not something that is separate from the genuine Dao as a whole but one dimension or layer of the Dao: its eternal and infinite dimension that consists in the Dao going on forever and continuously transcending any finite manifestations of the Dao in "wan-wu" (ten thousand particular, concrete, and individual things of the universe) in the course of its developing and changing process.[35]

Against this, Ames and Hall note "the absence of the 'One behind the many' metaphysics" of the *Daodejing* and write:

> As a parody of Parmenides, who claimed that "only Being is," we might say that for the Daoist, "Only beings are," or taking one step further in underscoring the reality of the process of change itself, "only becomings are." That is, the Daoist does not posit the existence of some permanent reality behind appearances, some unchanging substratum, some essential defining aspect behind the accidents of change.[36]

While there may seem to be no middle ground between the two interpretations of the Dao of the *Daodejing*, in fact neither is incorrect, but each must be assessed in relation to either the Laozi *Daodejing*, for which phenomenological interpretations are more appropriate, or the Huang-Lao *Daodejing*, for which metaphysical interpretations are more appropriate. If there is a judgment to be made between them, then it stems from the historical priority of the Laozi *Daodejing* over the second-generation Huang-Lao *Daodejing* and not the philosophical rightness or wrongness of either. The Huang-Lao *Daodejing*, although historically later, in the course of the second century BCE came to obliterate the very memory of the Laozi *Daodejing*, due unquestionably to the loss of the textual basis for the phenomenological reading of the pristine Dao.

A few phenomenological readings of the *Daodejing* have in fact historically appeared from time to time,[37] but their momentum was insufficient to affect the Chinese tradition of *Daodejing* exegesis, of either Heshang Gong's metaphysical sort or Wang Bi's meontological sort, both of whose readings were foundational for the formation of Wei-Jin Xuanxue Daoism. Already by the start of the Song Dynasty, such conceptions of the cosmic Dao provided the foundational basis for the spread and development of Neo-Confucian metaphysics, whose most important notion, *taiji* 太极, evolved directly from the cosmic Dao of the *Daodejing*.[38]

Metaphysics is a term with a particularly loaded content in the history of philosophy and religion in the West, where scholars in the field have hesitated to label the *Daodejing* as a work of metaphysics largely because of the failure to perceive a philosophically stable backbone in its thought (one consequence of the still reigning syncretic model) that could compete with the logical rationality of Western metaphysics. This is according to the assessments of modern philosophers, who typically judge the classics of Asian philosophy and religion against their own conceptions of what grounds philosophy: primarily a metaphysics of Being, as Heidegger argues. Since twentieth-century sinologists, recognized as those best qualified to speak about the *Daodejing*, were not particularly trained in philosophy, they too were unable to appropriately manage its philosophy, much less properly introduce it into the circles of Western philosophers.

Chinese metaphysics is different from Western metaphysics, even from a linguistic standpoint. Two common phrases for "metaphysics" in Chinese philosophy are *xing er shang* 形而上 ("above form" or "not-yet formed") associated with Heshang Gong's Nothingness, and *xuanxue* 玄學 ("dark" or "profound learning") associated with Wang Bi's Non-being; however, neither is exactly identifiable with traditional Western understandings of the metaphysics of Being. The notion of *xing er shang* points to the realm primarily characterized by the absence of forms, the not-yet formed, or the formless. This is in distinction to *xing er xia* 形而下 ("below form" or "already-formed"), which refers to the realm characterized by physical forms or the formed. Such notions are originally at home in the *Yijing*, which anyway does not establish a strictly transcendental divide between the two realms, since both are situated within the same world, only that the former is higher and earlier than the latter, but this too is a form of metaphysics.

As a title, *xuanxue* 玄學 refers to a tradition of Wei-Jin thought that takes *xuan* 玄 ("dark" or "mysterious") from the *Daodejing*, where it is used several times in close conjunction with the Dao. This tradition, whose metaphysics is only sometimes recognized as such, was spearheaded by Wang Bi, who identified the Dao with *wu* 無 as Non-being from which was produced *you* 有 as Being from which in turn were produced the myriad beings. One might therefore ask, if Wang Bi in fact established a metaphysics at the philosophical core of the Huang-Lao *Daodejing*, then why is its philosophy not then normally recognized as metaphysics? The simple answer is that his metaphysics of Non-being is not easily managed by the Western philosophical tradition with its metaphysics of Being. It typically understands any metaphysics of Non-being (but also any metaphysics of Nothingness such as conceived by Heshang Gong or even a similar metaphysics such as conceived by Buddhism) as a form of nihilism, which the Western tradition prima facie resists entertaining. And Heidegger's philosophy was also often accused of nihilism.

Wang Bi's interpretation of the *Daodejing* as a metaphysics of Non-being is not entirely original but rather innovative, since it inherited Heshang Gong's interpretation of it as a metaphysics of Nothingness. Both of their metaphysics were grounded on the Huang-Lao *Daodejing*'s notion of the cosmic Dao that refers to a substantive or essentialized entity (as either Nothingness or Non-being), standing as both eternal and external source for the production of the world and all its beings.

Heshang Gong's interpretation of the *Daodejing* was standard throughout most of traditional China, but Wang Bi's started its slow path to dominance when the Neo-Confucians recognized it as orthodox around the beginning of the Song Dynasty. Western sinologists maintained that dominance at the expense of Heshang Gong's interpretation. Among the main reasons for this was because Wang Bi's metaphysics (or meontology) was somewhat less foreign to the Western tradition of metaphysics than Heshang Gong's. Still, interpretations of the text based on any sort of metaphysics, whether of Being, Non-being, or Nothingness, have perennially struggled to produce viable readings of the Huang-Lao *Daodejing*. It is not surprising since the notion of the cosmic Dao allowed few possibilities for the original phenomenology of the Laozi *Daodejing* to show itself; but the cracks are there.

Heidegger's was the first decisive Western interpretation of the *Daodejing* that, largely due to its ignoring the metaphysical notion of the cosmic Dao, uncovered the text's fundamental phenomenology that was grounded on the notion of the pristine Dao. Zhang Xianglong writes, "To my judgment,

Heidegger's understanding of Dao is essentially 'closer' to the original meaning of 'Dao' than any metaphysical interpretations. Dao, as the Way, is ontologically regional-ecstatical rather than conceptual and linear."[39]

Sinology, Philosophy, and History of Religions

Between the Western sinologist's unwillingness or inability to adequately represent the core philosophy of the *Daodejing* and the Western philosopher's dismissal of it as insufficiently philosophical, Heidegger opened a third path to approach it, that of comparative philosophy. More and more scholars are finding philosophical ways around traditional metaphysical interpretations of the *Daodejing*, and, when they do, it is most often by recourse to similar kinds of phenomenological interpretations that Heidegger brought to the *Daodejing* when he was putting his imprint on the enterprise of comparative philosophy.

Over the past twenty years that the *Laozi* manuscripts have been stewing, almost behind the scenes as it were, in the awareness of scholars in the field, a couple of developments are worth noting. The most exciting developments in sinology concern the ever-continuing discoveries of early Chinese excavated texts and the meticulous work of making sense of them. Sinologists have completed much of the work of making sense of the *Laozi* manuscripts, and they are turning to more recently discovered manuscripts, particularly the Huang-Lao manuscripts.

The most exciting developments in philosophy concern the growing resistance to traditional metaphysical readings of the *Daodejing*, and a healthy number of scholars are at work pursuing the kinds of non-metaphysical approaches to the *Daodejing* pioneered by Heidegger (not to be confused with Heideggerian readings of the text, a project whose value has so far not proven very high). Nonetheless, scholarly efforts to make sense of the *Daodejing* remain hindered by phenomenologically interpreting a metaphysical entity but doing so does not make that metaphysical entity any more phenomenological. The recognition that there is both a Laozi *Daodejing* whose philosophical core is the phenomenological pristine Dao and a Huang-Lao *Daodejing* whose philosophical core is the metaphysical cosmic Dao may prove helpful for bringing *Laozi* studies to new levels of progress and, we may hope, to new levels of contemporary relevance.

This study closes by pointing to various paths not here followed. One is the path of excavated manuscripts, whose continuing discoveries hold the keys to a better historical understanding of early Chinese Daoism. Another is the path of exploring the further textual differences between the two versions of the *Daodejing* and, even more important, beginning the process of producing modern scholarly editions of each one separately, fully informed by the manuscripts themselves, with a clear eye to the differences and distinctions between them. All this is the province of sinology.

The paths of comparative philosophy left unfollowed in this study are even more numerous and in many ways were more difficult to resist; however, two of them in particular deserve special recognition. In the late 1980s, David Hall and Roger Ames first began to champion what they saw as the radical differences between Western and Chinese thought, which they presented with the provocative claim that Chinese philosophy was a tradition without transcendence. Their claim established an enduring framework within which professional research in the field has largely been directed, a major consequence of which was to depict Chinese philosophy as non-religious in the common understanding of the term. This view is also in keeping with more long-standing cultural claims, often coming from the West, that China is a godless civilization, at least with respect to a transcendent creator god, and Chinese philosophy is often treated as a tradition of respectable naturalism. The recognition that the cosmic Dao is beyond doubt a transcendent entity should no longer go unnoticed, despite that the language used in this study centered on "metaphysics" more than "transcendence," but there is great overlap between them.

In addition to debates about transcendence, the second unfollowed path of comparative philosophy in this study is the entire issue of metaphysics itself. Heidegger was not unusual in thinking that metaphysics is one of the unique cultural features of the West, and he did not consider various other kinds of it, especially Chinese ones. This study not only recognizes two distinct kinds of Chinese metaphysics, but it also conceives their origins as not separate from the Huang-Lao appropriation of the Laozi *Daodejing*. Their metaphysicalization of the Dao paved the way to Heshang Gong's metaphysics of Nothingness, followed by Wang Bi's metaphysics of Non-being. This path would explore the different values, philosophically and otherwise, of three different metaphysics: the Western metaphysics of Being, the Huang-Lao metaphysics of Nothingness, and the Xuanxue metaphysics of Non-being, the last two of which are exclusively accessed by way of the *Daodejing*.

This leaves two final paths left unfollowed herein to be recognized, both of which fall into the general arena of history of religions. The first is further and deeper research on *yangsheng*, and the notable area that most loudly hollers for attention is the shared ground between the *Daodejing* and the Mawangdui *yangsheng* writings within the context of the tradition of Chinese medicine more generally. One of the particular features of the Chinese medical tradition is its recognition and management of the same rhythmic systems of circulation that the Laozi *Daodejing* identified with *de*.

Very much related to this area is the second path, that of the Daoist body. This path is already well trod and has received a lot of scholarly attention, but the role and value of Daoist *yangsheng* for Chinese conceptions of the body both traditional and modern have been greatly neglected.

As mentioned at the beginning of this study, among all cultural traditions, Daoism is among the most misunderstood. At the same time, it has also of late been generating tremendous enthusiasm among scholars from various disciplines. The present study hopes to contribute to that enthusiasm and also to further the project of cross-cultural studies between China and the West.

Notes

Chapter 1

1. Han 2013 offers one of the few good studies of the Beida *Laozi*.
2. Wagner 1989, 30.
3. Hansen 1992, 215.
4. Burik 2009, 77.
5. Burik 2009, 89.
6. Heidegger 1971b, 92, quoted from Ma 2008, 151.

Chapter 2

1. For more on Daoist *yangsheng*, see Zhang R. (2003), Despeux (2004), Kohn (2008); for Ge Hong's understanding of it, see Hu (1989), Michael (2016).
2. *SKQS:SXZ* 1.7b-8a.
3. *NP* 5,114.
4. Xuan Nü and Su Nü are two semi-mythical females said to have instructed Huangdi in the sexual arts; see also van Gulik (2003, 74–5, *passim*). Wile (1992) has provided the most thorough study of these two figures; see also Cahill (2013).
5. *NP* 6, 124.
6. *NP* 6, 124.
7. *LWMS:SXZ* 10.4a.
8. Zhu Y 2008, 151.
9. *NP* 14, 256.
10. *NP* 6, 129; 18, 324.
11. *NP* 18, 324–5.
12. *NP* 8, 149.
13. *NP* 8, 150.
14. *NP* 4, 71.
15. *NP* 8, 151.
16. Zhu Y 2008, 150–1.
17. Campany 2002, 175 comments that *cainü* was a general term for harem women, but this particular woman was renowned in later Daoist writings where she was called Cainü.
18. *SKQS:SXZ* 1.4a.

19 *SKQS:SXZ* 1:7b. For more detail on these titles, see Campany 2002, 180.
20 *SKQS:SXZ* 1.7a.
21 *SKQS:SXZ* 1.7b.
22 *SKQS:SXZ* 1:4b-5a.
23 *NP* 13:242.

Chapter 3

1 Ariel and Raz 2010, 392.
2 Ariel and Raz 2010, 410.
3 Identifying the *Daodejing* with the Dao itself is not as outlandish as it might first appear. Schaberg (2015, 101) also arrives at a similar understanding: "[It] is possible to think of exercises in *Laozi*-verse not as external to their subject (reflections on, analyses of), but as attempts to create a verbal model of the subject, a microcosmic version of it that illustrates some of its functions by putting them in play in the words themselves. Since this would not be analysis, nothing like deduction would be necessary or even desirable. The satisfactions of patterning that come with the interlocking parallel style, the repetitions and successive modulations, would not be about *dao*, but would be *dao* in a miniature, experimental."
4 Schipper 1993, 185.
5 Hendrischke 2019, 164.
6 Billeter 1985, 31.
7 The Guodian *Laozi* is unusual in having "those who excel at being noble" 善為士者 instead of "those who excel in the practice of the Dao" 善為道者; see, for example, Henricks (2000, 39). Billeter notes that the reference to "this Dao" 此道 later in the chapter makes no sense without the Dao in this line to serve as its referent.
8 Billeter 1985, 15.
9 Billeter 1985, 23.
10 Billeter 1985, 25.
11 See Girardot 1988.
12 Billeter 1985, 31.
13 Billeter 1985, 32-3.
14 One noteworthy exception is Zhang R. (2003), in whose Chapter 7 is found a reading of *Daodejing* chapter 15 much in keeping with Billeter's, although somewhat less rigorous.
15 Ariel and Raz 2010, 413.
16 Hansen 2007.
17 See Michael 2017 discusses these two models more closely.

18 Although this is a position championed by Graham 1989, it substantially suffered with the 1993 discovery of the Guodian *Laozi*; nevertheless, Kim 2013 does his best to weave it into his refined rearticulation of the position.
19 Sivin 1978, 305.
20 Strickmann 1979, 165.
21 Hansen 2007.
22 Lau 1964.
23 LaFargue 1994.
24 Graham 1998.
25 But the most extreme version of the syncretic model would even deny to the Guodian *Laozi* the distinction of serving as the kernel of the *Daodejing*; as Boltz 1999, 594 writes: "Rather than claiming that this is 'an early version of the *Daodejing*,' we can only argue that this is a collection of passages that came over the course of the third century to be mixed in an unpredictable sequence with an approximately equal number of passages not seen in these manuscripts, ending up as a *mixtum compositum* that has been transmitted as the *Daodejing*."
26 Shaughnessy 2005, 451.
27 Boltz 1999, 594.
28 Shaughnessy 2005.
29 Chen 1988, 2015.
30 For more on this component of the *Lüshi Chunqiu*, see Sellmann 2002.
31 These exceptions notably include some portions of the text that discuss the art of war and appear to be non-essential additions either to the philosophy of the Dao or to bodily cultivation. Michael 2020 considers the possibility that those who were involved with the earliest circulations of the Laozi *Daodejing* were in close conversation with those who were involved with the earliest circulations of the militarist philosophy represented in the *Sunzi Bingfa*, and who themselves comprised a particular community of their own.
32 Roth offers an interesting case. On the surface, he holds to the syncretic model since he affirms that the written text of the *Daodejing* was the late Warring States product of an editor who collected and compiled various verses that he calls "the lore of the Way." However, he also maintains the staple assumptions of the synthetic model: about coherency, he writes, "The foundational texts of the Daoist tradition were produced within one or more closely related master-disciple lineages" (1998, 61–2); about oral antiquity, he writes, "This 'lore of the Way' may reach back in time well before it was recorded in written form in the mid-fourth century BCE" (1999, 202); and about community, he writes that this "lore of the Way" was "recited by masters to their students" (1999, 41).
33 Shaughnessy 2005, 452.
34 Graham 1998 and Kim 2013.
35 Hansen 2007 and Meyer 2009.

36 Ariel and Raz 2010.
37 Fung Yu-lan 1966.
38 Schipper 1993, Roth 1999, and Michael 2015a.
39 Levi 1984, 86.
40 Billeter 1985, 8.
41 For example, Roth 1999, 202 writes, "The transmission of the practices and philosophy of inner cultivation in regular, often tetrasyllabic and rhymed metrical verse that formed distinct units suggests that, before early Daoist texts like the *Inward Training* [*Neiye*] and the *Daodejing* were written down, they were transmitted orally within lineages of masters and disciples."
42 Meyer 2009, 838.
43 Meyer 2012, 227.
44 Meyer 2012, 228.
45 Meyer 2009, 843.
46 Chan 2008.
47 LaFargue 1994, 48–9.
48 Roth 1999, 186.
49 Hendrischke 2019, 164–5.
50 Liao and Li 2017, 147.
51 Hendrischke 2019, 165.
52 Schipper 1993, 184–5.
53 Baxter 1998, 249.
54 Schipper 1993, 191.
55 Schipper 1993, 186.
56 Schipper 1993, 195.
57 Roth 1999, 168.
58 Schaberg 2015, 104.
59 Roth 1999, 89.
60 Schipper 1993, 195.
61 Roth 1999, 61–2.
62 A detailed examination of these *yangsheng* masters found in the *Zhuangzi* is Michael 2015b.
63 Wang B 2014, 197–410.
64 Eno 1990.
65 Schaberg 2015, 102.
66 Roth 1999, 202.
67 Sun 2008, 182.
68 For more on the position of *yangsheng* in these texts, see Cook 2006.
69 The "Yiwenzhi" of the *Hanshu* lists many additional titles of lost *fangji* texts in four categories: medicine 醫, pharmacopoeia 經方, the sexual arts 房中, and divine longevity 神仙.
70 Harper 1998, 52.

71 Original quotations from the *Shiji* and the *Hanshu* are from ctext.org.
72 Hu 1999, 270–1.
73 Michael 2015a, 119–32.
74 Hu 1999, 271.
75 Harper 1998, 6.
76 Harper 1998, 42–3.
77 Harper 1987, 544.
78 What Harper means by "scholarly convention" is unclear since Anglo-American scholarship (with the likes of Roth and Kohn as exceptions) only rarely recognizes an early Daoist community from which *yangsheng* could have originated. The French scholarship represented by Maspero and Schipper certainly recognize such a community.
79 Harper 1998, 114.
80 Harper 1995, 383–4.
81 Harper 1998, 114.
82 Other *Daodejing* chapters dominated by *Laozi*-style tetrasyllables include 9, 19, 30, and 41.
83 Schaberg 2015, 88.
84 Schaberg 2015, 89.
85 This phenomenon is richly explored by Queen 1996.
86 Schaberg 2015, 90.
87 Schaberg 2015, 103.
88 Schaberg 2015, 102.
89 Harper 1998, 111.
90 Schaberg 2015, 104.
91 Outstanding Western sinological work on the excavated texts include Henricks 1989, 2000; Mair 1990; Boltz 1999; and Cook 2012; outstanding Chinese works include Chen G 2015 and Liu 2003.
92 Ding 2017, 162–3.
93 Lau 1964, xi.
94 Graham 1998.
95 Boltz 1993.
96 LaFargue 1994.
97 Michael 2017 compares Kim's 2013 syncretic model with my synthetic model.
98 Schipper 1993.
99 Baxter 1998.
100 Wagner 2003.
101 Wagner 2003.
102 Michael 2015a.
103 See for example Roth 1999; Schaberg 2015, and Hendrischke 2019.
104 Baxter 1998, 186.
105 Baxter 1998, 249.

106 Schaberg 2015, 89–90.
107 LaFargue 1994, 301–36 argues that the accumulation of introductory, transitional, and summarizing comments demonstrates the work of later editors who compiled the disparate materials into the syncretic *Daodejing*. In his defense, LaFargue did not have access to the Guodian *Laozi* at the time his work was published.
108 Ding Sixin 2017, 176, holds to a quite similar understanding:

> I propose to use the concept of "atomic section division" (or "atomic sections") to describe the distinctive feature of the *Daodejing* text at this stage. What I call "atomic section division" refers to an ideal state of section division in the *Daodejing*, where the constitution of every section and its specific textual segmentation is grounded in a singular "meaning" (or "unit of thought"), and cannot be subdivided any further. The [Guodian *Laozi*] is qualified precisely by "atomic section divisions," and every section of this version is "singular" in terms of unit of thought and unit of text. We see that each section of the [Guodian *Laozi*] either maintained its original condition ("the original section") and was not yet altered in the [the Beida *Laozi*] or only a part of a section was spliced into a new section one. There are no exceptions to these two options.

109 Meyer 2009, 836.
110 Meyer 2009, 843.
111 Meyer 2012, 205.
112 Meyer 2009, 843.
113 Meyer 2009, 192.
114 Meyer 2012, 206.
115 Meyer 2012, 194.
116 Liao and Li 2017, 151.
117 Liao and Li 2017, 153.
118 Ding 2017, 161–2.
119 Liu 2003, 338–9, examines other causes of difference between versions: "'linguistic assimilation' (that) describes the general tendency of editors of the *Daodejing* to replace some words, phrases, or passages with common terms or patterns according to their understanding of the message and style of the text (and) 'conceptual focusing' (that) refers to processes designed to bring out the intellectual insights and key concepts of the *Daodejing*."
120 Meyer 2012, 193.
121 Meyer 2012, 194.
122 Ding 2017, 177.
123 Wang Q 2001, 202.

Chapter 4

1. Chen 2013, 30.
2. Ames and Hall 2003, 77.
3. Original quotations from *Ziyi* are from Cook 2012.
4. This translation is greatly underrepresented in Western scholarship, but important discussions of it include Hansen 1992, 214–22, Yu 2003, 170–6, and Michael 2015a, 17–21.
5. Bo 2003, 247.
6. Kaltenmark 1965, 29–30.
7. Hansen 1992, 215.
8. Bo 2003, 249–50.
9. Patt-Shamir 2009, 409.
10. Chen 2017, 48.
11. Original quotations from the *Shijing* are from ctext.org. While I have consulted James Legge's translations of the *Shijing*, also found at ctext.org, all translations are my own.
12. Original quotations from the *Yijing* are from ctext.org.
13. Original quotations from the *Shuowen* are from ctext.org.
14. Wang Q 2001, 50.
15. Wang Q 2001, 57.
16. Wang Q 2001, 57.
17. Wang Q 2000, 149.
18. Wang Q 2001, 57–8.
19. Hansen 1992, 218.
20. Original quotations from the *Mozi* are from ctext.org.
21. Hansen 1992, 210.
22. Hansen 1992, 120.
23. Chen 2014, 19.
24. Chen 2014, 20.
25. Michael 2015a, 164–73 provides a more detailed analysis of *de* in the *Daodejing*.
26. On the present point, Harper 1995, 383 writes: "It is clear that the bellows analogy has physiological significance in *Daodejing* chapter 5. 'Guarding the inside' (*shouzhong* 守中) is attending to the physio-spiritual needs of the body, in preference to parading one's intelligence and talent; the ideal is presumably a microcosmic 'inner emptiness' which is simultaneously a source of vitality, comparable to the bellows bag (*tuo* 橐) and tube (*yue* 籥). However, the *Daodejing* does not appear to correlate the bellows bag and tube with the physiology of the body itself, nor does it indicate how such a physiological bellows might be activated through cultivation techniques." Harper's discussion of the presence of *yangsheng* in *Daodejing* chapter 5 intends to show that it was derived or inspired from external sources such as the Mawangdui *Yinshu*. However, the *Daodejing* is not a practice

manual, and anyway its explanation of why the bellows bag correlates to the physiological body is given with remaining content of the chapter.

27 Billeter 1985, 13–4.
28 This final line is not found in the Guodian *Laozi*. Mawangdui A has lacunae for the final three characters, but there is little reason to suppose they differ from Mawangdui B and the received text. Mawangdui B has "flea" 蚤 (*zao*), a homonym for "early" 早 (*zao*).
29 The confusion between longevity and immortality is longstanding in Daoist studies. Robert Company 2002 provides an example of this, against which both Zhang J 2012 and Michael 2016, 119–21 have called foul.
30 Chen 2017, 49.
31 Michael 2015a, 205–11.
32 Mawangdui A has "emotion" 情 instead of "stillness" 靜 as found in Mawangdui B and the received text, certainly a scribal error.
33 Mawangdui B seems to be the only edition with the correct character, "overseer" 督. Mawangdui A has "surface" 表, again certainly a scribal error, while the received text oddly has "sincere" 篤.
34 Both Mawangdui manuscripts have "side by side" 旁, the received text has "together" 並.
35 The received text has "natural" 天 instead of "now the ... " 夫, a likely scribal error.
36 The predominantly *yangsheng* uses of "stillness" occur in *Daodejing* chapters 15, 16, and 57, and the predominantly philosophical ones occur in *Daodejing* chapters 26, 37, 45, and 67.
37 Michael 2015a, 197–221 examines the notion of bad knowledge in the *Daodejing*.
38 Mawangdui manuscript A has "to accord with *chang*" 襲常, manuscript B has a lacuna, and the received text has "to practice *chang*" 習常, which makes no sense and is certainly a scribal error.

Chapter 5

1 Wang B 2005, 38–9.
2 Wang Q 2001, 56.
3 Chen 2014, 23.
4 Wang Z 2019, 1–2.
5 Chen 1988.
6 Wang Z 2011.
7 Wang Z 2013, 2016b.
8 Wang B 2005.
9 Wang Q 2001, 55.

10 Wang Q 2000, 150–1.
11 Wang Z 2016a, 42, 2019, 21. The first reference is to the original Chinese article (2016a), and the second is to the English-language translation (2019).
12 Wang Z 2016a, 42, 2019, 21. Ding's 2016 study of *heng* relies on Wang's explanation of the original character as "the crescent moon," although he cites it from a separate article by Wang Z 2008. Ding provides visual presentations of the ancient variations of *heng* 恆, gen 亙, and ji 極 in the ancient Chu script of the *Hengxian*.
13 Shaughnessy 2014, 167–9 charts the various hexagram numbers and sequences from the received *Zhou yi*, the *Mawangdui Zhou yi*, the *Wangjiatai Zhou yi*, and the *Ma Guohan Gui cang* next to the incomplete *Shanghai Zhou yi* and *Fuyang Zhou yi*.
14 Wang Q 2000, 152 cites the sequences of the Xu Commentary (followed by all other commentaries in the received *Yijing*), the Za Commentary, the Meng Xi/Jing Fang, and the Mawangdui.
15 Next to Shaughnessy 2014 and Li 2013, the *Gui cang* has received little scholarly attention.
16 Shaughnessy 2014, 181, slightly modified.
17 Shaughnessy 2014, 163.
18 Original quotations from *Zuozhuan* are from ctext.org.
19 Original quotations from the *Mencius* are from ctext.org.
20 Original quotations from the *Zhanguoce* are from ctext.org.
21 Original quotations from the *Zhuangzi* are from ctext.org.
22 Original quotations from the *Lunyu* are from ctext.org.
23 Wang Z 2016a, 43, 2019, 22.
24 Compare James Legge's translation of *heng* as "permanent": "Ah! ye gentlemen! Do not reckon on your rest being permanent. Quietly fulfil the duties of your offices … Do not reckon on your repose being permanent. Quietly fulfil the duties of your offices."
25 Original quotations from the *Guoyu* are from ctext.org.
26 Original quotation from Li Ling 2013, 50–1.
27 Wang Z 2016a, 37.
28 Wang Q 2000, 152.
29 Wang Q 2000, 153.
30 See Ding 2016 for an informed summary of these scholars' findings on the issue.
31 Wang Q 2000, 153.
32 Qiu 2009 remains very relevant to the issue.
33 Wang Z 2016a, 38, 2019, 6.
34 Wang Z 2016a, 37, 2019, 8, notes that the editors of the excavated manuscript have changed *heng* to *ji* in this passage; see also Cook 2012, 286.
35 Wang Z 2016a, 41, 2019, 17.
36 Wang Q 2000, 154.

37. This final line is not included in the Guodian *Laozi*.
38. Wang Q 2000, 155, gives a slightly different interpretation of this passage, which is nonetheless closer to mine than Henricks' 1989, 190 that remains squarely epistemological: "These are all constants." Ames and Hall 2003, 80, translate the phrase 恆也 idiosyncratically as "This is really how it all works." That the Guodian *Laozi* does not have this line anyway leads Henricks 1989, 272, to write, "Without this *heng ye*, however, those lines remain incomplete." Cook 2012, 250, also remarks: "Given all the 之 above, we would expect some concluding thought here to a series of what read as dependent clauses; however, only Mawangdui here has 恆也, 'these are constancies,' to complete the sentence."
39. Wang Q 2000, 161.
40. Wang Q 2000, 154.
41. This line is not in the Guodian *Laozi*, and the received edition has 大道汎兮其可左右.
42. Note that this line is not included in either the Guodian or the Mawangdui *Laozi* manuscripts.
43. The Guodian uses an unknown character usually interpreted as 狀 that is also very close to *dao* 道. Cook 2012, 256, surveys various interpretations, none of which support its use as signifying an actual thing or entity, as in the Mawangdui and received editions.
44. Girardot 1988 famously explores the Daoist notion of "chaos" *hun* 混 or *hundun* 混沌.
45. This chapter is particularly rife with variants; Cook 2012, 257, writes that they "all bear close phonetic relationships with each other," but I remark only on the most important.
46. Cook 2012, 257.
47. Ames and Hall 2003, 210.
48. Chen 2011, 102. For a more nuanced view of these issues, see Chai 2018.
49. Wang 2018, 5.
50. Wang Z 2019, 7.
51. Wang Z 2019, 8.
52. Michael 2015a, 175–96, gives an alternative view on the Daoist notion of salvation 救.
53. Wang Q 2000, 154.
54. Wang Q 2000, 154.
55. Wang Q 2000, 154.
56. Wang Q 2000, 154–5.
57. Wang Q 2000, 155.
58. Wang Q 2000, 156.
59. The Mawangdui *Laozi* situates the four greats within "the state" 國 not the "realm" 域.
60. Fried 2018, 130.

61 Chen 2017, 134.
62 Liu 2006, 315.
63 Perkins 2109, 28.
64 Hendrischke 2019, 170.
65 Chen 2017, 141.
66 Chen 2017, 136.
67 Chen 2017, 136–7.
68 Chen 2017, 136.
69 Chen 2017, 138–9.
70 Chen 2015, 159–63.
71 Wang Z 2016a, 171.
72 See, for example, Schönfeld (2020).
73 Heidegger 1971c, 176.
74 Wang Z 2016a, 171.
75 Ames and Hall 2003, 116.

Chapter 6

1 Original quotations from both works are from ctext.org.
2 Ding 2017, 176.
3 Classic studies on *Zhuangzi* chapter attributions are Graham 1981 and Liu 1994.
4 See Roth 1992 and Klein 2010.
5 Translated by Major et al. 2012. See Queen and Puett 2014.
6 Roth 1991, 308.
7 See Els 2018.
8 See Defoort 1997.
9 Seidel Falkenhausen 2008, 135.
10 Roth 1991, 295.
11 For studies on the confluence of Huang-Lao and Daoism in the official histories, see Van Ess 1993, Loewe 1994, Smith 2003, and Csikszentmihalyi and Nylan 2003.
12 Benjamin Schwartz 1985, 237–54, among others, discusses several of the most easily identified of them including Song Xing, Tian Pian, Shen Dao, and Shen Buhai.
13 The Four Classics were given titles after excavation and are "Jingfa" 經法 (Classic of Law), "Shiliujing" 十六經 (Sixteen Classics), "Cheng" 稱 (Assessments), and "Daoyuan" 道原 (Origin of the Dao). English translations include Ryden 1997, Yates 1997, and Chang and Yu 1998.
14 Peerenboom 1993, 4.
15 The recent work of Zheng Kai 2019 focuses on the deeper philosophical connections between Huang-Lao and Daoist thought and deserves close attention.
16 The classic study of these texts is Wang Z 2011.

17 Brindley 2019 is a detailed study of *Taiyi shengshui*, Pang 2004 and Chen 2008 of *Hengxian*, and Perkins 2017 of *Fanwu Liuxing*.
18 Ding 2008, 53.
19 Namely "Liu Fan," "Nei chu shuo xia," and "Nan San." See Kim 2010. The "Tian Lun" 天論 chapter of *Xunzi* 荀子 appears among the first early Chinese writings to mention Laozi by name, and Hanfeizi once served as Xunzi's student.
20 Queen 2013, 214.
21 Queen 2014, 215.
22 *Guoyu* 國語, "Luyu xia" 魯語下 10:7b–10:8a: "Those sharing the same surname are brothers. Huangdi had 25 sons … Those who were born from the same father [Huangdi] but were given different surnames were the sons of four different mothers and were distinguished by the twelve surnames. The sons of Huangdi formed 25 ancestral lines." See also Chen 1991.
23 The "Jingfa" of the *Huangdi Sijing*: "In antiquity, Huangdi in his essential nature began to love constancy; he made himself into a stellar model and oriented his four faces, concentrating his heart-mind. Reaching out in four directions from the center, he set the three marks in the front, he set the three marks in the back, he set the three marks to his left, he set the three marks to his right. He manifested his position placed within the center of the marks, and therefore was able to be ancestor of all under Heaven."
24 *Shiji* 1, 1:2b–1:3b: "In the time of Huangdi, Shen Nong had allowed the world to fall into decline; all of the rulers attacked and invaded each other's territories and oppressed the hundred families. Shen Nong could not bring this under control. Then Huangdi practiced the management of shields and lances to bring to submission those who refused to pay homage to the court; the rulers all came with respect and obedience. However, Chi You was the most terrible and remained invincible … He wreaked havoc and paid no heed to the imperial orders. Then Huangdi called the rulers to arms and gave battle to Chi You in the country of Zhuolu. He seized Chi You and put him to death. Then the rulers elevated Huangdi to the rank of the Son of Heaven." See also Lévi 1996.
25 *Huainanzi* 6: 6.6b–7a: "In ancient times Huangdi ruled all under Heaven … He measured out the course of sun and moon and regulated the *qi* of *yin* and *yang*, apportioned the length of the seasons and rectified the numbers of the calendar, separated men and women and distinguished male and female [animals], made clear the distinction between those above and those below and classified the ranks of noble and common." See also Le Blanc 1985.
26 For more on the role of Huangdi in this text, see Unschuld 2003.
27 Original text from Yates 1997, 112–6.
28 Chan 1998, 106.
29 Xiong and Liu 2004, 54–5 discuss the Huang-Lao influence on Lu Jia's writings.

30 Chan 1998, 105 and Xiong and Liu 2004, 55 cite Yang Shuda 1936 for these fifty names of Han Huang-Lao proponents active in and around the court.
31 Xiong and Liu 2004, 54.
32 Xiong et al. 2005, 205.
33 The standard modern English translation is Queen and Major 2015.
34 Concerning these events, Vankeerberghen 2001 focuses on Liu An, Wang A 2000 focuses on Dong Zhongshu, and Cai 2014 focuses on Emperor Wu.
35 Xiong et al. 2005, 197.
36 Chan 1998, 124.
37 Yan Zun's dates are unclear; Chen 2019 examines his extant biographies.
38 Berkowitz 2000, 93; see also Vervoorn 1988 and Berkowitz 2000.
39 Seventy-two is a significant number in the *yin-yang* numerology: *yang* nine times *yin* eight is seventy-two. Wang B 2013 examines the commentary's cosmological structures, and Fan 2014 examines the Preface to the commentary that also explains the work's cosmological structure, but it was likely a later addition.
40 Fan 2013, 1.
41 Chan 1998, 107.
42 Shang de bu de pian 2.
43 My continued use of identifying the *Chunqiu Fanlu* with Dong Zhongshu is for convenience; Queen and Major 2015, 16, write that the text is "a composite work, compiled by an unknown editor from diverse sources long after Dong Zhongshu's death."
44 Wang R 2005, 93. Queen (1996) is another valuable study of its cosmology.
45 Chan 1998, 126.
46 Chan 1998, 122.
47 Ding 2018, 57.
48 Ding 2018, 2.
49 Robinet 1981, 20–1.
50 Creel 1970, 1–24.
51 Zhi bu zhi pian 2.
52 *Daodejing* chapter 17.
53 *Daodejing* chapters 37 and 48.
54 Ding 2018, 57.
55 Many scholars say that if there is an ideology in the *Daodejing*, it is anarchism. See Ames 1983, Feldt 2010, Rapp 2012, and Stamatov 2014.
56 Chan 1991, 144.
57 Chan 1991, 147.
58 Xiong et al. 2005, 56.
59 Zhang ZG 2008, 202.
60 Chan 1998, 123.
61 Chan 1998, 117.

62 Ding 2018, 61.
63 Liu 2008, 55.
64 Wang B 2017, 116–9.
65 Zheng 2000, 98; see Xiong et al. 2005, 150–60, for a study of historical people active in this.
66 Shen 2001 concisely examines the religious beliefs and practices in the commentary.
67 Xiong and Liu 2004, 56.
68 Liu 2008, 57.
69 Robinet 1981, 30.
70 Chan 1998, 124.
71 Chan 1991, 107–18.
72 Tadd 2013, 1–27.
73 Chan 1991, 131.
74 Tadd 2018, 13.
75 Tadd 2018, 14.
76 Lin 2014, 135–6.
77 Lin 2014, 136.
78 Lin 2014, 135.
79 Lin 2014, 136.
80 Lin 2014, 144.
81 Tadd 2019 is a detailed study of *ziran* in the commentary.
82 The question of a third, Tianshi *Daodejing* with its own commentary, the *Xiang'er*, is beyond the scope of this study since its impact on Chinese philosophy was negligible.

Chapter 7

1 See Isabelle Robinet 1981, 1997.
2 See Hu 1989 and Li 2012.
3 Michael 2016 examines Ge Hong's elevation of alchemy into Yangsheng Daoism.
4 Teng and Tang 2011, 73.
5 Zhang ZG 2008, 194.
6 See Michael 2015b, 2016 and Pregadio 2019 for a closer analysis of Ge Hong's conception of *yangsheng* and alchemy.
7 Graham 1959, 1989.
8 Li 2012, 87–8.
9 Li 2012, 88.
10 Zhong and Luo 2008, 155.

11 Chinese studies on Ge Hong's engagement with early Chinese philosophy show that he was not a simple iconoclast; see Hu 1989, 2006; and Li 2012.
12 See Xu 2008 for an incisive study of this issue.
13 Sun 2011, 56–9.
14 All quotations from Wang Bi's commentary (道德真經註) are from ctext.org.
15 Creel 1970 both initiated and exemplified this habit of Western sinology.
16 Li 2012, 89.
17 The excavated *Laozi* manuscripts show that there actually is no contradiction between Ge Hong's Yangsheng reading and *Daodejing* chapter 40, but that is a separate study.
18 Creel 1970.
19 Yuan 1989, 15.
20 Li 2008, 29.
21 Li 2012, 91.
22 Michael 2011 analyzes the development of *taichu* terminology in early Daoism.
23 *NP* 7.
24 *NP* 7.
25 *NP* 9.
26 *NP* 18; Ge Hong does not for some reason include the "vitalities" of *Daodejing* chapter 21.
27 *NP* 9.
28 *NP* 1.
29 Li 2012, 36.
30 Li 2012, 34.
31 Michael 2005, 61–8 and Burik 2009 analyze the notion of Daoist "gateways."
32 *NP* 1.
33 *NP* 18.
34 *NP* 1.
35 Li 2012, 84 and passim.
36 Hu 1989, 206–28.
37 Zhu 2009, 58.
38 *NP* 18.
39 *NP* 5.
40 *NP* 3.
41 Yuan 1989, 14.
42 *NP* 5.
43 *NP* 1.
44 *NP* 1.
45 Li 2012, 37.
46 *NP* 5.
47 Li 2012, 60.

48 *NP* 18.
49 *NP* 1.
50 *NP* 2.
51 *NP* 2.

Chapter 8

1 Fung 1966, 37.
2 *Mencius* 7A.26.
3 Fung 1966, 60.
4 Fung 1966, 61.
5 Kaltenmark 1953 is a complete translation of the *Liexian zhuan* and Giles 1948 a partial one, Campany (2002) is a complete translation of the *Shenxian zhuan*, and Ware 1966 a complete translation of the *Neipian*. I have consulted each of them, but all translations herein are my own. While all three texts are available at ctext.org, my base texts are *Liexian zhuan jiao yi* (*LXZ*), the *Siku Quanshu* edition of the *Shenxian zhuan* (*SKQS:SXZ*), the *Longwei Mishu* edition of the *Shenxian zhuan* (*LWMS:SXZ*), and *Baopuzi neipian jiaoshi* (*NP*). For *Liexian zhuan*, see Kaltenmark 1953, Campany 2002, and Penny 2008. For *Shenxian zhuan*, see Bumbacher 2000, Campany 2002, and Barrett 2003.
6 Translated by Nienhauser 1995.
7 Partially translated by Berkowitz 2014.
8 Yao 2009, 18.
9 With the exception of the *Lienü zhuan* 列女傳, attributed to Liu Xiang and translated by Kinney 2014, standard early Chinese biographies are exclusively devoted to males, while some *xian* biographies are devoted to females; see Chen 2003.
10 Zhang Y 2014, 151.
11 Chen 2010, 108.
12 Yao 2009, 19.
13 Chen 2010, 206.
14 Knapp (n.d.).
15 Yao 2009, 19.
16 Chen 2010, 108.
17 Yao 2009, 20.
18 Chen 2010, 108.
19 Yao 2009, 18.
20 Strickmann 1977 dates it to 465, but Michael 2015a, 93–100, challenges this claim. Wei-Jin reclusion has been extensively covered in the literature, but Ge Hong is rarely mentioned. On the Western side, Vervoorn 1990 and Berkowitz 2000

only passingly refer to him, and on the Chinese side, where Ge Hong studies are something of an industry, Wang Debao 1997, Wang Guangxin 2010, and Wei Zhaoqi 2015 also hardly mention him.
21 Zhang Y 2014, 151.
22 Chen 2010, 106.
23 Sun 2008, 190.
24 Campany 2002, 103–4.
25 Campany 2002, 102–8 examines further sources not mentioned by Ge Hong.
26 *SKQS:SXZ Yuanxu* 1a–2a. Company 2000, 103–4, partially translates the preface.
27 Standard works on Chinese alchemy are Sivin 1968 and Pregadio 2006.
28 *NP* 4, 71.
29 *LWMS:SXZ* 1:7a.
30 *NP* 14, 253.
31 *NP* 3, 52.
32 *NP* 5, 111.
33 *NP* 8, 148.
34 *NP* 15, 268.
35 *NP* 10, 185.
36 *NP* 17, 313.
37 *NP* 10, 186.
38 *NP* 8, 148.
39 *NP* 10, 187.
40 *NP* 17, 300.
41 *NP* 4, 85.
42 *NP* 4, 85.
43 Strassberg 2002 explores conceptions of the strange creatures inhabiting mountains.
44 *NP* 17, 299.
45 *NP* 16, 285–6.
46 Kohn 2009, 153.
47 *NP* 4, 86.
48 Chen 2008, 107.
49 *LXZ* 73.
50 *LXZ* 14.
51 This association is reinforced by the recently excavated fourth- to third-century BCE manuscript *Rong Cheng Shi* that presents an overview of ancient Chinese history as understood at the time of the writer; see Pines 2010 and Dorofeeva-Lichtman 2010.
52 English translation slightly modified from Harper 1998, 393; Chinese text from https://languechinoise.wordpress.com/x-nuages-et-pluie/liste-des-textes/shi-wen/
53 *NP* 20:347.
54 Kaltenmark 1953, 56.

55 *LXZ* 14.
56 *LXZ* 14.
57 *LXZ* 14.
58 https://ctext.org/shiji/lao-zi-han-fei-lie-zhuan
59 *LXZ* 18.
60 *LXZ* 24.
61 *NP* 13, 241.
62 *LXZ* 38.
63 *LXZ* 38.
64 *LXZ* 40.
65 *LXZ* 40.
66 *LXZ* 48.
67 *LXZ* 48.
68 *LXZ* 60.
69 *NP* 3, 49.
70 See Lai 1998 and Company 2005 for different interpretations of the *dixian*.
71 *NP* 3, 52.
72 Company 2002, 52–60.
73 Michael 2011, 2015a, 2016.
74 Zhang J 2012, 106.
75 *SKQS:SXZ* 1.5b.
76 Harper 1998, 110–1.
77 *SKQS:SXZ* 10.9a.
78 *SKQS:SXZ* 2.3b.
79 *SKQS:SXZ* 7.5a.
80 *SKQS:SXZ* 4.7a-b.
81 *SKQS:SXZ* 10.1a-b.
82 *SKQS:SXZ* 7.3a, *LWMS:SXZ* 7.6a-b.
83 *SKQS:SXZ* 7.3b.
84 *SKQS:SXZ* 7.5b.
85 *LWMS:SXZ* 10.4a.
86 *SKQS:SXZ* 9.7b.
87 *SKQS:SXZ* 9.13a.
88 *SKQS:SXZ* 8.14a.
89 *SKQS:SXZ* 2.2b.
90 *SKQS:SXZ* 2.3a.
91 *SKQS:SXZ* 2.3b.
92 Company 2002, 311–4, 498, also does not include it among the earliest biographies.
93 *LWMS:SXZ* 9.2b.

94 *LWMS:SXZ* 9.2b.
95 *LWMS:SXZ* 9.2b.
96 *LWMS:SXZ* 9.2b.
97 Michael 2015a, 109–18, presents a similar history in more detail.
98 Zhang R 2003, 34–5.
99 Text from Li 2001, 343–4.
100 See Gao 1995.
101 Robinet 1984.
102 Robinet 1997, 91.

Epilogue

1 Heidegger 1975.
2 Heidegger 1981, 61.
3 Heidegger 1981, 63.
4 Heidegger 1977c, 309.
5 Heidegger 1971b, 89.
6 See Heidegger 2012a.
7 Ma and van Brakel 2014, 548.
8 Ma and van Brakel 2014, 545.
9 Littlejohn (IEP).
10 Ma 2008, 11 writes, "Most of the Japanese students who studied with Heidegger were intellectually related to Nishida Kitarō," and Maraldo writes, "Nishida Kitarō was the most significant and influential Japanese philosopher of the twentieth-century. His work is pathbreaking in several respects: it established in Japan the creative discipline of philosophy as practised in Europe and the Americas; it enriched that discipline by infusing Anglo-European philosophy with Asian sources of thought; it provided a new basis for philosophical treatments of East Asian Buddhist thought; and it produced novel theories of self and world with rich implications for contemporary philosophizing." See Krummel 2018 for a discussion of Nishida's and Heidegger's separate notions of Nothingness.
11 Nelson 2017 is an historical examination of the early twentieth-century German reception of Asian thought and Heidegger's position therein.
12 Heidegger 1971a.
13 Ma and van Brakel 2014, 184–7.
14 Standard resources on Heidegger's engagement with the *Daodejing*, and Asian thought more generally, include Poggeler 1987, May 1996, and Ma 2008.
15 Heidegger 2012b, 137.
16 See Ma 2008, 121–2

17 According to May 1996, 6.
18 See Ma 2008, 17.
19 Heidegger 1977c, 317.
20 Heidegger 1977c, 325.
21 Heidegger 2012b, 95.
22 Heidegger 1977c, 332.
23 Heidegger 1977a, 94.
24 Heidegger 2012b, 46.
25 Heidegger 2012b, 20.
26 Heidegger 1971a, 8.
27 Heidegger 1968, 224.
28 See, for example, Heidegger, 1971c. Among many studies of Heidegger's notion of "poetic thinking," Halliburton 1981 stands out.
29 Defoort 2001 and van Norden 2017 examine Western philosophy's general dismissal of Chinese philosophy, including the *Daodejing*.
30 Ma 2008, 103.
31 Heidegger 1971d, 92.
32 Heidegger 1977c, 317.
33 Heidegger 2012b, 201.
34 Heidegger 1977b, 265.
35 Bo 2003, 249–50.
36 Ames and Hall 2003, 13–14.
37 Ames and Hall 2003, 116–117, particularly recognize the work of Tang Junyi.
38 See Liu 2014.
39 Zhang X (n.d.).

Works Cited

Ames, Roger T. (1983). "Is Political Taoism Anarchism?" *Journal of Chinese Philosophy* 10(1): 27–47.

Ames, Roger and David Hall (2003). *Dao De Jing "Making Life Significant": A Philosophical Translation*. New York: Ballantine Books.

Ariel, Yoav and Gil Raz (2010). "Anaphors or Cataphors? A Discussion of the Two *Qi* 其 Graphs in the First Chapter of the *Daodejing*." *Philosophy East and West* 60(13): 391–421.

Barrett, Timothy H. (2003). "On the Reconstruction of the *Shenxian zhuan*." *Bulletin of the School of Oriental and African Studies* 66: 229–35.

Baxter, William (1998). "Situating the Language of the *Lao-tzu*: The Probable Date of the *Tao-te-ching*." In *Lao-tzu and the Tao-te-ching*, edited by Livia Kohn and Michael LaFargue, pp. 231–53. Albany: State University of New York Press.

Berkowitz, Alan (2000). *Patterns of Disengagement: The Practice and Portrayal of Reclusion in Early Medieval China*. Redwood City, CA: Stanford University Press.

Berkowitz, Alan (2014). "Biographies of Recluses: Huangfu Mi's Accounts of High-Minded Men." In *Early Medieval China: A Sourcebook*, edited by Wendy Swartz, Robert Ford Company, Yang Lu, Jessey J. C. Choo, pp. 333–49. New York: Columbia University Press.

Billeter, Jean François (1985). "Essai d'interprétation du chapitre 15 du *Laozi*." *Asiatische Studien/Études asiatiques* 39(1/2): 7–44.

Bo Mou (2003). "Eternal Dao, Constant Name, and Language Engagement: On the Opening Message of the *Dao-De-Jing*." In *Comparative Approaches to Chinese Philosophy*, edited by Bo Mou, pp. 245–62. London and New York: Routledge.

Boltz, William G. (1993). "*Lao tzu Tao te ching*." In *Early Chinese Texts: A Bibliographical Guide*, edited by Michael Loewe, pp. 269–92. Berkeley: The Society for the Study of Early China and The Institute of East Asian Studies, University of California, Berkeley.

Boltz, William G. (1999). "The Fourth-Century B.C. Guodiann Manuscripts from Chuu and the Composition of the Laotzyy." *Journal of the American Oriental Society* 119(4): 590–608.

Brindley, Erika (2019). "The *Taiyi shengshui* 太一生水: Cosmogony and Its Role in Early Chinese Thought." In *Dao Companion to the Excavated Guodian Bamboo Manuscripts*, edited by Shirley Chan, pp. 153–62. Cham, Switzerland: Springer.

Bumbacher, Stephan Peter (2000). "On the *Shenxian zhuan*." *Asiatiche Studien/Études Asiatiques* 54: 729–814.

Burik, Steven (2009). "Thinking on the Edge: Heidegger, Derrida, and the Daoist Gateway." *Philosophy East and West* 64(4): 499–516.

Cahill, Suzanne E. (2013). "Sublimation in Medieval China: The Case of the Mysterious Woman of the Nine Heavens." *Journal of Chinese Religions* 20(1): 91–102.

Cai, Liang (2014). *Witchcraft and the Rise of the First Confucian Empire*. Albany: State University of New York Press.

Campany, Robert (2002). *To Live as Long as Heaven and Earth: A Translation and Study of Ge Hong's Traditions of Divine Transcendents*. Berkeley: University of California Press.

Campany, Robert (2003). "On the Very Idea of Religions (In the Modern West and in Early Medieval China)." *History of Religions* 42(4): 287–319.

Campany, Robert (2005). "Two Religious Thinkers of the Early Eastern Jin: Gan Bao and Ge Hong in Multiple Contexts." *Asia Major* 18(3): 175–224.

Chai, David (2019). *Zhuangzi and the Becoming of Nothingness*. Albany: State University of New York Press.

Chan, Alan (1991). *Two Visions of the Way: A Study of the Wang Pi and the Ho-shang-kung Commentaries on the Laozi*. Albany: State University of New York Press.

Chan, Alan (2013). "Laozi." *Stanford Encyclopedia of Philosophy*. Last modified May 2, 2013. http://plato.stanford.edu/entries/laozi/.

Chan, Alan (2017). "The *Daode Jing* and Its Tradition." In *Daoism Handbook*, edited by Livia Kohn, pp. 1–29. Leiden: Brill, 2000.

Chan, Alan K. L. 陳金 (1998). "The Essential Meaning of the Way and Virtue: Yan Zun and 'Laozi Learning.'" *Monumenta Serica* 46: 105–27.

Chang, Chung-yuan (2014). *Tao: A New Way of Thinking*. London: Singing Dragon.

Chang, Leo S. and Yu Feng (1998). *The Four Political Treatises of the Yellow Emperor*. Honolulu: University of Hawai'i Press.

Chen, Ellen (2011). *In Praise of Nothing: An Exploration of Daoist Fundamental Ontology*. NP: Xlibris Corporation.

Chen Guying 陳鼓應 (1988). "老学先于孔学" (Laozi Preceded Kongzi). *Zhexue yanjiu*: 180–201.

Chen Guying 陳鼓應 (1993). "繫辭傳的道論及太極, 大恒説" (On Taiji and Daheng and the Xici zhuan's Theory of the Dao). *Daojia Wenhua Yanjiu* 3: 64–72.

Chen Guying 陳鼓應 (1998). "從郭店簡本看老子尚仁守中思想" (The Thought of Esteeming Benevolence and Protecting the Center from the Guodian *Laozi*). *Daojia Wenhua Yanjiu* 17: 64–80.

Chen Guying (2013). *Rediscovering the Roots of Chinese Thought: Laozi's Philosophy*. St. Petersburg, Florida: Three Pines Press.

Chen Guying 陳鼓應 (2015). 老子注译及评介 (*Laozi*: Commentary, Interpretation, and Explanation). Beijing: Zhonghua Shuju Chubanshe.

Chen Hong 陈洪 (2010). "列仙传的道教意蕴与文学史意义." *Wenxue pinglun* 3: 106–11.

Chen Jing 陈静 (2003). 道教的女仙——兼论人仙和神仙的不同 (Daoist Female *Xian*: On the Difference between Human *Xian* and Divine *Xian*). *Zongjiaoxue Yanjiu* 3: 22–40.

Chen Jing (2008). "Interpretation of *Hengxian*: An Explanation from a Point of View of Intellectual History." *Frontiers of Philosophy* 3(3): 366–88.

Chen Jing (2017). "'There Are Four Greats in the Realm': Looking at the Evolution of the *Laozi* Text with Respect to Different Orderings of the 'Four Greats.'" *Contemporary Chinese Thought* 48(3): 129–42.

Chen Ligui 陳麗桂 (1991). 戰國時期的黃老思想 (Huang-Lao Thought in the Period of the Warring States). Taibei: Lianjing Chupan Shiyi Gongsi.

Chen Ligui 陳麗桂 (2014). "道的異稱及其義涵衍化: 一與亙" (Synonyms of "Tao" and Their Derivative Implications—The "One" and "Permanence"). *Chengdao Zhongwen Xuebao* 46: 1–32.

Chen Ligui 陳麗桂 (2017). "由老子的 '常' '復' 到 亙先的 '恆' '復'" (From *Laozi*'s *Chang* and *Fu* to the *Hengxian*'s *Heng* and *Fu*). *Laozi Xuekan* 15: 48–57.

Chen Zhi (2019). "Biographical Genres and Biography: The Case of Yan Zun 嚴遵." In *China and the World—the World and China: Essays in Honor of Rudolf G. Wagner*, edited by Barbara Mittler and Natascha Gentz, pp. 67–82. Ostasiem Verlag: Deutsche Ostasienstudien 37.

Cheng, Tsan-shan (Zheng Canshan) 鄭燦山 (2000, Minguo 1989). "河上公注成書時代及其思想史, 道教史之意義" (The Age of the *Heshanggong Commentary* and Its Significance in Intellectual and Daoist History). *Hanxue yanjiu* 18(2): 85–112.

Cook, Constance (2006). *Death in Ancient China: The Tale of One's Man Journey*. The Netherlands: Brill.

Cook, Scott (2012). *The Bamboo Texts of Guodian: A Study & Complete Translation*, Vol. 1. New York: Cornell University East Asia Series.

Creel, Herlee G. (1970). *What Is Taoism? And Other Studies in Chinese Cultural History*. Chicago: University of Chicago Press.

Csikszentmihalyi, Mark and Michael Nylan (2003). "Constructing Lineages and Inventing Traditions through Exemplary Figures in Early China." *T'oung Pao* 89(1/3): 59–99.

Defoort, Carine (1997). *The Pheasant Cap Master: A Rhetorical Reading*. Albany: State University of New York Press.

Defoort, Carine (2001). "Is There Such a Thing as Chinese Philosophy? Arguments of an Implicit Debate." *Philosophy East and West* 51(3): 393–413.

Despeux, Catherine (1989). "Gymnastics: The Ancient Tradition." In *Taoist Meditation and Longevity Techniques*, edited by Livia Kohn, pp. 225–61. Ann Arbor, MI: The University of Michigan Center for Chinese Studies.

Despeux, Catherine (2004). "Le gymnastique *daoyin* 導引 dans la Chine ancienne." *Études chinoises* 23: 45–86.

Ding Sixin (2016). "A Study of the Key Concepts 'Heng' and 'Hengxian' in the *Hengxian* on Chu Bamboo Slips Housed at the Shanghai Museum." *Frontiers of Philosophy in China* 11(2): 206–21.

Ding Sixin (2017). "The Section Division of the *Laozi* and Its Examination." *Contemporary Chinese Thought* 48(3): 159–79.

Ding Sixin 顶四心 (2018). "严遵老子指归的無為自然概念及其政治哲学" (The Notions of *Wuwei* and *Ziran* in Yan Zun's *Laozi zhigui* and Its Political Philosophy). *Zhexue Yanjiu* 7: 53–128.

Dorofeeva-Lichtman (2010). "The Rong Cheng shi Version of the 'Nine Provinces': Parallels with Transmitted Texts." *East Asian Science, Technology, and Medicine* 32: 15–58.

Els, Paul van (2018). *The Wenzi: Creativity and Intertextuality in Early Chinese Philosophy; Studies in the History of Chinese Texts no. 9*. Leiden: Brill.

Eno, Robert (1990). *The Confucian Creation of Heaven: Philosophy and the Defense of Ritual Mastery*. Albany: State University of New York.

Fan Bocheng 樊波成 (2013). "老子指归当为严遵老子章句: 严遵老子注的发现以及老子指归的性质" (The *Laozi zhigui* as Yan Zun's Commentary to the *Laozi*: The Discovery of Yan Zun's Commentary to the *Laozi* and the Nature of the *Laozi zhigui*). *Wenshi Xintan* 84: 19–27.

Fan Bocheng 樊波成 (2014). "道藏本老子指归序,目真伪重探 —兼论西汉严遵本老子的上下经 次序" (A Re-examination of the Authenticity of the Preface and Introduction of the *Daozang* Edition of the *Laozi zhigui*, with a Concurrent Discussion of the Order of the Upper and Lower Classics of the Western Han *Laozi* of Yan Zun). *Wenxian* 2: 147–52.

Feldt, Alex (2010). "Governing Through the Dao: A Non-Anarchistic Interpretation of the *Laozi*." *Dao: A Journal of Comparative Philosophy* 9: 323–37.

Fried, Daniel (2018). *Dao and Sign in History: Daoist Arche-Semiotics in Ancient and Medieval China*. Albany: State University of New York Press.

Fung Yu-lan (1966). *A Short History of Chinese Philosophy*. Edited and translated by Derk Bodde. New York: The Free Press.

Gao Dalun 高大倫 (1995). 张家山漢簡引書研究 (Research into Zhangjiashan Han Bamboo Slip Yinshu). Changdu: Ba Shu Shushe.

Ge Hong 葛洪. (1796). *Longwei mishu: Shenxian zhuan* (*LWMS:SXZ*) 龍威祕書: 神仙傳. Edited by Ma Junliang 馬俊良 n.p: Shidetang 世德堂.

Ge Hong 葛洪. *Neipian* (*NP*), from 抱朴子內篇校釋 (*Collated Annotations on the Inner Chapters of Baopuzi*). Edited by Wang Ming 王明 Beijing: Zhonghua Shuhu.

Ge Hong 葛洪. (1599–1659). *Siku quanshu Shenxian zhuan* (*SKQS: SXZ*), from 四庫全書: 神仙傳. Edited by Mao Jin 毛晉.

Giles, Lional (1948). *A Chinese Gallery of Immortals: Selected Biographies Translated from Chinese Sources*. London: John Murray Publishers LTD.

Girardot, Norman (1988). *Myth and Meaning in Early Daoism*. Berkeley: University of California Press.

Graham, A.C. (1959). "Being in Western Philosophy Compared with *Shi/Fei* and *Yu/Wu* in Chinese Philosophy." *Asia Major* 7(1-2): 79–112.

Graham, A.C. (1981). *Chuang-tzu: The Inner Chapters*. New York: Hackett Publishing Company.

Graham, A. C. (1989). *Disputers of the Tao: Philosophical Argumentation in Ancient China*. La Salle, IL: Open Court Press.

Graham, A. C. (1998). "The Origins of the Legend of Lao Tan." In *Lao-tzu and the Tao-te-ching*, edited by Livia Kohn and Michael LaFargue, pp. 23–40. Albany: State University of New York Press.

Hall, Roger and David Ames (1981). *Thinking through Confucius*. Albany: State University of New York Press.

Halliburton, David (1981). *Poetic Thinking: An Approach to Heidegger*. Chicago: University of Chicago Press.

Han Yi 韩義 (2013). 西漢竹書老子 的文本特徵和學術價值(The Textual Characteristics and Academic Value of the Western Han Bamboo *Laozi*). *Daojia Wenhua Yanjiu* 27: 1–35.

Hansen, Chad (1992). *A Daoist Theory of Chinese Thought: A Philosophical Interpretation*. Oxford: Oxford University Press.

Hansen, Chad (2007). "Daoism." *Stanford Encyclopedia of Philosophy*. http://plato.stanford.edu/entries/daoism/.

Harper, Donald (1987). "The Sexual Arts of Ancient China as Described in a Manuscript of the Second Century B.C." *Harvard Journal of Asiatic Studies* 47: 539–93.

Harper, Donald (1995). "The Bellows Analogy in *Laozi* V and Warring States Macrobiotic Hygiene." *Early China* 20: 381–92.

Harper, Donald (1998). *Early Chinese Medical Literature*. London: Kegan Paul.

Heidegger, Martin (1968). *What Is Called Thinking?* Translated by Fred D. Wieck and J. Glenn Gray. New York: Harper and Row.

Heidegger, Martin (1971a). "A Dialogue on Language between a Japanese and an Inquirer." In *Poetry, Language, Thought*, translated by Albert Hofstadter, pp. 1–54. New York: Harper Perennial.

Heidegger, Martin (1971b). "What Are Poets For?" In *Poetry, Language, Thought*, translated by Albert Hofstadter, pp. 89–139. New York: Harper Perennial.

Heidegger, Martin (1971c). "… Poetically Man Dwells …." In *Poetry, Language, Thought*, translated by Albert Hofstadter, pp. 211–27. New York: Harper Perennial.

Heidegger, Martin (1971d). "The Nature of Language." In *On the Way to Language*, translated by Peter D. Hertz, pp. 57–108. New York: Harper and Row.

Heidegger, Martin (1975). Early Greek Thinking. Translated by David Farrell Krell. New York: Harper SanFrancisco.

Heidegger, Martin (1977a). "What Is Metaphysics?" In *Basic Writings*, translated by David Farrell Krell, pp. 93–110. New York: Harper Collins.

Heidegger, Martin (1977b). "Letter on Humanism." In *Basic Writings*, translated by David Farrell Krell, pp. 213–65. New York: Harper Collins.

Heidegger, Martin (1977c). "The Question Concerning Technology." In *Basic Writings*, translated by David Farrell Krell, pp. 307–42. New York: Harper Collins.

Heidegger, Martin (1981). "Only a God Can Save Us: The *Spiegel* Interview (1966)." In *Heidegger: The Man and the Thinker*, edited by Thomas Sheehan, translated by William Richardson, pp. 45–67. New York: Routledge.

Heidegger, Martin (2012a). *Bremen and Freiburg Lectures: Insight into That Which Is and Basic Principles of Thinking*. Translated by Andrew J. Mitchell. Bloomington, Indiana: Indiana University Press.

Heidegger, Martin (2012b). *Contributions to Philosophy (Of the Event)*. Translated by Richard Rojcewicz and Daniela Vallega-Neu. Bloomington: Indiana University Press.

Hendrischke, Barbara (2019). "Daoist Philosophy as Viewed from the Guodian Manuscripts." In *Dao Companion to the Excavated Guodian Bamboo Manuscripts*, edited by Shirley Chan, pp. 163–86. Cham, Switzerland: Springer.

Henricks, Robert G. (1989). *Lao-Tzu Te-Tao Ching: A New Translation Based on the Recently Discovered Ma-wang-tui Texts*. New York: Ballantine Books.

Henricks, Robert G. (2000). *Lao Tzu's Tao Te Ching: A Translation of the Startling Documents Found at Guodian*. New York: Columbia University Press.

Hu, Fuchen 胡孚琛. (1989). 魏晉神仙道教: 抱朴子内篇研究 (The Daoist Religion of Immortality in the Wei-Jin: Studies in the *Baopuzi Neipian*). Beijing: Renmin Chubanshe.

Hu, Fuchen 胡孚琛 (1999). 道學通論道家道教仙學 (A General Theory of Daoism: The Study of *Daojia*, *Daojiao*, and the *Xian*). Beijing: Shehui kexue wenxian chubanshe.

Hu, Fuchen 胡孚琛 (2006). 葛洪的哲学思想概說: 抱朴子内篇中的道教哲學研究之一 (A General Account of Ge Hong's Philosophical Thought: The Key to Researching the Religious Daoist Philosophy of the *Baopuzi Neipian*). In *Ge Hong yanjiu lunji* (Collected Research Papers on Ge Hong), edited by Liu Gusheng 刘固盛, pp. 151–63. Hubei: Huazhong Shifan Daxue Chubanshe.

Kaltenmark, Max (1953). *Le Lie-sien tchouan: Biographies légendaires des immortels taoïstes de l'antiquité*. Beijing: Université de Paris, Publications du Centre d'études sinologiques de Pékin. 1987 reprint Paris: Collège de France.

Kaltenmark, Max (1965). *Lao Tseu et le taoïsme*. Paris: Éditions du Seuil.

Kim, Hongkyung (2013). *The Old Master: A Syncretic Reading of the Laozi from the Mawangdui Text A Onward*. Albany: State University of New York Press.

Kim, Tae Hyun (2010). "Other *Laozi* Parallels in the *Hanfeizi*." *Sino-Platonic Papers* No. 199.

Kinney, Anne Behnke (2014). *Exemplary Women of Early China: The Lienü zhuan of Liu Xiang*. New York: Columbia University Press.

Klein, Esther (2010), "Were There 'Inner Chapters' in the Warring States? A New Examination of Evidence about the *Zhuangzi*." *T'oung Pao* 96(4/5): 299–369.

Knapp, Keith. (n.d.). "Ge Hong (Ko Hung), 283-343 C.E." From *Internet Encyclopedia of Philosophy*: https://www.iep.utm.edu/gehong/.

Kohn, Livia (2008). *Chinese Healing Exercises: The Tradition of Daoyin*. Honolulu: University of Hawai'i Press.

Kohn, Livia (2009). "Healing and the Earth: Daoist Cultivation in Comparative Perspective." In *Environmental Ethics: Intercultural Perspectives*, edited by Ip King-tok, pp. 147–71. Amsterdam, NLD: Editions Ropodi.

Krummel, John (2018). "On (the) Nothing: Heidegger and Nishida." *Continental Philosophy Review* 51(2): 239–68.

LaFargue, Michael (1992). *The Tao of the Tao-te-ching*. Albany: State University of New York Press.

LaFargue, Michael (1994). *Tao and Method: A Reasoned Approach to the Tao Te Ching*. Albany: State University of New York Press.

LaFargue, Michael (1998). "Recovering the *Tao-te-ching*'s Original Meaning: Some Remarks on Historical Hermeneutics." In *Lao-tzu and the Tao-te-ching*, edited by Livia Kohn and Michael LaFargue, pp. 255–75. Albany: State University of New York Press.

Lai Chi-tim (1998). "Ko Hung's Discourse of *Hsien* Immortality: A Taoist Configuration of an Alternate Ideal Self-Identity." *Numen* 45:1–38.

Lau, D. C. (1964). *Lao Tzu Tao Te Ching*. New York: Penguin Classics.

Le Blanc, Charles (1985). "A Re-Examination of the Myth of Huang-ti." *Journal of Chinese Religions* 13(1): 45–63.

Legge, James. Translation of *Shijing*. https://ctext.org/book-of-poetry.

Lévi, Jean (1984). "Connais le masculin, garde le féminin: Stratégies du Yin et du Yang. Le sexe des nombres." *Le Genre humain* 1(10): 75–89.

Lévi, Jean (1996), "Pluie et brouillard: un paradigme de la Fondation en Chine ancienne." *Homme* 137: 23–40.

Li, Jiahao (2013). "Identifying the Wangjiatai Qin (221-206 BCE-206 BCE) Bamboo Slip 'Yi Divinations' (Yi zhan) as the Gui cang." *Contemporary Chinese Thought* 44(3): 42–59.

Li Ling 李零 (2001). *Zhongguo Fangshu Kao* 中國方術考. Beijing: Donghua chubanshe.

Li Ling 李零 (2013). 楚帛书研究 (Studies on the Chu Silk Manuscripts). Shanghai: Zhongxi Shuju.

Li Songrong 李鬆榮 (2008). "逍遥與成仙: 莊子, 抱朴子內篇生死關比較." (Carefree Wandering and Becoming *Xian*: Comparative Perspectives on Life and Death in the *Zhuangzi* and the *Baopuzi Neipian*). *Anhui Daxue Xuekan* 32(4): 29–33.

Li Zongding 李宗定 (2012). 葛洪抱朴子內篇與魏晉玄學 (Ge Hong's *Baopuzi Neipian* and Wei-Jin Xuanxue). Taibei: Taiwan Xuesheng Shuju.

Liao, Mingchun and Li Cheng (2017). "A New Explanation of the Order of Parts in the *Laozi*." *Contemporary Chinese Thought* 48(3): 143–58.

Lin Mingzhao 林明照 (2014). "老子河上公章句治身與治國關係之思辯模式析論" (A New Discussion of the Speculative Method Concerning the Relation between Regulating the Body and Regulating the State in the *Heshang Gong Commentary to the Laozi*). *Guoli Zhengzhi Daxue Zhexue Xuebao* 7: 129–69.

Lin Mingzhao 林明照 (2015). "老子河上公章句, 老子指歸 中的治道推演" (Deducing the Regulations of the Dao in the *Heshang Gong Commentary to the Laozi* and the *Laozi zhigui*). *Daojia Wenhua Yanjiu* 19: 146–67.

Littlejohn, Ronnie (n.d.). "Comparative Philosophy." In *The Internet Encyclopedia of Philosophy*: https://www.iep.utm.edu/comparat/.

Liu Gusheng 刘固盛 (2008). 道教老学史 (The History of Daoist *Laozi* Studies). Wuhan: Huazhong Shifan Daxue Chubanshe.

Liu, JeeLoo (2014). "Was There Something in Nothingness? The Debate on the Primordial State between Daoism and Neo-Confucianism." In *Nothingness in Asian Philosophy*, edited by JeeLoo Liu and Douglas L. Berger, pp. 181–96. New York: Routledge.

Liu, Xiaogan (1994). *Classifying the Zhuangzi Chapters*. Michigan: Center for Chinese Studies, The University of Michigan, 1994.

Liu, Xiaogan (2003). "From Bamboo Slips to Received Versions: Common Features in Transformation of the *Laozi*." *Harvard Journal of Asiatic Studies* 63(2): 337–82.

Liu, Xiaogan 刘笑敢 (2006). 老子古今 (*Laozi* Past and Present), Vol. 1. Beijing: Chinese Social Sciences Publishing.

Loewe, Michael (1994). "Huang Lao Thought and the *Huainanzi*." *Journal of the Royal Asiatic Society of Great Britain & Ireland (Third Series)* 4: 377–95.

Ma, Lin (2008). *Heidegger on East-West Dialogue: Anticipating the Event*. New York: Routledge.

Ma, Lin and Jaap Van Brakel (2014). "Out of the *Ge-stell*? The Role of the East in Heidegger's 'Das Andere Denken.'" *Philosophy East and West* 64(3): 527–62.

Mair, Victor (1990). "[The] File [on the Cosmic] Track [and Individual] Dough[tiness]: Introduction and Notes for a Translation of the Ma-wang-tui Manuscripts of the LaoTzu [Old Master]." *Sino-Platonic Papers* No. 20.

Major, John S., Sarah Queen, Andrew Meyer, Harold Roth (2012). *The Huainanzi: A Guide to the Theory and Practice of Government in Early Han China, by Liu An, King of Huainan*. New York: Columbia University Press.

Maraldo, John C. "Kitarō." *The Stanford Encyclopedia of Philosophy*, available at<https://plato.stanford.edu/archives/win2019/entries/nishida-kitaro/>.

Maspero, Henri (1971). *Le Taoïsme et les religions chinoises*. Paris: Éditions Gallimard.

Maspero, Henri (1981). *Taoism and Chinese Religion*. Translated by Frank A. Kierman Jr. Amherst: University of Massachusetts Press.

May, Reinhard (1996). *Heidegger's Hidden Sources: East Asian Influences on His Work*. Translated by Graham Parkes. New York: Routledge.

Meyer, Dirk (2009). "Texts, Textual Communities, and Meaning: The *Genius Loci* of the Warring States Chu Tomb Guodian One." *Asiatische Studien/Études asiatiques* 63(4): 827–56.

Meyer, Dirk (2012). *Philosophy on Bamboo: Text and the Production of Meaning in Early China*. Leiden: Brill.

Michael, Thomas (2005). *The Pristine Dao: Metaphysics in Early Daoist Discourse*. Albany: State University of New York Press.

Michael, Thomas (2011). "The That-Beyond-Which of the Pristine Dao: Cosmogony in the *Liezi*." In *Riding the Wind with Liezi: New Essays on the Daoist Classic*, edited by Ronnie Littlejohn and Jeffrey Dippmann, pp. 101–26. Albany: State University of New York Press.

Michael, Thomas (2015a). *In the Shadows of the Dao: Laozi, the Sage, and the Daodejing*. Albany: State University of New York.

Michael, Thomas (2015b). "Hermits, Mountains, and *Yangsheng* in Early Daoism: Perspectives from the *Zhuangzi*." In *New Visions of the Zhuangzi*, edited by Livia Kohn, pp. 149–64. St. Petersburg, FL: Three Pines Press.

Michael, Thomas (2015c). "Ge Hong's *Xian*: Private Hermits and Public Alchemists." *Journal of Daoist Studies* 8: 24–51.

Michael, Thomas (2016). "Mountains and Early Daoism in the Writings of Ge Hong." *History of Religions* 56(1): 23–54.

Michael, Thomas (2017). "Approaching *Laozi*: Comparing a Syncretic Reading to a Synthetic One." *Frontiers of Philosophy in China* 12(1): 10–25.

Michael, Thomas (2018). "Explorations in Authority in the *Daodejing*: A Daoist Engagement with Hannah Arendt." *Religions* 9(12): 1–26.

Michael, Thomas (2020). "Strategic Sages and Cosmic Generals: A Daoist Perspective on the Intertextuality of the *Daodejing* and the *Sunzi*." *Dao A Journal of Comparative Philosophy* 19(1): 11–31.

Nelson, Eric S. (2017). *Chinese and Buddhist Philosophy in Early Twentieth-Century German Thought*. London: Bloomsbury.

Nienhauser, Willian J. (1995). *The Grand Scribe's Records, Vol. 7: The Memoirs of Pre-Han China*. Indiana: Indiana Universwity Press.

Pang Pu 庞朴 (2004). "恒先试读" (A Tentative Reading of the Hengxian). Zhongguo Sixiangshi Qianyan: Jingdian Quanshi Fangfa (2008), edited by Liang Tao, pp. 151–4. Xi'an: Shaanxi Shifan Daxue Chubanshe.

Patt-Shamir, Galia (2009). "To Live a Riddle: The Transformative Aspect of the *Laozi*." *Journal of Chinese Philosophy* 36(3): 408–23.

Peerenboom, R. P. (1993). *Law and Morality in Ancient China: The Silk Manuscripts of Huang-Lao*. Albany: State University of New York Press.

Penny, Benjamin (2008). "*Liexian zhuan* 列仙傳 Biographies of Exemplary Immortals." In *The Encyclopedia of Taoism*, edited by Fabrizio Pregadio, pp. 653–4. New York: Routledge.

Perkins, Franklin (2017). "*Fanwu Liuxing* 凡物流形 ('All Things Flow into Form') and the 'One' in the *Laozi*." *Early China* 38: 195–232.

Perkins, Franklin (2019). "The Guodian *Laozi* Materials." In *Dao Companion to the Excavated Guodian Bamboo Manuscripts*, edited by Shirley Chan, pp. 1–20. Cham, Switzerland: Springer.

Pines, Yuri (2010). "Political Mythology and Dynastic Legitimacy in the Rong Cheng shi Manuscript." *Bulletin of the School of Oriental and African Studies* 73(3): 503–29.

Poggeler, Otto (1987). "West-East Dialogue: Heidegger and Lao-tzu." In *Heidegger and Asian Thought*, edited by Graham Parkes, pp. 47–78. Honolulu: University of Hawai'i Press.

Pregadio, Febrizio (2006). *Great Clarity: Daoism and Alchemy in Early Medieval China*. Stanford: Stanford University Press.

Pregadio, Fabrizio (2019). "Seeking Immortality in Ge Hong's *Baopuzi neipian*." In *Dao Companion to Xuanxue*, edited by David Chai (in press). New York: Springer.

Qiu Xigui 裘锡圭 (2009). "是恒先还是極先?" (Hengxian or Jixian?). http://www.gwz.fudan.edu.cn/SrcShow.asp?Src_ID=806.

Queen, Sarah (1996). *From Chronicle to Canon: The Hermeneutics of the Spring and Autumn, According to Tung Chung-shu*. Cambridge: University of Cambridge Press.

Queen, Sarah (2013). "Han Feizi and the Old Master: A Comparative Analysis and Translation of Han Feizi Chapter 20, 'Jie Lao,' and Chapter 21, 'Yu Lao.'" In *Dao Companion to the Philosophy of Han Fei*, edited by Paul R. Goldin, pp. 197–256. Cham, Switzerland: Springer.

Queen, Sarah and John S. Major (2015). *Luxuriant Gems of the Spring and Autumn: Attributed to Dong Zhongshu*. New York: Columbia University Press.

Queen, Sarah and Michael Puett, eds (2014). *The Huainanzi and Textual Production in Early China*. Leiden: Brill.

Rao Zongyi 饒宗頤 (1993). "帛書繫辭傳大恒說" (On Daheng in the Silk Text of the Xici zhuan). *Daojia Wenhua Yanjiu* 3: 6–19.

Rapp, John A. (2012). *Daoism and Anarchism: Critiques of State Autonomy in Ancient and Modern China*. London: Bloomsbury Publishing.

Robinet, Isabelle (1981). *Les Commentaires du Tao To King jusqu'au VIIe Siècle*. Paris: Mémoires de l'Institut des Hautes Études Chinoises.

Robinet, Isabelle (1984). *La révélation du Shangqing dans l'histoire du taoïsme*, 2 vols. Paris: École française d'Extrême-Orient.

Robinet, Isabelle (1997). *Taoism: Growth of a Religion*. Translated by Phyllis Brooks. Stanford: Stanford University Press.

Roth, Harold (1991). "Psychology and Self-cultivation in Early Taoistic Thought." *Harvard Journal of Asiatic Studies* 51: 599–650.

Roth, Harold (1992). *The Textual History of the Huai-nan Tzu*. Ann Arbor: Association for Asian Studies Monograph No. 46.

Roth, Harold (1997). "Evidence for Stages of Meditation in Early Taoism." *Bulletin of the School of Oriental and African Studies* 60(2): 295–314.

Roth, Harold (1999). *Original Tao: Inward Training (Nei-yeh) and the Foundations of Taoist Mysticism*. New York: Columbia University Press.

Ryden, Edmund (1997). *The Yellow Emperor's Four Canons, a Literary Study and Edition of the Text from Mawangdui*. Taipei, Taiwan: Ricci Institute and Kuangchi Press.

Schaberg, David (2015). "On the Range and Performance of *Laozi*-Style Tetrasyllables." In *Literary Forms of Argument in Early China*, edited by Joachim Gentz and Dirk Meyer, pp. 87–111. Leiden: Brill.

Schipper, Kristofer (1993). *The Taoist Body*. Translated by Karen C. Duval. Berkeley: University of California Press.

Schönfeld, Martin (2020). "Grounding Phenomenology in Laozi's *Daodejing*: The Anthropocene, the Fourfold, and the Sage." In *Daoist Encounters with Phenomenology: Thinking Interculturally about Human Existence*, edited by David Chai, pp. 275–308. London: Bloomsbury.

Schwartz, Benjamin (1985). *The World of Thought in Ancient China*. Cambridge: The Belknap Press of Harvard University Press.

Seidel, Anna (1992). *La Divinisation de Lao Tseu dans le Taoisme des Han*. Paris: École Française d'Extrême-Orient.

Seidel, Anna and Lothar von Falkenhausen (2008). "The Emperor and His Councilor: Laozi and Han Dynasty Taoism." *Cahiers d'Extrême-Asie* 17: 125–65.

Sellmann, James (2002). *Timing and Rulership in Master Lü's Spring and Autumn Annals (Lüshi Chunqiu)*. Albany: State University of New York Press.

Shaughnessy, Edward (2005). "The Guodian Manuscripts and Their Place in Twentieth-Century Historiography on the *Laozi*." *Harvard Journal of Asiatic Studies* 65(2): 417–57.

Shaughnessy, Edward (2014). *Unearthing the Changes: Recently Discovered Manuscripts of the Yi Jing (I Ching) and Related Texts*. New York: Columbia University press.

Shen Guochang 申国昌 (2001). "老子河上公注养生教育思想探析" (Analysis of the Thought of *Yangsheng* Education). *Zhongguo Daojiao* 1(1): 19–22.

Sivin, Nathan (1968). *Chinese Alchemy: Preliminary Studies*. Cambridge: Harvard University Press.

Sivin, Nathan (1978). "On the Word 'Taoist' as a Source of Perplexity." *History of Religion* 17: 303–30.

Sivin, Nathan (1995). "State, Cosmos, and Body in the Last Three Centuries B. C." *Harvard Journal of Asiatic Studies* 55(1): 5–37.

Smith, Kidder (2003). "Sima Tan and the Invention of Daoism, 'Legalism,' et cetera." *Journal of Asian Studies* 62(1): 129–56.

Stamatov, Aleksandar (2014). "The *Laozi* and Anarchism." *Asian Philosophy* 24: 260–78.

Strassberg, Richard (2002). *A Chinese Bestiary: Strange Creatures from the Guideways through Mountains and Seas*. Berkeley: University of California Press.

Strickmann, Michel (1977). "The Mao Shan Revelations: Taoism and the Aristocracy." *T'oung Pao* 63: 1–63.

Strickmann, Michel (1979). "On the Alchemy of T'ao Hung-ching." In *Facets of Taoism: Essays in Chinese Religion*, edited by Holmes Welch and Anna Seidel, pp. 123–92. New Haven: Yale University Press.

Sun Yiping 孫亦平 (2008). "论葛洪对道教仙学的发展与贡献" (On Ge Hong's Development and Contribution to the *Xian* of Daoism). In *Ge Hong yanjiu er ji* (Researchs on Ge Hong, Volume 2), edited by Yang Shihua 杨世华, pp. 181–91. Wuhan: Huazhong Shifan Daxue Chubanshe.

Sun Yiping 孫亦平 (2011). "葛洪與魏晋玄学" (Ge Hong and Wei-Jin Xuanxue). *Zhongguo Zhexue* 21: 55–60.

Tadd, Misha (2013). "Alternatives to Monism and Dualism: Seeking Yang Substance with Yin Mode in *Heshanggong's Commentary on the Daodejing*." Ph. D. dissertation, Boston University.

Tadd, Misha (2018). "Varieties of Yin and Yang in the Han: Implicit Mode and Substance Divisions in *Heshanggong's Commentary on the Daodejing*." *Diogenes*: 1–21.

Tadd, Misha (2019). "Ziran: Authenticity or Authority?" *Religions* 10(207): 1–20.

Teng, Wei 滕巍 and Tang Juan 唐娟 (2011). "葛洪抱朴子內篇與魏晉士人的生命意識論析" (Analyzing Ge Hong's *Baopuzi Neipian* and Wei-Jin Intellectual's Doctrine of Life-Consciousness). *Xinan Nongye Daxue Xuebao* 9(9): 73–6.

Unschuld, Paul (2003). *Huang Di nei jing su wen: Nature, Knowledge, Imagery in an Ancient Chinese Medical Text*. Berkeley and Los Angeles: University of California Press.

Van Ess, Hans (1993). "The Meaning of Huang-Lao in *Shiji* and *Hanshu*." *Études chinoises* 12(2): 161–77.

Van Gulik, R. H. (2003). *Sexual Life in Ancient China: A Preliminary Study of Chinese Sex and Society from ca. 1500 B.C. till 1644 A.D.* Leiden: Brill.

Van Norden, Bryan W. (2017). *Taking Back Philosophy: A Multicultural Manifesto*. New York: Columbia University Press.

Van Xuyet, Ngo (1976). *Divination, magie et politique dans la Chine ancienne*. Paris: Presses Universitaires de France.

Vankeerberghen, Griet (2001). *The Huainanzi and Liu An's Claim to Moral Authority*. New York: State University of New York Press.

Vervoorn, Aat (1988). "Zhuang Zun: A Daoist Philosopher of the Late First Century B.C." *Monumenta Serica* 38: 69–94.

Vervoorn, Aat (1990). *Men of the Cliffs and Caves: The Development of the Chinese Eremitic Tradition to the End of the Han Dynasty*. Hong Kong: Chinese University Press.

Wagner, Rudolf (1980). "Interlocking Parallel Style: Laozi and Wang Bi." *Asiatische Studien/Etudes asiatiques* 34(1): 18–58.

Wagner, Rudolf (1989). "The Wang Bi Recension of the *Laozi*." *Early China* 14: 27–54.

Wagner, Rudolf (2000). *The Craft of the Chinese Commentator: Wang Bi on the Laozi*. Albany: State University of New York Press.

Wagner, Rudolf (2003). *A Chinese Reading of the Daodejing: Wang Bi's Commentary on the Laozi with Critical Text and Translation*. Albany: State University of New York Press.

Wang, Aihe (2000). *Cosmology and Political Culture in Early China*. Cambridge: University of Cambridge Press.

Wang, Bo 王博 (2000). "關於郭店楚墓竹簡分篇與連綴的幾點想法" (Thoughts on Sections and Connections in the Bamboo Strips from the Chu Tomb in Guodian). *Zhongguo Zhexue* 21: 247–73.

Wang, Bo 王博 (2005). "恒先與老子" (*Hengxian* and the *Laozi*). *Zhengda Zhongwen Xuebao* 3: 33–50.

Wang, Bo 王博 (2013). "西汉竹书老子与严遵老子指归" (The Western Han *Laozi* and Yan Zun's *Laozi zhigui*). *Zhongguo zhexue shi* 3: 5–43.

Wang, Bo (2014). *Zhuangzi: Thinking through the Inner Chapters*. Translated by Livia Kohn. St. Petersburg, FL: Three Pines Press.

Wang, Bo (2017). "The Textual Transformation of the *Laozi* through the Lens of History of Thought." *Contemporary Chinese Thought* 48(3): 115–28.

Wang, Debao 王德保 (1997). 任与隐 (Officials and Hermits). Beijing: Huawen Chubanshe.

Wang, Guangxin 王广心 (2010). 中国隐士的品格 (The Character of Chinese Hermits). Xi'an: Shanxi Chubanshe.

Wang, James Qingjie (2001). "*Heng* and Temporality of Dao: Laozi and Heidegger." *Dao: A Journal of Comparative Philosophy* 1: 55–71.

Wang, Ming 王明 (2002). 抱朴子内篇校释 (Annotated Examination of the *Baopuzi Neipian*). Beijing: Zhonghua Shuhu.

Wang, Qingjie (2000). "*Heng Dao* and Appropriation of Nature—A Hermeneutical Interpretation of Laozi." *Asian Philosophy* 10(2): 149–63.

Wang, Qingjie (James) (2003). "'It-self-so-ing' and 'Other-ing' in Lao Zi's Concept of Zi Ran." In *Comparative Approaches to Chinese Philosophy*, edited by Bo Mou, pp. 225–44. Hants, England: Ashgate.

Wang, Qingjie James (2016). "Thing-ing and No-Thing in Heidegger, Kant, and Laozi." *Dao: A Journal of Comparative Philosophy* 15: 159–74.

Wang, Robin (2005). "Dong Zhongshu's Transformation of Yin-Yang Theory and Contesting of Gender Identity." *Philosophy East and West* 55(2): 209–31.

Wang, Robin (2012). *Yinyang: The Way of Heaven and Earth in Chinese Thought and Culture*. Cambridge: Cambridge University Press.

Wang, Zhongjiang 王中江 (2008). "恒先宇宙观及人民观的构造" (The Structures of Cosmology and Outlook on Life in the *Hengxian*). *Wen Shi Xue* 5: 45–56.

Wang, Zhongjiang 王中江 (2011). 简帛文明与古代思想世界 (Civilization of Bamboo-Silk and the World of Ancient Thought). Beijing: Beijing Daxue Chubanshe.

Wang, Zhongjiang 王中江 (2013). 北大藏漢簡老子的某些特徵 (Certain Characteristics of the Han Bamboo *Laozi* of the Beida Collection). *Daojia Wenhua Yanjiu* 27: 58–82.

Wang, Zhongjiang (2015). *Daoism Excavated: Cosmos and Humanity in Early Manuscripts*. Translated by Livia Kohn. St. Petersburg, FL: Three Pines Press.

Wang, Zhongjiang 王中江 (2016a). "终极根源概念及其谱系: 上博简恒先的'恒'探微" (The Concept of Ultimate Origin and Its Genealogy: An Exploration of Heng in the Hengxian Text of the Shanghai Museum Bamboo Manuscripts). *Zhexue Yanjiu* 1: 35–46.

Wang, Zhongjiang (2016b). *Order in Early Chinese Excavated Texts: Natural, Supernatural, and Legal Approaches*. London: Palgrave Macmillan.

Wang, Zhongjiang (2018). "Abnormalities and Return: An Exploration of the Concept Fan 反 in the *Laozi*." *Religions* 10(32): 1–20.

Wang, Zhongjiang 王中江 (2019). "The Concept and Genealogy of the Ultimate Origin: An Exploration of Constancy in the Hengxian 恒先 Text of the Shanghai Museum Collection." *Journal of Chinese Philosophy* 46(2/3): 3–32.

Ware, James R. (1966). *Alchemy, Medicine, and Religion in the China of A.D. 320: The Nei P'ian of Ko Hung*. New York: Dover Publications.

Wei, Zhaoqi 汉兆琦 (2015). 中国古代的隱士 (Ancient Chinese Hermits). Beijing: Shangwu Yinshuguan Chuban.

Wile, Douglas (1992). *Art of the Bedchamber: The Chinese Sexual Yoga Classics Including Women's Solo Meditation Texts*. Albany: State University of New York Press.

Xiong, Tieji 熊铁基 and Liu Lingzi 刘玲姊 (2004). Lun Han Laozi ("Reading the Han Laozi"). *Zhexue yanjiu* 4: 52–8.

Xiong, Tieji 熊铁基, Ma Lianghuai 嗎良怀 and Liu Shaojun 刘韶军 (2005). 中国老学史 (The History of Chinese *Laozi* studies). Fuzhou: Fujian Renmin Chubanshe.

Xu, Kangsheng 許抗生 (2008). "葛洪道教思想研究" (Research into Ge Hong's Religious Daoist Thought). In *Ge Hong yanjiu erji* (Researchs on Ge Hong, Volume Two), edited by Yang Shihua 楊世華, pp. 23–39. Hubei: Huazhong Shifan Daxue Chubanshe.

Yang, Shuda 楊樹達 (1936). "漢代老學考" (Investigations in Han Dynasty *Laozi* Studies). In *Zengbu Laozi guyi*. Shanghai: Zhonghua shuju.

Yao, Shengliang 姚圣良 (2009). "史传体例寓言笔法:列仙传,神仙传叙事模式探析" (The Fable Style of Historical Biography: An Analysis of the Narrative Modes of the *Liexian zhuan*). *Fuyang Shifan Xueyuan Xuebao* 2: 18–21.

Yates, Robin (1997). *Five Lost Classics: Tao, Huang-lao, and Yin-yang in Han China*. New York: Ballantine Books.

Yu, Anthony (2003). "Reading the *Daodejing*: Ethics and Politics of the Rhetoric." *Chinese Literature: Essays, Articles, Reviews (CLEAR)* 25: 165–87.

Yuan, Long 袁朗 (1989). "葛洪抱朴子內篇對莊子的接受淺析" (A Preliminary Analysis of Ge Hong's Reception of the *Zhuangzi* as Seen in Ge Hong's *Baopuzi*). *Wenxue Yanjiu* 3: 12–15.

Zhang, Ji (2012). *One and Many: A Comparative Study of Plato's Philosophy and Daoism Represented by Ge Hong*. Albany: State University of New York Press.

Zhang, Rongming 张荣明 (2003). 中国古代气功与先秦哲学 (Ancient Chinese Qigong and Pre-Qin Philosophy). Taibei: Guiguan tushu gufen youxian gongsi.

Zhang, Xianglong (n.d.). "Heidegger and Taoism on Humanism." <http://www.confuchina.com/07%20xifangzhexue/Heidegger%20and%20Taoism.htm>.

Zhang, Xianglong (1992). *Heidegger and Daoism*. Albany, NY: State University of New York Press.

Zhang, Yulian 张玉莲 (2014). "列仙傳及其叙事学阐释" (The Liexian zhuan Biographies and Their Narrative Interpretation). *Henan Shifan Daxue Xuebao* 41(1): 151–5.

Zhang, Zhenguo 张振国 (2008). "葛洪神仙思想对人格塑造的影响" (The Influence of Ge Hong's Thought on Xian on Personality Modeling). In *Ge Hong yanjiu erji*

(Researchs on Ge Hong, Volume 2), edited by Yang Shihua 杨世华, pp. 192–8. Wuhan: Huazhong Shifan Daxue Chubanshe.

Zheng, Kai 郑开 (2019). 到家政治哲学发微 (Detailed Analysis of Daoist Political Philosophy). Beijing: Peking University Press.

Zhong, Sheng 钟盛 and Luo Yi 罗毅 (2008). "從抱朴子看葛洪對玄學的批判" (Ge Hong's Judgement of Xuanxue as Seen from the *Baopuzi*). *Zhonghua Wenhua Luntan* 1: 154–9.

Zhu, Yueli 朱越利 (2008). "东晋葛洪的房中术" (Dongjin Ge Hong's Arts of the Bedroom). In *Ge Hong yanjiu erji* (Researches on Ge Hong, Volume 2), edited by Yang Shihua 杨世华, pp. 149–61. Wuhan: Huazhong Shifan Daxue Chubanshe.

Zhu, Zhanyan 朱展焱 (2009). 道教生命觀看的哲學闡釋:以葛洪抱朴子內篇為中心 (Viewing the Philosophical Elucidation of Religious Daoism from Its Concept of Life: Taking Ge Hong's *Baopuzi Neipian* as the Core). *Jiangxi Shehui Kexue* 11(1): 58–61.

Index

Ames, Roger 65, 103, 105, 109–10, 114, 229, 233, 240, 244, 245, 247, 254, 247, 254
Analects 48, 73, 93, 94, 200, 243
Ariel, Yoav and Gil Raz 25–6, 35, 37, 236, 237
Aristotle 225

Ban Gu 183
Baopuzi Neipian 11, 15, 16, 153, 160, 169, 174, 184, 186–95, 197, 200, 202, 204, 250
Baopuzi Waipian 159
Barrett, Timothy 250
Baxter, William 45, 57, 58, 60, 68, 238
Berkowitz, Alan 128, 250, 251
Billeter, Jean Francois 29–34, 39, 57, 77, 236, 238, 241
Bo He 205
Bo Mou 66, 67, 229, 241, 254
Boltz, William 38, 57, 237, 239
Boyang. *See* Laozi.
Brindley, Erika 246
Buddhism 15, 223, 224, 231
Bumbacher, Stephan Peter 250
Burik, Steven 7–10, 235, 249

Cahill, Suzanne 235
Cai, Liang 247
Cainü 18, 235
Campany, Robert 188, 189, 202, 235, 242, 250, 251, 252, 252
Chai, David 244
Chan, Alan 39, 41, 48, 57, 126, 128, 129, 130, 134, 137, 138, 142, 143, 144, 238, 247, 248
Chang 66–7, 89, 95, 99, 101, 136, 137, 143, 167, 172, 217, 229, 242
 ancient uses 69–73
 in Laozi manuscripts 73–85.
 (*See also* Dao)
Chang Chung-yuan 225

Chang, Leo S. and Yu Feng 235
Chen Bo 207–8
Chen, Ellen 106, 244
Chen Guying 38, 65, 88, 111, 237, 239, 240, 242, 245
Chen Hong 185, 186, 187, 188, 196, 250
Chen Jing 109–11, 241, 242, 245, 246, 250, 251
Chen Ligui 12, 68, 73–4, 79–80, 88, 89, 221, 242, 257, 246
Chen Zhi 247
Cheng Tsan-shan (Zheng Canshan) 140, 248
Chi Songzi 192
Chinese Text Project (ctext.org) 11
Chuci 58
Chunqiu Fanlu 127, 128, 129, 247
Confucianism 48, 50, 93, 94, 111, 127, 128, 130, 146, 147, 199, 223
Confucius 48–50, 55, 65, 71, 92, 93, 94, 103, 162, 198, 200
Cook, Constance 238
Cook, Scott 105, 239, 240, 244
Creel, Herlee 52, 134, 169, 247, 248
Csikszentmihalyi, Mark and Michael Nyla 245

da (great/greating) 108–16
Dao, pristine *heng dao* and cosmic *chang dao* 10, 23–4, 63, 67–8, 71, 74, 85, 87–90, 92, 98–9, 101–02, 116, 123–4, 129, 135, 139, 152, 215–6, 217, 219–20. *See also chang, heng*
Daodejing. *See also* Laozi, Huang-Lao, Tianshi
 commentaries 6
 editions 6
 orality 4, 15–18, 38–47, 55, 56–63, 120, 191, 194, 200, 217, 237, 238
 staple assumptions 35–42, 59, 237
 synthetic and syncretic 35–45, 57–60, 73–85, 139, 230, 237, 239

versions 5, 6, 23-4, 122
Daoism. *See* Fangxian, Huang-Lao, Tianshi, Xuanxue, Yangsheng, Zuowang
Daoism and immortality 52, 79, 91, 93, 128, 137, 141, 159-62, 165, 168-70, 173, 175, 177-81, 189, 195, 202-7, 242
Daoism and long-life 13, 16, 18, 27, 51, 79, 101, 137, 140, 142, 148-50, 152, 160-1, 169, 170, 173, 178-81, 184, 187, 190-1, 195-6, 199, 202-4, 206
Daoism and longevity 14, 34, 43, 45, 49, 79, 82-3, 125, 136, 142, 159, 165, 190-1, 197, 199-200, 203, 208, 238, 242
Daoism and mountain reclusion 15, 43, 44, 48, 49, 50, 51, 54, 84, 128, 140, 152, 158-60, 178-86, 188, 190-6, 198, 200-4, 207-8, 251
Daojia wenhua yanjiu 88
Daoyin tu 18, 210
de (systems of circulation or charismatic virtue) 75-84, 104, 129, 146, 148, 152, 234, 241
Defoort, Carine 245, 254
Despeux, Catherine 235
Ding Sixin 56-57, 61-2, 63, 119, 120, 123, 130, 131, 132, 134, 138, 239, 240, 243, 245, 246, 247, 248
Ding Yuanzhi 105
Dong Feng 205
Dong Zhongjun 205
Dong Zhongshu 127, 129, 130, 131, 134, 146, 147, 247
Dorofeeva-Lichtman 251

Els, Paul van 245
Emperor Cheng 128
Emperor Jing 127
Emperor Wen 142
Emperor Wu 127, 128, 130, 141, 247
Empress Dou 127
Eno, Robert 48, 238

Fan Bocheng 129, 247
Fan Li 96-8, 207-8
fangji 43, 50-6, 60, 62, 238
fangshi 50-1, 188

Fangxian Daoism 43-4, 49-56, 60, 62, 122, 139, 188, 211
Feldt, Alex 247
Fried, Daniel 109, 245
Fung Yu-lan (Feng Youlan) 38, 183, 184, 237, 250

Gan Shi 204-5
Gao Dalun 253
Gaoshi zhuan 184
Ge Hong 11, 14-19, 102, 142, 153, 157-182, 183-4, 186-95, 198, 202-6, 208, 210, 235, 248, 249, 251
Ge Xuan 15, 142, 205
Ge You 196
Gengsang Chu 48
Giles, Lional 250
Girardot, Norman 236, 244
Government of Wen and Jing 127
Graham, A.C. 37, 57, 161, 236, 237, 239, 245, 249
Gu Jiegang 38
Gu Qiang 197
Guang Chengzi 48
Guben *Laozi* 5
Gui cang 91-2, 243
Gui Fu 196
Guo Xiang 158
Guoyu 96, 243, 246

Hall, David 66, 103, 105, 109, 113, 229, 233
Halliburton, David 254
Han Shu 51, 121, 126, 142, 197, 238, 239
Han Yi 235
Hanfeizi ("Yu Lao" and "Jie Lao") 124-6, 140, 246
Hansen, Chad 7-10, 35, 37, 66, 71-3, 235, 236, 237, 241
Harper, Donald 53-6, 76, 105, 203, 238, 239, 241
he (bodily ultimacy) 76-82
Heguanzi 121, 123, 126
Heidegger, Martin 8-10, 11, 91, 107, 108, 113, 114, 161, 215-33, 235, 245, 253-4
Hendrischke, Barbara 28, 42, 45, 60, 109, 236, 238, 239, 245
heng 63, 87, 89, 113, 115, 116, 243
ancient uses 89-95

and *ji* 99–100, 244. (*See also* Dao)
   and phenomenology 101–8
   and temporality 95–101
Heng E (Chang E) 91–2, 93
Heng hexagram 91–2, 93, 94, 99–101
Henricks, Robert 239, 244
Heraclitus 216
Heshang Gong 6, 11, 46, 56, 62, 108, 119, 121, 126, 134, 135–53, 173, 182, 217, 222, 223, 230, 231
Heshang Zhangren 142
Hou Ji 70
Hou Yi 91–2
Hu Fuchen 51–2, 177, 235, 238, 239, 248, 249
Hu Shi 38
Huainanzi 5, 109, 111, 121, 123, 126, 128, 133, 139, 153, 197, 246
Huangdi 121, 125–6, 193, 196, 197, 200, 235, 247
Huangdi Neijing 125
Huangdi Sijing 122, 123, 137, 139, 245, 246
Huangfu Mi 184
Huang-Lao *Daodejing* 5, 10, 23–4, 38, 43, 46, 56–7, 58, 63, 103, 104, 116, 119, 152, 216, 217, 219, 220, 222, 229, 231, 232–4
Huang-Lao Daoism 10, 11, 29, 36, 38, 43–4, 65, 119–28, 135, 138, 139, 140, 141, 142, 143, 152, 188, 199, 211
Huang-Lao manuscripts (*Taiyi Sheng Shui, Hengxian, Fanwu Liuxing*) 5, 6, 10, 88, 89, 90, 110, 120, 122, 123, 139, 243
Hundun 84

immortality 52, 79, 91.93, 128, 137, 141, 159–62, 165, 168–70, 173, 175, 177–81, 189, 195, 202–7, 242
"Inscription on *Qi* Circulation" 209

Ji Kang 158
Jia Yi 126
Jian Wu 200–1
Jiapian 98
Jie Xiang 206
Jie Yu 200–1
Jin Gao 192
jing (hot body fluids) 76–82
jing (tranquil, settled, calm) 123, 136

Jixia Academy 122
Juanzi 200–1

Kaltenmark, Max 66, 197–8, 241, 250, 252
Kim Hongkyung 57, 236, 237, 239
Kim Tae Hyun 246
Kinney, Anne Behnke 250
Klein, Esther 245
Knapp, Keith 186, 250
Kohn, Livia 195, 235, 239, 251
Kong Anguo 207
Krummel, John 253

LaFargue, Michael 37, 42, 57, 237, 238, 239, 240
Lai Chi-tim 252
Laoxue, Laozi Studies 4, 12, 126, 211, 223, 224
Laozi 15, 17, 37, 38, 41, 44, 48, 65, 121, 125, 183, 187, 192, 192, 197–200, 246
   "Old Master" versus "Old Masters" 44, 60
Laozi *Daodejing* 5, 10, 23–4, 38–44, 48, 53, 56–7, 63, 68, 73, 74, 87–9, 96, 101, 104, 111, 116, 119, 121, 148, 152, 216, 217, 219, 220, 222, 229, 231, 232–4, 237
Laozi manuscripts (Guodian, Mawangdui) 4, 5, 6, 10, 11, 12, 37, 56, 59, 63, 67, 71, 74, 87, 102, 103, 105, 122, 215, 217, 220, 221, 232, 236, 241–2, 249
   Beida 5, 62, 63, 105, 109–11, 240
   Guben 5
   Guodian 37, 38, 40, 42, 57, 58–63, 65, 109
   Mawangdui 50, 52, 62–3
Laozi zhigui. *See* Yan Zun
Lau, D. C. 37, 57, 87, 237, 239
Le Blanc, Charles 246
Legge, James 96, 241, 243
Levi, Jean 39, 238, 246
li (ordering principles) 123, 124, 130–1, 136, 137, 145
Li Jiahao 243
Li Ling 242
Li Songrong 169
Li Zhongfu 15, 205
Li Zongding 161, 166, 170, 174, 175, 177, 180–1, 248, 249, 250, 253
Lian Shu 200

Liang Qichao 38
Liao Mingchun and Li Cheng 45, 61, 238, 240
Lienü zhuan 250
Liexian zhuan 11, 43, 153, 184–91, 192–4, 195–202, 204, 250
Lin Mingzhao 149–53, 248
Littlejohn, Ronnie 223, 253
Liu An 127, 128, 200, 247
Liu Bang 63
Liu Gen 206
Liu Gusheng 138, 141, 248
Liu Heng (Emperor Wen) 63, 67, 119, 127, 152, 205, 219
Liu, JeeLoo 254
Liu Xiang 119, 183, 186, 189, 194, 250
Liu Xiaogan 109, 239, 240, 245
Liu Xinfang 105
Liu Xing 183
Loewe, Michael 245
Lü Buwei 38
Lü Gong 207
Lu Jia 126, 247
Lu Mu Gong Wen Zisi 93
Lu Tong 200–1
Lüshi Chunqiu 38, 237

Ma, Lin 225, 227, 235, 253, 254
Ma, Lin and Jaap Van Brakel 218, 222, 223, 253
Ma Shihuang 196
Mair, Victor 40, 239
Major, John S., Sarah Queen, Andrew Meyer, Harold Roth 245
Mao Nü 196
Maraldo, John 253
Maspero, Henri 46, 239
Master Qingjing 18–19
Matrix 7, 17, 24, 26–9, 68, 101, 135, 137, 138, 139, 140, 153, 188
May, Reinhard 254
Mencius 93, 94, 243, 250
Meyer, Dirk 40, 41, 59–60, 62, 237, 238, 240
Michael, Thomas 235, 236, 237, 238, 239, 241, 244, 248, 249, 251, 252, 252
Mid-Autumn Moon Festival 92
ming (natural condition or destined lifespan) 131
ming (proprioceptive sensitivity) 76–85

Mozi, Mohism 71–3, 241
Mystery (*xuan*) 24, 25, 135, 170–7, 178, 179–81, 190

Neipian. See *Baopuzi*
Nelson, Eric 253
Neo-Confucianism 230, 231
Nienhauser, Willian J. 250
Nishida Kitaro 223, 253
Nü Wa 91
Nü Wan 196

Pang Pu 246
Parmenides 216, 229
Patt-Shamir, Galia 67, 241
Peerenboom, R. P. 122, 246
Penny, Benjamin 250
Peng Zu 17–18, 192, 193, 200, 201, 203
Perkins, Franklin 109, 245
Pines, Yuri 251
Plato 225
Poggeler, Otto 254
Pregadio, Febrizio 248, 251
Pre-Socratics 216, 218, 222, 225–8

qi 13–14, 27–8, 31–3, 48, 76–9, 136, 144, 145, 146, 152
Qian Mu 38
Qin Gao 201–2
Qiong Shu 200
Qiu Xigui 243
Queen Mother of the West 92
Queen, Sarah 124–5, 239, 246, 247
Queen, Sarah and John S. Major 247
Queen, Sarah and Michael Puett 245

Radhakrishnan, Sarvepalli 223
Rapp, John 247
Rao Zongyi 88, 91, 242
Robinet, Isabelle 133, 142, 151, 210, 247, 248, 253
Rong Cheng/ Rong Cheng Gong 17, 196–200, 204, 251
Roth, Harold 42, 46–9, 58, 121, 237, 238, 239, 245
Ruan Ji 158
Ryden, Edmund 245

Sage 28, 29, 30, 47, 49, 51, 76, 82, 84, 100–1, 115, 125, 158, 170

sage-king 124, 129–36, 141, 143, 145, 152, 162
Sartre, Jean-Paul 161
Schaberg, David 47, 49, 52–6, 236, 238, 239
Schipper, Kristofer 28, 45–7, 57, 236, 237, 238, 239
Schönfeld, Martin 246
Schwartz, Benjamin 121, 245
Seidel, Anna 121, 122, 125, 245
Seidel, Anna and Lothar von Falkenhausen 245
Sellmann, James 237
Shaughnessy, Edward 37, 38, 39, 92, 237, 243
Shen Guochang 248
Shen Jian 205
sheng 115–16
Shenxian zhuan 11, 13–18, 43, 153, 184–90, 192, 194–5, 199, 200, 202–8, 250
Shih-yi, Paul Hsiao 224
Shiji 43, 50, 51, 121, 142, 153, 184, 185, 198, 199, 238, 246
Shijing 54, 55, 58, 68, 69–70, 85, 95–6, 241
Shiwen 125, 197, 203
Shuowen jiezi 70–1, 87, 90, 91, 92, 241
Siku Quanshu 184
Sima Tan 121
Sivin, Nathan 36, 37, 53, 120, 237, 251
Smith, Kidder 245
Sri Aurobindo 223
Stamatov, Aleksandar 247
Strassberg, Richard 251
Strickmann, Michel 36, 53, 120, 237, 251
Su Nü 17, 204, 235
Sun Yiping 50, 162, 188, 238, 249, 251
Sun Zhen 205
Sunzi Bingfa 237

Tadd, Misha 143, 146, 147, 151, 248
Taibo Zhenren 15, 205, 206
taiji 230
Teng Wei and Tang Juan 160, 248
Tianmenzi 205
Tianshi Daoism (Xiang'er) 5, 6, 36, 43–4, 62, 122, 139, 140, 160, 249

unconcealment 102, 108, 111–16, 218–19, 225–6, 228

Unschuld, Paul 247

Van Ess, Hans 245
Van Gulik, Robert 52, 235
Van Norden, Bryan 254
Vankeerberghen, Griet 247
Vervoorn, Aat 247, 251

Wagner, Rudolf 6, 57, 60, 235, 239
Wang, Aihe 247
Wang Bi 6, 11, 56, 62, 143, 182, 217, 222, 223, 230, 231, 249
Wang Bo 48, 60, 87, 89, 139, 238, 242, 247, 248
Wang Debao 251
Wang Guangxin 251
Wang, James Qingjie 63, 70–3, 87, 88, 89–90, 91, 95, 99, 102, 103, 107, 108, 111–15, 221, 240, 241, 242, 245
Wang Jun 15, 205
Wang, Robin 130
Wang Yuan 15
Wang Zhongdu 15, 205, 206
Wang Zhongjiang 12, 88, 90–1, 93, 94, 98, 99, 102, 106, 107, 108, 114, 242, 245, 246
Wang Ziqiao 196
Ware, James 250
Wei Zhaoqi 251
Wenzi 121, 126, 139
Wile, Douglas 235
Wo Quan 196
Wu Cheng 192
Wu Chengliu 70
wuwei 123, 132, 133, 137, 147

xian 19, 50–2, 53, 141–2, 153, 159–62, 169, 181, 184–92, 194–6, 200, 201–7, 250, 252
Xinshu 126
Xinyu 126
xinzhai 136
Xiong, Tieji and Liu Lingzi 126, 141, 247n29, 247 248
Xiong Tieji, Ma Lianghuai and Liu Shaojun (Xiong et al.) 127, 128, 137, 247, 248
Xu Kangsheng 249
Xuan. See Xuanxue

Xuan Nü 17, 204, 235
Xuanxue 157–63, 165, 177, 181–4, 199, 230–1, 233
Xunzi 6, 73, 246

Yan Zun 6, 11, 62, 119, 121, 126, 128–35, 138, 139, 140, 147, 182, 247
Yang Shuda 247
Yang Zhu 183, 184
yangsheng 10, 13–19, 27–34, 41–56, 57, 60, 68, 73–85, 101–2, 104, 120, 121–5, 135–42, 147, 148, 152–3, 157, 159, 160, 169, 170, 178, 180–1, 184, 188–211, 233–4, 238, 239, 241, 242, 248
Yangsheng Daoism 10, 11, 15, 17, 24, 28–9, 35, 42–57, 60, 65, 73, 102, 104, 120, 121, 122, 123, 129, 138, 139, 143, 148, 149, 152, 153, 211
  nexus 188, 190, 195, 196, 200, 201, 206, 207, 210
Yao Shengliang 185, 250, 251
Yates, Robin 245
Yijing 70, 73, 91–2, 93–4, 99–101, 128, 230
Yin and yang 129, 132, 133, 145, 146, 147, 148, 151–2, 247
Yinshu 210
Yu, Anthony 241
Yu Hua 192
Yuan Long 169, 179, 249

Zhang Daoling 36, 43
Zhang Ji 203, 242, 252

Zhang Rongming 209, 235, 236, 253
Zhang Xianglong 231, 254
Zhang Yulian 185, 188, 250, 251
Zhang Zhan 158
Zhang Zhenguo 137, 160, 248
Zhanguoce 93, 242
Zheng Canshan. *See* Cheng Tsan-shan.
Zheng Kai 246
Zheng Yin 15, 16, 17, 205
zhi shen/zhi guo (regulate the body/regulate the world) 135, 137–8, 143, 148, 149, 151–2
Zhong Sheng and Luo Yi 162, 249
Zhu Huang 196
Zhu Yueli 15, 17, 235
Zhu Zhanyan 177, 249
Zhu Zhu 196
zhuang (prime) 78–9
Zhuangzi 5, 37, 44, 48, 49, 84, 93, 94–5, 120, 121, 128, 133, 136, 140, 153, 165, 168–9, 179, 183, 197, 200–1, 208–9, 238, 243, 245
Zi Du 17
ziran 95, 107, 111–15, 123–4, 129, 132, 134, 137, 147, 152, 174, 248
Ziyi 65, 240
zhi (proprioceptive knowledge) 76–9
Zou Yan 50
Zuo Ci 15, 205
zuowang 120, 124, 136, 138, 139, 140, 152
Zuowang Daoism 44, 48, 49, 120, 121, 122, 139, 140
Zuozhuan 92–3, 242

www.ingramcontent.com/pod-product-compliance
Lightning Source LLC
Chambersburg PA
CBHW052218300426
44115CB00011B/1732